The Prophet Motive

Cover design by Brad Roberts and Susan A. Barnes.

Unless otherwise indicated, Scripture quotations are from the King James Version.

Published by the Gospel Advocate Company
PO Box 150, Nashville, TN 37202

ISBN 0-89225-458-0

The Prophet Motive

EXAMINING THE RELIABILITY
of the BIBLICAL PROPHETS

KENNY BARFIELD

GOSPEL ADVOCATE COMPANY
P. O. Box 150
Nashville, Tennessee 37202

Dedication and Appreciation

The clock edges toward midnight. Biting winds knife through the trees behind our house. A January freeze locks the South in its grasp. Forecasters say temperatures will plummet into the single digits. And, while that may not be cold to those from more northern climates, it sends shock waves rippling through northwest Alabama. That snow "flurries" are merely possible in the next twenty-four hours sends thousands of shoppers into "panic mode." Grocery shelves are stripped of bread and milk. Southerners want to be prepared in case an inch of snow makes our highways "impassable." It all reminds me of how desperately we want to feel that we are in control.

No author is ever totally in control of a manuscript. These pages rise on others' foundations. I would be remiss if I did not pause to recognize their contributions.

My wife, Nancy, and my two daughters, Amber and Lora, deserve much of the credit. Their patience overwhelms me. They allow me to forage in libraries and bookstores for hours. They don't even cringe (at least openly) when they see me pack my laptop computer in the trunk as we prepare to leave on vacation. Often, when I make "pilgrimages" to regional and university libraries, one of them will hop in the car, ride for two to five hours, sit patiently in the library while I work, then talk to me as we drive home in the darkness to be sure that I don't fall asleep at the wheel. Without their love and understanding, there would be no book.

A special thank you to Amber and to Lora for constantly keeping track of my materials. I could not ask for a kinder, more understanding wife. Nancy is God's greatest earthly blessing. Her parents taught her that true love comes through service to others.

I have been blessed with supportive and loving parents. Though never very wealthy, they have always been willing to sacrifice to see that I had the opportunity to reach for my goals. They have always been special.

Dad passed from this life on his birthday in February, 1994. I will never forget his care and the love he shared with his family. I shall treasure the memories. Mom is one of the sweetest, kindest women I have ever known. I have never heard her say a bad word about anyone. I humbly dedicate this book to them.

Many others played important roles. To Neil and Kerry Anderson and Susan Barnes and the staff at Christian Communications/Gospel Advocate, I extend my deep appreciation. They encouraged me. They offered sound advice. They gave me the opportunity to do that which I dearly love—the opportunity to write a defense of the faith that has meant so much to me through the years. I am in their debt.

Elaine Bryant and Ray Minardi offered invaluable assistance in arranging for the use of photos from the Fon Schofield Collection at the E. C. Dargan Research Library. They were so patient and courteous. I am grateful for their gift of time. Marlin Connelly of David Lipscomb University in Nashville graciously supplied slides of various sites which he made on his many trips to the Middle East. They add greatly to the quality of this book.

I also stand indebted to those whose scholarship and encouragement broadened my horizons and gave me a deep interest in learning. Marlin Connelly, Carroll Ellis, Willard Collins, and the late Batsell Barrett Baxter of David Lipscomb University in Nashville taught me to love research and helped me develop the talent God provided. Jack Wilhelm, Lawrence Williams, Milton Sewell, and David Vester, and the late Ralph Snell served as my administrators at Mars Hill Bible School in Florence. Without their support and patient understanding, this work would remain unfinished. They are/were motivators, moulders of minds, teachers, and scholars. They exert(ed) a profound influence over my life. They are/were genuinely good men—givers, and not takers. Many others should be mentioned as well, but limited space precludes exhaustive accolades. I gratefully acknowledge the help of so many and trust they will understand that these words of appreciation are for them, too.

Table of Contents

Abbreviations

ABT	American Biology Teacher
AEHL	Archaeological Encyclopedia of the Holy Land (Negev)
AJA	American Journal of Archaeology
AJSL	American Journal of Semitic Languages and Literature
AL	Archivum Linguisticum
ANET	Ancient Near Eastern Texts (Pritchard)
ARC	Archaeology
AS	American Scientist
AUSS	Andrews University Seminary Studies
BA	Biblical Archaeologist
BAR	Biblical Archaeology Review
BASOR	Bulletin of the American Schools of Oriental Research
BJRL	Bulletin of the John Rylands University Library
BS	Bibliotheca Sacra
BZAW	Beihefte zur Zeitschrift fur die alttestamentliche Wissenschaft
CAH	Cambridge Ancient History
CAHR	Cambridge Ancient History (revised edition)
CanJTh	Canadian Journal of Theology
CBQ	Catholic Biblical Quarterly
CBTL	Cyclopaedia of Biblical, Theological, and Ecclesiastical Literature (McClintock and Strong)
CEN	Creation Ex Nihilo
ChT	Christianity Today
CSR	Christian Scholars Review
CTR	Criswell Theological Review
DJG	Dictionary of Jesus and the Gospels (Green, McKnight, and

	Marshall)
DJMT	Dialogue: A Journal of Mormon Thought
EAEHL	Encyclopedia of Archaeological Excavations in the Holy Land, (Avi-Yonah)
EB	Encyclopedia Britannica. 9th edition
EBMAC	Encyclopedia Britannica. Macropedia
EBP	Encyclopedia of Biblical Prophecy (Payne)
EI	Eretz Israel
EQ	Evangelical Quarterly
FP	Faith and Philosophy
HBD	Harper's Bible Dictionary
HTR	Harvard Theological Review
HUCA	Hebrew Union College Annual
IBD	Illustrated Bible Dictionary
ICC	International Critical Commentary
IDB	Interpreter's Dictionary of the Bible
IDBS	Interpreter's Dictionary of the Bible-Supplement
IEJ	Israel Exploration Journal
Int	Interpretation
ISBE	International Standard Bible Encyclopedia
ISBER	International Standard Bible Encyclopedia (revised edition)
JANES	Journal of the Ancient Near Eastern Society
JAOS	Journal of the American Oriental Society
JASA	Journal of the American Scientific Affiliation
JBC	Jerome Bible Commentary
JBL	Journal of Biblical Literature
JBR	Journal of Bible and Religion
JCS	Journal of Church & Society
JEA	Journal of Egyptian Archaeology
JETS	Journal of the Evangelical Theological Society
JFA	Journal of Field Archaeology
JNES	Journal of Near Eastern Studies
JNSL	Journal of Northwest Semitic Languages
JRGSL	Journal of the Royal Geographical Society of London
JRS	Journal of Roman Studies
JSOR	Journal of the Society for Oriental Research

JSOT	Journal for the Study of the Old Testament
JSS	Journal of Semitic Studies
JTB	Journal of Theoretical Biology
JTS	Journal of Theological Studies
MDB	Mercer Dictionary of the Bible
MTJ	Michigan Theological Journal
NBD	New Bible Dictionary
NEASB	Near East Archaeological Society Bulletin
NIDB	New International Dictionary of the Bible
NIDBA	New International Dictionary of Biblical Archaeology
NS	New Scientist
NTS	New Testament Studies
PEQ	Palestine Exploration Quarterly
PR	The Philosophical Review
PT	Philosophy Today
QDAP	Quarterly of the Department of Antiquities of Palestine
RdQ	Revue de Qumran
RR	Reason and Revelation
RS	Religious Studies
SA	Scientific American
SD	Science Digest
SDB	Smith's Dictionary of the Bible
SHERK	The New Shaff-Herzog Encyclopedia of Religious Knowledge
SJT	Scottish Journal of Theology
SNTSMS	Society for New Testament Studies Monograph Series
TB	Tyndale Bulletin
TNS	The New Scholasticism
USQR	Union Seminary Quarterly Review
VT	Vetus Testamentum
VTS	Vetus Testamentum Supplement
WBC	Wycliffe Bible Commentary
WT	The Watchtower
WTJ	Westminster Theological Journal
ZAW	Zeitschrift fur die alttestamentliche Wissenschaft
ZPEB	Zondervan Pictorial Encyclopedia of the Bible

1

A Brief Introduction
to Biblical Prophecy

As the busy Huntsville intersection of University Drive and Jordan Lane drew closer, I spotted two young men standing on the concrete islands. Each held a home-made placard. Less than a week remained before the late June run-off in Alabama's typically hot elections, so I supposed they were campaigning. I was wrong. Stopping for the traffic signal, I noticed the placards contained Bible verses, one on each side, warning passersby of the eternal fate of those who refuse to obey God. People reacted in different ways. Most seemed indifferent. Several pointed with obvious scorn. Others seemed amused. A few were openly hostile, yelling obscenities or flashing a derogatory sign. One or two waved in support or agreement.

As I watched, I understood, ever so slightly, how Old Testament prophets must have felt as they delivered similar messages in the long ago. I sympathized with the indifference Noah, Isaiah, Jeremiah, Ezekiel, and other prophets must have felt. The life of a prophet/messenger is not a simple one. Loneliness, pain, and frustration are never handled easily. Yet, for all the inherent frustrations, the role of the prophet has been common in history. It is also one most of us have yearned for on occasion, even if the reasons are purely selfish.

How many times have we wished that we could look into the future? How many times have we felt uneasy after finalizing an important decision? How many times have we wondered if our choice was really the best one? If we're honest with ourselves, we'll admit that it would be nice to know the outcomes of key decisions before we make them. What most of us wouldn't give to squeeze out just a tiny drop of tomorrow and examine it in advance. Somehow, a feeling inside tells us if we really knew the future, we might circumvent or alter many of life's major problems. Unfortunately, we don't have the ability to foresee the results of our choices. Regardless of how well we may review our options, some will fail.

Perhaps that's why attempting to look into the future has always been one of our most intense obsessions. We understand that correctly predicting future events will give us a definite advantage over our peers. As a result, we have attempted everything imaginable to procure that ability. We have summoned the future from livers, scraps of bone, drops of oil, shooting stars, palms, horoscopes, and tarot cards; we have relied on ecstatic seers, astrologers, diviners, mystics, and the prognostications of modern-day experts. More often than not, we have returned from our search cynical and bewildered.

Looking into the crystal ball and returning with accurate predictions is no easy task. Ask any governmental official whose future employment depends on correctly guessing the direction foreign events will take, or one who is responsible for developing an economic system that will correctly appraise the direction of the economy. Ask people who have a wealth of information at their disposal how readily the future can be predicted. They will quickly tell you how few of their guesses correspond to reality. Even those lucky enough to score an occasional bull's-eye with their forecasts must savor their accomplishment for years because hundreds of additional predictions end as embarrassments, miscalculations, and failures.

Even in today's "Age of Information," experts falter badly in their efforts to foresee future events. In recent times, the sudden surge toward democracy in Eastern Europe and the tragedies in Bosnia caught western scholars off guard. Few correctly predicted the Iraqi invasion of Kuwait or the swiftness and decisiveness of Desert Storm. Specifics of recent natural disasters such as the October 1989 San Francisco earthquake or the devastating typhoon in Bangladesh were never detailed in advance. The list of unpredicted or unpredictable events from the final decades of the twentieth century alone will fill, not books, but libraries.

Still, despite the failures, humanity has always been awestruck by those who, in one sense or another, claim the gift of prophecy. Self-proclaimed psychic Jeanne Dixon, for example, enamored the American public for years with her predictions. She obtained notoriety by supposedly predicting the assassination of President John F. Kennedy in Dallas in November 1963. Although she made thousands of additional predictions, the only one worth remembering was the one regarding Kennedy. The life of a prophet is not an easy one.

The lines waiting at the door of prophetdom, however, appear as endless as the characters are diverse. For some, the motives seem noble; for others they seem self-serving. With all the pitfalls and frustrations associated with the claim of prophethood, the profession, by its very nature, commands multitudes of followers. Many are willing to pay dearly for information seers claim to provide. Sadly, such promises of great wealth and large followings produce far more charlatans than true prophets. Perhaps that's why the young men on the busy street corner were greeted as they were. Perhaps we have grown so accustomed to impostors we now believe there is no such thing as true prophecy. It's easy to reach that point.

Reasons for Skepticism Regarding Prophecy

A world-renowned scholar, seeking to explain humanity's distinctiveness, chose the term "time-binder." By this, he referred to our unique ability to pass along information from one generation to another without the necessity of repeating each experience. Modern usage simply explains, "You don't have to reinvent the wheel!" We remember. We use our communication skills to amass and disperse knowledge. We recall with delight our pleasant experiences and recoil in horror over our failures. We echo over and over, "Those who do not remember the past are forced to repeat it!" We are especially appalled when conned or deceived by those around us. Such experiences grate on our self-confidence and chafe our soul. As a result, through a process psychologists refer to as transference, we become wary of anyone who possesses even the slightest resemblance to our deceivers. Realizing this natural aversion to being deceived, four current trends feed the modern tendency to reject legitimate prophecy.

First, individuals who attempt to foretell the future are usually in error. Not only is this true in contemporary society, it was equally true in earlier times.

Second, most prophetic efforts are associated with religious activity. That is no surprise. I was raised in the Christian faith. When I was a child, sermons and Sunday School stories introduced me to Isaiah, Jeremiah, Daniel, and other biblical prophets. As I grew older and my readings became more diverse, I learned that many other religious movements were initiated by charismatic leaders who either claimed to be prophets or shared personality traits with those who were. This raised some difficult questions: Were biblical prophets really unique after all? If so, was the uniqueness merely based upon some cultural trait, or was there something infinitely deeper than mere culture involved? Was it possible to explain the successes of prophecy in terms other than supernatural ones? Were the prophecies composed ex post facto (after-the-fact)? Were predictions based on information that was common to any writer of the time period? Grappling with such questions can be daunting; they demand answers.

Third, many people reject the Bible and Christianity because those pretending to understand biblical prophecies advance wildly inaccurate interpretations of prophetic scriptures. Time and again, for instance, self-styled scholars have assured anyone willing to listen that the end of the world was imminent. Time and again, they were incorrect. Were these biblical interpreters led astray by errant biblical prophecies or by their fertile imaginations? Were biblical prophets just as prone to mistakes as others?

Fourth, many contemporary scholars presume there is no meaningful distinction between biblical prophets and prophets from other cultures, especially certain Greek oracles. Are they correct? Is it possible, for instance, that Isaiah and the Oracle of Apollo at Delphi share many commonalities and differ, if at all, only in degree? Were biblical prophets really any different from others who coveted the same title? Were they really spokesmen for a divine being, or were they merely another group of socially-active reformers with admirable intentions who possessed nothing more than the charisma common to many talented human beings?

A Rationale for the Study of Prophecy

Given the increasingly skeptical attitude toward the supernatural and prophecy, a rational examination of the evidence is needed. To assume, without an objective investigation, that there is no God or that predicting the future is impossible runs counter to our democratic principles of fairness which demand that all sides be equally heard. We take pride in our ability to calmly investigate evidence and arrive at unbiased conclusions. If we are to live up to that claim in this arena, we must thoughtfully evaluate the likelihood that individuals really have accurately predicted future events. If evidence indicates they have, the search must continue for a reasonable explanation as to how they were able to do so.

Defining Prophecy:
A Prophet is a Prophet
is a Prophet ...

What is a "prophet"?

More specifically, what is a biblical "prophet"?

For those unacquainted with the scholarly debate on the issue, the question may appear superfluous; yet, nothing could be less accurate. Even the English term "prophet" appears in widely diverse circumstances. It refers to Egyptian priests, to temple officials in the ancient city of Mari, to astrologers and sorcerers, to diviners, and to a horde of others who claimed either some form of intensely personal contact with supernatural beings or some extraordinary ability to look into the future.[1] In more recent years, the term "prophet" extends to almost any religious leader.[2]

It also surfaces in areas totally unrelated to religion. For example, one often hears references to "weather prophets," "psychics," and "palm readers" in the same context as biblical prophets. Instead of launching an encyclopedic investigation into the many uses of the term "prophet", we will simply explore the various Hebrew terms used to designate these seers of antiquity and compare their efforts to others who espouse similar claims.

Poets or Prophets?

Before examining Hebrew terms used to describe and/or identify prophets, we should first note recent attacks on the classical understanding of the prophets leveled by such scholars as A. G. Auld. Auld argues that the biblical spokesmen who now carry the label "prophet" would have been appalled by such designations. They were, he claims, "poets" not prophets.[3] He asserts that the term "prophet" never appeared in the original writings/teachings of Jeremiah, Isaiah, Ezekiel, and others called prophets. He also asserts that those living during the days of these poets would never have considered them to be prophets. Rather, scribes and editors intent on implementing some hidden political and/or religious agenda, inserted all such "prophetic" material into the books sometime after the return from Babylonian captivity.[4] As a result, prophets like Amos "only became a good prophet when he was a dead one."[5] In this manner, Auld has built his case on the presupposition that prophecy of the type encountered in Scripture could not possibly exist in Israel prior to the Exile.

A number of serious weaknesses cut deeply into Auld's theories. First, the concept of divine messengers permeated cultures around Israel long before her captivity in Babylon. Throughout the Semitic world, phrases similar to "the Word of God" or "the Word of JHWH" appear in materials prior to the times of the biblical prophets.[6] Under such circumstances, Auld's foundation seems to be without historical justification.

Second, discoveries in Mesopotamia indicate that Assyrian kings commonly "consulted the gods" before any battle. These discoveries likewise pre-date biblical prophets. Auld's presupposition that prophecy in the sense of predicting future events was unknown among the Hebrews during this period is highly suspect.[7]

Third, discoveries at the Israelite city of Lachish of pottery shards dating from the time of Jeremiah strongly indicate that those responsible for the inscriptions were keenly aware of some prophet active in Judah during the time of the Babylonian invasion. This prophet clearly foretold dire future consequences for the Hebrews.[8] So, while Auld's theories will no doubt gain approval among critical scholars committed to deny all or most supernatural involvement in the composition of Scripture, they are built primarily on assertions and presuppositions rather than on concrete facts.[9]

Hebrew Terms Describing the Prophets

Five Hebrew terms describe those generally spoken of in the Judeo-Christian Scriptures as prophets: *ro'eh* and *hozeh* (both of which are translated by the English term, 'seer'), *nabi* ('prophet'), *'ish 'elohim* ('man of God'), and *'ish ha-ruah* ('man of the spirit'). Additional generic terms such as *sopeh* ('watchman') and *mal'ak* ('messenger') also refer, on occasions, to biblical prophets. Of these, the vast majority of modern scholars acknowledge that nabi—which occurs in some form over 500 times—is the term customarily associated with the so-called literary, or writing, prophets of biblical times.

Although there has been a concerted effort in recent years to trace the etymology of *nabi*, the results remain as uncertain as ever.[10] No one knows with certainty exactly where and when the term originated, but, a short summary of the meanings provided by a diversity of scholars through the years will help develop at least a reasonable understanding of what the term may have meant.

Over a century ago, Kuenan[11] and others argued that the term sprang from a concept that implied a "bubbling forth," or an ecstatic presentation by the prophet(ess). Since such behavior occurred with significant frequency among Greek oracles, scholars assumed that biblical prophets must have adopted similar patterns. Thus, Pedersen[12] and Robinson[13] argued that the term evolved as a description of "ecstatic incoherent cries" made by the prophets. Their arguments have fallen from favor in recent years. Rowley, using a wealth of recent archaeological information regarding linguistic materials in antiquity, suggested that *nabi* more likely meant "to act like a prophet" than "to act like one beside himself."[14]

On the other hand, Arnold[15] and other scholars believed the term originated from a word meaning "to enter" and argued it suggested human consciousness being entered or overwhelmed by a spirit. Eiselin[16] contended that the word traced its roots to an Arabic term that either meant to announce a message or referred to one who announced the message of another. Koehler and Baumgartner[17] also defend this position while Bewer[18] connects the word with an Accadian term that means "to tear away." For Bewer, the word connoted an individual pulled or carried away by the influence of another. Many contemporary scholars[19] believe the term refers to one who is called by another, specifically, in this instance, one called by God. Ringgren,[20] concluded,

> Based on Old Testament evidence, prophecy may tentatively be defined as the proclamation of divine messages in a state of inspiration. The Old Testament prophets proclaim messages from Yahweh speaking in his name and using the messenger formula Ko'amar YHWH, "Thus says Yahweh."

Ringgren's definition agrees with that of Edersheim, who also recognized prophecy as "a medium of divine communication."[21]

Thus, a cursory review of the possible derivations of the Hebrew word for prophet leaves only an enigma. Several options relating to the origin and precise meaning of the term compete for acceptance. Frankly, no position is indisputable, though the bulk of current archaeological and linguistic evidence questions that of the prophet being an ecstatic babbler. Further, despite difficulties in pinning down the derivation of the term, it is obvious to the most casual reader that biblical prophets often differed extensively from their counterparts in surrounding cultures. Even should we conclude the ancient Hebrews borrowed the cognate of the expression used to identify their prophets from some other source, that factor would not establish the term's meaning within a biblical context. Words transported from culture to culture often undergo fundamental changes in their meanings. While a study of the background and ultimate origin of *nabi* may prove enlightening, it is not sufficient, in itself, to establish the meaning of the word in Scripture. Only one thing is certain. Prophets dominate much of the history of the Hebrew nation. They emerge, to some degree, in every major period of Israelite history from the days of Abraham to the times of Malachi.[22]

Diversity Among the Hebrew Prophets

One possible explanation for the rich diversity of terms used to describe these messengers can be found in the enormously dissimilar backgrounds from which they came and in the colorful styles and mediums through which they revealed their messages.

Some (Moses, Samuel, Daniel) claimed to acquire their revelations through direct communication with God; others (Joseph, Balaam, Gideon) maintained they were recipients of messages delivered through dreams or visions. Often, prophets received information without requesting it. On other occasions, when prophets were inquiring about specific choices, or when a simple "yes" or "no" sufficed, the casting of lots, a procedure not unlike the rolling of dice, transmitted the eagerly-sought information. At other times, the highly mysterious Urim and Thummim (Ex. 28:30; Num. 27:21; Deut. 33:8; Prov. 16:33) became the source of inquiries.

Some prophets (Samuel, Jeremiah, Ezekiel, Zechariah) were priests. Some (Elijah, Elisha) were itinerant holy men, or sages, who wandered through the nation pronouncing God's judgments and provoking the anger of the nation's establishment. Some, such as Isaiah and Jeremiah, were court prophets, living among the nation's elite while delivering their declarations in the temple. Some, such as Amos, were simple herdsmen, perhaps from impoverished backgrounds. Amos held two jobs to support his family, and Scripture records that he engaged in the menial job of "pinching sycamore trees."[23] On the other hand, Isaiah and Zephaniah were likely descendants of royalty while Nahum, Obadiah, and Elijah hailed from unknown backgrounds. Some (Elijah, Elisha) invoked miraculous powers as they performed their day-to-day activities; others enhanced their messages through imaginative object lessons such as Hosea's ill-fated, then reconciled, marriage to a prostitute (Hosea 1-3), Jeremiah's wearing of a yoke through the streets of Jerusalem (Jeremiah 27-28), and Ezekiel's lying on his left side for 390 days (Ezekiel 4).

Some prophets (2 Kings 1:8; Zech. 13:4) donned outlandish dress. Others (Elijah, Jonah, Daniel) gained notoriety as a result of unique events that shaped their lives and the lives of those around them. Who can forget the story of Jonah and the great fish or Daniel's encounter with lions? Who can imagine more picturesque stories than those of Elijah's confrontation with Ahab and Jezebel or Ezekiel's fantastic visions of "the flying wheel" or the "valley of living bones?" Our fascination with the prophets is understandable.

Simply, biblical prophets were a vastly divergent group. They became, to a degree, products of their environments, and they clothed their messages in language and allusions appropriate to their cultures. It is understandable that terminology describing these seers and their work proved to be just as diverse. To acknowledge such in no way detracts from the central core of their message; through all the differences a single strand is obvious—they claimed to deliver messages that were not theirs, but had originated with divinity.

Impact of the Hebrew Prophets

Our fascination with the prophets is not based simply on their claim to predict the future. While sharing some attributes and characteristics with seers in surrounding societies, biblical prophets were vastly different and far more influential.

Note their accomplishments. Three world religions—Judaism, Christianity, and Islam—find their origin deeply embedded in the soil of biblical prophecy. Their influence permeates much of western civilization. Our philosophies are nourished by their teachings. Spokesmen for moral stricture and social consciousness exalt the lives and preaching of these ancient Hebrews as fit role models for modern man. Kraeling's glowing tribute is applicable, even if somewhat overstated:

> The influence of the Hebrew prophets on human history has been so vast that it is impossible to appraise or describe it. Without the prophets there would have been no Judaism, no Jesus called the Christ, no apostles and martyrs. ... There would have been no crusades, no Reformation. All history would have been different and far poorer.[24]

Biblical prophets were extraordinary personalities.

Unlike Greek oracles or Mesopotamian astrologers, the prophets addressed the concerns and needs (spiritual, political, social, and economic) of common people. They lashed out at immorality and greed wherever they occurred. They challenged the sovereignty of the mighty who used their power for greed or self-aggrandizement. They chastised the populace for unfaithfulness to God as well as for their deviation from the Law. They pleaded. They begged. They warned. They demanded change, always assuring their listeners of the wanton devastation that would follow if they refused to heed the warnings of the Almighty. This social, preaching function of the prophets—their denunciation of evil and injustice—led many scholars in the nineteenth and early twentieth centuries to argue that the only way to understand biblical writer-prophets was in their roles as social reformers. The job of the prophets, these scholars insisted, was that of proclaiming God's outrage toward a selfish society. In their view, the predictive element in the prophets' writings was of little, if any, value.[25] These scholars labeled the prophets "forthtellers" rather than "foretellers." Thus, Charles claimed, "Prophecy is a declaration, a forthtelling, of the will of God—not a foretelling."[26]

The Hebrew Prophets, Evil, and Injustice

Though our chief concern is not primarily with the prophets' role in reforming society, to neglect this major aspect of their work would be irresponsible. Their indignation, their messages from God, their irregular and highly controversial lifestyles, and even their predictions must be understood in the context of their culture and their beliefs. They were "preachers" of the highest order. Their message, like the message of modern-day reformers and preachers, must be understood in that context. These spokesmen for God were ordained to serve during particular time periods and to meet specific needs. While their words are appropriate for all humanity at all times, certain messages are more meaningful in their historical context. Habbakkuk eloquently expresses our concerns when evil seems rampant in society. Amos and Micah effectively communicate the need to correct social injustice. Malachi carries us to war against our tendencies to become materialistic. To the extent society faces similar problems today, the words of the prophets are reborn as we wrestle with our human flaws and attempt to overcome them.

Similar processes are at work in the secular world. Those who study rhetorical criticism have often surmised that the world's great orations are as much the product of a crucial moment in history as the product of an orator. Winston Churchill, whose fiery speeches and tenacious resolve challenged the free world during the dark days of World War II, is said to have "marshaled the English language and sent it into battle." A half century later, phrases from his speeches still dance gleefully from the pages of history:

"I have nothing to offer but blood, sweat, and tears."
"We shall not flag or fail. We shall fight in France, we shall fight on the

seas and oceans ... we shall fight on the beaches, we shall fight on the landing grounds, we shall fight in the fields and in the streets, we shall fight in
the hills; we shall never surrender."

"Let us therefore brace ourselves to our duties, and so bear ourselves that,
if the British Empire and its Commonwealth last for a thousand years, men
will still say: 'This was their finest hour'!"[27]

For all his reputed skill as an orator, however, when the great conflict ground to a halt, so, seemingly, did Churchill's oratorical genius.
Lacking a real issue, his orations moved swiftly from the sublime to
the forgettable.

In the same sense, Israel's prophets rose to greatness in troubled times
as they squared off against problems that threatened the fiber of their
society. Convinced their civilization's future depended upon its people
being good people who lived according to God's commands, they—like
Coleridge's "Ancient Mariner"—felt compelled to speak against the can-
cers that ate away at their society. To speak out was their obsession.
Jeremiah (20:9) eloquently explained his mission as a "fire" in his bones.
Centuries later, the apostle Paul, gripped by similar inspirational compulsion, sighed, "Woe unto me if I preach not the Gospel of Jesus Christ" (I
Cor. 9:16). A similar compulsion seems to have waged war with all the
prophets, and it thrust them into the forefront of society's battles.

No one has a deeper understanding of their outspoken attacks on evil
and injustice than Abraham Heschel. In the opening pages of his book,
Heschel noted:

> Instead of dealing with the timeless issues of being and becoming, of mat-
> ter and form, of definitions and demonstrations, he (the student of the
> prophetical writings) is thrown into orations about widows and orphans, about
> the corruption of judges and affairs of the marketplace. Instead of showing us
> a way through the elegant mansions of the mind, the prophets take us to the
> slums. ... The prophet's words are outbursts of violent emotions. His rebuke
> is harsh and relentless. ... The prophet is a man who feels fiercely. God has
> thrust a burden on his soul, and he is bowed and stunned at man's fierce
> greed. Frightful is the agony of man; no human voice can convey its full ter-
> ror. Prophecy is the voice that God has lent to the silent agony, a voice to the
> plundered poor, to the profaned riches of the world. It is a form of living, a
> crossing point of God and man. God is raging in the prophet's words.[28]

Before turning our focus toward the uncanny accuracy of predictions
delivered by biblical prophets, we must remember that they were, to a
degree, products of the times in which they lived. Still, we must not
ignore their claim of intimacy with a being far beyond human compre-
hension. Anyone reading Scripture without a preconceived bias will rec-

ognize that "the prophets found their legitimacy and valid credentials first of all in Yahweh's call."[29] It was an integral part of their lives. Aune's declaration that prophecy "consists of intelligible verbal messages believed to originate with God and communicated through inspired human intermediaries"[30] is an excellent starting point for formulating our own definition of a prophet. It is, however, only a starting point.

The prophets' belief that they were communicating with Deity provides a far more encompassing base for our definition than if we assume that they were mere reformers of the social structure. They did, in fact, speak of the future with as much candor and force as they did of the needs of their own society. No one can deny that function involved more than prediction; that declaration was their sole function is, as we shall soon see, simply untrue. Sandmel[31] explained,

> A prophet, simply stated, was someone deemed close to the Deity who through special revelation was able to predict the future. The remarkably elevated content of the literary prophecy of the Tanak [the Old Testament Scriptures] led scholars toward the end of the 19th century to minimize the element of prediction in prophecy. From that generation we have inherited the misleading epigram that the prophets were not "foretellers" but "forthtellers." They were both.

While this proposition will unfold more completely in the next chapter, we must realize that predictions of the future occur with as much frequency as any other theme in the writings of the prophets. On this basis, Meyrick defined "prophets" as the "instruments of revealing God's will to men, specially by predicting future events, and, in particular, by foretelling the incarnation of the Lord Jesus Christ and the redemption effected by him."[32] In following Sandmel and Meyrick, this study will define a "prophet" as "a spokesman who delivers intelligible verbal messages, believed to originate with Deity, that often include references to future events and actions."

The Predictive Element
in Biblical Prophecy

While recognizing the social and religious functions of the prophets, many modern scholars refuse to acknowledge a predictive element in their presentations.[1] Such conclusions simply cannot be substantiated. Bullock explained,

> Although it can accurately be said that the prophets were basically preachers, that is, they spoke to their own times and situations, interpreting current events of history in light of God's will, the predictive element was a distinctive part of their message.[2]

In fact, the predictive element played a significant, rather than miniscule, role in the lives and teachings of the prophets. It is manipulative to say otherwise. As Ramm concluded, "Forth-telling often involved foretelling, for knowledge of the *future* dispositions of God was necessary to influence *present* conduct."[3] Though admitting that previous generations of scholars mistakenly restricted their discussions to the predictive element of the prophetic writings, he added,

> If it was a mistake to emphasize the apologetic element out of all proportion and in neglect of the religious and spiritual ministries of the prophet, it is as much a mistake to ignore the predictive elements to heighten the ethical and spiritual elements. Both elements are there. ...[4]

Thus, in defending the inclusion of the predictive element, we readily admit multiple objectives for prophetic speeches and writings. Given that admission, we now focus on the predictive material delivered by the biblical authors.

Prediction Is Inherent in the Prophetic Writings

A cursory reading of the Scriptures easily establishes that prediction was a prime ingredient of prophetic writings. Payne's massive study of the Old Testament reveals that the 6,641 verses contain 1,239 predictions (about 18.7% of the total).[5] Similarly, the New Testament contains 578 predictions in 1,711 verses. In all of Scripture, slightly more than one verse in five (21.5%) involves prediction.[6] To attempt to rationalize such a massive amount of material is pretentious. Maybe Goebbels, Nazi Germany's propaganda minister, was correct when he claimed that people will come more nearly accepting the "big lie" than several smaller ones.

Prediction in Old Testament Narratives

A quick tour through the Old Testament reveals the key function played by predictions of the future. Even the oldest biblical narrative, the story of creation, ends with a prediction for the future: "And I will put enmity between you and the woman, and between your offspring and hers; he will crush your head, and you will strike his heel" (Gen. 3:15). Noah learns in advance of an impending and catastrophic flood (Gen. 6). The pivotal story of Abraham is replete with predictions regarding the future as God promises: "I will make you into a great nation and I will bless you; I will make your name great, and you will be a blessing. I will bless those who bless you, and whoever curses you I will curse; and all peoples on earth will be blessed because of you" (Gen. 12:2-3). Years later, the promise was repeated (Gen. 15:1-6; 18:10-14). The writer of Hebrews recalled the episode centuries afterward, adding,

> By faith Abraham, even though he was past age—and Sarah herself was barren—was enabled to become a father because he considered him faithful who had made the promise. And so from this one man, and he as good as dead, came descendants as numerous as the stars in the sky and as countless as the sand on the seashore (Heb. 11:11-12).

Nor does the thread of prediction end with Abraham. Isaac and Jacob received the same promise (Gen. 26:2-4; 28:13-15). Later, Joseph saw his future in dreams, though he failed to comprehend the significance until he was promoted to Pharaoh's second-in-command (Gen. 37:1-11; 45:5-7). He also foretold future events to Egyptian servants through their dreams (Gen. 40) and predicted the future of Egyptian agriculture and the cycles of nature over a 14-year period (Gen. 41). As the events in Genesis drew to a close, Joseph gives instructions on the removal of his bones from Egypt when Israel returned to the promised land (Gen. 50:25). To remove the elements of supernatural prediction from these stories depletes their meaning.

Extensive predictions also characterize the stories of Moses in the book of Exodus. As he vacillated in undertaking God's bidding to lead a rag-tag group of slaves from bondage, he was told, "When you have brought the people out of Egypt, you will worship God on this mountain" (Exo. 3:12). When his prolonged protests were answered, he was told Aaron was already on his way to meet him (Exo. 4:14). His ultimate response had been known in advance. The thread of prophecy weaves its way through the entire narrative. The Scriptures record that God announced every plague before it occurred (Exo. 7:17-20; 8:1-4, 16, 20-24; 9:2-6, 8-9, 13-15; 10:3-6, 21-23; 11:1-7; 12:12; 14:1-14). Moreover, to ascertain that the plagues were more than coincidence, each announcement was highly descriptive. No vague generalities bewildered the Egyptians. To the contrary, specific details saturated the announced judgments.

On and on the story goes. Throughout the Old Testament, whether one is reading Genesis or Malachi, the Psalms or Isaiah, the predictive element cannot be overlooked. Even so-called non-literary prophets utilized predictive theology as well as demands for social justice. Elijah, stung by rampant corruption and evil in Ahab's kingdom, strode defiantly into the presence of the selfish monarch and proclaimed, "As the Lord, the God of Israel, lives, whom I serve, there will be neither dew nor rain in the next few years except at my word" (I Kings 17:1).

Add to these references the myriad of predictive statements drawn from writings of the prophets, and you must conclude that foretelling was a weighty function enjoined upon the Hebrew prophets. Isaiah considered the predictive component so critical that he challenged the many "false prophets" in his day to predict future happenings in order to validate their credentials. In issuing the challenge, he clearly set forth the claim that his God could predict future occurrences:

> Present your case, says the Lord. Set forth your arguments says Jacob's King. Bring in your idols to tell us what is going to happen. Tell us what the former things were, so that we may consider them and know their final outcome. Or declare to us the things to come, tell us what the future holds, so we may know that you are gods. Do something, whether good or bad, so that we may be dismayed and filled with fear. But you are less than nothing and your works are utterly worthless; he who chooses you is detestable. (Isa. 41:21-24)

After reviewing similar themes throughout Isaiah's writings, Oehler writes, "When it is said in Isaiah 42:9, 'New things do I declare: before they spring forth I tell you of them,' the idea of pure prediction could hardly be more precisely expressed."[7]

In addition to Isaiah, the writer of Deuteronomy plainly informed his readers that one characteristic of a true prophet was the validity of his predictions:

The remains of Ahab's palace at Samaria call to mind the prediction that the evil king would not return from battle (II Chronicles 18). Photo courtesy, Fon Scofield Collection, E.C. Dargan Research Library of the Sunday School Board, SBC.

Isaiah, Jeremiah, and Ezekiel offered detailed predictions regarding the future of ancient Babylon. See chapter 8 for a discussion of the accuracy of these predictions. Photo courtesy, Fon Scofield Collection, E. C. Dargan Research Library of the Sunday School Board, SBC.

I will raise up for them a prophet like you from among their brothers; I will put my words in his mouth, and he will tell them everything I command him. If anyone does not listen to my words that the prophet speaks in my name, I myself will call him to account. But a prophet who presumes to speak in my name anything I have commanded him to say, or a prophet who speaks in the name of other gods, must be put to death. You may say to yourselves, How can we know when a message has not been spoken by the Lord? If what a prophet proclaims in the name of the Lord does not take place or come true, that is a message the Lord has not spoken. That prophet has spoken presumptuously. Do not be afraid of him. (Deut. 18:18-22)

These and many additional passages in the Old Testament would become incomprehensible if we deny their inherent predictive element. How could we logically explain Jeremiah's (28:9) words that, "When the word of that prophet comes to pass, it will be known that the Lord has truly sent the prophet" unless he believed the role of prophet included prediction? Likewise, how could we interpret Ezekiel's (33:33) statement, "When this comes—and come it will—then will they know that a prophet has been among them" if we choose to ignore their claim to predict future events? Surely, Old Testament prophets believed they were foretelling future events.

Prediction in New Testament Times

In New Testament times, one encounters the same elements. The first confrontation between Jesus and Jewish social and religious leaders occurred when Jesus visited his hometown synagogue, took the scroll of Isaiah, and read:

The Spirit of the Lord is on me, because he has anointed me to preach good news to the poor. He has sent me to proclaim freedom for the prisoners and recovery of sight for the blind, to release the oppressed, to proclaim the year of the Lord's favor (Isa. 61:1-2).

Having completed the reading, he gazed intently at his audience, then electrified them by adding, "Today this Scripture is fulfilled in your hearing" (Luke 4:21). Such segments of the gospels would be of little worth if Isaiah contained no predictive elements. In another confrontation with his accusers, Jesus responded, "You diligently study the Scriptures because you think that by them you possess eternal life. These are the Scriptures that testify about me" (John 5:39). Matthew records no less than thirteen instances where Jesus proclaims that certain events occurred "to fulfill" the Scriptures. Jesus even foretold his own death to help his disciples come to grips with the tragedy. "I have told you now before it happens," he said, "So that when it does happen you will believe" (John 14:29; 16:4).

When Jesus no longer walked Palestine's dusty trails, the apostles and New Testament writers continued the relentless discussion of fulfilled prophecy. In delivering the church's foundational sermon on Pentecost, Peter liberally punctuated it with exclamations of fulfilled prophecy, quoting both David (Psa. 16:8-11, 110:1) and Joel (2:28-32), insisting that Jesus was the one predicted by the prophetic writings. A short time later, when Jewish authorities hauled Peter and John before their tribunal to answer charges that they were preaching in the name of Jesus, they responded by quoting from the Psalms (118:22) and applying the reference to Christ.

The well-known encounter between Philip the evangelist and the treasurer from Ethiopia further illustrates the belief in Old Testament prediction. Joining himself to the slow-moving procession, Philip discovered the governmental official struggling to understand Isaiah's prophecy of the suffering servant (Isa. 53). When given the opportunity to interpret the meaning of the passage, Philip unhesitatingly applied it to Jesus.

Both Peter and Paul made the fulfillment of Scripture central in their argumentation. While preaching to Cornelius, Peter explained, "All the prophets testify about him" (Acts 10:43). Paul always took the opportunity to explain to his hearers, "What God promised our fathers he has fulfilled for us" (Acts 13:32-33). He defended his faith before rulers with explanations such as, "I am saying nothing beyond what the prophets and Moses said would happen" (Acts 26:22). Thus, to ignore the centrality of predictive prophecy in Scripture is a mockery of scholarship.

Thankfully, more and more scholars are beginning to understand that abandoning the predictive element in the prophetic writings is inexcusable. As Jack Lewis observed, "The stress upon prediction in the Old Testament is too striking to be ignored."[8] Other widely-respected authorities have taken similar positions: "… whether modern scholars like it or not, prediction was the way the New Testament writers themselves related the Testaments."[9] Expunging the predictive element from either the Old or the New Testament would be invalid.

Prediction Is Essential to the Prophets' Character

To deny the predictive element in the prophetic writings also denies the very nature of the messengers themselves. For centuries, they carried the title of "prophets." Antiquity's scholars labeled them so. Churchmen throughout the Christian era, at least until modern times, unanimously followed the lead. Books by the thousands focus on the Old Testament "prophets." Guillaume's succinct observation is oft-quoted: "There is no prophet in the Old Testament who was not a fore-

Biblical prophets predicted the demise of the Philistine city of Ashdod (see chapter 9). These ruins at the site of the ancient city testify to the accuracy of their predictions. Photo courtesy, Fon Scofield Collection, E.C. Dargan Research Library of the Sunday School Board, SBC.

teller of the future. ... When a prophet ceases to prophesy in this sense he ceases to be a prophet and becomes a preacher. ... The power of predicting the future was regarded by the Hebrews as the distinguishing mark of prophetic activity."[10]

Realizing it would be naive to attempt a study of the prophets without noting their predilection for future events, Sawyer added, "... prediction is an integral part of the biblical tradition of the prophets."[11] He then turned to the passage regarding true and false prophets found in Deuteronomy (18:18-22) and concluded: "... the fulfillment of prophecy is a major concern of the Deuteronomist, and he argues throughout that God is true to his word."[12] To deny the predictive element is to deny the very core of the biblical message; the Bible makes no sense if we remove all the predictions.

Moreover, when biblical prophets were compared to those who might have been considered their peers in antiquity, they were always discussed side-by-side with oracles, diviners, astrologers, and soothsayers, all of whom gained prominence through prediction. It is noteworthy that none of their peers acquired fame through preaching. Had the biblical prophets been mere preachers, constant comparisons with augurs, oracles, and astrologers would be difficult to comprehend.

Finally, the prophets obviously regarded prediction as an essential part of their work. Rowley[13] concluded that they "regarded the foretelling of the future as the essence of their function." They claimed to see the future. Therefore, since prediction is such an integral part of their work, any comparison between them and others who aspired to be their counterparts or their superiors must address the similarities and differences in this arena as well. It is inadequate to compare only their messages of social reform or their outward styles.

The Conditional Element in Biblical Prophecy

Examples of Conditional Prophecies

A full understanding of the biblical prophets also requires an awareness of the conditional nature of many of their prophecies. Just as these reformers denounced corruption and injustice and worked feverishly to eradicate them, they constantly echoed a promise that repentance on the part of the people would soften their punishment at the hands of an angry God. Coupled with prophetic demands for reform came an unbroken series of predictions said to be contingent upon the behavior of those who listened to the messages. If listeners were repentant and attempted to correct their reprobate lifestyles, predicted disasters could be set aside or greatly reduced; if warnings went unheeded, a series of predicted calamities awaited. Note the conditional nature of the future incorporated into Moses' statements as he prepared Israel to enter Canaan[1]:

> If you follow my decrees and are careful to obey my commands ... you will eat all the food you want and live in safety in your land. I will grant peace in the land, and you will lie down and no one will make you afraid. ... But if you will not listen to me and carry out all these commands, and if you reject my decrees and abhor my laws and fail to carry out all my commands, and so violate my covenant, then I will do this to you. ... I will turn your cities into ruins and lay waste your sanctuaries. ... I will waste the land. ... I will scatter you among the nations. ... Your land will be laid waste (Lev. 26: 3, 5-6,14-16,31-33).

> If you pay attention to these laws and are careful to follow them, then the Lord your God will keep his covenant of love with you, as he swore to your forefathers (Deut. 7:12).

> The Lord will establish you as his holy people, as he promised you on oath, if you keep the commands of the Lord your God and walk in his ways (Deut. 28:9).

Not only were promises given through Moses said to be conditional, Moses' successor, Joshua, after years of serving as a harbinger between

God and Israel, echoed the same message just prior to his death: "If you forsake the Lord and serve foreign gods, he will turn and bring disaster on you ... after he has been good to you" (Josh. 24:20).

Other spokesmen for Yahweh entered the fray. Like Moses and Joshua, their predictions for the future of nations, cities, and peoples were also predicated upon the principle of conditionality. The following statements illustrate the ongoing nature of that principle during the days of the writing prophets:

> Tell them everything I command you. Do not omit a word. Perhaps they will listen and each will turn from his evil way. Then I will relent and not bring on them the disaster I was planning. ... Now reform your ways and your actions and obey the Lord your God (Jer. 26:2-3,13).
>
> But if a wicked man turns away from all the sins he has committed and keeps all my decrees and does what is just and right, he will surely live; he will not die. None of the offenses he has committed will be remembered against him. Because of the righteous things he has done, he will live. Do I take any pleasure in the death of the wicked? declares the Sovereign Lord. Rather, am I not pleased when they turn from their ways and live (Eze. 18:21-23)?
>
> And if I say to the wicked man, 'You will surely die,' but he then turns from his sin and does what is just and right—if he gives back what he took in pledge for a loan, returns what he has stolen, follows the decrees that give life, and does no evil, he will surely live; he will not die (Eze. 33:14-15).
>
> Return to the Lord your God, for he is gracious and compassionate, slow to anger and abounding in love, and he relents from sending calamity (Joel 2:13).
>
> When God saw what they did and how they turned from their evil ways, he had compassion and did not bring upon them the destruction he had threatened (Jonah 3:10).
>
> If at any time I announce that a nation or kingdom is to be uprooted, torn down and destroyed, and if that nation I warned repents of its evil, then I will relent and not inflict on it the disaster I had planned (Jer. 18:7-8).

The last reference furnishes the most straightforward argument for conditional prophecy found in Scripture. Jeremiah clearly states that predictions regarding the temporal future of nations and people are not unalterable. Rather, predictions easily could be set aside as a result of repentant attitudes. After reviewing several excerpts from Jeremiah (17:19-27; 22:1-8; 26:1-15; 38:17-18; and 42:10-17) regarding conditional prophecies, Kearley concludes,

> Surely, these conditional statements flavor the entire message of Jeremiah with a conditional nature. Indeed, all other specific, similar prophecies in Jeremiah must carry the same kind of conditions, especially in light of the fact that Jeremiah announced the conditional principle as an exegetical principle by which people might understand his message.[2]

Furthermore, God couched his promises to individuals in conditional language. At the outset of Solomon's reign over Israel, He informed the monarch, "... if you will walk in my ways and obey my statutes and commands as David your father did, I will give you a long life" (I Kings 3:14).

Biblical prophecies, though conditional, were clear as to what would happen to Israel if she rejected God. Even the startling fortifications and exemplary defense of the twenty-three-acre flat-top mesa at Masada could not thwart the warnings of Deuteronomy 28:15, 49, 52: "...if you do not obey the Lord your God...all these curses will come upon you...The Lord will bring a nation against you from far away, from the ends of the earth...They will lay siege to all the cities throughout the land until the high fortified walls in which you trust fall down." (Photo courtesy, Fon Scofield Collection, E. C. Dargan Research Library of the Sunday School Board, SBC.)

Later, Solomon was told, "... if you walk before me in integrity of heart and uprightness, as David your father did, and observe my decrees and laws, I will establish your royal throne over Israel forever, as I promised David your father" (I Kings 9:4-5). Near the end of Solomon's reign, after he had strayed from his father's religion and his father's God, an inevitable verdict followed: "Since this is your attitude and you have not kept my covenant and my decrees, which I commanded you, I will most certainly tear the kingdom ... out of the hand of your son" (I Kings 11:11-12). Payne provides an appropriate summary for the immense role conditionality played in the writings of the biblical prophets:

> It is not that God's standards, His decrees, or His nature are changeable; it is, in fact, the very immutability of the character of deity which necessitates the application of differing aspects of His fixed principles, in accordance with such changes as may be exhibited by fickle men. Prophecy in particular

has been designed by God for moral ends, so as to motivate men into confor-
mity with divine holiness.[3] We would do well to remember that the conditional nature of biblical prophecy also differentiates God's prophets from
mere pretenders since its purpose is to encourage repentance.

Given the existence of conditional prophecy, two questions arise. First,
how many biblical prophecies are conditional? Second, how do we distinguish between predictions that are conditional and those that are not?

The Extent of Conditionality in Scripture

Initially, we must determine the extent of conditionality in Scripture.
Here, several mistaken views have surfaced. One asserts that no prophecies are conditional; all are absolute dictums. Such is inconsistent with
what the Scriptures claim. A wealth of verses either presupposes or
openly declares their conditional nature.

A second view holds that only prophetic statements that specifically
claim conditionality can be considered as such. Again, in light of explicit
passages such as those described in Jeremiah 18, the biblical standard is at
odds with such a position. That standard implies that any prophecy related
to temporal nations, cities, and people can be considered conditional.

Berkhof advocates a third alternative in which he contends two specific requirements must be met for a prophecy to be considered conditional:
(1) the time of the prophecy must be close at hand, and (2) the prediction
must be capable of satisfaction by the prophet's contemporaries.[4] Again,
no definitive statements in Scripture lend credence to this alternative.

A fourth view holds that all biblical prophecies are conditional. This view
is also difficult to defend, however, as promises regarding the coming of the
"Chosen One" or the Messiah seem to be totally unrelated to any condition.

Two Types of Prophecies Identified

Kearley proposes the most sensible resolution of the problem.[5] He suggests there are two basic types of prophecies. The first, and most important, relates to what biblical writers call "the mystery" (Eph. 1:9; 3:4).
God's primary interest, according to Scripture, centers around spiritual
redemption and man's salvation—the reconciliation of the creature and
the Creator. Kearley maintains that all prophecies regarding "God's eternal purpose" are immutable. On the other hand, he holds that all other
predictions pertain to issues that are trivial in light of eternity.

Contrast, for instance, the predictions regarding the destruction of
Assyrian Nineveh and those detailing events surrounding the coming of
the Messiah. Both are described in detail in Scripture. The destruction of

Nineveh, however, was unrelated to the birth of the Messiah and the plan of salvation. As such, references to Nineveh were conditional. God's eternal plan for man's redemption could have been carried out regardless of the future of Assyria's capital city.

When Jonah delivered God's message of doom upon the city, it was understood that the decreed destruction was not unalterable. Jonah's actions in fleeing from his appointed task signified his understanding of the conditional nature of the prophecy. Assyria terrorized Israel's northern tribes for years and the prophet, no doubt, was unwilling to offer the inhabitants of Nineveh an opportunity to escape the full fury of God's wrath. Later, when he reluctantly delivered God's warnings, Jonah wandered a safe distance from the city and smugly settled back to witness the impending slaughter. Perhaps a monster earthquake would swallow the city. Perhaps fire and brimstone would plunge from the skies, incinerating everything that moved. Much to his chagrin, and with his worst fears realized, Nineveh repented. Its destruction was averted.

Had Nineveh's repentance been long-lasting, the city conceivably could have been an important population center hundreds of years later. That Nineveh failed to be destroyed when its inhabitants repented at the preaching of Jonah (4:10) supplies ample evidence that such predictions were contingent upon the reactions of the people rather than upon some unalterable timetable. Had Nineveh rejected the preaching of the prophet, the timetable of destruction in forty days would doubtless have been enforced. Thus, whether a nation retained power over a piece of temporal real estate, appears insignificant alongside eternity, and prophecies relating to such issues were always capable of being altered. Kaiser wrote, "... almost every prophecy, except for those involved with the provision of our salvation and with the creation, maintenance, and renewal of the universe, has an 'unless' or 'if' ... connected with it."[6]

On the other hand, some prophecies in Scripture do seem constant. These predictions revolve around the coming of the "Anointed One" (*mashiach*) or the "Messiah." Within Old Testament Scriptures are many hints that His arrival in the world would occur within a fairly explicit time frame. The event was pre-set; the time was exact. No hints of possible postponements are recorded. As early as the patriarchs, prophecy revealed that the tribe of Judah would still possess certain self-governing abilities when the Messiah entered the world (Gen. 49:10).[7] Other predictions presuppose the existence of the Jewish Temple during the lifetime of the Messiah (Psa. 69:9; Mal. 3:1). Furthermore, mysterious timetables in Daniel (2; 7; and 9:24-27) strongly implied that the long-awaited ruler would appear during the time of the Roman Empire.

Neither humanity's reaction to God's laws nor the acceptance or rejection of His plan ever became a determining factor in God's scheme of reconciliation. In fact, not only did God devise His strategy prior to the creation, He understood even then that much of humanity would openly reject the Messiah (Isa. 53) when he entered the world. Such passages suggest God's plan was immune to human tampering. In other words, whether humanity accepted the plan or not, God orchestrated the procession of events so that the plan became reality. According to Scripture, this plan of redemption is part of God's character and nature. He would have offered it even if no one accepted.

Contrast the two types of prophecies. On one hand are prophecies based on the unchangeable character of God. Since His character does not change, neither will the outcome of the predictions. On the other hand, since changeable human response determines the outcome of other predictions, logically those predictions should be conditional. Girdlestone argues that predictions relating to specific (and limited) groups of people, individuals, or nations can be modified, depending upon the action of those involved, while predictions given to humanity as a whole are never altered. These irreversible promises do not depend on man's goodness, but on God's.[8]

Positions like Kearley's and Girdlestone's are consistent with another theme in Scripture—the conditional nature of salvation. According to the Bible, the opportunity for salvation is available for everyone, yet, over and over, biblical writers tie salvation to an obedient faith on the part of humanity. The promises are grand—eternal life, happiness, contentment, our every need taken care of—and, yet, these promises are not realized if we reject God's love and grace. Since prophecies involve God's promises for the future, the conditional nature of those promises is consistent with the conditional nature of salvation.

Summary

Three ideas are key to the study. First, biblical prophets expressed deep concern with the conditions of society in which they lived. They were reformers as well as prophets. Second, alongside their work in proclaiming the anger of God regarding evil and injustice and their demand for repentance, these prophets did reveal numerous predictions regarding the future. It is impossible to read their writings without sensing the predictive element. Third, Scripture substantiates the conditionality of many prophecies. Those relating to God's redemptive causes appear unchangeable; those that deal with temporal motifs are flexible.

The Apologetic Value of Biblical Prophecy

The preliminaries are behind.

Acknowledging the predictive element in Scripture assures us that a link exists between that element and apologetics. It exposes the very heart of Scripture to attacks by the non-believer. More importantly, however, it offers opportunities for the believer to test the validity of his or her faith in a world rife with skepticism. Unlike any other religious dogma, it offers a rational justification for its doctrine. If Scripture predicts future events with any degree of regularity in a manner subject to open evaluation, then serious consideration of all its other doctrines is warranted. Herein lies the essence of contemporary disagreement regarding the nature of Scripture.

Like a child clutching a favorite, worn-out toy, much of modern scholarship still clings tenaciously to nineteenth century ideas that writings of the biblical prophets are no more than the products of human genius — the result of an evolving awareness of social justice wrenched from a mere handful of men who were intellectually "far above their neighbors or their conquerors, above all the rest of the world ... for hundreds and hundreds of years."[1] These scholars carve up the prophets and serve them as merely the best of humanity's whims and wishes, quaint historical relics, of value primarily to nostalgia buffs and historian-philosophers.

Inadequacy of Nineteenth Century Theology

This school contends the prophets were delivering only personal ideas that they thought, in some vague manner, were messages from God. It asserts that true prediction is impossible and suggests that anyone who declares biblical prophets engaged in such is advancing arguments detrimental to faith. One proponent of this theory is Gurdon Oxtoby. He explained:[2]

Is it credible that a man living in the sixth or seventh century before Christ could, with any accuracy, predict what would not occur until hundreds of years had passed? If his world was one in which Assyria or Babylonia was the leading world power, could he foresee conditions that would prevail when Greece or Rome had succeeded them? To many honest inquirers, there is something of the magical or superstitious in such assumptions. ... A detailed representation of the future ... seems to many of us to put the Bible into a difficult, not to say a questionable, position. It seems to obligate the reader of the Bible to attitudes and presuppositions that he rejects in all other areas of his experience. No wonder there is a widespread feeling that religion is superstition, that faith is unreasonable, and that the Old Testament prophets really belong to the age of enchanters and sorcerers of Babylon, or the priestesses of the famous oracles of ancient Greece.

Oxtoby's position, like that of most modern theologians, is cradled in several highly untenable assumptions.

Attacking Strawmen

First, those who espouse such a philosophy construct a strawman rather than deal with precise statements of Scripture. I know of no conservative scholar who asserts that the prophets, on their own, or assisted by some vague, inner guidance system more like indigestion than inspiration, were able to look "hundreds of years into the future" and describe minute aspects of future society. To assert that evangelical scholars accept such a scenario is ludicrous.

Denying the Power of God

Second, Oxtoby's rejection of prophecy allows no room for a supernatural being. Surely, a God powerful enough to create the vast universe in which we live, who understands its minute inner workings, and who brought man into existence and presented him with an eternal soul, can know the future. If not, then the issues that demand discussion are far more intricate than the reality of prophecy. Much more at issue are questions that ask:

> "Is there really a God?"
> "If so, what is the nature and power of God?"
> "Is God capable of determining the future?"
> "Is God capable of communicating with man?"
> "Does God want to communicate with man?"

If God has power to create the universe, with the natural laws that govern it, then why is it thought incredible that He also has the power to foresee future events? If one denies the creative power of God or His ability to foresee the future, then one must ask why the Bible and its teachings are worthy of study at all. The real issue, then, becomes one's conception and understanding of God.

For some, the hang-up occurs in areas of communication. William Temple argued, "There is no such thing as revealed truth. There are truths of revelation, that is to say propositions that express the results of correct thinking regarding revelation; but they are not themselves directly revealed."[3] Scholars like Temple accept the power of God but suggest that He is either unable or unwilling to communicate with man except in an indeterminate, generalized fashion. The same line of reasoning is obvious in the writings of C. H. Dodd who alleged that Jeremiah was not commissioned by God but experienced some type of "hallucination."[4] Again, the issue really goes back to one's concept of God. If God created the universe, life, and man, surely He understands enough about man and the rest of His creation to communicate about that creation to man.[5]

Refusing to Consider Opposing Views

Third, those who hold the position articulated by Oxtoby demonstrate an unquestioning faith in all aspects of higher criticism. They defend higher criticism's tenets with all the veracity they so quickly condemn in those who defend the Scriptures. They criticize those who accept Scripture as the inerrant Word of God because they claim those who do so are unwilling to consider opposing evidence. Yet, the same authors who declare objectivity to be a virtue refuse to consider evidence in opposition to higher criticism. Packer succinctly describes the problem:[6]

> Mesmerized by the problems of rationalistic criticism, we can no longer hear the Bible as the Word of God. Liberal theology, in its pride, has long insisted that we are wiser than our fathers about the Bible, and must not read it as they did, but must base our approach to it on the "assured results" of criticism, making due allowance for the human imperfections and errors of its authors. This insistence has a threefold effect. It produces a new papalism—the infallibility of the scholars, from whom we learn what the "assured results" are. It raises doubt whether every biblical passage truly embodies revelation or not. It also destroys the reverent, receptive, self-distrusting attitude of approach to the Bible. ...

Obviously, several problems inhere with blind acceptance of the critical method. Unfortunately, the time and space to review them at this juncture is lacking. Those interested in such can find in-depth discussions in many sources.

What is the point? What difference does it make if the Bible is or is not filled with predictions? It makes a world of difference. If we remove the predictions, we have no rational reason for accepting the rest of the material. Remove the predictions and the prophets are just another group of men whose opinions are mere entertainment for others; but, if they accurately predict future events, humanity must rationally explain how these spokesmen were able to accomplish such remarkable feats.

Ancient Jerusalem became the object of numerous predictions found in both Old and New Testaments. The accuracy of these predictions serve as important evidence of the inspiration of Scripture. See, especially, the discussion in chapter 17. (Photo courtesy, Mr. Lawrence Williams.)

Standards for Evaluating Prophetic Claims

How are we to determine the validity of the prophets' claims? Is it possible that their predictive successes go beyond the possibilities of mere chance? To answer questions like these, we must establish objective, verifiable standards.

In prescribing these standards by which prospective prophets are to be judged, only the predictive element will be considered. This approach is essential because, in the broadest understanding of the concept which declares prophecy to be merely the forthtelling of someone's message, anyone with an unusual or unique teaching can declare himself/herself as a prophet/prophetess. If the broad understanding is accepted, there is no objective manner by which such claims can be evaluated. How can we know whether the message originated with deity or not? How can we distinguish the prophet from the charlatan?

What are the standards?

What would a reasonably intelligent person need to know in order to conclude that an individual truly predicted a future event? Numerous answers have been proposed. Davison,[7] for example, listed the following as his "Criterion for Prophecy:"

> First, the known promulgation of prophecy prior to the event; secondly, the clear and palpable fulfillment of it; lastly, the nature of the event itself—if when the prediction was given, it lay remote from human view, and was such as could not be foreseen by any supposable effort of reason, or be deduced upon principles of calculation derived from probability and experience.

Culver,[8] on the other hand, approached the standards by what he called distinctive characteristics: "They will not be mere sage remarks, or scientific prediction (sic) based on laws of nature," he penned. "Neither will they reflect a humanly controlled situation wherein the prophet or his supporters fulfill the prophecy. They must be predictions of the future."

One eighteenth century writer declared, "Prophecy is a miracle of knowledge, a declaration, a description or representation of something future, beyond the power of human sagacity to determine or calculate, and it is the highest evidence that can be given of ... communion with ... God."[9] While disagreement occurs over the wording of the standards, certain criteria do seem essential. Kuenan,[10] for example, observed: "It must first be proved that the prediction actually preceded the event. ..." Using his observation as a base, the following standards seem to be reasonable criteria for assessing the claims of predictive prophecy.

First, the prediction should occur well in advance of the fulfillment. There should be no valid reason to suspect the prophecy was after-the-fact.

Second, the prediction should be accurate. It must conform to historical fact.

Third, fulfillment should occur in an impartial manner. There should be no evidence of collusion or manipulation of the events.

Fourth, the fulfillment should be obvious to a reasonable person. Absent bias toward either position, an individual should be able to weigh evidence on both sides of the argument and conclude that a prediction was made prior to an event and was later confirmed to have occurred through valid testimony. This does not suggest that the prediction has to be totally free from ambiguity, but that the fulfillment should be obvious.

Fifth, predictive prophecy should be dynamic. It must be ongoing, repetitive, and consistent. Anyone can be lucky, so, to eliminate the chance of an accidental fulfillment, the number of accurate predictions should be significant.

Sixth, the prediction should suggest supernatural guidance. Prediction capable of being based on human reasoning or genius is not sufficient to establish one's claim as a prophet.

With these qualifications in hand, let us examine the predictive writings of the biblical prophets. Did they accurately predict future events with any degree of regularity? The answer to this query will take us on an extended tour of the ancient world. Our first stop will be in Egypt.

6

Egypt in Prophecy:
Predicting the Decline and Fall
of History's Greatest Civilization

No land of antiquity could match Egypt. Born amid the fertile Nile Valley, it matured rapidly and dominated the western world longer than any nation in history. It assumed the role of the supreme power in the Mediterranean. Where Greece and Rome counted their supremacy by the centuries, Egypt numbered hers by the millennia. Appropriately, our study of biblical predictions starts in the land of the Pharaohs.

Egypt's Claim to Grandeur

Grand temples and awesome tombs dotted ancient Egypt. To outsiders they presented both the illusion of the eternal and the mystery of the ethereal. Respect for Egyptian power pervaded the Mediterranean world. Seemingly, there had never been a time this great nation did not exist. Writing originated in Egypt. The earliest records of Western man were penned there. Etched on the tablets of history can be found their achievements in the arts, in architecture, and in engineering. Egyptian armies strode defiantly through the region. During her peak, Egyptian power was relentless.

When biblical prophets offered their predictions, Egypt's mystique dominated the Western world. Though her military might was no longer invincible, no other prophets in antiquity seemed ready to announce her demise. For most, not even the Assyrian and Babylonian empires seemed capable of successfully challenging the might of her armies. Pro-Egyptian feelings dominated Israel during the days of the prophets. Many in Israel trusted that an alliance with their southern neighbor would protect them from invasion (Eze. 17:15-17; II Kings 17:4-7). Within this milieu, biblical prophets spun their tales of Egypt's future.

Predictions Regarding Ancient Egypt

One prophet after another enumerated his predictions. Eight complete chapters of the Old Testament (680 verses) resound with the echoes of their rebukes. Other scattered verses add to the sheer volume of material produced by these ancient messengers. No other country received as much press from the prophets as did ancient Egypt.

Because of the sheer volume of material, knowing where to begin might be confusing. Still, among predictive material relating to Egypt, no references are more significant than those in Isaiah 19. One commentator termed the chapter "the most important prophetic utterance concerning Egypt in all the Old Testament."[1] Seven major predictive themes surface as the torrents of God's judgments prepared to deluge antiquity's greatest kingdom: (1) Egypt would be harassed with civil conflicts; (2) the Nile's life-giving properties would lessen; (3) Egypt's celebrated canals would become putrid and unusable; (4) prolific vegetation growing along the waterways would diminish; (5) a drastic decline in Egypt's fisheries would follow; (6) the fabled artistry of her workers and craftsmen would be lost; and (7) her renowned military would be crushed.

Each prediction offered specific details. Each prediction's fulfillment can be thoroughly documented.

Prediction of Civil Conflict

Any nation can have internal disagreements that can turn violent and lead to bloodshed. It is a paradox that Earth's most intelligent inhabitant should be cursed to be its most argumentative and sanguinary. From modern perspective, a prediction of civil conflict would hardly be worth our notice. Jeremiah's lament (8:11), "They cry, 'peace, peace' when there is no peace" appropriately summarizes our world at the close of the twentieth century.

Yet, such a prediction leveled against Egypt at the time of the prophets prove far more difficult. Obviously, Egypt has not been immune to such influences, but, surprisingly, those influences seldom appear in her early history. Records of ancient Egypt portray a land of immense political stability. She seemed to sense that her grandeur relied upon a strong central government. Both Herodotus and Diodorus Siculus reported the need for stability to be so intense that the Egyptians refused to continue for any length of time without a king.[2] Besides, records from ancient Egypt suggest that when trouble erupted, non-indigenous inhabitants usually started the troubles.

When the land divided into smaller, independent states, the resulting confederacies expressed open congeniality. Even during the 21st dynasty, when Theban high priests usurped the throne, the challenge did not result in civil warfare.[3] Only one significant civil disturbance occurred during Egypt's history prior to the time of the biblical prophets. That came during the reign of Takelothis II (circa 850-825 B.C.) and was drastically limited in scope.[4]

Thus, when Isaiah forecast violent civil wars throughout the land, no personal experiences dictated his prophecies. Egypt had been notoriously stable. Yet, Isaiah (19:2) wrote, "And I (God) will incite Egypt against Egypt, and a man will fight against his brother, and a man against his neighbor, city against city, kingdom against kingdom." The prophecy proved amazingly accurate.

Not long after Isaiah's prediction, Egypt witnessed a period "punctuated by civil war and ... increasing local separatism."[5] This divisiveness paved the way for the first successful invasion of the country in nearly a thousand years when an Ethiopian king, Pi-ankhi, encouraged by the weakened defenses, sought to end Egyptian dominance in the region. Little of outward consequence resulted from Pi-ankhi's short-lived campaign. Egypt's internal squabbling intensified. Diodorus described the period just before the ascension of Psammetichus I as if he were reading Isaiah's prophecy: "There was anarchy in Egypt," he wrote. "The people fall into broils and tumults and slaughter one of another."[6]

Though Psammetichus temporarily reversed the trend, an irrevocable pattern became apparent. Eventually, internal strife sufficiently weakened Egypt to allow capture and subjugation by her enemies. With her loss of self-determination, Egypt's fabled culture vanished. Isaiah (19:3) saw the future.

Predictions Regarding the Nile River

Hidden deep within Africa's heartland, hundreds of miles from the Mediterranean, the sources of the Nile River—and the sources of life for Egypt—emerge. The Greeks called Egypt "the gift of the Nile." They were correct. Without the river, Egypt would have been a barren, dusty wasteland dotted with sand dunes and menacing deserts. Egypt owed everything to the Nile. She never forgot its importance.

Egyptian Reverence for the Nile. Even in the earliest records, Egyptians worshiped the Nile. Old inscriptions name the river "Hapi, father of the gods, lord of sustenance."[7] Later, when Egypt's armies marched up the river in their periodic conquests, they searched dutifully for its origin. When they reached Khartoum, they observed that, though the river divided in half, each stream seemed equal to the other. One stream, the Blue Nile, flowed northward from distant mountains. The other, the White Nile, could be traced to the immense equatorial plain.

Yet, as far as their armies traveled, the river "always appeared as wide, as full, as irresistible in its progress as ever. It was a fresh water sea, and sea (*iauma ioma*) was the name by which they called it."[8] For the Egyptians, the Nile originated in heaven.

The earliest records suggest a belief that the river cascaded to the earth via a giant waterfall located somewhere south of the first cataract. "Conquests carried into the heart of Africa later forced the Egyptians to recognize their error, but did not weaken their faith in the supernatural origin of the river. They only placed its source further south, and surrounded it with greater marvels. ... The Nile was said to have its source in Paradise."[9] Because the Nile supposedly emanated from celestial sources, ancient Egyptians felt the need to sacrifice to the river. Traditions "assert that the prelude to the opening of the canals, in the time of the Pharaohs, was the solemn casting to the waters of a young girl decked as for her bridal—the 'Bride of the Nile'."[10]

Not only did the inhabitants of Egypt view the Nile as a god, they also imparted to the plants and animals that grew along its banks and roamed the regions near the river the same characteristics. So many deities surfaced that "one would think that the country had been inhabited for the most part by gods, and contained just sufficient men and women to satisfy the requirements of their worship."[11] Although believing the river and its inhabitants to be gods, the people used both to survive and advance. Networks of canals channeled water deep into the desert and transformed burning sands into productive agricultural land. The Egyptians became so successful at harvesting the river that, centuries afterward, Rome transformed Egypt into the "breadbasket of the world."[12]

Breadbasket or not, biblical prophets leveled some stunning predictions at the Nile and her dependents. Specifically, the prophets noted: (1) irrigation canals would be dried up; (2) the river would stink; (3) papyrus growing along its banks would diminish; (4) lotus plants would no longer flourish; and (5) Egypt's splendid fisheries would all but disappear. Each prophecy proved accurate.

The Decline of the Canals. Both Ezekiel (30:12) and Isaiah (19:5-6) predict the decline and disappearance of the canals. At the time of these predictions, the canals had been in continuous use for centuries. Even when Egypt first succumbed to foreign invaders, the invaders carefully maintained the intricate system of waterways. Conquerors recognized the need for Egyptian agriculture to remain vibrant and productive. They understood that a world often wracked with famine needed Egypt as an unfailing food supply. The likelihood that anyone would allow the system to deteriorate seemed nil.

Yet, that did happen. When Muslim armies seized Egypt six centuries after the death of Christ, they neglected the canals. They diverted, for personal uses, monies intended to keep them in repair. One historian described correspondence between a Muslim conqueror and the caliph detailing the maintenance of the canals. Unfortunately, the caliph ignored the instructions. The writer concludes, "the canals have ... been 'minished and dried up'."[13] Today, most canals remain covered— clogged with sand and debris from centuries of neglect. Those that remain possess little value. A nineteenth century writer observed, "They all want deepening ... (and) run dry at the critical season of the year."[14] If these canals were clean and kept in good repair, Egypt's agricultural production would soar. For several reasons—some political, some economic, some religious—this has not happened. Her canals remain worthless, silt-filled gullies. The unthinkable has happened. A thousand years of neglect testify to the Bible's accuracy.

Putrification of the Canals. Declining use of the canals accounts for the fulfillment of the second part of the prophecy. The waters became odorous. Instead of allowing water to flow freely, remnants of the ancient canals serve as traps and allow it to stagnate. One writer, speaking of canals in Cairo, observed that it would be more desirable to fill the remains than to leave them partially exposed. Such action, he explained, would free "the houses on its banks from the noxious vapors that rise when the water has retired and left a bed of liquid mud."[15]

Decline of the Nile's Ecosystem. With the canals' disappearance, flora alongside the Nile vanished as well. The prophets foretold that, too. "The reeds and the flags shall wither," Isaiah (19:6-7) predicted. "The paper reeds by the brooks ... and everything sown by the brooks shall wither." The prophecy refers to papyrus—a plant that adorned the banks of the ancient canals in large numbers.

The ancient historian Pliny said the plant grew "in the marsh lands" and described it in detail:

> The root of the plant is the thickness of a man's arm; it has a triangular stalk, growing not higher than ten cubits [approximately fifteen feet], and decreasing in breadth toward the summit. ... They [the Egyptians] employ the root as firewood and for making various utensils. They even construct small boats of the plant; and out of the rind, sails, mats, clothes, bedding, ropes; they eat it either crude or cooked, swallowing only the juice; and when they manufacture paper from it, they divide the stem by means of a kind of needle into thin plates.[16]

The luxurious nature of the vegetation and abundance of fish in the ancient Nile is depicted in this painting on plaster from what is believed to be the tomb of Nebamum at Thebes. (Taken from *Egyptian Designs* by Catherine Calhoun. Used by permission of Stemmer House Publishers, Inc., Owings Mills, Maryland.)

Among Egypt's most valued possessions, papyrus plants thrived in the golden sunshine and well-watered valley. They were hardy and well-suited for their environment. As one scholar noted, "the lotus, the papyrus, and other similar productions of the land ... were ... one of the greatest blessings nature ever provided for any people."[17] Those blessings proved temporary, however, and "the papyrus, and the three varieties of blue, white, and rose lotus which once flourished ... have now almost entirely disappeared."[18] Their loss devastated the Egyptian economy.

Travelers to Egypt a little over a century ago marveled when they noted "no water plants or weeds grow on the banks of the Nile."[19] Biblical predictions again proved accurate.

Decline of Egyptian Culture

Among the more intriguing predictions are those relating to the future decline of a highly-skilled culture. In reality, Egypt's greatness stemmed, not so much from her formidable military prowess as from her cunning workers and craftsmen. Tailors, seamstresses, craftsmen, architects, engineers, artists, and tradesmen flourished. Their handiwork astounds even the most cynical critics. In recent years, touring exhibits from the tombs of Tutankhamen and Ramesses have allowed throngs of Westerners to gape in awe at the almost unimaginable artistry that permeated Egyptian life. The dedication of Egyptian craftsmen to their trades even led them to insist that no artisan work at more than one task. They were among the world's earliest specialists.

This artistry from the Old Kingdom illustrates a metalworkers' workshop. Craftsmen are shown weighing the precious metals (top left), using blowpipes to produce the necessary liquid state, and casting and hammering the cooling metals into shape (top right). The lower drawing illustrates the fashioning of the materials into necklaces and expensive ornaments. From Rawlinson, *A History of Egypt.*

Merchants sought as vigorously for garments made in ancient Egypt as they did for gold and silver. One writer observed: "By the end of the First Dynasty, the Egyptians were producing the finest linen of the ancient world."[20] Solomon imported linen from Egypt and listed it among his treasures (I Kings 10:28). Later, Phoenician traders became wealthy because of their commerce in "fine linen with broidered cloth from Egypt" (Eze. 27:7). Centuries afterward, the Greeks still purchased byssus (the finest linen) woven on Egyptian looms. Merchants from

Europe discovered prosperity through traffic in Egyptian-made apparel. Commerce with Arabia and India flourished.[21]

The demand for Egyptian gear seems justified. One historian elaborated:

> Nor was the praise ... unmerited; and the quality of one piece of linen found near Memphis ... excites equal admiration at the present day, being to the touch comparable to silk and not inferior in texture to our finest cambric. ... Some idea may be given to its texture from the number of threads in the inch, which is 540 (270 double threads) in the warp (and) 110 in the woof. ... It is covered with small figures and hieroglyphs, so finely drawn that here and there the lines are with difficulty followed by the eye. ... The perfection of its threads is equally surprising; the knots and breaks seen

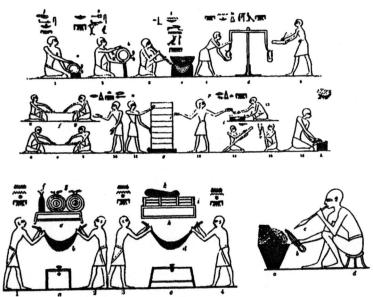

Egyptian artistry from Thebes shows craftsmen producing gold and jewelry. From Rawlinson, *A History of Egypt.*

in our best cambric, are not found in holding it to the light.[22]

Nor was the discovered fabric unique. Other early writers describe a linen corselet made in Egypt whose threads contained an astounding 365 fibers.[23] So exquisite are the garments produced in early Egyptians that their creators would still be in demand today. Yet, the skills of Egypt's leading weavers disappeared with her culture.

When the prophets pronounced God's thunderous judgments on Egypt, not even her magnificent culture escaped. Isaiah (19:9) had written: "They that work in fine flax, and they that weave networks shall be confounded." Again, the predictions were fulfilled.

The Demise of Theban Power

Deep in the heartland of Egypt, nestled between protective deserts and nurtured by the life-giving properties of the Nile, lie the remains of once-magnificent Thebes. The ruins, coupled with records of ancient travelers and historians, speak of a proud and cultured city. Theban kings extended their political influence throughout the land. Theban armies marched northward to the Mediterranean, along the coast into Palestine, and southward deep into Africa to exact tribute and slaves from their enemies. Leaders of Thebes, certain of their city's preeminence, declared first Egypt, then Thebes, as the geographical center of the world.

The Temples of Thebes. With the emergence of Thebes, intimidating temples appeared along the eastern banks of the river. Pylon after pylon pointed their shafts skyward. No edifice could match that of El-Karnak, the greatest of Egypt's surviving temple complexes.

Surrounded by a large brick wall, complete with a 360-foot-wide entrance way, the area housed twenty of Egypt's most impressive sanctuaries. Of these, the Temple of Amun appeared the most awe-inspiring.[24] Its chief attraction, an incredible hypostyle hall leading into its sanctuary, measured 170 feet in length by 329 feet in width. The roof's support came from 134 giant columns, the largest of which soared seventy feet into the air and measured some twelve feet in diameter. It quickly became "the most magnificent work of its class in Egypt."[25]

Between the hall and the sanctuary, four imposing obelisks jutted skyward. A sacred lake lay just south of the sanctuary, giving the entire scene an atmosphere of majesty and serenity. Throughout the complex, statues and bas reliefs expounded the glories of ancient Egypt. Several smaller temples, situated north, east, and south of the main enclosure, added an extra aura of magnificence to the setting as broad avenues, lined with hundreds of ram- and human-headed sphinxes joined the main complex.

A nineteenth-century writer eloquently described the scene:

> It is a place that has been much written about and often painted; but of which no writing and no art can convey more than a dwarfed and pallid impression. To describe it ... by means of words is impossible. The scale is too vast; the effect too tremendous; the sense of one's own dumbness, and littleness, and incapacity too complete and crushing. It is a place that strikes you into silence; that empties you, as it were, not only of words, but of ideas ... I found I never had a word to say in the Great Hall ... I could only look and be silent.[26]

Just three kilometers south of el-Karnak, at modern Luxor, stood the Temple of Amun. Yet another avenue of sphinxes joined this complex to the former. Here, inside another walled enclosure, temples dedicated to Hathor,[27] and Serapis,[28] two red granite obelisks, several colossal statues of Ramesses II, a peristyle court of 74 large columns, a processional colonnade composed of fourteen giant columns, and other smaller halls and sanctuaries could be found. Tutankhamen claimed responsibility for the decorations that adorned the walls.

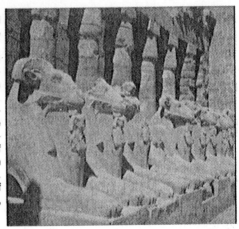

Ram-headed sphinxes lined broad avenues leading to many Egyptian temples. Temples at modern Luxor and Karnak, some three kilometers apart, were joined by such sphinxes. Only a few remain. Many have disappeared completely. Others lie broken in the sands. Biblical prophets foretold the "breaking up" of Thebes. (Photo courtesy, Fon Scofield Collection, E. C. Dargan Research Library of the Sunday School Board, SBC.)

Temples Across the Nile. Immediately across the Nile, additional temples dotted the landscape. For approximately eight kilometers along the river's western banks, travelers came in constant contact with at least one such edifice. Many buildings on the western shore were mortuary temples built for pharaohs whose tombs can be located just to the west in the storied Valley of the Kings. Non-mortuary temples dedicated to Hathor, Thoth, Amun, and Isis also adorned the west bank.

The most impressive buildings on the western shore, however, recognized Queen Hatshepsut and Ramesses II. Partly free-standing and partly carved from massive rock cliffs, the Temple of Hatshepsut was the most pretentious. The temple lay at the base of a ruggedly beautiful cliff and easily dominated the surrounding landscape. It rose in terraces and could be approached only by a "monumental causeway, some 37 meters wide, lined by sphinxes." The site is among the most impressive in all Egypt.[29]

Ramesses' monument, though not as large, was imposing enough. Known as the Ramesseum, the building housed a gigantic statue of the Egyptian monarch that is the largest statue ever uncovered in the land of the Nile. The statue, carved from a single block of granite, weighed nearly 900 tons, and stood sixty feet tall.[30]

Impact of the Temples. The impact overwhelmed visitors as they gazed at the massive structures and their delicate artistry. Diodorus Siculus, who came calling during the first century, B.C. when Thebes' greatness retained only a shell of its original glory, stood in awe at its magnificence: "Never was there a city which received so many offerings in silver, gold, and ivory, colossal statues, and obelisks,"[31] he wrote. Considering Diodorus visits included treks to Athens, Rome, and Babylon, his compliment establishes Thebes' credentials as one of the great cities of the ancient world.

Later visitors found themselves equally amazed. Eighteen centuries after Diodorus, another visitor raved about the city:

> The pyramids, the Catacombs, and some other things to be seen in lower Egypt, are look'd upon as great Wonders; and are justly held in Preference to whatever the rest of the world can boast of. But if these challenge the Preeminence to all the extra-Egyptian world ... they must Yield the Glory of Superiority to the many ancient Temples etc. of (Thebes and Upper Egypt).[32]

Another scholar added, "All here is sublime and majestic."[33] Modern writers agree. Baines and Malik point out: "Its (Thebes') temples were the most important and the wealthiest in the land and the tombs prepared for the elite ... on the west bank were the most luxurious Egypt ever saw."[34]

Population of Thebes. Besides Thebes' architectural beauty, the city also could raise a powerful army. Drawing from the hundreds of thousands of people living in the region, Thebes could quickly field a huge army to oppose any invaders.[35] As late as the period of Roman conquest, the city remained powerful enough to become the chief military headquarters for Rome's occupation legions. Remarkably, at the very time Theban power reached its zenith, biblical prophets outlined predictions of the future far afield from the common perception, even in Israel. Ezekiel (30:14-16) described three distinct occurrences: (1) God would "execute judgments" in Thebes; (2) the "multitudes" of people would be "cut off"; and (3) the city itself would be "broken up." As before, the accuracy of each prediction is easily substantiated.

Judgments Against Thebes. First came the judgments. Ezekiel spoke of these events in the plural. More than once Thebes would feel the sting of oppression and war. Around 525 B.C., the Persian monarch, Cambyses, the first non-Egyptian to subjugate the city, defeated the combined armies of Upper Egypt at Pelusium and marched his armies victoriously into Thebes. Upon occupying the city, Cambyses first inclined to be perceived as a gracious, benevolent dictator. Unfortunately, two setbacks, totally unrelated to the Egyptian people, shattered the serenity of his rule.

Cambyses first dispatched some 15,000 troops to overpower the Oasis of Ammon that lay in the western desert. Disaster struck. The Persian troops, ill-equipped for the desert, succumbed to the hostile environment. Not long afterward, Cambyses decided to attack the Ethiopians to the south. To ensure no foul-ups occurred, he personally took charge of his troops. Again disaster struck. Less than one-fifth of the way to their objective, his army ran out of provisions. Reduced to cannibalism, only a remnant limped back into Thebes. As Cambyses' party struggled into the city, they encountered an Egyptian celebration dedicating a new sacred bull (Apis) to the gods. Mistaking their gaiety as revelry regarding his misfortunes, Cambyses flew into a rage and began to desecrate all religious monuments in the city. In the ensuing fracas, parts of the city burned, the giant walls (twenty-four feet thick and sixty-six feet high) that surrounded Thebes were partially destroyed, and most of its great temples were damaged. Though not a deathblow to the city, the once-proud metropolis was permanently crippled.

An even more devastating jolt occurred in the first century, B.C. Ptolemy Lathyrus, the grandfather of Cleopatra, laid siege to the city. Thebes resisted for three years. When the bitter struggle ended, the full wrath of Lathyrus fell. Much of the city was leveled. Every temple was damaged.[36]

In the intervening centuries between the time of the Romans and our day, many other conquerors strode the wide avenues of this once-proud city. Ezekiel's prediction came to pass.

Multitudes to be "Cut Off." Ezekiel's second prediction foresaw the decline of the city's vast population base. That, too, occurred just as predicted. No longer do vast multitudes reside within its boundaries. In place of a bustling, thriving metropolis, modern visitors find several smaller vil-

The imposing Temple of Hatshepsut at Deir el Bahri is dwarfed by great cliffs to the west. When Edouard Naville visited the site in 1892, he found a jumbled mass of ruins. Reconstruction began in 1893 and continues to the present. (Photo courtesy, Dr. Marlin Connelly.)

The imposing Temple of Hatshepsut at Deir el Bahri is dwarfed by great cliffs to the west. When Edouard Naville visited the site in 1892, he found a jumbled mass of ruins. Reconstruction began in 1893 and continues to the present. (Photo courtesy, Dr. Marlin Connelly.)

lages near the river itself and almost nothing of importance in the surrounding deserts. The multitudes are gone. Even Western tourists, who used to come in large numbers before the current unrest, arrive in smaller numbers.

The "Breaking Up of the City." Though the prophets' declaration that Thebes would be 'broken up' is somewhat ambiguous, even a superficial understanding of the city's status verifies the accuracy of Ezekiel's prediction.

First, the population center is broken. Instead of a single, booming metropolis known to those who frequented the city in earlier centuries, Thebes is now the site for at least four, much smaller, fragmented villages.

Second, the city's remains are also scattered and broken. Some statues are standing; most are not; all are damaged. Some temples remain; some have vanished. At el-Karnak, four giant obelisks once stood at the entrance to Amun's temple. Only one remains. Broken fragments of the others are scattered in the hot sands. The hypostyle roof exists only in fragments. Only parts of Hatshepsut's temple remain. Only portions of the Ramesseum survive.

If any phrase could adequately describe modern Thebes, the one chosen by Ezekiel ('broken up') is the one. Other terms such as "destroyed," "vanished," or "annihilated" simply do not apply. What a coincidence that this sixth century, B.C. prophet chose exactly the right phrase. Or, is it more than mere coincidence?

The Destruction of Memphis

Far to the north of Thebes, in Lower Egypt, the equally impressive city of Memphis rose from the sands. While Thebes came to the foreground in Egypt's later years, Memphis seems to have been born with the nation itself. While Theban temples were constructed by well-known historical figures, early structures at Memphis were attributed to semi-mythological personages about whom little is known.

Home to Temples and the Pyramids. What is known is that the city stood on the western bank of the Nile just south of modern Cairo. Ancient records inform us that it

> ... was the royal residence and capital of Egypt during the Early Dynastic Period and the Old Kingdom, and many later kings maintained a palace there. The city's temples were among the most important in the land. Memphis remained one of the most populous and renowned sites in Egypt and, indeed, in the ancient world.[37]

At Memphis, the famed royal pyramids emerged from the desert sands at Abu Rawash, Giza, Abu Ghurab, Abusir, Saqqara, and Dahshur. At Memphis, hundreds of temples thrust their majestic profiles heavenward as if to commune with the powerful god of the sun. At Memphis, thousands of statues adorned temple halls, lined wide avenues, and stood silent vigils over tombs of the nobility.[38] At Memphis, the elite of the world rubbed shoulders with Egyptian merchants and priests.

Memphis became known as "the great temple city of Egypt."[39] The testimony of history reveals that her edifices, at the least, equaled those in Thebes. The most conspicuous seems to have been the Great Temple of Ptah which "occupied an area about as large as that of the Great Temple of Amon at Karnak."[40] Ancient visitors at the site describe a number of colossal statues that graced the entrances to this important landmark.

The population rivaled that of Thebes as well. The Greek geographer, Strabo, described the city—as late as the first century, B.C.—as "large and populous."[41] Six centuries later, Memphis still basked in glory as the Roman governor of Egypt chose it as the site of his palace. From all outward appearances, Memphis seemed destined to be an eternal city.

Predictions of Memphian Demise. Yet, at the very moment Memphis reached its pinnacle, the invectives of the biblical prophets lashed the city. Ezekiel (30:13) sounded the initial warning: "Thus says the Lord God, 'I will also destroy the idols and make the images cease from Memphis." Destroying the idols of Memphis proved to be a herculean task. They existed by the thousands. Many rock colossi weighed several tons. Most had stood in their places for centuries.

Thus, the two great cities of Egypt stood under widely divergent sentences. One would be 'broken' and 'diminished'; the other would be destroyed. No natural reason exists for the distinction. If based on human expertise, it is extremely difficult to justify the differences. A solid case can be made for reversing the predictions: The region surrounding Memphis served as home to a much larger population. Also, the city was located in a region more likely to see future development due to its strategic importance. More statues and temples existed at Memphis than at Thebes.

Listen to a recognized scholar of Egyptian antiquities:

> Memphis was a great mass of huge temples. Even in the XXth Dynasty, the Temple of Ptah was the (third) largest in the country. ... Down into the thirteenth century of our own era, many temples could still be seen standing. (Yet) No one of the great cities of the old world has so utterly disappeared as Memphis. There is neither sacred building nor palace nor a trace of a common house. All are gone but the broken colossi.[42]

Memphis' end came swiftly and silently. Modern scholarship still cannot answer when the city disappeared or why. So complete was the obliteration that even the site of ancient Memphis became a matter of dispute during the eighteenth and nineteenth centuries. As Ezekiel said, the temples are no longer seen; the idols have vanished. De Camp concludes of most of the Memphian structures, "no details of their construction have survived. In some cases we do not even know where they stood."[43]

Predicting Egypt's Long-Term Future

Gazing intently across the ages, biblical writers next turned to Egypt's long-term destiny. The threads of their distinctive predictions wove a detailed pattern of continuing judgment on one of antiquity's greatest powers. Egypt's grandeur was finished.

Joel (3:19) predicted the ultimate tragedy sometime in the eighth century, B.C. Whereas Joel outlined the general boundaries of Egypt's future, later prophets colored in the details: (1) Nebuchadnezzar would invade the land; (2) Egyptian power would enter a period of decline from which it would not recover; (3) The land would be ruled by foreigners and many of its valued treasures would be removed; (4) The nation and its people would continue to survive as an outward confirmation of the prophecies (Isa. 19-20; Jer. 25, 42-46; Eze. 29-32; Zech. 11). Each prophecy's fulfillment can be attested.

Nebuchadnezzar's Invasion. Biblical prophets next directed the spotlight of the future toward a rising nemesis far to Egypt's east. Jeremiah (42-44) sounded the initial notes of warning: Babylonian armies were on the prowl and Egypt would be among the victims. Soon afterward, Ezekiel (29-32) echoed the warning. Nebuchadnezzar would rule the land of the Pharaohs. There is no way we can know if Egyptian authorities heard the words of these Hebrew prophets. One element is certain. If they became aware of the predictions, the Egyptians didn't believe them, for, in 608 B.C., Pharaoh Neco II launched a major invasion of Palestine and Syria, openly challenging the Babylonian armies. Four years later, at Carchemesh, the battle joined. Egypt's armies staggered home in defeat. The highway to Egypt was open.

Babylon emerged from obscurity to become the dominant military force in the ancient world. Within a few years, her mighty armies stood poised on the borders of Egypt. The rapid turn of events caught many smaller kingdoms—including Judah—by surprise. Assuming they were heading to safety, many Israelites fled to Egypt in hopes of escaping Babylon's hordes. Even those who remained behind continued to counsel a military alliance with Egypt as their ticket to freedom. Isaiah's warning (36:6) passed unnoticed: "Behold thou that trusteth upon the staff of this bruised reed, even upon Egypt, whereon if a man lean, it will go into his hand and pierce it: so is Pharaoh, king of Egypt to all that trust on him."

While the exact period of Nebuchadnezzar's intrusion into Egypt is debated, it is certain that the Mesopotamian monarch did not march on the Egyptian homeland immediately after the battle at Carchemesh. His delay caused several earlier scholars[44] to assume Nebuchadnezzar's forces never invaded Egypt. Leading the denials, Thomas K. Cheyne argued, "no monumental evidence has as yet been found of anything approaching an invasion."[45]

Cheyne's argument ignored a sizable body of evidence that confirmed biblical predictions. First, the Syrian-Babylonian historian Berosus claimed to witness the invasion.[46] Second, the Jewish historian Josephus argued that Nebuchadnezzar's forays into Egypt transformed the nation into a Babylonian province.[47] Third, two small Babylonian tablets, located in a trove of materials at the British Museum, bluntly state: "In the thirty-seventh year, Nebuchadnezzar, king of Babylon, marched against Egypt," defeated Egyptian defenders, and killed or carried away soldiers and horses.[48] Fourth, an inscription on a statue now housed in the Louvre states that an army of northerners invaded Egypt during the time in question.[49] Evidence supports the accuracy of biblical predictions.

The Decline of Egyptian Power. Egypt's declining power also appeared in the forecast from the prophets. Ezekiel (29:15) minced no words in declaring that Egypt "shall not any more lift itself up above the nations." His message concluded: "(God) will diminish them that they shall rule no more over the nations." A later prediction (30:4,6) recorded, "Her foundations shall be broken down ... the pride of her power shall come down." Ezekiel spoke accurately. First came Esarhaddon and the Assyrians in 670 B.C. A hundred years later, Nebuchadnezzar's army pillaged the land. In 525 B.C., Cambyses joined the growing list of Egypt's conquerors. Alexander the Great followed the Persians. Then came the Ptolemies and the Romans. In 641 A.D. control passed to the Saracens. Six centuries later, the Mamelukes deposed the Saracens. The Turks followed, as did the French (under Napoleon) and the English. For 2,500 years, the only authority in the land came from strangers.

Even an opponent of Christianity[50] stood amazed at the accuracy of Ezekiel's forecast:

> Deprived twenty-three centuries ago of her natural proprietors, she has seen her fertile fields successively a prey to the Persians, the Macedonians, the Romans, the Greeks, the Arabs, the Georgians, and, at length, the race of Tartars distinguished by the name Ottoman Turks. The Mamelukes, purchased as slaves and introduced as soldiers, soon usurped the power, and elected a leader. They were replaced by slaves brought from their original country. The system of oppression was methodical. Everything the traveler sees or hears, reminds him that he in the country of slavery and tyranny.

In modern times, only superficial changes have occurred. Though Egypt gained her independence after the close of the Second World War, she is no longer considered a world power. Her strength resides in alliances with others. Her neighbors no longer cower at her name or fear her armies. Twice, while allied with hard-line communist states, she entered war with Israel. Twice, Israeli victories came somewhat easily. In 1973, only threatened intervention prevented total annihilation of her armies. Egypt's power has diminished.

The Loss of Egyptian Royalty. Egyptian royalty also came under the gun. Ezekiel's (30:13) judgments continued: "There shall be no more a native prince out of the land of Egypt." Except for one brief period, native kings occupied the thronerooms of Egypt for as long as anyone could remember. No fixture had been more enduring than the Egyptian pharaohs.

Only one titular ruler, King Farouk, has led the nation since the Persian invasion better than 2,500 years ago. Farouk's nationality is Ethiopian, not Egyptian. With Farouk's overthrow in the 1950s, Egypt's leaders spurned royalty. Nasser found the title offensive, as did Sadat and Mubarik.

The Spoiling of the Land by Strangers. Another judgment added to Egypt's prophetic burden. Her treasures and wealth would be removed as strangers laid "waste the land." Of all the predictions, none has been more graphically fulfilled.

As early as the seventh century, B.C., Esarhaddon began plundering her treasures. The Assyrian king removed fifty-five of Memphis' fabled statues—probably those made from precious metals—with many other materials. [51] A century later, Nebuchadnezzar exacted tribute from Egypt. Cambyses, angered by a misunderstanding, carried away little but left the nation in shambles. The Greek conqueror Alexander used part of the wealth he obtained in Egypt to finance his conquests. Likewise, Octavius used the riches of Egypt to pay debts he incurred while defeating Antony and Cleopatra.

For seven hundred years after Alexander, Roman legions exploited the land. So did the Muslims who followed. With each passing day, more of Egypt's past disappeared. Alexandria's magnificent library was razed. More objects were simply ignored, allowing the blowing sands and other natural forces to erode away remnants of the nation's storied history.

Rising interest in antiquities at the opening of the modern era sent archaeologists and historians into the land by the thousands. Later, ships and caravans departed Egypt with hoards of artifacts from Egypt's "glory years." Early treasure-hunters pillaged the land. Around the globe, hardly a museum of note fails to house Egyptian antiquities.

Survival of the Egyptian People. One sidenote is worthy of consideration: Egypt's continued presence among the community of nations is intimated by the prophets. The vast majority of ancient nations passed into oblivion or found themselves assimilated into other cultures long ago. That Egypt outlives her Old Testament contemporaries was foretold by Ezekiel (30:14) in plain, blunt language: "They shall be there, a base kingdom." Hittites, Assyrians, Babylonians, and Persians no longer exist as national entities. No modern people can trace their ancestry back to the Philistines, the Edomites, the Moabites, or the Perizites. Yet, like the Jews, the Egyptians survive. They, too, encountered oppression, slavery, and poverty. Still, they answer the roll call of nations. It is as the prophet predicted.

Possible Explanations

So, what does all this suggest? How is it possible that these Jewish prophets so accurately provided the future of Egypt and her people centuries before the events transpired?

Many answers emerge. Some argue that writers composed the prophecies long after the events. Others assert the fulfillments were circumstantial. The apologetic weight afforded fulfilled prophecies is said to be offset by failures and blatant errors. Some attempt to negate the material by explaining predictions as common-sense guesses made by a few enlightened sages. Still others (myself included) believe that the evidence suggests the intervention of a supernatural force or power far beyond faculties possessed by humanity.

Assyria in Prophecy:
Predicting the Defeat
of a Military Juggernaut

On the eastern bank of the Tigris River, some 220 miles northwest of modern Baghdad, lie the pretentious remains of one of the world's most renowned cities. References in the early Cappadocian Tablets (circa 2000 B.C.), in the Code of Hammurabi, and in Scripture attest to its age.[1]

The bewildering dearth of information regarding its origin, coupled with the later immensity of its dominion, the splendor and gigantic bulk of its suburbs and royal fortresses, and the utter destruction that eventually settled upon it invest it with all the mystery of an eastern fable. While scattered records document the city's methodical rise to greatness and its meteoric plummet into desolation, those same records leave many unanswered questions.

That questions exist at all testifies to the thoroughness with which the Medo-Babylonian alliance destroyed the city in 612 B.C. That conquest, and the easily erodable nature of Assyrian building materials, provides the basis for a scholarly controversy. Was Nineveh a huge metropolis or just another ancient city?

The Controversy
Between Ancient and Modern Descriptions

Diodorus Siculus, an early geographer, first described Nineveh as a quadrangle with a perimeter of nearly sixty miles.[2] Strabo insisted that the city's size surpassed even Babylon.[3] Both dovetail nicely with descriptions drawn by the prophet Jonah (3:3), who revealed it required three days to cross. Since the average distance traveled in a day was fifteen to twenty miles, "three days' journey" implies the city's circumference must have been forty-five to sixty miles, the same size attributed to it in early historical records.

Beginning with the original mapping of the ruins by Claudius James Rich in the 1820s, modern archaeologists have identified a much smaller area

eight miles in circumference as the remains of the ancient Assyrian capital.[4] Which is correct? Must we assume that ancient chroniclers made
enormous errors? Could it be that much of the ancient area of Nineveh
lies undiscovered? Is it possible to reconcile the two viewpoints?

Portions of ancient Nineveh lie buried under this mound near the Tigris River.
When Xenophon passed by here two and a half centuries after the city's destruction
by Medo-Babylonian armies, he was unaware of the significance of the mounds.
(Photo courtesy, Fon Scofield Collection, E. C. Dargan Research Library of the
Sunday School Board, SBC.)

Merging the Two Descriptions

Interestingly, evidence does point to the possible merging of the two
views. Proposed originally by a widely respected Old Testament scholar,
the reconciliation focuses on phraseology from Genesis 10:11-12. The
record states that Nimrod "went to Assyria, and built Nineveh, Rehoboth
Ir, Calah, and Resen, which is between Nineveh and Calah; that is the
great city."[5] Hebrew grammatical structure strongly implies that the total
area was considered a homogeneous entity. Thus, the "Hebrews were
accustomed to include under the name Nineveh (like the complex entities that form modern New York), Calah, eighteen miles south, Resen,
between Calah and Nineveh proper, and Rehobeth-Ir ... west of the capital. ... (as) composing 'the great city'." So, when Jonah spoke of
"Nineveh," he spoke of an entire metropolitan area and not the strongly
fortified citadel unearthed by modern archaeology.

A second consideration deserves notice. The entire region may well have found itself enclosed in a smaller, earthen wall. Bolstered by the occasional presence of forts and towers, that might well give the appearance of a contiguous city. Within these boundaries could be found an extensive population with sizable pasture lands and lush gardens.

Has the Outer Wall been Found?

Portions of a much longer and smaller structure, possibly some type of defensive fortification (an outer wall?), rise over the plain to the northeast of what is sometimes called "lesser Nineveh."[6] Whether this structure once extended around the entire region is unclear. At a minimum, Nineveh's city limits might well be stretched beyond the immediate vicinity of the citadel.

The Evidence of Forts along the Perimeter

Intervals of intense fortifications dotted the outer regions of "the great city." Within these fortifications, evidence suggests a blossoming area of Assyrian culture. Encircled by strategically-placed forts, these extensive ruins convinced Nineveh's most celebrated excavator, Austin Henry Layard, to espouse the compromise position. Layard observed that a "vast number of small mounds (are) everywhere visible" within the perimeter. "Scarcely a husbandman drives his plough over the soil, without exposing the vestiges of former habitations."[7] The remains led him to argue, "If we take the four great mounds of Nimroud, Kouyunjik, Khorsabad, and Karamles, as the corners of a square ... its four sides correspond pretty accurately with the sixty miles of the geographer, which make the three days' journey of the prophet."

Describing the Inner City

Though historians may have described the entire urban sprawl as "Nineveh," the glue that held it together came from the central core. This core, sometimes spoken of as "lesser Nineveh," engaged the fancies and conversations of foreigners. Through the gates of "lesser Nineveh" marched the iron-like pincers of her powerful armies. Through her gates rumbled hundreds of her fearful war-chariots. Through her gates rode her twelve thousand horsemen-archers.[8] Speaking of this "lesser Nineveh," Andre Parrot exclaimed,

> The Assyrians were invincible; from Elam to the island of Cyprus, the whole of Eastern Asia lay under their sway. Their troops were stationed on the frontiers of Egypt. In their huge palaces on the banks of the Tigris was gathered the wealth of the whole world, and thousands of slaves cringed beneath their whips.[9]

Wall reliefs from remains at Nineveh graphically depict the Assyrian pride at the torture doled out to their victims. Captives were flayed, mutilated and beheaded. From A. H. Layard, *Nineveh and Its Remains*.

Here, at the central core of the empire, towering walls, more like small mountains than man-made defenses, soared one hundred feet above the surrounding plain. Stretching to a width of nearly sixty feet, they appeared imposing to any would-be aggressor. Ninevites affectionately named their wall, "the one which terrifies the enemy."[10] It required eight years and 140,000 slave laborers to build.[11]

Cataloging Assyrian Cruelties

Throughout the ancient Near East, Assyrian armies gained a reputation as cruel and barbarous conquerors. They flaunted their atrocities before the world. As early as the ninth century, B.C., Ashurnarsipal II gloated,

> I destroyed them, tore down the wall, and burned the town with fire; I caught the survivors and impaled them on stakes in front of their towns. ... I fed their corpses, cut into small pieces, to dogs, pigs, vultures. ... Of some, I cut off the hands and limbs; of others the noses, ears, and arms; of many soldiers I put out the eyes. ... I flayed them and covered with their skins the walls of the town. ... The heads of their warriors I cut off, and I formed them into a pillar over against their city; their young men and maidens I burned in the fire. ... Three thousand captives I burned with fire; I left not a single one alive to serve as a hostage.[12]

Examining Assyrian Culture

Within Nineveh's massive walls emerged a culture, seemingly incongruous with the barbarity and cruelty that permeated much of her society. Sculptors and artisans decorated her buildings. Architects and engineers

The advanced quality of Assyrian culture surfaces in detailed bas-reliefs and sculptures like these remains from Khorsabad that show the original state of the Grand Entrance at Kouyunik. From A. H. Layard, *Nineveh and Its Remains.*

planned and constructed gigantic buildings. Huge libraries recorded the successes of her kings and armies. During his reign, Ashurbanipal assembled

> ... a large library of cuneiform texts of all sorts and dispatched agents to search out tablets in the archives and schools of the temples of Babylonia and to bring back copies to Nineveh. Ashurbanipal's library included the reference works and standard lists used by Mesopotamian scribes and scholars, bilingual vocabularies, wordlists and lists of signs and synonyms, lists of medical diagnoses, compendia of rituals, omens, and incantations, and works of literature such as the Epic of Creation and the Epic of Gilgamesh.[13]

Among Nineveh's splendid palaces, none impressed the visitor more than the one built by Sennacherib. Pfeiffer describes it as

> ... built on a platform well above the level of the city. Marble stairs led up on all four sides to magnificent entrances decorated with colossal stone figures such as human-headed bulls and winged sphinxes. The palace was enormous. ... It had two large halls forty feet wide and 180 feet long which led into its interior made up of ... large courts and more than seventy spacious rooms. Its walls were beautifully adorned with sculptured slabs, and (contained) 9,880 feet of decorated walls. ... Winged bulls of ten to thirty tons each were prominent. ... In one part of the palace these bulls and sphinxes framed or guarded at least twenty-seven portals. ... (It) approached, if not equaled, the great palace-temple of Karnak in size and splendor.[14]

Visitors must have been astonished by its beauty. Even Layard, who described the ruins with superlatives like "colossal lions and bulls of white alabaster," "magnificent" and "imposing"[15] stood in awe at the remains. Seemingly interminable hallways covered with alabaster sculptures portrayed the exploits of Assyrian kings. Silver and gold lettering on the slabs chronicled the events of their reigns. Tall ceilings "painted with flowers, inlaid with ivory and surrounded with elegant borders and moldings"[16] with gigantic beams of cedar overlaid in gold supplied the finishing touches.

No doubt many Assyrian fathers toured the halls with their sons, showing them the bas-reliefs that told of their national legacy, proudly preparing them for glorious campaigns still in the future. Awed by their success and prodded to even nobler accomplishments for the glory of their homeland, Assyria's armies gave their kings yet more triumphs about which they could boast. Boast they

Sennacherib as pictured in Assyrian artwork. From A. H. Layard, *Nineveh and Its Remains.*

did. Sennacherib labeled himself "the great king, the mighty king, king of the universe, king of Assyria, king of the four world-regions."[17] His son, Esarhaddon, raved: "I am powerful, I am all-powerful, I am a hero, I am gigantic, I am colossal, I am honored, I am magnified, I am without equal among all kings, the chosen one of Assur, Nabu, and Marduk, called of Sin, favorite of Anu, beloved of ... Ishtar."[18]

Analyzing the Prophecies Concerning Nineveh

Against this backdrop of culture amidst cruelty, the biblical prophets leveled a series of inconceivable predictions. Nineveh's days were numbered. Nahum (1:8) penned the eulogy: "With an overwhelming flood (God) will make an end of Nineveh." Regarding the kings and armies, he wrote (1:12), "Although they are unscathed and numerous, they will be cut down and pass away."

Nor would the wrath of God be assuaged by merely diminishing her power. God's judgment would be a fatal blow. Never again would her proud chariots pass through her gates. Never again would her monarchs parade their cruelty in front of the world. Nineveh's breath would be stilled forever. "You will have no descendants to bear your name," Nahum (1:14) wrote. And though Nineveh guarded her fortresses and watched her roads and placed her armies in readiness for battle, nothing could avert the death-blows predicted by the prophet. The battle belonged to a higher power. Assyria's reign of terror plunged into oblivion.

Predictions regarding Nineveh's collapse flowed from Nahum's pen in prolific detail: (1) The city would be destroyed by a flood (2:6,8); (2) Nineveh would be burned and her riches taken as spoil (1:10; 2:9-10,13; 3:13,15); (3) Her defenders would be drunken at crucial times in the approaching war (1:10; 3:11); (4) A horrible slaughter of her leading citizens will follow (3:10,18); (5) The city will remain in ruins for centuries (1:14; 3:7); and (6) Assyria's people will vanish (1:14; 2:13). Each happened exactly as predicted.

Nineveh's Decline and Fall

Though annoyingly incomplete, historical sources paint a credible story about the city's final days. With the death of Ashurbanipal in 626 B.C., Assyria began her headlong descent into disaster. Three weak, inconsequential kings trudged to the throne. Their reigns were a mixture of debasement, poor planning, and outright ineptness. Coincidental with their rule, the pent-up frustrations of years of Assyrian domination and servitude reaped their harvest. Phraortes, king of the Medes, launched the first wave of military reprisals. He attacked too soon, however, and the still formidable Assyrian armies soundly defeated his forces and killed him. Still, the spark had been unleashed. Soon an inferno of rebellion licked at the empire.

Babylon Gains Her Freedom

The southern holdings gained their freedom first. Nabopolassar seized the initiative and led an insurrection that thrust his masters from Babylon. The Assyrians hurriedly recoiled northward behind the protection of their potent fortresses. Simultaneously, Babylon struck an alliance with the Medes who, though still smarting from their recent defeat, were already laying the groundwork for another attack.

Early Failures by the Alliance

Twice, the rebel armies composed of Persians, Medes, Babylonians, and Arabians dared to engage the elite of Assyria's armies. Twice, the rebel armies bowed to the superiority of the Assyrian forces. The defenders grew ecstatic. Confident that the rebel forces fled in full retreat and positive that no army would dare attack in the darkness, the commanders proclaimed a celebration. Unaware that rebel spies observed their every move, the army "broke out the wine." Its soldiers soon rollicked in a drunken stupor. When word of the army's incapacitation reached the retreating rebel forces, they reversed their plans and agreed upon a swift nighttime attack. The attack succeeded and the remnants of an inebriated and confused army limped toward their capital.

Still, the Ninevites refused to panic. Nineveh's defenses remained strong. The city could be easily defended. Besides, the Medes had never been known for their stamina in sustaining a siege. Though the future may not have been rosy, neither was it bleak. For three months the rebel army waited, poised to strike. No opportunity came.

Forces of Nature Enter the Battle

Finally, in the late spring of 612 B.C., the forces of nature aligned themselves against Nineveh. An unusually heavy snow cover in the mountains started to melt. At the same time, torrential rains fell on the city and its environs. Rivers that passed through or near the city rose rapidly. Raging torrents lapped at the walls and undermined the foundations. Soon, the walls began to disintegrate. As they did, the rebel armies discovered breaches in the defenses and poured through. Nineveh's fate was sealed.

Realizing his predicament, the Assyrian monarch, chose to avoid humiliation and certain torture at the hands of his captors. "Despairing of his fate," he heaped all his gold and royal clothing on a funeral pyre (approximately 400 feet high), gathered his family and close associates around him, and ordered the pyre set ablaze.[19] Not long afterward, enemy troops entered the city, stripped it of its valuables, and reduced it to shambles. Nineveh was no phoenix. She never rose from the ashes.

An Analysis of Nahum's Predictions

The Destructive Flood

Nahum (1:8; 2:7,9) connected Nineveh's destruction with a devastating flood. History agrees. But, is there any reason to believe an astute observer in those times could not have made an identical prediction? After all, three flood-prone rivers either traversed the city (the Khosr) or flowed near its walls (the Tebiltu and the Tigris). Even so, predicting the city's destruction by flood would have been highly speculative.

First, the city had existed for centuries in this general location without experiencing any such disaster. That Sennacherib altered the course of the tiny Tebiltu to provide more fresh water for the city (the muddy waters of the larger Tigris were uninviting) seemed inconsequential. Second, the main city walls were located well over a half-mile from the banks of the Tigris.[20] Third, Nineveh's rulers took many precautions to ensure that the floods never threatened the city walls. They constructed giant reservoirs in the nearby hills to intercept heavy floodwaters.[21] Huge dams, so well constructed that they still function after nearly three thousand years, spanned the rivers to help in flood control. Fourth, even with these precautions, Assyrian workers constantly shored up the area around the walls to thwart any conceivable flood.

Thus, the likelihood of Nineveh's destruction by floodwaters seemed small. So sure were the Assyrians of the improbability of an event that they jokingly claimed their city would be destroyed only when the river itself became their enemy. In the era of Assyrian power, those jokes brought laughter in the marketplace. In 612 B.C., with rebel armies surrounding their city and rain falling in torrents from the skies, the laughter ceased.

The Destructive Fire

Another, seemingly incredulous, prophecy lay alongside the first. Fire and water would join as co-agents of destruction.

Surely one must be in error. How could a city be destroyed by a fire and a flood simultaneously? In reality, history easily harmonized what must have appeared in antiquity as a major discrepancy. According to historical documents, floodwaters undermined the massive walls surrounding the city, causing certain sections to collapse. Seeing his most critical line of defense in jeopardy and unwilling to accept from others the same torture his soldiers had meted out, Assyria's king gathered his wealth, his immediate family, and his eunuchs inside the palace. After the hasty construction of a huge pyre, the command was given to burn the building. Those inside perished. As the rebel armies gained control over other portions of the city, they torched other structures.

Excavations document the bath of fire that washed the city. Layard's digging confirmed that Sennacherib's palace

> ... had been destroyed by fire. The alabaster slabs were almost reduced to lime, and many of them fell to pieces as soon as uncovered. The palaces which others had occupied could only be traced by a thin white deposit, like a coat of plaster, left by the burnt alabaster upon the wall of sun-dried bricks.[22]

Rawlinson added, "Excavations have shown that fire was a great instrument in the destruction of the Nineveh palaces. Calcined alabaster, masses of charred wood and charcoal, colossal statues slit through with heat ... attest the (truth) of the prophecy."[23] At every major dig, charred debris and clear traces of burning have been noted.[24]

Destruction by Drunkenness

Nahum (1:10; 3:11) also correlates the city's eventual destruction with the intoxication of her defenders. Again, the prophet proved unimpeachable. Had Assyrian leaders been more cautious in their celebrations, the onslaught of rebel forces would have been postponed if not eliminated. Yet, following a second victory over rebel forces, military commanders distributed an abundant supply of intoxicants to their troops. Diodorus describes the result:

> ... the Assyrian king ... gave way to negligence and distributed to his soldiers ... liberal supplies ... to make merry upon. While ... carousing, the friends of Arbakes (the leader of the rebel army) learned from some deserters of the slackness and drunkenness which prevailed ... and made an unexpected attack by night.[25]

Yet again, alcohol exacted her price.

As for Nahum's ability to predict such an unpropitious end to one of the world's greatest war-machines, one would do well to remember that for centuries Assyrian armies had been the world's most disciplined fighting unit. Whatever improprieties they may have shown, drunkenness while on duty was not included.

Wholesale Slaughter of the Assyrian Defenders

Next, Nahum (2:10-11) forecast the ravishing of Assyria by her captors. Torture and carnage had been the signature of her armies. Now Nineveh suffered an identical fate. Nahum's visions (3:3) pictured "Many casualties, piles of dead, bodies without number." It would be so severe rebel armies would be "stumbling over corpses." Diodorus writes of the butchery: "So great was the multitude of the slain that the (river), mingled with their blood, changed its color."[26] Violence from the attacking Medes became so out of control, it drew criticism from their Babylonian allies.[27] The Medes were not interested in slaves. They craved revenge.

Nineveh's Approaching Desolation

Called into the judgment hall of her accusers to pay for her atrocities, Nineveh found no mercy. Justice demanded the death penalty. A once proud and haughty city found herself destined for a rubbish-pile memorial. Nahum expressed his finis to the city (1:14; 3:6-7) in unequivocal terms: "You will have no descendants to bear your name ... I will prepare your grave, for you are vile. ... I will treat you with contempt and make you a spectacle. All who see you will flee from you and say, Nineveh is in ruins—who will mourn for her?"

Nineveh's conquerors left the city in ruined heaps, without inhabitants. Soon, the forces of nature joined in the destruction. Howling winter winds and blistering summer heat took their toll. What had been geometrical mountains of brick deteriorated into shapeless hills of dirt. The Greek adventurer, Xenophon, chancing to pass the ruins two hundred years later, did not realize he had encountered one of antiquity's premiere attractions.[28]

Later writers like Lucian[29] and Strabo[30] speak of the city as if she had completely disappeared. Even Herodotus wrote that the Tigris was the river on which "Nineveh formerly stood."[31] As late as 1776, travelers in the region believed the giant mounds to be naturally-formed hills.[32] Not until 1842, with the work of Paul Emile Botta, did the world finally recognize the hills of dirt to be the remains of the former Assyrian capital. No less an authority than A. H. Sayce wrote, "Nineveh, the bloody city, fell, never to rise again, and the doom pronounced by Nahum was fulfilled. For centuries the very site ... remained unknown."[33] The scholarly *Cambridge Ancient History* summarized the thoroughness of Nineveh's disappearance by noting, "No other land seems to have been sacked and pillaged so completely as was Assyria."[34]

Words of another Hebrew prophet (Zeph. 2:13-15) coincide perfectly with those of Nahum:

(God) will stretch out his hand against the north and destroy Assyria, leaving Nineveh utterly desolate and as dry as the desert. Flocks and herds will lie down there, creatures of every kind. The desert owl and the screech owl will roost on her columns. Their calls will echo through the windows, rubble will be in the doorways, the beams of cedar will be exposed. This is the carefree city that lived in safety. She said to herself, "I am, and there is none besides me." What a ruin she has become, a lair for wild beasts! All who pass by her scoff and shake their fists.

Assyria's Great Vanishing Act: The Disappearance of Her People

With the desolation of the city assured, Nahum directed his discussion toward the Assyrian people. He saw them (3:18) "scattered on the mountains with no one to gather them together," and (2:13) the "voices of your messengers will no longer be heard." Finally, he notes (3:17), "Your guards are like locusts, your officials like swarms of locusts that settle in the walls on a cold day—but when the heat appears they fly away, and no one knows where."

Thus, their Goliath of a city in shambles, those who could do so, in harrowing fear for their lives, distanced themselves from Nineveh. Neighboring populations assimilated the remnant of her population. The same sentence Assyria imposed on others—the uprooting and transplanting of civilizations and the obliteration of cultures—was imposed on them. Within a few years no one admitted Assyrian citizenship. The vanishing act was complete.

Maier expresses the uniqueness of the prophecy:

> Not all captured and devastated cities have suffered this fate. ... Jerusalem was besieged and captured by Nebuchadnezzar; masses of its people were led into captivity; but they returned and rebuilt the city, which has been perpetuated ever since. The captive and dispersed citizens of Nineveh, however, never returned. ... Its inhabitants disappeared so completely that they left no impress on subsequent ages. No people lost their identity more completely and quickly than did the Ninevites.[36]

The *Cambridge Ancient History* concluded, "The disappearance of the Assyrian people will always remain an unique and striking phenomenon in ancient history."

Babylon in Prophecy: Predicting the Demise of History's Greatest City

Babylon. After more than two thousand years, the city still bedevils inquirers. Her name conveys a mixture of evil, opulence, and power. To Isaiah, she was "the glory of the Chaldee's excellency" (13:19). In the Revelation to John the apostle, she epitomized evil.

The ancient city reached its pinnacle in the latter seventh and early sixth centuries B.C. during the reigns of Nabopolassar and his son Nebuchadnezzar. During those "glory years," she became, arguably, the most striking city in antiquity. Located in the center of one of the world's most fruitful regions, Babylon drew water and sustenance from both the Tigris and Euphrates Rivers. Miles of canals crisscrossed her avenues and suburbs. Her agriculture flourished, blessed by an abundant water supply, a warm climate, and rich, seemingly inexhaustible, soil. Yields of staple products such as corn and barley multiplied.[1] So prolific did her fields and vineyards become that the region earned the title of "the fertile crescent."

Ancient Descriptions of Babylon

Ancient visitors to Babylon acquired their deepest impressions not from the richness of the soil, but from the magnificence of the city. From a great distance, travelers distinguished her imposing battlements and formidable walls towering above the surrounding plains. No other city in antiquity came close to duplicating them.

Our earliest detailed description of the city comes from the pen of the fifth century, B.C., historian and traveler Herodotus. "My job," Herodotus explained, "is to write what has been said, but I do not have to believe it."[2] His narrative style and the tendency to record everything he heard drew the ire of earlier critics. Yet, Herodotus was no gullible sap. In areas where he obtained his information firsthand, his accuracy proved remarkable.[3] Since he was a visitor to Babylon, his descriptions carry a demonstrable flavor of truth.

Herodotus and other ancient authors (Pliny and Solinus), describe the city walls as fourteen miles long on each of four sides. They claim these defenses, as tall as many modern skyscrapers, soared about three hundred feet over the surrounding plain while reaching a width of seventy-five feet.[4] A military causeway wide enough for four-horse chariots crowned the walled area. Battle towers jutted skyward at approximately sixty feet intervals. Even writers (Quintus Curtius, Ctesias, Clitarchus, Diodorus Siculus) who record a slightly smaller size for the city place the length of the walls at between eight and twelve miles. Moreover, the Greek geographer Strabo deeply impressed by their colossal appearance, cataloged them among the seven wonders of the world.[5] If any of these records can be trusted, would-be aggressors surely shuddered at the logistics of trying to neutralize or overcome these man-made behemoths.

Still smaller measurements offered by modern authorities (Lloyd suggests the walls enclosed approximately 6-1/4 square miles of real estate),[6] do not seriously challenge the stunning magnificence of the city nor the effectiveness of her defenses. There can be no doubt they "presented an overpowering spectacle even from a long way off"[7] and "the many kilometers of heavy walls, towers and multistoried temples must have been very impressive to travelers."[8]

Though not part of the city per se, several miles north of Babylon proper, a miniature "Great Wall," tabbed by modern scholars as the Median Wall, presented invaders with their initial challenge. Xenophon, the Greek adventurer who visited the site around 400 B.C., described it as twenty-two feet thick and approximately one hundred feet tall. It stretched from the city of Opis on the Tigris westward to a point north of Sippar on the Euphrates, a distance of some twenty-four miles.[9] Given the uncertain nomenclature in ancient times, it is possible that the entire region south from the Median Wall to what is recognized by modern scholars as Babylon, may have been included within the parameters of the ancient city by certain authors. At the least, a formidable obstacle stood guard over the entrance into Babylon. First came "the wall." Then came the real test at the city itself.

Archaeological Evidence Relating to Babylon

Exactly what do we know about the city? Evidence from historical sources and archaeologists confirms the existence of a large double wall surrounding the central city that far surpasses the first wall to the north. The inner wall enclosing the central city reached a minimum of twenty-one feet thick while the outer wall measured another twelve feet. Nebuchadnezzar filled the twenty-four feet between the two walls with earth, giving the bulwark a total thickness of nearly sixty feet. Immediately preceding World War I, a German research expedition, directed by Robert Koldewey,[10] painstakingly verified the general dimensions of these fortifications. The description from Koldewey and his associates, coupled with Ravn's assessment[11] of earlier information from Herodotus, "gives an overall description of the area enclosed by the walls" that has proved to be "an accurate topographical record."[12]

Besides the walls, a moat, supplied by the Euphrates and ranging in width from sixty to 250 feet, meandered lazily toward the Persian Gulf, completely encircling the city.[13] The moat provided yet another dimension of security for Babylon's citizenry. In an age lacking aircraft and artillery, the defenses appeared impregnable. Only the eight major gates offered entrance into the city. One was the fabled Ishtar Gate. This gate, now partially restored, with its two flanking towers decorated with "blue and black glazed bricks with alternate rows in yellow relief of 575 (symbols) of Marduk, a combination of a serpent with the legs of lions and eagles and the bulls of (H)adad,"[14] furnished an imposing access to Babylon's interior.

Inside the City: Babylon's Amazing Buildings

Once inside, Babylon's guests could gape at the city's beauty. More than fifty temples, including fifteen built by Nebuchadnezzar, pointed majestically skyward in both the old city on the east of the Euphrates and the new city to the west. None appeared more striking than a giant ziggurat at the city's center. Its massive courtyard alone measured 1,380 feet by 1,230 feet while the building's base registered 300 feet square. Its layers of multicolored brick bulged 280 feet above the surrounding plain.

In the ziggurat's shadow sat the Temple of Esagila, a smaller shrine whose walls had been covered with gold and studded with jewels by Nebuchadnezzar. The garish exterior barely hinted at the even more opulent interior. Local priests informed Herodotus that its statues and tables were forged from 800 talents of gold (16.8 metric tons).[15]

Just the streets of Babylon astounded visitors. The city's main Processional Way traversed the Euphrates River via a ten-foot-wide stone bridge with a removable center span. Colored bricks, stamped with Nebuchadnezzar's name, covered the main street and many smaller avenues. Palm trees, like so many dominoes, lined the arteries.

Nebuchadnezzar's architects attained their crowning achievement in the famed Hanging Gardens. Said to be one of the Seven Wonders of the

Ancient World, tradition recounts them as a labor of love for
Nebuchadnezzar's Median Queen, Amytis, who longed for the forests
and mountains of her homeland.[16] Unfortunately, no first-hand evidence
of the fabled gardens survived; only descriptions from later writers and
speculations of archaeologists satisfy our curiosity.

Portions of what is sometimes called the "northern mound" of ancient Babylon
demonstrate the accuracy of predictions by the prophets that described the city
being in "heaps." (Photo courtesy, Fon Scofield Collection, E. C. Dargan Research
Library of the Sunday School Board, SBC.)

Berosus' (a contemporary of Alexander the Great) gives the earliest
glimpse of the marvel. The Jewish historian Josephus preserves his
description:

> At his (Nebuchadnezzar's) palace he had knolls made of stone that he
> shaped like mountains and planted with all kinds of trees. Furthermore, he
> had a so-called pensile paradise planted because his wife, who came from
> Media, longed for such, which was the custom in her homeland.[17]
> ... within this palace he erected stone terraces, in which he closely repro-
> duced mountain scenery, completing the resemblance by planting them
> with all manner of trees and constructing the so-called Hanging Gardens;
> because his wife, having been brought up in Media, had a passion for
> mountain surroundings.[18]

Another account, from Diodorus Siculus, says the Gardens attained a
height of seventy-five feet, were "constructed at a great expense," and in
such a manner that guests could walk under them through a series of
passageways:

The roofs of the galleries were covered over with beams of stone sixteen feet long ... and four feet wide. The roof above these beams had first a layer of reeds laid in great quantities of bitumen, over this two courses of baked brick bonded by cement, and as a third layer a covering of lead, to the end that the moisture from the soil might not penetrate beneath. On all this again the earth had been piled to a depth sufficient for the roots of the largest trees; and the ground, when leveled off, was thickly planted with trees of every kind. ... And since the galleries, each projecting beyond another, all received the light, they contained many royal lodges of every description; and there was one gallery which contained openings leading from the topmost surface and machines for supplying the garden with water, the machines raising the water in great abundance from the river, although no one outside could see it being done.[19]

Given Nebuchadnezzar's immense building projects, his boastful assertion, recorded by Daniel (4:30), "Is not this great Babylon which I have built?" possesses a definite ring of authenticity. Modern archaeologists corroborate Nebuchadnezzar's claims, and excavations sanction both his role as a builder and Babylon's preeminent position among the cities of antiquity.

Predictions Regarding Babylon's Future

Babylonian pride in her defensive capabilities led to the rejection of prophetic calls to repentance and their concomitant warnings of impending doom. Just as Israel's reliance on her abilities and an alliance with Egypt lulled her into overlooking the threat from Babylon years earlier, Babylonian pride generated a comparable outcome. As Keith observed,

If ever there was a city that seemed to bid defiance to any prediction of its fall, that city was Babylon. It was for a long time the most famous city in the world, and its walls which were reckoned among the wonders of the world appeared rather like the bulwarks of nature than the workmanship of man. The Temple of Belus, half a mile in circumference and a furlong in height—the hanging gardens which, piled in successive terraces, towered as high as the walls—the embankments which restrained the Euphrates—the hundred brazen gates—and the adjoining artificial lake—all displayed the mightiest works of mortals. ... Yet, while in ... its power and according to the most accurate chronologers, 160 years before the foot of an enemy had entered it, the voice of prophecy pronounced the doom of the mighty and unconquered Babylon.[20]

Though not taken seriously, biblical prophets enumerated a lengthy list of predictions regarding the city of Babylon and its inhabitants. The accuracy of their efforts is a matter of record.

Many Nations Will Help Subdue Babylon

The initial prediction came easily. Alliances in antiquity flourished as they do today. So, when Jeremiah (50:9) announced that God would "raise and cause to come up against Babylon an assembly of great nations from the north country," hardly an eyebrow lifted. Militancy dominated peoples north of the fertile crescent. Still, years later, when a Medo-Persian alliance, artfully crafted by Cyrus, rose to challenge Babylon's supremacy, it succeeded primarily because of the ineptness of Babylon's rulers. In less than a decade Nabonidus and his son Belshazzar lost the friendship of their allies, insulted the powerful religious establishment, and lost the popular support of their people.[21] Without the bumbling indiscretions of her rulers, alliances might never have formed.

> By successive alliances and conquests, by proclaiming liberty to the slaves, by a humane policy, consummate skill, and ... a boundless generosity, he changed, within a space of twenty years, a confederacy which the king of Babylon had raised up against the Medes and the Persians ... into a confederacy of the same nations against Babylon itself.[22]

Soon, flags of war danced over numerous armies. Kingdoms and peoples joined ranks in opposing Babylon's power. The assembly of mighty armies from countries north of the city planned their strike.

The Method of Capture Is Predicted

Jeremiah's forecast continued. He described the precise pattern of attack to be adopted by the city's attackers: "They shall hold the bow and the lance," he wrote. "They shall ride upon horses" (Jere. 50:42). When Cyrus descended upon the plains of the Euphrates, his war machine numbered 40,000 armed horsemen and "tens of thousands of archers and those who throw the javelin."[23] Realizing the strength of Cyrus' army, Babylon drew her forces behind the seemingly impregnable defenses, confident they could resist the Persian thrusts.

What happened next is difficult to sort out from our vantage point twenty-six centuries later. Some sources[24] imply that the real battle for Babylon raged near the Median Wall. After outflanking the defenders by diverting water from the Tigris and overwhelming Babylon's forces, Cyrus' army is said to have marched unimpeded into the city. A second set of sources,[25] while not denying the battle at the wall, argue that the key confrontation occurred at the city itself soon after the preliminary skirmish. This latter account, based primarily upon records of Herodotus, asserts that the Babylonians, after suffering initial setbacks in the field, withdrew behind the massive walls of the city, confident in their ability to withstand a siege. Irrespective of the length or exact location of a siege (the Median Wall, Babylon, or both), the most accurate historical sources available testify to its occurrence. Jeremiah's prediction (50:14) came to pass: "They camped against it round about. They put themselves in array against Babylon."

The Lack of Resistance in Babylon

For Cyrus and his forces, victory at Babylon came swiftly. So swiftly that attempts to establish the exact procedures used by the Medo-Persia alliance and the reasons for the near-total ineffectiveness of Babylon's massive defenses are mere conjectures.

Its Capture by Betrayal. Some modern writers point to the likelihood that the citizens simply opened the gates to the invaders who marched unopposed into city. Hinz[26] takes the position that an important Babylonian general, Gubaru, defected to the Persian alliance, then entered Babylon without anyone realizing his change of allegiance. Such a position is unlikely, however, since it is not mentioned by any of the earlier histories.

The idea of a conspiracy in the eventual overthrow of the city finds strong support in most collateral circumstances. First, both Nabonidus and his son, Belshazzar, became extremely unpopular with the masses. Nabonidus incurred the wrath of the religious establishment by failing to honor the traditional New Year's celebration, perhaps their most important festival. The celebration required the physical presence of the king. Nabonidus, however, spurned the event, choosing to absent himself from the city for nearly a decade.[27]

Second, Nabonidus undermined his popularity by championing a wave of religious reform. During his reign, he devoted significant resources toward elevating the moon-god Sin, the chief god of his home in Harran, to a position of honor.

Third, additional reforms proved catastrophic to the local economy. Prices surged nearly fifty percent in one decade.[28] As Oates concludes, "Clearly Nabonidus' religious and administrative reforms provoked great resentment."[29]

Fourth, during early skirmishes in the war, a brief civil struggle erupted in the city itself.[30]

Fifth, Cyrus' welcome into the city more resembled that of a liberator than that of an alien conqueror. A clay cylinder discovered in the ruins of the city in 1879 declared that Cyrus and his armies were welcomed into the city and green branches were spread before him. Although there is some evidence that this cylinder, like so many efforts in history, smacks of propaganda in attempting to legitimatize Cyrus' rule,[31] it is consistent with additional information drawn from Herodotus and Xenophon. Thus, the preponderance of evidence admits that Cyrus entered the city "amid much public acclaim."[32]

A Likely Breach in the Defenses. Still, the oldest data suggests that a breach of readiness and security by the Babylonians (Daniel 5) became a key factor in the city's capture. After all, the city was constructed to withstand assaults from any would-be aggressor. Her defenses appeared nearly impregnable. Waters of the Euphrates bisected the city bringing an ample supply of water and fish. At least one source suggests the government had stored enough provisions within the city to withstand a twenty-year siege. So, safe behind her fortifications, Babylon remained calm.

Daniel's writings record that the city fell in a night, while her leading citizens engaged in a drunken orgy. Their wickedness, false confidence, and profligate lifestyle remained to the end. No repentance tumbled from their lips. Jeremiah's prediction (51:30) that Babylon's fighting men would "remain in their holds" joined the list of fulfillments. To the end she trusted in her Maginot Line, unaware its Achilles' heel had been discovered.

To achieve conquest, Medo-Persian strategists faced two obstacles: (1) Waters of the Euphrates, nearly a quarter of a mile wide with a depth of twelve feet at the point they entered the city, had to be diverted long enough to allow their armies to scurry under the city walls, and (2) this had to be done with as much subterfuge as possible. The task was not simple. Babylon long recognized the river to be a likely point of attack and had taken great pains to secure the entrance. Nebuchadnezzar's builders had designed iron gates to prevent enemies from using the river as an entrance into the city. Yet, another of Jeremiah's predictions (51:36) rang clear: "I will dry up her sea," God had said. "I will dry up the rivers."

Herodotus and Xenophon confirm that the diversion of the river allowed the elite troops from Cyrus' army to enter the city at night. Their records and those of Daniel (5:3-4) testify that the event occurred while the city reveled in a drunken celebration. Herodotus writes:

> The Persians came on them by surprise and so took the city. Owing to the vast size of the place, the inhabitants of the central parts, as the residents of Babylon declare, long after the outer portions of the town were taken, knew nothing of what had chanced, but as they were engaged in a festival, continued dancing and reveling until they learnt the capture but too certainly (i.191).

Ruins of ancient Babylon offer eloquent testimony to the accuracy of the biblical prophets. (Photo courtesy, Fon Scofield Collection, E. C. Dargan Research Library of the Sunday School Board, SBC.)

Drunkenness of Defenders a Factor in Her Fall

Once Cyrus' troops were inside the city, he guessed that any soldiers still loyal to Belshazzar and Nabonidus would likely be drunk. So, he ordered his men to mimic revelers as they moved through the darkened city. When finally recognized as enemies, there would be no time to mount an adequate defense. Jeremiah (51:39) had predicted that as well: "I will make them drunken, that they may ... sleep a perpetual sleep, and not wake, saith the Lord." Thus, with breathtaking ease, the Medo-Persian alliance entered Babylon unchallenged.

When word of the invasion finally surfaced, messengers sped through the city to alert defenders. Again, a prophecy found fulfillment. "One post shall run to another," the prophet wrote (Jere. 51:31), "and one messenger to meet another to show the king of Babylon that his city is taken at one end." As news of the successful invasion wound its way through the city streets, the spirit of loyalist forces rapidly faded (Jere. 51:32). The few pockets of resistance that sprang up succumbed quickly.

Soon the invaders stood at the gates of the citadel. Hearing tumult outside and noting the hue and cry to be different from that expected, Belshazzar, in a moment of drunken stupidity, is said to have opened the gates of his fortress to dispatch a small body of soldiers to find the cause of the disturbance. When the Persians observed the gate opening, they poured through the gap. Belshazzar's fate was sealed. Jeremiah (51:57) foresaw even the final detail: "I will make drunk her princes (saith the Lord) and her wise men; her captains and her rulers, and the mighty men, and they shall sleep a perpetual sleep." Jeremiah's prediction (50:24) rings loud and clear: "It was taken and it was not aware."

Philistia in Prophecy:
Predicting the Disappearance
of the Sea Peoples

"Philistine." Even the name evokes an emotional response from students of Scripture. It calls to mind classic confrontations between arrogant giants (Goliath) and poetic shepherd boys (David), between manipulative temptresses (Delilah) and Herculean strong men (Samson). It reminds us of Saul's last, fatal battle and of the mysterious events surrounding the capture of the ark of the covenant. Yet, for all these memorable stories, the Philistines hardly should be remembered as fierce, war-loving savages who swarmed over Palestine. Though often locked in combat with their Israelite neighbors, they never launched a full-scale invasion.

Philistine Origins and Their Land

Much of our knowledge of the Philistines is speculative and of no crucial concern to our current study. However, scholars generally agree that they comprised at least a portion of the "sea-peoples" who stormed Egypt during the reign of Ramesses III.[1] Believed to originate either in Cyprus, Crete, or the Aegean islands,[2] the primary migratory wave, after being repulsed by the Egyptians, retreated northward and settled along Palestine's coastal plain.[3]

The land occupied by the Philistines seldom measured more than forty miles north to south or more than twenty miles inland from the Mediterranean. Five key cities dominated the nation. Three (Gaza, Ashkelon, and Ashdod) rose near the coast. Two (Gath and Ekron) were farther inland. Other, minor hamlets dotted the district around these major cities. On occasions, Philistine dominance even reached as far inland as Bethshan, Gibeah, and Bethshemesh.

Though the Philistines never controlled a sizable land area, they did exert tremendous influence. Philistia's location at a critical point along

Ruins of ancient Gath, home of the fabled giant Goliath, confirm God's judgments on the Philistines and their cities. (Photo courtesy, Fon Scofield Collection, E. C. Dargan Research Library of the Sunday School Board, SBC.)

the north-south coastal highway multiplied her strategic value. Coupled with these natural blessings, the Philistines brought with them the ability to manufacture iron (I Sam. 13:19-22), a talent in which they held a monopoly in the early history of the area.[4] So exaggerated did she appear to outsiders that the name for Philistia eventually became almost synonymous with the entire region:

> The Philistines' Hebrew name was *pelishtim*, and their conquered territory was called *eretz pelishtim* ("land of the Philistines") or *pelesheth* ("Philistia"). The name "Palestine" is derived from *Palastinoi*, a Greek designation for the Philistines' descendants.[5]

Biblical Records of the Philistine-Israelite Conflict

From a biblical standpoint, Philistia's surge to notoriety began with her incursion into portions of the land of Israel during the period of Samson (Judg. 13f). Samson's personal, and colorful, victories over the Philistines failed to stem the encroachment. Later, during the judgeship of Eli, they advanced at least as far west as Mizpah (I Sam. 4:1) where they captured the ark of the covenant. Philistia's incursions ebbed slightly during the early years of Samuel (I Sam. 7:12), only to explode in intensity and coverage in his later years. These incursions continued throughout the reign of King Saul (I Sam. 13:17-23). Finally, after David assumed the throne, Israel threw off Philistine dominance and recaptured the disputed land areas. From that point, Philistia never again proved a serious national threat.[6]

Predictions Regarding Philistine Cities

Hebrew prophets explain the reason for their denunciation of the Philistines by focusing on two charges: (1) The Philistines' trade in slaves (Amos 1:6; Joel 3:3-5), and (2) their unbending hostile and malicious stance toward Israel (Ezek. 25:15-17). Biblical predictions regarding Philistia also may be divided into two groups: (1) Specific predictions regarding their leading cities, and (2) predictions regarding the future disappearance of the nation.

Predictions Regarding Gaza

Among the five leading Philistine cities, Gaza emerged as the strongest. Located in the extreme southwestern corner of Canaan some three miles inland from the Mediterranean and about fifty miles southwest of Jerusalem, she had a long and storied history before the arrival of the Philistines. She was one of the last remaining homes of the "Anakim," the ancient race of giants (Josh. 11:22). Gaza also appears "as an Egyptian administrative center for Egypt's possessions in Canaan ... in documents of Pharaoh Thutmose III" during the middle of the fifteenth century B.C.[7] During the period of Egyptian dominance, several Egyptian fortresses surrounded the area. These fortifications offered a buffer between Egypt and increasingly warlike peoples to the north.[8]

Gaza owed much to her strategic position as well. Located astride the Via Maris ("Way of the Sea," Isa. 9:1), she provided protection for caravans and military maneuvers moving along the great international highway. Her location also offered economic and commercial advantages and she served as both "the principal mart for north Arabia"[9] and the "center of the slave trade" for the region.[10]

Not only did Gaza serve as home to a considerable population, she also became the most heavily fortified of the Philistine cities. When the armies of Alexander trampled the region in the fourth century B.C., only Gaza dared to oppose the Greek juggernaut. Two months of repeated assaults followed before the city finally succumbed to the onslaught.[11]

Specifically indicted for her role in the slave trade that often involved Israelites,[12] the prophets augured that (1) the city would be burned (Amos 1:7), (2) would become bald like a "shaven head" (Jer. 47:5), and (3) would "be abandoned" (Zeph. 2:4). Each prediction proved dependable.

Gaza to Be Burned. The prophecy's initial fulfillment occurred during the last quarter of the fourth century, B.C. Alexander's mighty armies prowled through Palestine looking for additional conquests. Although other Philistine cities quickly capitulated, Gaza, backed by strong defenses and her courageous army, defiantly refused Alexander's demands. The Greek monarch, still smarting from his long and costly siege at Tyre (see chapter 10), was in no mood for compromise. Gaza's defenders exacted a heavy toll. Finally, two months of intense fighting awarded control of the city to Alexander.[13] The struggle had been ferocious. Twice, Alexander lay wounded, and historians record that each city defender died at his post.[14]

Alexander's rage at Gaza's opposition would not be assuaged by the mere capture of the city. Gaza's intransigence demanded far more. After removing everything of value, Alexander burned the city. Still, Gaza's desirable location could not be overlooked, and, soon, another city rose from the ashes. Antiochus torched that city, too.[15] Again, the city endured the pangs of rebirth. Again, invaders burned the city—this time at the charge of Jonathan Maccabeus (I Macc. 10:84). The cycle continued. She was rebuilt, then burned to the ground during the Jewish rebellion in 55 A.D.[16] On at least two other occasions—during the Arabic civil wars and the crusades—flames devoured her population.[17] Gaza has found fire to be one of her more consistent companions.

Gaza to Become "Bald" and "Abandoned." For years, modern scholars grappled with Jeremiah's prophecy. While "shaven heads" often symbolically describe servitude, there seemed to be more to the prophet's lament. A possible interpretation arose during the nineteenth century when Dr. Alexander Keith's travels through the region encountered unexpected troubles near the city bearing Gaza's name. He meant to spend the evening in the storied city, but the presence of plague altered his plans. Instead, he and his company scoured the region "for the smoothest place ... whereon to pitch a tent,"[18] eventually choosing nearby sand dunes not far from the city. Here, they accidentally stumbled upon the remains of an ancient city hidden under the sand. Keith had discovered ancient Gaza. Covered for centuries by the desert sands, the location had become as smooth as a bald head.

As Urquhart so aptly observed years later, "The great Gaza of the Philistines ... is now a series of sandhills, covered with minute but manifold remains. It is so forsaken that there is not a single hut resting on its site. It is so bald that neither pillar nor standing stone marks the place where the city stood, nor is there a single blade of grass on which the weary eye can rest."[19]

These discoveries coincide beautifully with ancient records. The geographer Strabo described "the port of Gaza, and at the distance (from the then existing city) of seven furlongs the city, formerly illustrious, but destroyed ... and remaining desert."[20] Other writers spoke of "new Gaza" and "desert Gaza."[21] Now, such references are easily understandable. They also fit precisely into biblical predictions. Stoner's question is appropriate: "What better description could you give of a city buried under sand dunes than to say that it had become bald?"[22] Only during the last half of the twentieth century has the area become resettled.

Predictions Regarding Ashkelon

Ashkelon (I Sam. 6:17) lay on the Mediterranean coast about forty-five miles southwest of Jerusalem. "It was the only city (of the Philistine pentapolis) on the southern coastal plain directly on the seaboard."[23] The city is spoken of ten other times in the Old Testament and in several Egyptian sources before the days of the Philistines.[24]

Three prophets describe the future of the city: "left in ruins" (Zeph. 2:4), "deserted" (Zech. 9:5), and "silenced" (Jer. 47:5). Unlike predictions regarding Babylon, Nineveh, and Tyre, no hint of the length of the desolation surfaces.

There is no question about the fulfillment of the prophecies. Ashkelon revolted against the Assyrian Tiglath-Pileser in 733-732 B.C., against Sennacherib in 701 B.C., and again in 671 B.C. In each instance, the Assyrian war machine easily put down the revolt. Though damaged, the city survived the three Assyrian conquests, as well as one by the Egyptians in 612 B.C. and another by the Scythians two years later. Then, in 609 B.C., Babylonian armies finally decimated the city.[25] After the Babylonian period, Ashkelon disappeared from historical records. She reappeared in the Hellenistic period and endured a violent and bloody history for 1,500 years. The Mamelukes destroyed the city in 1270 A.D. This time, Ashkelon remained in ruins, awaiting the curious travelers and archaeologists of the modern era.[26]

Some evidence suggests that, like Gaza, more recent ruins at Ashkelon—including material from the Hellenistic to Crusader times—do not date from the Philistine era.[27] Barnes quotes a twelfth-century traveler, Benjamin of Tudela, as saying, "From Ashdod are two parasangs to Ashkelonah; this is the new Ashkelon ... and it is distant from the old Ashkelon, which is desolate."[28] The most recent excavations, by Lawrence Stager of Harvard University and the Oriental Institute of the University of Chicago, offer additional credence to the theory.[29] Regardless of whether two or more Ashkelons graced the coastal landscape, the ancient sites stand desolate and silent. Barnes wrote:

> The present Ashkelon is a ghastly skeleton; all the frame-work of a city, but none there. The soil is good, but the peasants who cultivate it prefer living outside (the remains of the old city) ... because they think that God has abandoned it, and that evil spirits (the Jan and the Ghul) dwell there. ... It lies in such a living death, that it is one of the most mournful scenes of utter desolation which a traveler even in this land of ruins has beheld.[30]

Predictions Regarding Ekron

Today, after centuries of squabbling over the location of Ekron, scholars generally agree that the remains of the ancient Philistine city can be viewed at Tel-Miqneh (Khirbet el-Muqanna). That would place it approximately thirteen miles east of Ashdod and twenty-five miles west of Jerusalem.[31] Recent archaeological work at the site documents the city's founding at some point in the twelfth century B.C. as a "large, 50-acre metropolis."[32]

Like other Philistine cities, Ekron attracts sizable attention in the Old Testament. After the defeat of Goliath, the Philistines retreated behind Ekron's fortifications (I Sam. 17:52). Later, the writer of II Kings (1:2) speaks of a temple of Baal-Zebub located there.

Thanks to extensive excavations at the site since 1981 led by Trude Dothan and Seymour Gitin, much is known about the city. The researchers found, for instance, that "In the seventh century B.C., Ekron became the largest known center for olive oil production in the ancient Near East."[33] Over a hundred facilities, with a production capacity in excess of 290,000 gallons annually, have already been unearthed though only three percent of the area has been excavated. Amid the ruins, Gitin and his fellow researchers also found traces of a possible textile industry.[34]

Zephaniah (2:4) offered one simple prediction regarding the city: "Ekron (will be) uprooted." Even the prophecy offered a jab, for the city's name means "firm-rooted." Amos (1:7) was just as blunt: "I will turn my hand against Ekron till the last of the Philistines is dead, says the Sovereign Lord."

The predictions came to pass. Babylon's military pushed the Philistines from Ekron at the end of the seventh century. Her citizens faced deportation. Those few who managed to escape mixed with other people in the region. Ekron disappeared, along with her Philistine inhabitants. Gitin summarizes:

> ... signs of the great Babylonian destruction were unmistakable. The massive fortification system was breached and destroyed; entire building com-

plexes were toppled; industrial installations and private residences, and all of their contents, were set to the torch and buried under a thick blanket of ash and collapsed mud-brick and stone structures. ... For the people of Ekron, the Babylonian conquest was more than a horrible military disaster. It was a blow from which the Philistine culture could never recover. Once the traditional boundaries of Philistia and its cities had been destroyed, their populations either dispersed or deported, the Philistines, including the Ekronites ... were easily assimilated into the cultures that remained.[35]

Remains of the ancient Philistine city of Ashdod are located under this mound in southwestern Palestine. (Photo courtesy, Fon Scofield Collection, E. C. Dargan Research Library of the Sunday School Board, SBC.)

Predictions Regarding Ashdod

Unlike other cities in the Philistine pentapolis, Ashdod's location never came in question. Located thirty-five miles north of Gaza on the Via Maris, and three miles inland, the city attained biblical prominence when Philistines captured the ark of the covenant and brought it to the house of Dagon in the city (I Sam. 5:1ff). That temple remained for hundreds of years before being destroyed by Jonathan Maccabeus (I Macc. 20:84).

In addition to the early encounter, conflicts between Israel and the citizens of Ashdod are recorded during the reigns of both Uzziah and Ahaz (II Chron. 26:6; II Chron. 28:18). People from Ashdod also opposed Nehemiah's (4:1ff) building activities in the days immediately after Babylonian captivity.

Physically, Ashdod boasted powerful defenses. According to
Herodotus, the city withstood history's longest recorded siege (29 years
from Pharaoh Psammetichus).[36] Recent archaeological discoveries confirm the city's defensive capabilities: "The fortifications consisted of a
brick wall (15 feet wide), strengthened at places with stone, and a gate
(45 feet by 53 feet) defended by two solid towers."[37] Though not as formidable as those of Nineveh, Babylon, or Jerusalem, they were, never-
theless, significant.

Again, the prophets forecast the city's future. Amos (1:8) decreed that
God would "destroy the inhabitants of Ashdod" and Zephaniah (2:4)
echoed, "At midday, Ashdod will be emptied." Ashdod often felt the rod
of conquering armies. "Assyria conquered it in 712 B.C.E.; Egypt took it
after a long siege in the early seventh century; and it fell to Babylon
when Judah did in the early sixth century."[38]

Like other Philistine cities, Ashdod was built slightly inland from the
sea, perhaps from fear of pirates, invasion, or natural disasters such as
storms and earthquakes. As a result, she required a port facility on the
Mediterranean to service her needs. By New Testament times, the port
city (Azotus Paralus) outstripped its inland sister (Azotus Mesogeius) in
both size and importance. Babylon delivered the major blow to the
inland city in the sixth century. After that conquest, the site remained
virtually uninhabited during the Persian period. Though partially rebuilt,
the city suffered her fatal wound during the Jewish revolt in 67 A.D.
Ashdod was destroyed and her citizens faded into oblivion.

Predictions Regarding the Philistine Nation

Having detailed the fall of key cities, biblical prophets conclude their
pronouncements by foretelling the disappearance of the nation. Jeremiah
(47:4) minced no words: "The Lord is about to destroy all the
Philistines." Zephaniah (2:5) added, simply, "none will be left."
Zechariah's terse comment (9:6-7) predicted the Philistines would go the
way of the Jebusites.

The prediction has been fulfilled to the letter. As George Davis
explained, "The Philistines have been destroyed so completely that
there is not a single Philistine living anywhere in the world today."[39]
Bierling concludes his recent treatise by musing, "Both Jews and
Philistines adapted to the local Canaanite culture, but when both peoples went into captivity, the Philistines left the stage of Near Eastern
history and disappeared."[40]

The complete disappearance of the Philistine nation is called an "enigma" by modern scholars struggling to understand why a powerful and

innovative people failed to survive. Referring to the "textual evidence" that describes their destruction by the Babylonians, Gitin writes, "it does not explain its disastrous finality. It does not explain why the Philistines, who had endured previous Egyptian, Judean, and Assyrian conquests, did not survive the Babylonian conquest."[41] A simple explanation exists. Philistia did not survive because Deity decreed it would not survive. The decree came in advance as proof that the prophets delivered words from a supernatural source.

Tyre, Sidon and Phoenicia in Prophecy: Predicting the Collapse of the Great Traders

The ancient city of Tyre earned the titles "Queen of the Seas" and "Emporium of the Ancient World." Tyrian ships traversed the blue Mediterranean, traced the shoreline of Africa from the Pillars of Hercules to Ethiopia, and carried merchants to the ends of the then-known earth.

The antiquity of the city is unquestioned. Isaiah (23:7) describes her as "the old, old city." Strabo adds that Tyre is "the largest and oldest city of the Phoenicians."[1] Herodotus was told by local priests when he visited the city some four centuries before the birth of Christ that the city was founded some 2,300 years prior to his visit.[2]

The Growth of Tyrian Power and Prestige

Tyre easily became the most celebrated of a cluster of Phoenician cities that clung to Palestine's Mediterranean coastline like pearls on a string.[3] Her disinterest in empire-building enabled her to coexist alongside the great empires of antiquity. The success of her merchants filled the coffers of Egypt, Assyria, Babylon, and Persia as well as her own. Left to her commercial endeavors, Tyre and Phoenicia created much wealth and no trouble for the great powers. Besides, the military prowess of the empires offered Phoenician traders protection and opportunities for unimpeded travel. As Katzenstein observed, "incorporation of Tyre into the Persian empire was a great blessing for the Phoenician merchant princes."[4] The system worked well for both, unless the dictators became too greedy.

So impressed did the ancients become with the skills of the Phoenicians, they attributed to them navigation, the origin of writing, glass-making, embroidery, and purple-dyeing. Though modern scholarship questions some of these claims, there can be no doubt that the Phoenicians "brought these arts to perfection."[5] The city lay claim to being "the theatre of an immense commerce and navigation, the nursery of arts and science, and the city of perhaps the most industrious and active people ever known."[6]

Six centuries before Christ, the prophet Ezekiel (27:3-25) enthusiastically described the city:

> You say, O Tyre, "I am perfect in beauty." Your domain was on the high seas; your builders brought your beauty to perfection. They made all your timbers of pine trees from Senir, they took a cedar from Lebanon to make a mast for you. Of oaks from Bashan they made your oars; of cyprus wood from the coasts of Cyprus they made your deck, inlaid with ivory. Fine embroidered linen from Egypt was your sail and served as your banner; your awnings were of blue and purple from the coasts of Elishah. Men of Sidon and Arvad were your oarsmen; your skilled men, O Tyre, were aboard as your seamen. Veteran craftsmen of Gebal were on board as shipwrights to caulk your seams. All the ships of the sea and their sailors came alongside to trade for your wares. ...
>
> Tarshish did business with you because of your great wealth of goods; they exchanged silver, iron, tin and lead for your merchandise. Greece, Tubal, and Meshech traded with you; they exchanged slaves and articles of bronze for your wares. Men of Beth Togarmah exchanged work horses, war horses, and mules for your merchandise. The men of Rhodes traded with you, and many coastlands were your customers; they paid you with ivory tusks and ebony. Aram did business with you because of your many products; they exchanged turquoise, purple fabric, embroidered work, fine linen, coral and rubies for your merchandise. Judah and Israel traded with you; they exchanged wheat from Minnith and confections, honey, oil and balm for your wares. Damascus, because of your many products and great wealth of goods, did business with you in wine from Helbon and wool from Zahar. Danites and Greeks from Uzal bought your merchandise; they exchanged wrought iron, cassia and calmus for your wares. Dedan traded in saddle blankets with you. Arabia and all the princes of Kedar were your customers; they did business with you in lambs, rams and goats. The merchants of Sheba and Raamah traded with you; for your merchandise they exchanged the finest of all kinds of spices and precious stones, and gold. Haran, Canneh and Eden and merchants of Sheba, Asshur and Kilmad traded with you. In your marketplace they traded with you beautiful garments, blue fabric, embroidered work and multicolored rugs with cords twisted and tightly knotted. The ships of Tarshish serve as carriers for your wares. You are filled with heavy cargo in the heart of the sea.

Reasons for Tyre's Success

Several factors account for Tyre's rise to preeminence. First, she became the most prolific in planting colonies outside the homeland. Tyrian settlements sprang up at Tarsus, in the Aegean islands, in Thera and Rhodes, in Spain, and along the Atlantic seaboard in Europe and Africa. Strabo claims she planted three hundred cities on the Mauritanean coast west of the Pillars of Hercules.[7] None gained more notoriety than the north African colony at Carthage. Eventually, she rose to challenge Rome's dreams of world conquest.

Second, Tyre achieved superiority because of her near-impregnable defenses. While all Phoenician cities were fortified, not all proved equally defendable. The Sidonians found that true when Philistines overran their city around 1200 B.C. Tyre's exceptionally strong defenses came partly because of her location. Like other powerful Phoenician cities, the waters of the Mediterranean shielded the mainland city—Ushu or "Old Tyre"—on one side while towering stone walls protected the three remaining sides.[8] More important, however, two islands, approximately one-half mile from the mainland, secured her existence. Separated from the mainland by a channel that reached some twenty feet deep, the islands provided a type of insurance policy should the mainland city come under attack. A contemporary of David and Solomon, King Hiram, ingenuously joined the two islands into a unit and began construction on their defenses.[9]

Through the years, the island fortress proved nearly invincible. Assyrian, Babylonian, and Persian armies found their plans thwarted by an inability to reach and subdue the city's island hub. The island defenses often demanded a pragmatic approach of taxation and peaceful coexistence. Walls for the island city, constructed from huge stones, soared 150 feet skyward. Menacing battlements jutted from the walls at regular intervals.[10] The island's bedrock foundations also made possible the construction of tall buildings. Houses, perhaps "the pleasant houses" of Ezekiel (26:12), often rose several stories high and could be easily seen towering above the walls.[11]

Third, Tyre attained prominence through her ability to attract skilled artisans and craftsmen. Some came to work with the many merchants and traders. Others found jobs working on the city's public buildings. Curtius, for instance, describes the city as "excelling all the cities of Syria and Phoenicia in its size and glory."[12] Katzenstein describes three temples to Baal-Shamem, Melqart, and Astarte, the royal palace, the archives, and "large marketplaces" as part of the island city. He concluded: "The kings of Tyre adorned their city with many magnificent buildings."[13]

Although not as grand as those of Thebes or Babylon, these buildings gained renown for their exquisite workmanship and artistic beauty. So marvelous were the carvings and so widespread the fame of the craftsmen that when time came to build the Temple in Jerusalem, the call went to Tyre. Solomon wrote to Hiram (II Chron. 2:4-5,7):

> Now I am about to build a temple for the Name of the Lord my God and to dedicate it to him. ... The temple I am going to build will be great, because our God is greater than all other gods. ... Send me, therefore, a man skilled to work in gold and silver, bronze and iron, and in purple, crimson and blue yarn, and experienced in the art of engraving.

So, skilled artisans from Tyre brought their expertise to Israel. Their decorative additions to Solomon's temple drew praise from all who saw them. According to Josephus,

> ... the temple was made, with great skill, of polished stones, and those laid together so very harmoniously and smoothly, that there appeared to the spectators no signs of any hammer, or other instrument of architecture, but as if, without any use of them, the entire materials had naturally united themselves together.[14]

Fourth, Tyre flourished because of its trade. Besides its merchants, the city housed "installations for the building and overhauling of ships and vessels. There were 'dockyards' and sheds in which boats were kept, when they were taken out of the water or for repairs."[15]

Fifth, and finally, Tyre boasted perhaps the greatest fishing industry in the Western world.[16] Thus, with much in its favor, Tyre grew to be the most important of the Phoenician cities.

Reasons for the Prophetic Condemnations

Unfortunately, Tyre's outward strength and beauty turned vile and ugly inside. Her society's weaknesses could not be masked by artists who gave beauty to brass and silver and gold. She ruthlessly pursued wealth. In a philosophy reminiscent of future societies, Tyre felt no moral obligation about the method of achieving her riches. Economic considerations and moral concerns found themselves irreconcilably divorced. Tyre bartered and sold human slaves in her markets. Slavery was profitable. Moreover, the Tyrian religion—worship of Melqart—encouraged a low view of human life. Children were wrenched from their parents and offered as sacrifices to their gods.

Consequently, Ezekiel (26:3-5,7,12,14) painted her future in dark and ominous colors. Six distinct hues of his prophecy can be isolated. (1) Nebuchadnezzar would besiege the city, but his siege would fail to achieve its total purpose. (2) Tyre would be attacked by many nations who would reduce it to nothing. (3) Even the stones, timber, and dust of the old city would be deposited in the sea. In this prediction, Zechariah (9:3-4) echoed the one by Ezekiel. (4) The site of the city would become as flat as the top of a rock. (5) She would never be rebuilt. (6) The city would become a place for fishermen's nets.

Of the six prophecies, only the first occurred during the lifetime of the prophet. All others happened much later.

Tyre's Strategy for Survival against Assyria

For centuries, Tyre used her wealth and neutrality to avoid open warfare. Tribute flowed from her treasuries to the great powers. Egypt became the first beneficiary. Then, when the Assyrian war-machine under Asshurnazirpal reached the coastal plain in the ninth century B.C., Tyre altered her allegiance. Well aware of Assyrian military abilities, Tyre understood that, even if she withstood the onslaught, her trade would be irreparably disrupted. She chose to switch rather than fight. It was, after all, as easy to pay tribute to Assyria as to Egypt.

Katzenstein concluded,

> Taxes and/or tribute were reckoned as a commercial expense, and the Phoenicians were prepared to pay for the right of transit; for, as traders par excellence, they understood very well that commerce is a two-way street. Their practical mercantile sense was very much developed, and it dictated the course of their actions.[17]

Life in Tyre continued. Assyrian domination offered safe caravan routes for the city's traders. During this era, Tyrian wealth and commerce expanded tremendously[18] as Assyrian hegemony created safe overland routes for Phoenician traders. Isaiah (23:3,8) described the beneficial relationship: "she became the marketplace of the nations. ... (her) merchants are princes, (her) traders are renowned in the earth." Likewise, Zechariah (9:3) retorted, "Tyre ... has heaped up silver like dust, and gold like the dirt of the streets." Ezekiel (28:4-5) added, "you have gained wealth for yourself and amassed gold and silver in your treasuries. By your great skill in trading you have increased your wealth."

Eventually, Assyria's grip loosened. Tyre and the rest of Phoenicia edged toward independence. When Shalmaneser IV of Assyria decided that the relaxed confederation had passed acceptable limits, Assyrian hordes streamed westward, expecting to subjugate the area as before. Most of Phoenicia gave in to the pressure. Tyre refused. With problems increasing on her eastern and southern borders as well as within Assyria itself, the Assyrian monarch glumly recalled his troops, exacting only a minimal agreement with the Tyrians. Even that agreement soon evaporated.

When Assyria successfully dealt with her other concerns, she sent her armies racing westward yet again. Mainland Tyre fell to the advancing armies and angered by Tyre's obstinateness and piqued by her inability to subdue the island fortress, Assyria embarked on a disastrous course. Commandeering sixty ships and 800 sailors from other Phoenician cities, she launched a naval attack on the island. Only twelve ships from the Tyrian fleet advanced to meet the challenge. The superiority of those twelve ships and their crews overwhelmed the attacking forces. Tyre's fleet sank or captured most of the Assyrian fleet. Over 500 prisoners fell into Tyrian hands.

Failing to reach the island, Assyria next attempted to cut off her water supply. Until the invasion, the island city's water supply came from daily ferries from springs at the site of the mainland city. That strategy failed as well. The island's inhabitants rationed their supplies, used giant cisterns to capture rain, and dug huge wells. Five years passed. Finally, the Assyrian armies gave up and returned home.[19]

In 701 B.C., Sennacherib returned with an even larger army. The island fortress remained invulnerable.[20] Two decades later, another Assyrian monarch, Esarhaddon, mustered one last attempt to capture "Tyre-in-the-sea." He proved no more successful than his predecessors. Fleming describes the results:

> The Assyrian could occupy the mainland; he could ... cut off the city's usual water supply; he could attempt to fight the island dwellers with starvation. But the half mile of water in the channel was an effective barrier against assault, and the Assyrian army could not shut Tyre in from the open sea. And while the sea was open, Tyre could not be starved into submission.[21]

Esarhaddon and the Assyrians withdrew.

Still, the constant defensive effort exacted its toll on Tyre's commercial endeavors. Upon the death of Esarhaddon, Tyre struck an agreement with Ashurbanipal that freed her "from military expenditure, ensured the country against invasion, and gave settled conditions and protections ... for the development of trade. To a commercial people these advantages more than balanced their cost in tribute and the loss of political independence."[22]

Nebuchadnezzar Tries His Luck

When Assyria's power faded, Egypt and Babylon sparred for the opportunity to add Phoenicia to their crowns. Egyptian forces, almost forgotten during Assyria's rule, raced northward along the coastal plain. Babylonian forces under Nebuchadnezzar moved westward to meet the challenge. Stung by the effectiveness of Babylonian traders who were already cutting into their markets, Tyre cast her lot with Egypt. Egyptian armies were soundly defeated by the Babylonians and retreated southward while Nebuchadnezzar turned to deal with Egyptian allies.[23] Jerusalem fell. So did the other cities who sided with Egypt. Finally, Nebuchadnezzar turned his attention to Tyre.

Though Ezekiel (29:18) prophesied the Babylonians would take spoils from Tyre, he did not predict total conquest of the city. He wrote: "Nebuchadnezzar ... drove his army in a hard campaign against Tyre; every head was rubbed bare and every shoulder made raw. Yet he and his army got no reward from the campaign he led." For thirteen long years, Babylonian soldiers besieged the city. The mainland city fell, but the island fortress remained. In the end, like the Assyrians before, Nebuchadnezzar agreed to accept an alliance.

Thirteen years of warfare proved devastating. Commerce declined. Leadership of the Phoenician league passed to Sidon. The mainland city lay in ruins.[24] A sustained depression followed. More than a century would pass before Tyre regained her former glory. By then, Persia had supplanted Babylon, and Tyre concluded that it was in her interest to accept an alliance with Cyrus.

Alexander's Campaign Against the City

Near the close of the fourth century B.C., Alexander's Greek-led confederacy challenged Persian dominance. Two great battles, at the Granicus River and the city of Issus, established the superiority of Alexander's armies and shattered the Persian Empire. After the victory at Issus, Alexander disdained an immediate strike at the retreating Persian army. Instead, he turned toward Egypt in an attempt to render Persia's allies powerless. As usual, Phoenicia lacked interest in a fight. Sidon and the other cities quickly capitulated. Tyre followed—to a degree. Emissaries rushed to greet the young conqueror bearing a crown of gold, lavish presents, and an agreement of submission.[25]

Unsatisfied, Alexander responded that he, supposedly a descendant of the god Heracles (the equivalent of the Tyrian god Melqart), would enter the island city to sacrifice at the god's widely renowned temple. Tyre's leaders found themselves in a quandary. Allowing the Macedonian army inside their gates ensured permanent occupation to a degree they found unacceptable. They decided to make a stand. After all, neither the Assyrians nor the Babylonians had been able to capture the island fortress. There was no reason to suspect Alexander would fare better. As Fleming explains:

They could expect the hostile armies of Babylon soon to engage Alexander's attention. Alexander had no fleet with which to attack them. In the event of a siege, the Persian fleet, in which their own vessels were serving, might be counted on for help. At least their own fleet ... could be recalled. There was no reason to believe that ships of other Phoenician cities would show any great enthusiasm in attacking their kinsfolk. Egypt, next to be invaded, would have weighty reasons for aiding Tyre. An embassy from Carthage ... counseled resistance and promised that the squadrons of Carthage would soon come to the city's assistance. In former times the city had shown itself well nigh impregnable. That Alexander's method of attack was not anticipated is not strange, for there was no precedent for it in the annals of warfare.[26]

Buoyed by their defenses and confident of success, Tyre's leaders sent word that Alexander would be welcome at the much older mainland temple of Melqart. He would not, however, be granted permission to enter the island fortress.[27] The man, who later in his life, supposedly wept because he had nothing left to conquer, grittily seized the challenge and prepared for war. His armies swiftly gained control of the mainland city while Alexander and his strategists mulled over ways to attack the island citadel.

Fulfilling Ezekiel's Predictions

Tyre's Stones, Timbers, and Dust Thrown in the Water

No one knows who devised the precise method of attack. Some credit Alexander. Regardless, the choice proved ingenious. Engineers would construct a causeway from the mainland to the island giving Alexander's giant war machines a chance to breach the walls. Parties of workers would be dispatched to the nearby mountains to collect wood for the pilings. Others would tear down the buildings of mainland Tyre and use those materials as well.[28] The great stones and pillars that graced the magnificent buildings on the mainland would serve as the foundation for the mole.

Although it was a unique and completely unexpected method of attack, the Tyrians refused to capitulate. Tyrian troops staged guerrilla raids on those bringing stone. Allies to the east disrupted the work in the mountains. Progress on the mole slowed to a crawl.[29] Sensing an opportunity to thwart the Macedonian, Tyre committed her ace to the fray. Tyrian warships, filled with archers and slingers, entered the channel. Their deadly accuracy exacted a heavy price on the exposed work parties.[30] Meanwhile, Tyre's great war machines hurled missile after missile at the mole. The work stopped.

To address the challenge, Alexander's engineers built two large wood-en towers and moved them to the end of the mole. They provided both protection for the workers and an offensive capability that allowed Alexander to respond to the Tyrian attacks. Also, workers next installed a barrier made from sails and animal hides to provide extra cover.

Alexander used materials from the buildings of ancient Tyre to construct his causeway to the island fortress. Ezekiel predicted it would happen. (Photo courtesy, Fon Scofield Collection, E. C. Dargan Research Library of the Sunday School Board, SBC.)

Again, Tyre countered. They outfitted a large merchant ship as a fire-bomb. Highly flammable materials, possibly naphtha, filled the hold while two masts, serving as a giant spearhead, jutted from the bow. Cauldrons of bitumen, sulfur, and other combustibles hung from the masts. When all was ready and the currents were flowing toward the mole, two triremes manned by the city's finest sailors, towed the floating bomb into position and began their run toward the target. At the last moment, the two triremes veered to the sides and released the cargo ship in a collision course with the mole. Sailors on board the vessel ignited the fires and jumped overboard to await rescue by other Tyrian warships.

The blazing inferno slammed into the mole. Cauldrons filled with flammable materials spilled onto the Greek barrier and burst into flames. Within minutes, flames engulfed the mole. Marksmen on Tyrian war-ships effectively prevented reinforcements from extinguishing the blaze.[31] Simultaneously, divers successfully removed many stakes protecting the mole from the current. Soon, Alexander's masterpiece began to disintegrate.[32]

Though his advisers counseled abandoning the task, Alexander's pride had been stung. More determined than ever, he vowed to destroy the island fortress. Ordering a second mole, even wider than the first,[33] he directed that everything remaining from the mainland city be dumped into the sea. Workers even scraped topsoil from the old city to gain material for the causeway. Ezekiel's prediction had been fulfilled.

The City Will Fall

To be successful, Alexander realized that the Tyrian fleet had to be taken out of the battle. Like the Assyrians before him, he scavenged the coast for ships. Luckily, fleets from the other Phoenician cities entered the harbor at Sidon just when Alexander needed them. These Phoenician ships matched those of Tyre in quality. Soon Alexander had eighty ships at his command. Other ships from Lycia, Rhodes, Soli, and Malus joined the fleet. Days later, Cyprus added 120 ships to the cause.[34] Alexander could now overwhelm the Tyrian vessels. He bottled up their fleet in their two harbors and stepped up the work on the mole.

Though Tyre's defenders fought well and hard, only some massive, unexpected diversion of Alexander's efforts could spare the city. It never came. After seven, long, arduous months, Alexander's armies breached the walls. The city fell. Eight thousand defenders died. Two thousand were crucified.[35] Thirty thousand more were sold into slavery.[36] Much of the city was burnt and left in ruins. Green's recent summary is appropriate:

> Against Alexander's mole, quiet now under the summer sky, sand began to drift from the coastal dunes, softening the sharp outline of blocks and joists, linking Tyre ever more closely to the mainland. The flail of the Lord had done his work all too well. With each passing century the peninsula grew wider. Today ... the stone core of that fantastic causeway still stands: one of Alexander's most tangible and permanent legacies to posterity.[37]

Many Nations Will Attack the City

Ezekiel's prophecy that "many nations" would attack the city found fulfillment in many ways. First, Nebuchadnezzar, Persia, and Alexander marched against the city. Second, Alexander's army was truly an international force. He drew soldiers from many other nations. Third, in the years after Alexander, other nations have subdued the Mediterranean coastal region. Ptolemy invaded Phoenicia after the death of Alexander.[38] Less than a decade later, with the city starting to undergo partial restoration, Antigonus led his armies to victory over the region's inhabitants.[39] Others (the Seleucid kings,[40] King Tigranes of Armenia,[41] the Roman legions) followed suit. In 1289, the Mamelukes delivered the region another decisive defeat.[42] Many nations came. Many nations conquered.

Tyre Will Not be Rebuilt

Mainland Tyre had grown fat with prosperity when Nebuchadnezzar's armies encircled the city. There was every reason to think that, despite the outcome, the city would continue to thrive. The only question seemed to be who would control her. Her location was ideal for trade. The harbors (two on the island and perhaps one at the mainland city) were commodious. A constant stream of fresh water—averaging 10,000,000 gallons a day and a rarity in the region—gushed from the Ras-el-Ain springs.[43]

With a perfect location for commerce, an adequate water supply, and a long history, Tyre seemed destined to exist forever. Besides, victors rebuilt and repopulated most cities destroyed in warfare. They were far more interested in tribute and slaves than in deserted ruins. Moreover, builders in antiquity chose their sites with great care and did not abandon them hastily. Yet, Ezekiel confidently declared that Tyre would not be rebuilt.

The Complete Desolation of the Mainland City. Under Alexander, every vestige of a city on the mainland was hurled into the sea. The harbor disappeared under tons of debris. Alexander's efforts altered an entire landscape. Mainland Tyre no longer exists. The Greek strategy so completely blotted it from the earth that it is impossible to reconstruct its appearance. Hamilton explains,

> Old Tyre today stands as it has for twenty-five centuries, a bare rock, uninhabited by man! Today anyone who wants to see the site ... can have it pointed out to him along the shore, but there is not a ruin to mark the spot. It has been scraped clean and never been rebuilt.[44]

If the prophecy referred to Old Tyre, the fulfillment is obvious.

The Complete Transformation of the Island Fortress. It is also possible that Ezekiel spoke of the island citadel. If so, that prophecy, too, was accurate. With Alexander's causeway, the character of the region unalterably changed. Tyre's defenses, centered on her island fortress, no longer exist. The ancient harbors, around which the city made her fortune, find themselves choked with sand and debris. The islands no longer exist. Whatever might exist on the peninsula could bear no resemblance to the ancient Phoenician stronghold.

The fishing village that currently sits on a portion of Alexander's peninsula possesses none of the characteristics of the city about which Ezekiel prophesied. No fortifications or walls surround it. No international markets thrive in its streets. No great temples rise from its land area. No exquisite artistry adorns its buildings. No riches pour into its coffers. In short, no one would consider it a "rebuilt replica" of ancient Tyre. Hall argues that one must only understand the words of Ezekiel to mean that subsequent cities built on the site would lack the greatness of Tyre.[45]

Consider All Parts of the Prophecy. We must remember that the same prophet who declared, at the same time, in the same writing, that ancient Tyre would never be rebuilt, also declared that the site would be a place for fishermen. Obviously, Ezekiel did not mean to imply that humans would never again live at the location of the old city. That, today, a small fishing village exists at the very location where it was prophesied to exist does not seem to be a serious objection to the validity of the prophecy's fulfillment.

A Place for Fishermen

The prediction that Tyre would become "a place to spread fishnets" (Ezek. 26:14), has also been fulfilled. The records of several travelers throughout the years confirm the prediction. Nelson writes, "I went to visit on a summer's day. ... Fishing nets were drying on the shore."[46] Other writers concur. Rackl adds, "Tyre has become a place to dry fish nets."[47] Ward concludes, "Since (1921), agriculture and fishing ... have turned Tyre ... into a backwater."[48] Even a committed early opponent of Christianity admitted,

> Instead of the ancient commerce, so active and extensive, (Tyre), reduced to a miserable village, has no ... (more) trade than ... exportation of a few sacks of corn. ... The whole village contains only fifty or sixty poor families who live on the produce of their little grounds and a trifling fishery.[49]

Peripheral Predictions Regarding Sidon

Ezekiel's prophecies relating to Tyre's chief rival, Sidon, also merit discussion. Sidon claimed to be the oldest of the Phoenician cities, antedating Tyre by a hundred years or more, sometime around 2000 B.C.

Great similarities characterized the two cities. Comparable fortifications protected both. Both served as home port for large fleets. Both housed large merchant populations. Both were home to extensive populations. Both gained fame because of the artisans and craftsmen who worked there. They were also close neighbors.

Given their proximity and similarities, we might suppose their futures would also converge. What would be true of one likely would also be true of the other. Despite the expected, however, Ezekiel's predictions regarding Sidon differed drastically from his predictions of Tyre. He wrote (28:22-23): "This is what the Sovereign Lord says: I am against you, O Sidon. ... I will send a plague upon her and make blood flow in her streets. The slain will fall within her, with the sword against her on every side." Hardly an auspicious future, yet, no word came from the prophet about her total destruction. Evidently Sidon would continue while Tyre vanished. The weaker city would survive; the stronger would not.

Today, Sidon continues to thrive and appear in world headlines as a base for operations by the Palestine Liberation Organization and other Arab groups. She has seen blood shed in her streets throughout the centuries. Her enemies have come from every direction.

Babylonian armies came first, then the Persians. After years of tribute, Sidon rebelled. Persian armies laid siege to the city and were, for a time, unsuccessful. Then, to assure his safety should the siege fail, the Sidonian king betrayed the city. Rather than accept incredible hardships and torture because of their rebellion, 40,000 Sidonians barricaded themselves in their homes and burned them down over their heads.[50]

Confrontation after confrontation followed. The Ptolomies, the Seleucid kings, the Romans, Moslems, and the crusaders have all entered the city. Typical of its history is Hamilton's description of the crusades: "In the days of the crusades (Sidon) was taken and retaken again by opposing forces. Three times it was captured by crusaders, and three times it fell before Moslem armies."[51] Unlike Tyre, Sidon rebounded from every blow. In 1840, the combined fleets of England, France, and Turkey shelled the city.[52] The twentieth century has seen civil war after civil war rage in her streets as Druses, Turks, Arabs, Christians, Israelis, and Moslem militias dueled for possession of the city. Truly, Sidon "has had one of the bloodiest histories any city ever saw."[53] That she would have faced exactly that was the focus of Ezekiel's prophecy. He was right again.

Attempted Explanations for Ezekiel's Prophecies.

Given the close relation between Ezekiel's predictions and historical events, it is only natural that attempts to explain away the correlation will surface. Were they composed after the events occurred? Were they the product of mere chance? Were they no more than educated guesses? Or, were they indicative of a supernatural knowledge of the future?

Were the Prophecies Composed after the Events Happened?

Here, one must face two competing philosophies. One, biased toward any supernatural intervention in human affairs, assumes that predictive prophecy is impossible and that any correlation between predictions and actual events can only be explained by having the material in question composed after the fact. Scholars supporting such a thesis do not object to portions of Ezekiel being written very early. They do argue that, much later, some unknown author or group of authors added the section containing the prophecies. Still, the superstructure of this philosophy is built on a foundational assumption that no supernatural prophecies could ever happen. Discussion of the failures of this philosophy are dealt with in detail in many other sources and is beyond the scope of this work. .

Absent a supernatural bias, no evidence supports the thesis that Ezekiel's predictions were penned later than 400 B.C.[54] Moreover, the book (Ezek. 1:1; 8:1; 33:1; 40:1-4) claims to have been composed by the prophet sometime in the sixth century, B.C.,[55] and Josephus attributes the book to the Hebrew prophet during the time in question.[56] The tremendous lack of consistency among critical studies has led many modern scholars to return to the original consensus that existed before this century: Ezekiel and his writings are products of the sixth century, B.C.[57]

Were the Fulfillments Merely the Result of Luck?

As to chance playing a major role in Ezekiel's success, the odds are hardly encouraging. Mathematicians who have calculated the possibilities conclude, "If Ezekiel had looked at Tyre in his day and had made these predictions in human wisdom. ... there would have been only one chance in 75,000,000 of their all coming true."[58] Chance seems an unlikely explanation. We must remember also that these odds merely apply to Ezekiel's predictions regarding Tyre. Hundreds of other fulfilled prophecies throughout Scripture push the odds far beyond acceptable limits.

Did Ezekiel Make a Series of Educated Guesses?

Again, the solution is strained. Tyre had consistently defended herself. Her defensive arrangements were both unique and superbly constructed. No city had ever been tossed into the ocean to make a highway to an island. Rebuilding a city was far more likely than not. No, it is unlikely that Ezekiel produced a superlative series of educated guesses.

Do the Fulfillments Suggest Supernatural Guidance?

The only remaining alternative implies the need for supernatural assistance. No, it is not required by the evidence, but unless one has a preconceived bias in opposition, it is more consistent with the evidence than its competing alternatives. That it is a strongly intuitive position is obvious considering the many attempts by critics to date Ezekiel's prophecies after-the-fact.

Edom in Prophecy:
Predicting the Decline
of the Merchants

Nestled among the rocky crags and scorpion-infested sands south of the Dead Sea lie the ghostly remains of the once-proud Edomite/ Nabataean nation.[1] Today, its wild, untamed appearance offers quick rebuttal to any claim that it was once home to a vibrant and prosperous nation. Yet, such a hasty judgment proves untenable.

Edom never became a military giant. Mention of her name in Babylon, Thebes, or Nineveh evoked neither fear nor concern. Nor were her neighbors apprehensive regarding their common borders with Edom. No evidence suggested that she craved the territory of others. Her agricultural production failed to match either Babylon or Egypt. Though hardly the Garden of Eden, the desert blossomed sufficiently to become one of Edom's jealously guarded possessions.[2] Realizing this, Moses based his plea for Israelite passage through the land on their trek from Egypt to Palestine on a promise to "not go through any field or vineyard, or drink water from any well" (Num. 20:17). He added, "We will travel along the king's highway and not turn to the right or to the left until we have passed through your territory."

Either Israel's "blood kin" did not believe the promise or they used that supposed disbelief as a ruse to mask other motives. Edom denied passage. "You may not pass through here; if you try, we will march out and attack you with the sword" (Num. 20:18). Rather than fight Esau's descendants, Israel circled eastward. The two nations became bitter enemies.

Reasons for Edom's Prestige in Antiquity

While Edom/Idumaea never attained wealth or fame from either her military or her agriculture, her geographical location brought both.[3] Through the region passed two important caravan routes. The first, a north-south route, meandered through rugged countryside from Egypt to Damascus and earned the reputation as the "King's Highway." The second, an east-west route, stretched from India to the Mediterranean and allowed the treasures of the east access to western merchants.

As the volume of trade proliferated, so did the riches and importance of Edom. She became a prominent locus of trade. Merchants from Phoenicia, Egypt, Greece, and India bartered and sold in her markets. Her location provided a natural resting place for weary caravans that plodded across the great deserts. She also offered a perfect haven from bandits and raiders who plundered caravans at every opportunity. Surprisingly, Edom also yielded a plentiful supply of water for thirsty travelers in an otherwise parched and sandy region.

Partly because of its isolation and rugged terrain, the region attained a significant degree of independence:

> It is a difficult area, not easily accessible, and its many crevices and natural strongholds provide excellent places of refuge for the population in time of emergency. A chain of fortresses on the fringe of the desert gave added protection. Thus in both early and later periods it enjoyed considerable strength and independence.[4]

Several Edomite/Nabataen cities flourished at various times in antiquity. Yet, only one could claim to be the hub of world commerce. A unique setting, encircled by deep-hued rock cliffs, located some fifty miles south of the Dead Sea gained that honor. The Greeks called the city Petra, "the rock."

Somewhere during the second millennium, B.C., Petra burst from obscurity to become the "center of the great caravan trade."[5] One authority on ancient commerce glowingly declared

> ... caravans ... from ... Arabia and from the Gulf of Persia, from Hadramaut on the ocean, and some even from Sabea or Yemen ... pointed to Petra as a common centre; and from Petra the trade seems again to have branched out in every direction, to Egypt, Palestine, and Syria through Arsinoe, Gaza, Tyre, Jerusalem, Damascus, and a variety of subordinate routes that terminated on the Mediterranean.[6]

The same writer reported, "Petra is ... considered ... by all geographers, historians, and poets, as the source of all the precious commodities of the east."[7] Another scholar claimed Chinese traders frequented Petra's markets and bazaars centuries before the time of Christ.[8] Petra epitomized ancient Edom/Nabatea. As Fry observed, Petra became "the greatest commercial empire of the ancient Near East."[9]

An Adequate Water Supply

Besides her central location, Petra also offered an abundant supply of water. That any water of significance could have been available in the region surprises those who view its barren landscapes today. Yet, scholars confirm that her "supply was beyond the wildest dreams of the most optimistic caravanner."[10] Not only was the region dotted with springs, but the inhabitants constructed ingenuous reservoirs and catchment basins to preserve whatever water fell during the rainy season.

Petra's artificial water containment procedures drew high commendations from historians. One wrote that her people's effort at

> ... water engineering was in fact their most remarkable achievement: their architecture is remarkable, their pottery exceptionally fine, but their techniques of collecting, distributing, and conserving water display outstanding ingenuity, skill, and imagination which even the Romans could not do better.[11]

A Protective Haven for Travelers

In addition, Petra offered unique protection from bands of robbers and brigands. When the caravans entered Petra, they knew they were safe. Petra was situated inside a large box canyon. In every direction, towering and rugged sandstone cliffs jut their ragged edges hundreds of feet skyward.

Entry into the city of Petra was through a narrow gorge (left). After traveling several hundred feet along the serpentine passage, the viewer catches his first glimpse of the awesome beauty of the "rose red city, half as old as time" when the "Treasury," popularized by the hit movie "Indiana Jones and the Last Crusade," comes into view between the rock massifs. (Photos courtesy, Mr. Lawrence Williams.)

Realistically, only one viable entrance opens into the city. That comes through a narrow opening in the eastern cliffs known as the Sik ("shaft").[12] This defile, seldom more than a few yards wide, twists like a serpent through approximately one mile of rocky massifs. On both sides, the sheer face of the rocky cliffs climb upward from one to 500 feet above the canyon floor. So imposing were these cliffs, and so treacherous was any other entrance, that travelers inside the city enjoyed a sense of security unparalleled elsewhere along the trade routes. As one author explains,

> Rocks on either side are so high and the passage is so narrow that a dozen men in ancient times could, without difficulty, have held at bay a whole army. ... Yet, it was through these same sinuous windings that the conquerors and caravans of antiquity, and the kings and queens of different nations once filed in stately, dignified procession.[13]

he one hundred thirty-foot ll "Treasury" is but one evience of the grandeur of ncient Edom and Nabataea. Photo courtesy, Fon cofield Collection, E. C. argan Research Library of ie Sunday School Board, BC.)

Petra's Grandiose Tombs

Riches poured into Edom. Her location astride the world's mercantile highways provided an opportunity for opulence seldom encountered, even in antiquity. As treasure swelled the city's coffers, the leading citizens became increasingly interested in preserving their fame. Their wealth assured, they began the arduous task of carving massive tombs from the cliffs that encompassed Petra. These tombs were to be their niche in history, a way of preserving their memory. Soon, monuments pocketed the cliffs. Some were magnificent, artistically-engraved edifices; others were more modest. All spoke of wealth and grandeur.

The most auspicious of the tombs was also the first to greet the traveler. After zig-zagging for several hundred yards between the cliffs and rounding a bend in the Sik, visitors came face-to-face with the fabled Khaznet Fir 'aun. This structure, a gigantic mortuary known as "The Treasury" and carved from the face of the cliffs, is so awesome and intimidating that it has served as the locale for many films, including the popular "Indiana Jones and the Last Crusade." When not the target of film directors, it has drawn the attention of many of the world's leading scholars. Robinson labels it, "the handsomest, the most majestic, and the most elaborately carved of all the ... monuments ... a miracle in the desert."[14] Few would disagree. It measures ninety-two feet wide and 130 feet high. The door stands twenty-six feet tall. Six columns, each over forty feet high, provide an allusion to Greek architecture. The first modern traveler to enter the city, exclaimed, "Great must have been the opulence of a city which could dedicate such ornaments to the memory of its rulers."[15]

Tombs, temples, shrines, altars, and public buildings appear throughout the box canyon and into the hills and wadis that surround it. Each serves as mute testimony to a once powerful and rich civilization. Robinson concludes,

> The monumental remains of Petra rank among the most remarkable in the world. Caves, graves, temples, altars, shrines and buildings have been carved from the richly colored sandstone rocks ... with such amazing cleverness, that visitors ... stand in awe and amazement at the uniqueness of the place.[16]

Edom's Predicted Doom

Petra and Edom once occupied positions of importance. They also incurred the biting condemnation of the Hebrew prophets: (1) Israel would eventually possess the land (Obad. 17); (2) Edom's curse would result from treacherous dealings with Israel during a time of great calamity (Obad. 10-14); (3) Her land and cities would become waste and desolate (Jer. 49:17); (4) Evidence of her rulers would vanish (Isa. 34:12); (5) Thorns and thistles would thrive in her ruined towns (Isa. 34:11-15); (6) Wild birds and animals would inhabit her dwellings (Isa.

34:11-15); and (7) Edom would cease as a nation (Obad. 10, 18). Considering the region's wealth and importance for traders of all nations, such prophecies offered a unique test for prophetic accuracy.

Predicting Israel's Possession of Edomite Land

During the days of the kings, Israel and Edom were bitter antagonists. Although Edom never totally surrendered her independence, Israel's powerful military presence dominated her neighbor (I Sam. 16:47; II Sam. 7:14; I Kings 11:14-15). During the reign of Jehoram (circa 850 B.C.), hostilities intensified. First one side, then the other, temporarily gained an advantage (II Kings 8:20; 14:7,22; II Chron. 25:11). Then, during the reign of Ahaz, Edom finally wrested total independence from the Jews (II Chron. 28:17ff).

During this period of independence, the prophets announced that Israel would once again possess the land that belonged to the Edomite people. Still, for the next six centuries, the Edomites and their Nabataen successors, retained sovereignty over the land. Not until the last third of the second century B.C. did Jewish forces, directed by John Hyrcanus, subjugate their southern neighbors.[17] At that time, the Jews compelled all Edomite/Nabataen males to submit to circumcision. The region continued under Jewish rule while her people were "merged into the Jewish state."[18] Jewish settlers quickly filtered into the region. The first prediction was fulfilled.

Prediction of "Treacherous Dealings" with Israel

That Edom should create problems for her neighbors comes as no surprise. The animosity and contempt between the two cultures finds ample documentation. So, when Obadiah (10-15) described Edomite treachery, few found his words unexpected.

Treachery in the Babylonian Period. Some scholars believe fulfillment came in 587 B.C. when Babylonian armies encircled Jerusalem. Others find the text to be so accurate in its description of the events, that the verses detailing the treachery are said to be the work of an eyewitness to the actual events.[19] It is, in fact, impossible to determine from the text itself which option is correct. However, for current apologetic purposes, neither becomes critical. Even should the book of Obadiah have been composed after the events of 586 B.C., even the most critical scholars would place its writing prior to the fourth century, B.C. Even at that late date, all but one of the predictions are still future.

But, for a moment, let us return to events surrounding Babylon's sacking of Jerusalem in 586 B.C. The biblical record indicates that

King Zedekiah and a portion of his army fled "under cover of darkness, only to be overtaken on the plains of Jericho. ... Evidently their hopes were dashed by roadblocks set up by the Edomites. They collaborated with the enemy, and simply handed back those who fell into their hands."[20]

Allen's assessment of those events echoes those of Myers,[21] Bright,[22] Dahood,[23] and others. Bartlett[24] disagrees, choosing to reject references to such treachery found in the Psalms (137:7) and Lamentations (4:21). However, Bartlett's position in this area is hardly as conclusive as he suggests.[25] As Coggins concludes, "there is clear evidence of hostility between Judah and Edom from the time of David ... right through the monarchical period."[26]

Moreover, archaeological evidence demonstrates increased military activity by Edom somewhere around the time of the Babylonian invasion. Areas of southern Judah and the Negev passed under Edomite control:

> From the Biblical evidence and the evidence from Qitmit, it may fairly be assumed that Edom invaded and conquered extensive territory that belonged to Judah in the eastern Negev some time near the fall of Jerusalem, either before or after, taking advantage of Judah's weakness. This Edomite invasion of the eastern Negev was a prelude to the further expansion of Edomite settlement into the Hebron highlands, the southern Shephelah and the northern Negev.[27]

Edomite Treachery in 70 A.D. Centuries later, with Israel writhing in a life and death struggle with Rome's powerful legions, another group of Edomites/Idumaens infiltrated Jerusalem. Once inside, their sanguinary behavior produced as much devastation as the Roman army.

Josephus claims as many as 20,000 Idumaeans led a murderous rampage. When the reign of terror subsided, 8,500 bodies filled the outer court of the temple.[28] Even these deaths failed to satisfy. The terrorists "plundered every house, and slew every one they met. ... (including) the high priests."[29] Before the violence subsided, 12,000 inhabitants lay dead in the streets.[30] Obadiah foretold Edomite treachery. Had Israel's leaders only believed his words, many lives might have been spared.

Predicting the Land's Desolation

Hebrew prophets harbored no illusion about Edom's future. No less than six proclaimed Edom's doom.[31] Isaiah (34:10) wrote, "From generation to generation it will lie desolate; No one will ever pass through it again." Jeremiah (49:18) added, "No one will live there; no man will dwell in it." "This is what the sovereign Lord says," Ezekiel (25:13) concluded. "I will lay it waste." Later, he added (35:7) God's final judgment: "I will make Mt. Seir a desolate waste and cut off from it all who come and go."

Petra's citizenry lived in "apartments" such as these that were hewn from the sides of the rock cliffs. (Photo courtesy, Dr. Marlin Connelly.)

While the physical dirt and rocks that formed the geographical features of ancient Edom remain where they have for centuries, the Edomite people and cities no longer exist. Yet, when the predictions came from the prophets, Edom was thickly populated. Towns and cities dotted her landscape. Great caravans plied her highways. As late as the time of the Herods, she could raise an army of 50,000.[32] Soon afterward, however, those towns and villages were deserted and the population disappeared.

The Gradual Nature of Edom's Demise. Desolation settled gradually over Edom and Idumaea, much like the dusk that creeps slowly over her deserts when the sun slips below the western horizon. Unlike Nineveh, no sudden plunge into obscurity awaited Edom. Jews and Arabs slowly meshed her people into their cultures until she became completely assimilated in other nations.

Before the desolation, Nabatean cities flourished in the region. Between the second century B.C. and the end of the second century A.D., city after city sprang into existence. The famed archaeologist Nelson Glueck excitedly described "a story-book people with almost magical accomplishments ... exciting architecture, and imaginative agriculture. ... The towers and temples they built or hewed out of solid rock, as well as their innumerable cisterns and reservoirs and terraces testify to their extraordinary adventures."³³ Prophecies about desolation must have been viewed as pipe-dreams.

Roman Control of Edom. No noticeable demise appeared even when Roman legions forcibly incorporated the region into the Empire during the second century A.D. On the surface, Edom continued to flourish. This time, the prosperity would not last; for, with Roman control, other interests always demanded more attention than the desert areas south of Jerusalem. Monies formerly expended on Edom trickled into other purses.

Besides Roman neglect, other factors contributed to a declining population. Increasing forays of desert marauders made life in border cities more and more difficult. Leaders in 4th, 5th and 6th century Christian communities, obsessed with opulent edifices and buildings, bled the people with exorbitant taxes to complete their building projects. Rather than pay high levies and risk pummeling by bands of brigands, caravanners diverted their trade routes away from Edom.

The Moslem Invasion. By the seventh century, the region was ripe for the picking. Moslem armies occupied the region. The darkness and obscurity predicted by the prophets became reality. As Glueck observed, "Commerce dwindled, agriculture declined, and the people of the land began ... to drift away and seek their livelihood elsewhere." Cities that depended on the caravans for their lifeblood ceased to exist. In less than a century, "a pall of abandonment enveloped" the region. ³⁴

For fully a thousand years, the land lay undisturbed, visited only by occasional troupes of bedouins. Desert sands drifted over the garden cities. Once mighty Petra, stung by the bite of those hot blowing sands and the seldom interrupted blazing sun, eroded in silence. The only caravans to enter were the imprecise flocks of the bedouin tribes and wild goats looking for water. Clatter and clamor gave way to silence and the screeches of wild birds of prey.

Burckhardt's Return to Edom. Not until the nineteenth century did a Westerner return to Petra and live to tell about his excursion. Then, John L. Burckhardt, a young adventurer disguised as a Moslem, gained access to the region. Hearing that a mysterious, yet foreboding, rock city existed in the desert near Mt. Hor, the ancient burial site of Aaron, Burckhardt determined to verify the rumors. Though the expedition was fraught with danger, Burckhardt's knowledge of Arabic, the Koran, and the Moslem culture, coupled with an ingenuous ruse of traveling to Mt. Hor to offer sacrifice served him well. He found the "rose red city that time forgot" and emerged from the wilderness to tell the world.

Of the area, he wrote that it "must once have been thickly inhabited; for the traces of many towns and villages are met with. ... (whereas) at present all this country is desert."[35] Cheered by Burckhardt's success, others embarked on similar missions. All expressed amazement at the wild, desolate nature of the region. All were struck by the unexpected ruins of once marvelous cities now reduced to ruins. Yet, Ezekiel's prophecy (35:4) specifically announced that God had decreed, "I will turn your towns into ruins and you will be desolate. Then you will know that I am the Lord." Later he added (35:9), "your towns will not be inhabited."

Another traveler, the Frenchman de Bertou, traversed the region some three decades after Burckhardt. He stood in bewilderment at the bleakness: "This solemn waste ... (is) destitute of vegetation and inhabitants ... (and) all around is enveloped in this silence of death."[36]

Predictions Regarding Bozrah

Bozrah felt the same sting of denunciation from the prophets as did the land as a whole. Jeremiah penned (49:13), "Bozrah will become a ruin and an object of horror, of reproach and of cursing; and all its towns will be in ruins forever." Amos added (1:12) that God would "send fire upon Teman that will consume the fortresses of Bozrah."

Though some controversy has arisen over the precise location of the Edomite city, most modern scholars locate it some eighteen miles southeast of the Dead Sea on a long east-west ridge surrounded by deep wadis. As Robinson notes, the city "was well fortified by nature."[37] Like Petra and the other Edomite cities, ancient Bozrah lies in ruins. Robinson's terse comments hauntingly describe the region: "All along the ridge are scattered ruins of former greatness. ... Of all the places in Palestine, Syria, and the Desert which I have ever visited Bozrah is the most miserable, wretched, abject."[38]

One amazing sidelight demands closer scrutiny. Not only did the prophets correctly predict the desolation, they also delineated its extent. Ezekiel (25:13) identified the area as stretching from Teman to Dedan. Astoundingly, when Burckhardt entered the region in 1812, he reported, "Maan (Teman) is the only inhabited" city in the land.[39] Of all the ancient cities of Edom and Idumaea, only one, Teman, remains. Is it merely coincidence that it is the one city Ezekiel implies would not be destroyed?

Predictions Regarding Edom's Rulers

Petra's nobility and rulers seemed determined to preserve their names for posterity. Pretentious tombs emerged from the rock massifs at Petra.

Edomite/Nabatean rulers wanted to be remembered for their accomplishments. Isaiah's prophecy (34:12) vetoed those desires: "Her nobles will have nothing there to be called a kingdom." he wrote. "All her princes will vanish away."

When Western observers, adventurers, and scientists squeezed into Petra and Edom in the early nineteenth century, they found only the shells of tombs that had once held the remains of the region's rulers. Nothing was inside the tombs. Also, the effacing winds and desert sun had, over a thousand years, silently obliterated any names that might have been carved in the soft sandstone. Even the graves do not defy the prophecies. No nobles (or their remains) are to be found.

Predictions Regarding the Remaining Buildings

Isaiah's predictions also included the houses and public buildings. They would stand as a mute testimony to the fulfillment of his prophecies:

> The desert owl and the screech owl will possess it; the great owl and the raven will nest there. God will stretch out over Edom the measuring line of chaos and the plumb line of desolation. ... Thorns will overrun her citadels, nettles and brambles her strongholds. She will become a haunt for jackals, a home for owls. Desert creatures will meet with hyenas, and wild goats will bleat to each other; there the night creatures will also repose and find for themselves places of rest. ... there also the falcons will gather, each with its mate. Look in the scroll of the Lord and read: None of these will be missing (Isa. 34:11, 13-16).

Written records of visitors to the region confirm the prophecies. Petra, specifically, teemed with inhospitable creatures. John Wilson, who visited the city in the 1840s, explained,

> The creeping things which are found in the ruins of Petra are so numerous that (it) ... may be characteristically spoken of as "an habitation for dragons." The Fellahin, in a space of a few minutes, caught for us ... scores of lizards, chameleons, centipedes, and scorpions. (Petra) literally swarms with them.[40]

The same writer later added, "Among the birds which we noticed, or which the Fellahin told us are to be found there ... are the eagle, cssifrage, kite, hawk, great owl, small owl, and raven."[41]

Two English naval officers, Captains Irby and Mangles, spent two evenings inside Petra during the mid-nineteenth century. During their stay, a variety of birds of prey circled in the skies overhead. In their diary they noted the "eagles, hawks, and owls who were soaring above ... (their) heads in considerable numbers, (and) were seemingly annoyed at our approaching their lonely habitation."[42]

Other wild animals make their homes throughout the cliffs of Petra and the remainder of ancient Edom. Among those described by John Wilson as living in Petra's houses are "the wild goat, the wild boar ... the fox, wolf, jackal, hyena, lynx, leopard, and lion."[43] Lions, though not native to the region, were transported to Edom during the reign of the Emperor Decius. Decius was concerned by the increasing intrusion of the Saracens in the region and believed the lions would help serve as a natural barrier between the invaders and his armies.

Predicting the Extinction of the Edomite Nation

Obadiah (10,18) leveled one final burden: "Because of the violence against your brother Jacob, you will be covered with shame; you will be destroyed forever. ... There will be no survivors from the house of Esau." For well over a thousand years, the Edomites and their Nabatean cousins occupied regions south of Israel. They existed as an opulent, commercial people, well-known throughout the Roman world and to the borders of the Orient. Still, by the third century A.D., their national existence slowly slipped into the mists of eternity. McClintock and Strong observe, "From the ... overthrow of the Jewish nation (70 A.D.), the name of Idumaea no longer occurs but passes away in the wider denomination Arabia."[44] Other nationalities survived. Edom and Nabataea did not.

Moab and Ammon in Prophecy: Predicting the Ruin of Israel's Enemies

When the growing nation of Israel edged northward out of the Sinai in the last half of the second millennium B.C., opponents of the fledgling nation quickly barred their way. Their opposition led to a long series of protracted conflicts that hounded Israel until the crushing defeat by the Roman dreadnought in 70 A.D. While many tribes and nations played roles in the ensuing confrontations, Ammon and Moab assumed the role of two of the more prominent actors. Situated on Israel's southern and eastern borders, they often harassed her with violent forays into her territory and pressed the citizens of her border towns into slavery. Far more often than the military challenges, Israel's neighbors tempted her with moral and ethical incursions. These incursions, rather than the military ones, drew the invectives from the biblical prophets.

The Nation of Ammon and the Biblical Prophets

Ammon's Relation to Israel

Ammon traced her ancestry to Lot, the nephew of Abraham (Gen. 19:38). That made the Ammonites distant relatives of their new neighbors. Unfortunately, rather than provide for a harmonious relationship, their kinship provoked bitter hostility. Like Edom, Ammon denied Israel the right to pass through Ammonite lands as the Israelites plodded toward Palestine. They even hired the prophet Balaam to pronounce a curse on their wandering relatives (Deut. 23:3-6). Later during the days of the judges (Judg. 10), Saul (I Sam. 11:1-11), David (II Sam. 10; I Chron. 19), Jehoshaphat (II Chron. 20:1-30), Joash (II Chron. 24:26), Jehoiakim (II Kings 24:2), and Nehemiah (2:10,19; 4:3,7), they challenged Israel militarily. Ammonite armies crossed Israel's borders, won several skirmishes, and enslaved portions of Israel's population.

Cause for the Feud between Ammon and Israel

To some degree, this constant animosity stemmed from conflicting claims over land. Ammon and Moab claimed the eastern bank of the Jordan from the Dead Sea northward to the Jabbok River as their own. Yet, they lacked the strength to back their claims, and when Israel returned from Egyptian enslavement, Joshua found the area inhabited by another group known as the Amorites (Num. 21:13). Israel defeated the Amorites and began to settle the land. At this point, Ammon reinstated her claim to the land. That claim became a continual irritant.

A Physical Description of Ammon

Without the western lands contested by Israel, Ammon became relatively large and populous. The Ammonite capital, known in Old Testament days as Rabbah and in modern times as Amman, stood on both sides of the Jabbok, and earned the label the "city of waters." In later years, Ptolemy Philadelphus changed the city's name to Philadelphia and it grew to be one of the celebrated Roman cities of the Decapolis. Her rich soil and fertile agricultural setting earned her widespread notoriety in the ancient world.[1] The Bible (II Chron. 27:5) notes the extraordinarily large tribute of corn levied on the Ammonites during the reign of Jotham.

Roman ruins at Jerash (Gerasa) were so impressive that the much earlier ruins of an Ammonite city were overlooked. Biblical predictions regarding the disappearance of the Ammonites are explicit. (Photo courtesy, Dr. Marlin Connelly.)

Predictions Regarding Ammon

Prophecies directed at Ammon by biblical prophets are simple and straightforward: (1) Foreigners from the east will possess the land (Ezek. 25:4); (2) Rabbah will be destroyed (Jer. 49:2); (3) Rabbah will become a "pasture for camels and a resting place for sheep" (Ezek. 25:5); and (4) Ammon will cease to exist as a nation and a people (Ezek. 25:7).

Foreigners From the East to Possess the Land

Although Ezekiel chides Ammon for her glee when the Babylonian armies plundered Israel, Ammon seems to have suffered a similar fate. Under the iron rule of Nebuchadnezzar, the country shriveled from a populous citadel in the desert to a mere fragment of her original size and beauty. The decimation of her population centers also left her vulnerable to roving bands of desert marauders who swept in from the eastern deserts to plunder and pillage. So devastating was the combined effect of Babylon's armies and the brigands from the desert that Thompson claims the land's "occupation was interrupted by the Babylonian campaigns of the 6th century B.C. and did not resume until the 3rd century. Bedouin groups occupied the country."[2]

Beginning with the Tobiads in the third century B.C., Ammon rebounded to become, again, a significant and populous nation. Likewise, hostilities between Ammon and the Israelite "remnant" that returned from captivity in Babylon intensified. Tobiah, an influential Ammonite, led opposition to the restoration of Jerusalem (Neh. 2:10,19), and Judas Maccabaeus fought against the Ammonites in the second century B.C. (I Mac. 5:6).

Ammon's rebirth proved short-lived. Soon after the period of the Maccabees, strangers from the "east" again dominated her lands. The final devastation came from Moslem armies in the seventh century A.D. Again, the invaders came from the east. This time, the blow was fatal. With the Moslem takeover, the land quickly descended into an ever-deepening desolation. It lasted nearly twelve centuries. When the region's resettlement began at the onset of the twentieth century, the land's rulers hailed from "the east" again. Emir Abdullah, ruler of the Transjordan, built his palace at Rabbah.[3]

Destruction of Rabbah

Rabbah-Ammon served as the hub of the Ammonite nation. Situated some twenty miles east of the Jordan Valley, the city enjoyed a long and generally peaceful history. Twice the city submitted to opposing forces.

During the reign of David, Israelite forces under Joab captured the city (II Sam. 12:27). A half-millennium later, Nebuchadnezzar's forces repeated the conquest.[4] The latter defeat proved especially devastating. The city vanished from public records for more than two centuries. Though some suggest that the city lay totally uninhabited during this period, most scholars find the evidence to be too circumstantial to draw any firm conclusion. If this was the period of desolation described by the prophets, there is no way to prove it so based on the evidence currently available.

A second option more clearly fits the prediction. After Ptolemy Philadelphus rebuilt the city in the third century B.C., it remained a viable, thriving city until the Moslem invasion in 635 A.D. With that conquest, the city began a headlong slide into oblivion. By the middle ages, the population had all but disappeared. Centuries afterward, when Western travelers again traversed the region, they unanimously describe a region almost totally desolate.

Seetzen and Burckhardt were among the earliest adventurers to reach the site in modern times. Seetzen noted that the entire region lay "uninhabited, being abandoned to ... wandering Arabs, and the towns and villages are in a state of total ruin." Speaking specifically of Rabbah, he added, "Although this town has been destroyed and deserted for many ages, I still found there some remarkable ruins, which attest its ancient splendor."[5] Burckhardt, also, described the site as "covered with ruins of private buildings, nothing of them remaining except the foundations and some door-posts. The buildings ... are all in decay."[6] The desolation spoken of by the biblical prophets had become reality.

Today, modern Amman has again risen from the ruins. Its population swollen by Palestinian refugees, Amman is now home to hundreds of thousands of people. With its bulging neighborhoods and teeming markets, it would be easy to forget that, for over a millennium, its environs bore the burden of God's curse.

Rabbah to be a Place for Camels and Flocks

Early travelers to ancient Rabbah pack their writings with descriptions that confirm the accuracy of even the minutiae of biblical prophecies. One writer explained that, while making measurements of the ruins at Rabbah, "the number of goats and sheep which were driven in ... was exceedingly annoying."[7] Another noted that the entire area was

> ... one of vast pasturage, overspread with the flocks and herds of the Bedouins. The dreariness of its present aspect is quite indescribable, it looks like the abode of death, the valley stinks with dead camels ... (while) the ruins ... were absolutely covered in every direction with their dung. ...

Bones and skulls of camels were mouldering in the area of the theatre. ... Ammon is now quite deserted, except by the Bedouins, who water their flocks at the little river. We met sheep and goats by the thousands, and camels by the hundreds, coming down to drink.[8]

The Vanishing Ammonites

Finally, biblical prophets predicted that Ammon, as a distinct nation, would cease to exist. That, too, has found fulfillment. Current inhabitants trace their ancestry through Bedouins, Arabians, or Cicassians.[9] The Ammonites no longer exist. Yet, despite savage wars, forced dispersals, and slavery, their blood-enemies, the Jews, survive. Ezekiel (25:2-3,7) foretold it centuries before Jesus when he claimed the Lord told him, "Son of Man, set your face against the Ammonites and prophesy against them. Say to them ... I will cut you off from the nations and exterminate you from the countries."

The Nation of Moab and the Biblical Prophets

A Geographical Description of Moab

Immediately east of the southern end of the Salt Sea and immediately south of lands occupied by the tribes of Reuben and Gad in Transjordan, lay the small kingdom of Moab. At most, her boundaries stretched no more than forty miles in any direction. The imposing Syrian desert served as Moab's eastern border. The Salt Sea and then the Arabah comprised her western boundary. To the north, the Arnon gorge provided an effective physical border although, at times, Moab pushed her land claims farther north toward Heshbon. The Zered canyon separated Moab from Edom to the south. Physically, the region boasts a unique blend of deep, winding valleys and gently rolling farmland:

> The terrain of Moab may be described as gently rolling tableland, but numerous streams drain the plateau and have cut deep ravines that open into the Dead Sea valley. ... Moab has always been famous for its pasturage (cf. 2 Kgs. 3:4), but its soils and climate also allow for the growing of wheat and barley.[10]

Hostility between Moab and Israel

Like Ammon, Moab traced her ancestry through Lot (Gen. 19:37). Like Ammon, she proved an inhospitable relative and neighbor. The Moabite king Balak pleaded with, and finally bribed, Balaam to pronounce a curse on the young nation (Num. 22:24). Eglon, another Moabite king, organized an oppressive invasion of the southern part of the land (Judg. 3:13-14). Moab joined Ammon in declaring open warfare on Israel during the reign of Jehoshaphat (II Chron. 20). They led yet another raid when Judah found herself engaged in a military confrontation with Syria (II Kings 13:20).

Predictions Regarding Moab and Her People

Because of the caustic, and often violent, rivalry, references to Moab appear extensively throughout the prophetic writings. We are told that: (1) Moabite cities "will be laid waste; her towns will become desolate with no one to live in them" (Jer. 48:9); (2) Moab's production of wine will cease (Isa. 16:10) and others will control her agricultural riches (Jer. 48:32-33); (3) flocks, rather than people, will live in her ruined cities (Jer. 17:2); and (4) "Moab will be destroyed as a nation because she defied the Lord" (Jer. 48:42).

The predicted destruction of Moabite cities is confirmed by these ruins from the ancient city of Dibon. (Photo courtesy, Fon Scofield Collection, E. C. Dargan Research Library of the Sunday School Board, SBC.)

The Destruction of Moab's Cities. Abundant evidence documents the destruction of Moabite cities. Seetzen, Burckhardt, and Irby and Mangles chronicled the complete desolation they found when they visited the area in the nineteenth century. Burckhardt's journey carried him by the ruins of almost fifty cities.[11] Seetzen's more extensive travels revealed many ruins and only one inhabited village.[12] Both described a chilly shroud of desolation that engulfed all of ancient Moab.

The sites of Moabite cities such as Aroer, Bethgamul, Bethmeon, Dibon, Elealeh, Heshbon, Kerioth, Kiriathiam, and Medaba are well known in archaeological circles.[13] Ruins at each are considerable. Those at the ancient city of Bethgamul (Um el Jemal) serve as a typical example of fulfillment. An early traveler at the site expressed the seeming futility of the scene before him:

> I had before me an enormous city, standing alone in the desert. ... the most perfect of the old cities which I saw. It is surrounded by a high wall ... which seems to enclose more space than the modern Jerusalem. The streets are ... paved; and I saw here, what I do not think I saw anywhere else, open spaces within the city, such as we should call squares. There are some very large public buildings ... some of the houses were very large. ... On reaching this city, I ... wandered about quite alone in the old streets of the town ... entered the old houses. ... I almost fancied I was in a dream, wandering alone in this city of the dead, seeing all ... but not hearing a sound. There are enormous reservoirs here, but, like those in all the other towns about here, quite dry.[14]

Graham's last phrase brings to mind yet another of Jeremiah's predictions (48:34): "even the waters of Nimrim are dried up." His plaintive cry (48:21,24) that "judgment has come to the plateau ... to all the towns of Moab, far and near" has seen its fulfillment.

The Decline of Moab's Wine-Making Industry. As visitors learned from the Arab historians, the region of Moab

> ... was once rich in vines, and travelers of the present day can see how admirably adapted are the gentle slopes of the mountains, and the sunny plains along their base, for the growth of the vine and the fig. ... (Yet, the) fields, vineyards, pastures, villages, (and) cities (are) all ... deserted.[15]

Like Porter's description, other Westerners entering the region in the 1800s described an amazing incongruity. Burckhardt expressed amazement at the richness of the soil, yet remained perplexed as to why it was not tilled. Upon inquiring of the locals, he learned that cultivation was limited because the people felt "unable to secure the harvest against the incursions of enemies."[16] Even that observation echoed another of Jeremiah's predictions that foreigners would "empty her jars" (48:12) and "the destroyer has fallen on your ripened fruit and grapes" (48:32).

Porter's observations confirmed those of Burckhardt. He noted that "the few inhabitants ... drag out a miserable existence, oppressed by the robbers of the desert on the one hand, and the still more formidable robbers of the government on the other."[17] Even Volney, an outspoken opponent of Christianity and Theism, admitted, "the wretched peasants

live in perpetual dread of losing the fruit of their labors." He concluded
that when the peasants did manage to harvest crops they immediately
"retire among the rocks which border on the Dead Sea."[18] Volney's
description calls to mind another phrase from Jeremiah's prophetic treasure chest (48:28): "Abandon your towns and dwell among the rocks,
you who live in Moab." Seetzen, also, recorded that many families in the
region lived in caves. He called them "inhabitants of the rocks."[19]
Finally, Irby and Mangles in their observations near the site of ancient
Heshbon found there "many artificial caves in ... perpendicular cliffs"
laden with "chambers and small sleeping compartments."[20]

Moab Will be Filled with Flocks. Every early traveler to the region left
detailed descriptions of the Bedouin wanderers and their flocks and herds.
Reading any account will quickly document the accuracy of the prediction.

The Loss of Moab's National Identity, "Moab will be destroyed as a
nation," Jeremiah wrote (48:42). Today, no group of people caring the
name "Moabite" exists. Moab's end began with the Babylonian conquest
around 582 B.C.[21] Van Zyl writes,

> Nebuchadnessar marched against the Ammonites and the Moabites and
> defeated them in his 23rd year, i.e. in 582 B.C.. Some of them were carried
> off to Babylonia into exile, while others fled to Egypt, where they earned a
> living as hirelings. The voice of the Moabite nation was thus silenced; the
> impregnable fortress was conquered, and its walls were thrown down into
> the dust. The fate of Moab was severe. When the power of the state had
> once been broken by the Babylonians, the children of the East could
> encroach upon the cultivated land, for the former inhabitants of the line of
> fortresses, who had so boldly defended their country during the past cen-
> turies, had been abducted.[22]

Though scattered references persist for the next two to three hundred
years, the nation-state of Moab had been effectively dissolved. Even if
scattered remnants remained, they, too, lost their identity in the centuries
just prior to the Christian era when they were overrun and encompassed
by the Nabataeans.[23]

So ends the stories of Ammon and Moab. Their stories were real.
Their future had been foretold.

Predicting the Messiah's Arrival

Our world seethes with violence, abuse, pain, and selfishness. Despots, dictators, thieves, murderers, and liars monopolize its history. Blood from needless conflicts saturates its soil. Cannons, citadels, and cemeteries clutter its landscapes, mute testimonies to our obsession with the hounds of war. Poverty and hunger gnaw at our consciences. Cities and towns teem with lonely people. It is understandable why, for many, life becomes almost unbearable.

Perhaps that's why humanity desires to "get away from it all," to uncover some method or person capable of ending the ugliness pervading the globe. Perhaps that's why the elusive anticipation of a "savior," a "messiah," or a "benevolent ruler" danced through humanity's dreams during pre-New Testament times. In ancient societies, hope for a new world order centered on some superhuman, some great earthly ruler or leader capable of rectifying humanity's problems and ushering in an age of peace and justice. In more contemporary times, the search has shifted to science and education. The goal hasn't changed, only the anticipated manner in which it might be achieved.

The Expected Messiah

We should not be surprised that the world of the Old Testament prophets blossomed with expectations of a deliverer who would bring peace and tranquility. The same dream unfolded among Zoroastrians who spoke of a coming period of peace to be ushered in by one who would "judge the living and the dead, give new glory to the earth, and remove from a world of sorrows the germ of evil."[1] In addition, Babylonian, Egyptian, and Indian writings also glanced idyllically forward to a golden age that would supplant the evils of the current period. Nearly every culture nourished the hope of a better life to come. Even the Greeks, known for their orientation toward the present, philosophized about a golden age.[2]

Within this expectant atmosphere, a concerted symphony of voices directed antiquity's attention toward Palestine. The notion that a new ruler would appear in that region, during the Roman Empire, permeated the Western world.

Two of antiquity's more respected writers furnish the documentation. Suetonius observes, "There had spread all over the East an old and established belief that it was fated for men coming from Judaea at that time to rule the world."[3] Likewise, Tacitus records that the belief that a ruler of the world would emerge from the region was widespread throughout the known world. He admitted that "many persons entertained (that) persuasion."[4]

Nowhere were the expectations more impassioned than within the Jewish community. Until the discovery of the fabled Dead Sea Scrolls in 1947, it is unlikely modern scholars appreciated the scope of those expectations. Yet, in caves surrounding Qumran, manuscripts and fragments of manuscripts sketch a vivid picture of an anticipated deliverer or deliverers. A portion of one manuscript found in Cave IV at Qumran distinctly associated Isaiah 11:1 with a descendant of David "who is to arise in the latter days" to establish a worldwide kingdom.[5] Other manuscripts from the same cave also describe a future Messiah.[6] Coupled with information gleaned from other witnesses, it is obvious that the anticipation of some type of deliverer permeated the thinking of the day.

To say a "deliverer" was expected is not to say that a person like Jesus of Nazareth was expected. Even the Scriptures clearly teach he did not conform to the expected mold. Though more will be said in the following chapter, Fredriksen's observation of the reaction to Jesus by the Jewish leadership provides an apt summary of their bewilderment: "His opponents are merely baffled. They constantly ask him, 'where are you from?' and 'where are you going?' and inevitably they misunderstand the answer."[7]

Jesus' Claim to Fulfill the Messianic Prophecies

Within this milieu, Jesus of Nazareth is born, lives, and dies. In the region where the deliverer was expected and at the time suggested by the predictions, he makes his appearance. Both he and his followers declare that he is the long-promised deliverer. "Do not think that I am come to destroy the law, or the prophets," he says. "I have not come to destroy, but to fulfill" (Matt. 5:17). When confronting his enemies, he appeals to the prophecies: "Search the scriptures, for in them you think you have eternal life. And these are they which testify of me" (John 5:39). In the synagogue at Nazareth, he risks death by reading from

Isaiah's prophecies and declaring, "This day is this scripture fulfilled in your ears" (Luke 4:21).

Similarly, Jesus' disciples argue that events in the life of their master had been described aforetime in the prophetic writings. Matthew (2:4-6), Luke (Acts 3:18; 10:43; 13:29), Paul (Rom. 1:2; I Cor. 15:3-4), and Peter (I Pet. 2:5-6) all emphasize that Jesus fulfilled numerous Old Testament prophecies. They contend that he was the Messiah so long anticipated by their people. Moreover, they placed their lives on the line in order to spread their beliefs. Such claims deserve careful examination.

An Overview of the Messianic Prophecies

Analyzing the proposed references to the Messiah drawn from the Old Testament Scriptures is similar to observing a great artist compose a masterpiece. The first strokes are large, undifferentiated, and difficult to interpret. As time passes, however, a pattern becomes increasingly apparent. So it is with the evolving depiction of the Messiah found in the Old Testament prophets. Like master painters dipping their brushes in the hues of future events, these prophets produced an amazingly intricate portrait of the coming Messiah.

Though scattered tints were already in place, Isaiah (9:1-7) sketched the first detailed outline of the God-ordained deliverer. His particulars were extraordinary. To Moses' nebulous grays heralding a future victory of the "seed of the woman" over the "serpent" (Gen. 3:15), Isaiah added the bright pastels of "the virgin birth" (Isa. 7:14). He tempered the scarlets of Davidic royalty (Psa. 68; Psa. 72) with the depressing blues of the "suffering servant" (Isa. 53). Green hues, indicative of a new life, burst from his descriptions of "new heavens" and a "new earth" (Isa. 6). He even anticipated Daniel's plaintive hope for restoration (Dan. 7, 9).

Brush strokes from other prophets (Jeremiah, Daniel, Zechariah, et al.) add finishing touches to a comprehensive picture of the future ruler. The resulting mosaic became an astonishingly rich composite. Admittedly, some prophetic strokes are barely distinguishable. Others stand out in bold relief. Even scholars cannot be certain they have correctly isolated each reference to the coming Messiah.

At one end of the spectrum stands the venerable and meticulous 19th century scholar Alfred Edersheim. After seven years of exhaustive research, he published his acclaimed two-volume work, *The Life and Times of Jesus the Messiah*. Using his Jewish background as a foundation, Edersheim cataloged 456 references from the Old Testament that early rabbinical sources labeled as "Messianic."[8] Other writers concurred, in general, if not with Edersheim's exact figure. Pierson, while not claiming his list to be complete, identified more than 300 predictions regarding the Messiah taken from the Old Testament.[9] Likewise, without claiming an encyclopedic listing, James E. Smith itemized 72 prophecies he claimed were fulfilled by Jesus of Nazareth.[10] J. Barton Payne of Covenant Theological Seminary listed 127 predictions, drawn from approximately 3,000 verses of scripture, as future references to the Messiah.[11]

Regardless of the exact number, one can safely conclude that (1) scores of Old Testament statements describe a coming ruler/deliverer/priest, and that (2) those statements were articulated well before the birth of Christ. Obviously the non-encyclopedic nature of this work precludes an in-depth evaluation of each prediction. Instead, we will focus on only three areas: (1) the time frame for the expected appearance of the Messiah; (2) the unique features of the Messiah's life that would be difficult to predict in advance; and (3) the references to his death, burial, and resurrection.

Predictions Regarding the Time of the Messiah's Coming

At least four Old Testament references insinuate the time when the Messiah would appear. The patriarch Jacob furnished the earliest clue while bestowing the familial blessing on his twelve sons. Of Judah, he predicted, "The scepter shall not depart from Judah, nor a lawgiver from between his feet, until Shiloh come" (Gen. 49:10). Should this be Messianic, and many deny it, the reference would make sense only after the events occurred. On the other hand, dual predictions in the book of Daniel are more easily understood. The first (Dan. 2:44) set the Messiah's appearance during the days of the Roman Empire. The second (Dan. 9:24-27) predicted the Messiah's death would occur a precise number of years after a decree ordering the rebuilding of Jerusalem was issued. Malachi (3:1), last of the canonical prophets in the Old Testament period, added another indicator: the second temple would still be standing when the Messiah entered Jerusalem. With Malachi's prediction in place, the parameters for the Messiah's coming may now be carefully evaluated.

Implications of Genesis 49:10: Is 'Shiloh' the Messiah?

In regard to Genesis 49, one must first determine if sufficient proof supports the claim that "Shiloh" alludes to the Messiah. Prior to advancing such proof, we must realize that Old Testament Scripture applies a bewildering array of terms to the personification of the Messianic dream. Isaiah alone orchestrates a symphony of names by which the Messiah would be known: "Wonderful" (9:6), "Counselor" (9:6), "Prince of Peace" (9:6), "Branch" (4:2, see also Zech. 6:12), and "Immanuel" (7:14 and 8:8). Jeremiah (30:21) and Zechariah (9:7) name him "governor." Jeremiah also calls him "King" (23:5) and "The Lord our Righteousness" (23:6). The Psalmist (2:2) refers to him as God's "anointed." Daniel labels him "Son of Man" (8:17). Given this rich diversity of nomenclature, it would certainly be in character for the Scriptures to apply the term "Shiloh" to the Messiah as well. But, does evidence actually connect the two? The answer is "yes."

Evidence from Early Jewish Sources. Ancient Jewish sources affirm that the term "Shiloh" in Genesis 49 refers to the Messiah. Edersheim marshals support for this position from several venerable authorities. He writes, "... the Targum Onkelos, Pseudo-Jonathan, and the Jerusalem Targum, as well as Sanh. 98b, the Midrash on the passage, and that on Prov. xix.21, and on Lam. i.16 ... refer the expression ... to the Messiah."[12] The Targumin are very old Aramaic paraphrases of the Hebrew Bible. Although the Targumin were composed after the time of Christ, it is highly unlikely that these doctrinaire Jewish sources would have adopted Christian interpretations of prophecy unless the passages in question attained that status much earlier in history.

Specifically, Targum Jonathan on Genesis 49:10 claims that "rulers from the house of Jehuda, nor sopherim teaching the Law from his seed (shall not cease) till the time that the King, the Meshiha shall come."[13] In a similar vein, Targum Pseudo-Jonathan on Genesis 49:11 adds, "How noble is the King, Messiah, who is going to rise from the House of Judah."[14]

On the basis of such references, many scholars ascribe the term "Shiloh" to the predicted Messiah. McDowell writes, "... for centuries Jewish and Christian commentators alike have taken the word ... to be a name of the Messiah."[15] Leupold concurs by noting that all references "... from the days of the Septuagint onward felt very strongly the Messianic interpretations."[16]

Evidence from Qumran. That a Messianic interpretation was applied to the verse prior to the first century is authenticated, once again, by material drawn from the Dead Sea Scrolls. Among the earliest manuscripts to be translated was a fragment discovered in Cave IV at Qumran and known as Patriarchal Blessings. The paraphrase, as given by Bruce[17] reads,

> A ruler shall not depart from the tribe of Judah—When dominion comes for Israel [there shall never] fail an enthroned one therein for David. For the "ruler's staff" is the covenant of kingship, and the "feet" are the families of Israel.

Until he come who is the rightful Messiah, the shoot of David, for to him and to his descendants has been given the covenant of kingship over his people for everlasting generations.

Bruce concludes, "What is of chief importance is that Jacob's blessing of Judah is here regarded as a prediction of the coming of the Davidic Messiah."[18] Moreover, recent Carbon-14 tests on the fragments confirm the pre-Christian origin of the materials. Van Groningen's comments provide an apt summary:

> ... prior to Christ's ministry on earth ... Jewish scholars ... pointed to the personal Messiah concerning whom Jacob spoke. It is quite apparent that over the centuries Jewish scholars have become hesitant to grant that this prophecy refers to a Jewish kingdom for that opens the door to the idea of the personal Messiah.[19]

Evidence from Translators. Translators of respected versions such as the KJV, NKJV, ASV, and NASV recognize the Hebrew as a proper noun. Even the NIV which follows a somewhat different translation recognizes the older rendering in a footnote. Moreover, the NIV, rather than calling the Messianic interpretation into question, actually furthers the validity of the doctrine by reading, "The scepter will not depart from Judah, nor the ruler's staff from between his feet, until he comes to whom it belongs." Van Groningen's comprehensive discussion of the phrase leaves little question that a person is under consideration here:

> The subject of the verb yabo' (comes) is in the third person singular. In Hebrew sentence structure, the subject usually follows the verb; hence in the phrase, siloh would be considered the subject. The phrase would then mean that Judah would exercise royalty until siloh takes over.[20]

Evidence from the Wording. The passage also contains definite wording to suggest the fulfillment will occur much later. Again, Van Groningen's comments are apropos:

> The prophecy of Jacob concerning his twelve sons has some definite eschatological features. It is introduced by the familiar Old Testament phrase used repeatedly to introduce eschatological concepts. Jacob is said to have called his sons around his deathbed, so that he could tell them what was to take place "in the last days" (be aharit hayyamim). Thus, by a very specific introduction (Gen. 49:1b), the address was placed in an eschatological setting. Jacob spoke about future developments in the lives of his sons, most distinctly in respect to Judah.[21]

The phrase, "in the last days," as used in the Old Testament, generally speaks of the time when the Jewish kingdom would be judged by God and replaced with a new kingdom and covenant.[22] If true, Jacob then places the coming of the royal leader at a time customarily accepted by scholars as those years prior to Rome's obliteration of Jerusalem in 70 A.D.

Genesis 49:10 and Messianic Time Frames

Assuming Gen. 49 refers to the Messiah, it can be of immense assistance in setting the time parameters for his appearance, and so the reading, "The scepter shall not depart from Judah, nor a ruler's staff from between his feet UNTIL Shiloh (the Messiah) comes." The opening portion of the verse reads that Judah will not lose her tribal identity ("scepter") until the arrival of the Messiah,[23] while the latter part of the verse implies that Judah's ability to rule herself ("the lawgiver") will remain intact until the appearance of the Messiah.[24]

Both sections fit nicely with events in first-century Palestine. From the time Jacob pronounced his blessing until the destruction of the Jewish civil state by Rome, Judah did not relinquish her tribal identity. Extensive genealogical records permitted the citizenry to trace and verify their direct relationship to the patriarch. During the decimation of 70 A.D., those records were destroyed, presumably the victim of huge fires set after the city's capture. With the loss of these key records, the ability of Judah's descendants to trace their tribal lineage was wrestled forever from their grasp.

Moreover, from the time Judah entered Canaan until the first century A.D., her people retained the ability to formulate their own laws. Even during Babylonian servitude, they were not denied the right to determine their own laws or to select their own officials. It was not until the first century that these rights were first denied. Initial limitations were imposed in 11 A.D. when Rome deposed Archelaus and inserted her own officials in what previously had been Jewish civil positions. Rome also reserved to herself the sole right of administering capital punishment. That these intrusions were widely recognized at the time as relating to Jacob's blessing can be seen in the lament of Rabbi Rachmon who wrote,

> When the members of the Sanhedrin found themselves deprived of their right over life and death, a general consternation took possession of them; they covered their heads with ashes, and their bodies with sackcloth, exclaiming: "Woe unto us, for the scepter has departed from Judah, and the Messiah has not come."[25]

Josephus, writing of the same period, complains that even the Sanhedrin itself was not allowed to meet without express Roman authority.[26]

Thus, the Jews lost both the "scepter" and the ability to make their own laws hundreds of years after Jacob's blessings were offered. Could it be just a coincidence, that after such a protracted wait, both events transpired in the tiny little nation of Palestine in perfect harmony with the arrival of Jesus of Nazareth. I think not.

Daniel's Messiah: Setting Parameters for His Arrival

One widely-known prediction isolating the time when the Messiah should be expected appears in Daniel 2. Babylon's King Nebuchadnezzar visualized a colossus rising ominously from the desert sands. A head of gold crowned the image. Silver formed its arms and upper torso. Brass supplied the material for its lower torso and thighs while iron and clay composed the legs and feet. Glued in rapt attention to the unfolding drama, the monarch watched a rock (Dan. 2:34) strike and shatter the image. So complete was the decimation that only the rock survived. As the dream raced to its climax, Nebuchadnezzar observed the rock swell into a great mountain and fill the earth. Van Groningen concludes of the rock, "It not only replaces the image, but it becomes far greater, namely, the one great factor to be reckoned with in the world."[27]

Naturally, the controversy generated over the interpretation of the dream swirls through academia even today. About the only items agreed to by the majority of scholars is that the dream speaks of a succession of rulers and/or kingdoms and that the beginning point in the series must be Babylon and/or Nebuchadnezzar.

Two major interpretations must be considered. The youngest of the two claims the three kingdoms following Babylon are the Median, the Persian, and the Greek. This coincides with a widely held belief that the book of Daniel was composed under spurious circumstances during the second century B.C. The older theory identifies the successive kingdoms as the Medo-Persian, the Greek, and the Roman. Of the two, the latter is the more compelling.

Evidence from Ancient Sources. Leading writers in antiquity offer a concerted endorsement of the Persian-Greek-Roman thesis. Young finds it espoused by "Josephus, the church fathers, Chrysostrom, Jerome, Augustine" and others.[28]

Internal Evidence. The rationale for subdividing the Medo-Persian Empire ignores explicit internal evidence that directly contradicts the thesis. Historically and biblically (Dan. 5:28), the records confirm an intense mutual cooperation in the subjugation of ancient Babylon. The book refers (Dan. 6:8,12,15) to the kingdom replacing Babylon as the kingdom "of the Medes and the Persians." If the book was written at the time and for the purpose modern critics assert (to authenticate a second-century B.C. Jewish revolt), it is hard to understand why the forgers failed to render their wording in a manner obviously consistent with their purpose.

Failure of Alternative Hypothesis. After the fall of Babylon, a Median Empire, totally independent of Persia, is unknown in ancient records.[29] Surely later authors would have been cognizant of such an eventuality.

Evidence from Later Symbolism. A later prophecy in Daniel 8 clearly uses a single animal (a ram) to represent one composite Medo-Persian kingdom. Again, Young's comments must still be heard:

> The reader's attention is first directed to the ram (i.e., to the unity of the two kingdoms) and then to its diversified aspect as represented by the two horns. One of these horns came up after the other, which signifies the fact that it became predominant. This is historically true. Persia did as a matter of fact become predominant over Media, and hence in passages such as Dan. 10:13,20 the nation is referred to simply as Persia.[30]

Furthermore, parallel predictions of chapters 2 and 7 support the impression that the Medo-Persian Empire was understood as a unit. As Young argues, "The representations of these chapters are certainly congruous with the view that the second kingdom is Medo-Persian." He explains,

> The central meaning is that an empire, represented by the bear, is to conquer much territory. Now Media alone cannot rightly be represented as an empire whose principal characteristic was that it conquered much territory. ... If the writer of Daniel in 7:5 intended to represent Media alone, he has brought himself in sharp conflict with what he says in 8:3,20, where Persia is correctly represented as coming up after Media and obtaining the supremacy.
>
> On the other hand, the combined Medo-Persian empire (as in 8:3,4) did conquer much territory, and the description in 7:5 is apt.[31]

Moreover, the entire scenario depicted in Daniel 7 harmonizes stunningly with the above interpretation. The lion, as the initial symbol in the dream and by agreement of the overwhelming testimony of academicians, represents Babylon. As McDowell correctly discerns,

> The second figure, a bear, best represents the Medo-Persian empire—the three ribs that it devours correspond accurately with the empire's major conquests of Lydia, Babylon, and Egypt. The third figure, a four-headed leopard, represents Greece because Greece was divided into four kingdoms after Alexander's death.[32]

This simple "fit" leaves the fourth beast to symbolize Rome. As Archer now concludes,

From the standpoint of the symbolism of chapters 2, 7, and 8, therefore, the identification of the four empires with Babylon, Medo-Persia,
Greece, and Rome presents a perfect correspondence, whereas the identi-
fications involved in the Maccabean date theory presents the gravest
problems and discrepancies.[33]

Alternative Hypothesis Relies on Assumptions.

The thesis that sub-
divides the Medo-Persian empire becomes attractive only if one assumes
the book to have been forged in the second century B.C. Again, to make
such an assumption one must ignore substantial evidence to the contrary.
Specifically, the Aramaic found in older manuscripts is far more consistent with the theory that the material was composed prior to the
Maccabean period.[34] Whitcomb concludes,

> The Aramaic of Daniel (2:4b-7:28) closely resembles that of Ezra (4:7-
> 6:18; 7:12-26) and the 5th-century BC Elephantine papyri (cf. G. L. Archer
> in J. B. Payne (ed.) New Perspectives in the Old Testament, 1970, pp. 160-
> 169), while the Hebrew of Daniel resembles that of Ezekiel, Haggai, Ezra,
> and Chronicles more than that of Ecclesiasticus (180 BC; cf. G. L. Archer in
> J. H. Skilton (ed.), *The Law and the Prophets*, 1974, pp. 470-481).[35]

Persian and Greek Words Suggest Early Date.

Usage of certain
Persian and Greek words argues for the earlier composition.[36] So do
other features revealing significant information about Babylon unavailable to second century fabricators.[37] Also, early records affirm that both
Jewish authorities and the early church held the book to be authoritative.[38] It is very difficult to understand how this could be possible had the
book first appeared in the second century. Thus, Daniel's prediction that
the Messiah would appear sometime during Roman rule endures the
blows of the critic.

As a matter of record, Jesus of Nazareth entered history during the
days of the Roman Empire.

Daniel's "70 Weeks": More Clues about Timing

Another allusion to the timing of the Messiah's appearance emerges
in Daniel's highly controversial discussion of the "70 weeks" (Dan.
9:24-27). Here, the text portrays an aging prophet uncovering
Jeremiah's earlier prediction that Israel's captivity in Babylon would be
lifted after 70 years. Realizing those years were nearly complete and
that his people would soon commence their long trek homeward, a pas-
sionate prayer poured from his lips. The prophet acknowledged the sins
of his people and inquired of the Lord when those sins might be
removed. He believed Jeremiah's prophecy. His people would return to

their homeland. But, to Daniel, the big question remained. How could they obtain forgiveness? God's response supplies a second clue as to the timing of the Messiah's advent.

Speaking through an angel, God informed Daniel that, one day, in the distant future, forgiveness will come. "Seventy 'sevens' are decreed for your people and your holy city to finish transgression, to put an end to sin, to atone for wickedness, to bring in everlasting righteousness" (Dan. 9:24). The one who will accomplish this is said to be the "Anointed One" (Dan. 9:25). Two questions now demand our attention: (1) Who is this "Anointed One"? (2) When will the "Anointed One" appear?

Who is the "Anointed One" of Daniel 9? Current scholarship identifies the "Anointed One" either with some person living during the Maccabean period or with Jesus of Nazareth. Of the two, reference to Jesus better satisfies the text. For instance, given the activities of the "Anointed One,"—he will finish transgression, put an end to sin, atone for the iniquity of Israel, and usher in an age of everlasting righteousness—"it is very difficult to see how any such exalted purpose is explicable in terms of those interpretations which focus the prophecy on Antiochus Epiphanes. ... where, one might reasonably ask, is the finishing of transgression, the paying of the atoning price, the bringing in of everlasting righteousness?"[39] If the prophecy spoke of a Maccabean ruler, these ideas become meaningless.

When will the "Anointed One" Come? The "Anointed One" will appear sixty-nine "sevens" after a decree is issued to restore and rebuild Jerusalem (Dan. 9: 25). The text asserts Daniel received this message near the end of Israel's Babylonian captivity. Determining the date of the decree, then, becomes crucial in the search for Messianic parameters. A careful survey of decrees relating to the prophecy narrows the field to four: (1) 539/538 B.C., (2) 519/518 B.C., (3) 457/456 B.C., and (4) 445/444 B.C.

Whichever emerges as the terminus a quo (starting point) must satisfy three criteria: (1) It must date a decree or command, (2) It must authorize the rebuilding of the entire city of Jerusalem, and (3) It must mandate the restoration of the city to its former state. 445 B.C. is the superior option.

First, the decree in 539 B.C. merely granted permission to rebuild the temple, not the entire city. No references to the restoration of the city are included. Nothing suggests rebuilding defensive walls. Yet, the text in Daniel 9 clearly alludes to such activities in association with the decree.[40]

An even more telling argument surfaces in Ezra 4. Here, as Jewish returnees work feverishly to rebuild the temple (4:1-4), a formal complaint comes to the newly-crowned Persian monarch, Artaxerxes (4:7),

asking that he prohibit the rebuilding of the city walls. Had a former
Persian king commanded the city be rebuilt, it would have been unthinkable, under Persian law, for Artaxerxes to offer a command in direct
opposition to an earlier decree.[41] Moreover, no references in Ezra actually describe rebuilding Jerusalem's walls. In contrast, numerous references describe royal decrees authorizing the building of the temple.

Second, the 519 B.C. date suffers similar failures. Furthermore, this
so-called decree was actually a confirmation of the earlier decree rather
than a new command (Ezra 5:17-6:5).

Third, the 457 B.C. alternative flounders as well. No references
require building anything other than the temple.[42] A discriminating
review of the material reveals this was not a royal decree. Keil labels it a
"royal favor."[43]

Only the 445 B.C. date remains. In that year, Persian officials issued a
formal decree. It ordered the rebuilding of Jerusalem's defensive walls.
It directly provided for the restoration of the city to its earlier state. The
scriptural text (Neh. 2:3,5,8) specifically designates rebuilding city walls
and gates. No additional decrees ordering the rebuilding of the city occur
elsewhere.[44] The decree of 445 set in motion the complete restoration of
the city and its walls.

Calculating the Time of the Messiah's Appearance. Sixty-nine
"sevens" were to pass between the decree and the time of the
Messiah's appearance. Assuming the text to refer to 69x7 years, this
means 483 years would pass between the decree issued during
Nehemiah's lifetime and the Messiah. If we accept the traditional date
for Jesus' earthly ministry as 30-33 A.D. advocated by Hoehner,[45] then
445 + 33 = 478 years. This seems to suggest Jesus died five years
before the prophecy designates.

In an area of interpretation which must involve significant speculation
regardless of one's biases and presuppositions, two proposed scenarios
present at least as logical a solution as any offered by those who reject
the prophecy out of hand.

First, strong circumstantial evidence suggests that the prophecy speaks
of Jewish years of 360 days as opposed to modern determinations of
365+ days. Robert Anderson suggested the explanation late in the nineteenth century in his book *The Coming Prince*.[46] As Hoehner notes,

> This makes good sense for several reasons. First, ... in ancient times vari-
> ous systems (of determining a year) were used. When one investigates the
> calendars of India, Persia, Babylonia and Assyria, Egypt, Central and South
> America, and China it is interesting to notice that they uniformly had twelve
> thirty-day months (a few had eighteen twenty-day months) making a total of

360 days for the year. ... Although it may be strange to present-day thinking, it was common in those days to think of a 360-day year.[47]

Such measurements are used elsewhere in scripture. The author of The Revelation refers to 1,260 days (12:6), forty-two months (11:2), and what most scholars believe to be three and one-half years—"a time, times, and half a time" (12:7,14) as if they were synonymous. The 360-day year is obviously utilized.

Moreover, the book of Genesis does the same in describing the duration of flood waters—five months (Gen. 7:11 and 8:4) and 150 days (Gen. 7:24 and 8:3). Using the probable date for the decree as March 5, 444 B.C. and the probable date for Jesus' crucifixion in Jerusalem as April 3, 33 A.D., Hoehner demonstrates that Jesus would have entered Jerusalem precisely as the "69-sevens"—483 Jewish years—came to an end.[48] As there was a strong resurgence of sentiment at just this time that the Messiah's coming was imminent, it seems likely that others in the first century had studied the same prophecies.

Newman offers a second plausible alternative. Following sabbatical (seven-year) cycles, he argues that there were precisely sixty-nine of those cycles between the decree in 444 B.C. and the crucifixion in 33 A.D.[49] The angelic message delivered to Daniel specified that the Messiah would be killed "69-sevens" after the issuing of the decree to rebuild Jerusalem. By either reckoning, Jesus was executed in Jerusalem "69-sevens" after the decree was issued.

Not only did Jesus live at exactly the right time in history to fulfill the Messianic predictions, he also suffered crucifixion in Jerusalem at the time suggested. Can this be mere coincidence?

14

Predicting the Messiah's Miracles

Once the time for his appearance had been settled, the next question centered on how to recognize the Messiah. Would he be a king? A priest? A member of a particular tribe? What credentials would confirm his authenticity?

In this arena, the bulk of Old Testament prophecy emerges. The prophets foretell his lineage (Gen. 22:18; Isa. 11:1; Jer. 23:5), his birthplace (Mic. 5:2), and his style of teaching (Psa. 78:2). He was to be both king and priest (Psa. 72:8; 110:1,4), a descendant of David (II Sam. 7:13; Psa. 89:4; Isa. 9:7; 11:1; Jer. 23:5), and one who would suffer and die as God's servant (Isa. 53). His ministry was to reach the Gentiles as well as the Jews (Isa. 60:3; 49:6). Of all the identifying credentials, none creates more controversy nor, yet, is more critical to his claims than the prediction that he would work miracles (Isa. 35:5-6; 32:3-4).

To merely predict the arrival of some future individual is difficult enough, but to saddle that individual with the epithet of "miracle-worker" is incredible. Yet, New Testament authors uniformly testify Jesus achieved the incredible. He cured leprosy (Matt. 8:2-4). He gave sight to the blind (Mark 10:46-52). He provided hearing for the deaf (Mark 7:31-37). He raised the dead (John 11:1-44). He exercised inexplicable control over forces of nature (Matt. 8:23-27; Matt. 14:22-23; Luke 9:11-17). Each time he was party to the use of the miraculous, he was offering his credentials; he was defending his right to be named the predicted and long-awaited "Messiah."

Unfortunately, verifying the occurrence of a miracle, then and now, demands considerable effort.[1] Entire treatises have explored the likelihood of a miracle occurring at any point in history. It is not the intent of this essay to retrace those ventures. Rather, after a brief defense of the possibility of miracles, we will investigate specific evidence that Jesus of Nazareth performed them.[2]

Defining Terms

Exactly what is a miracle? No consensus definition emerges among scholars. Those interested in such should consult Colin Brown's seminal 1984 survey, *Miracles and the Critical Mind*. After an expansive review, he endorses as "a useful, rule-of-thumb definition" the one proposed by acclaimed British philosopher C. S. Lewis. Lewis declared that a miracle was simply "an interference with Nature by supernatural power."[3] Brown summarized the reasoning of Lewis and others as follows:

> ... our personal action, which does not suspend laws of nature, but rather orders them, may be an important clue as to how we may think of divine activity in the world. As personal beings, we do not stand outside the sequence of cause and effect. Personal action consists rather in initiating some sequences and terminating others. We stand within the process and at the same time enjoy a measure of transcendence.
>
> The same Creator may act within the world and he may act upon the world. ... The kind of miracles that Christians believe in are not pure random manifestations. They are manifestations of a divine ordering of nature with which we are familiar. ... (They would not) have come about if nature had been left to itself.[4]

The argument is simple. Imagine the rich farmlands of Iowa with their perfectly ordered cornfields. Row after row stand in precision-like, straight lines. The production of that symmetry involves an ordered interference in nature by an intelligent life form. Scientists would never call the growth of a stalk from a kernel of corn a miracle. It occurs whenever appropriate conditions exist. But the ordered appearance of row after row of corn and the absence of a mixture of other plant forms requires intelligent action by some being outside the plant kingdom and other non-human forces of nature.

In a similar vein, biblical authors portray God as operating at a higher level of existence than that of our three-dimensional universe. His intervention in our world occurs within laws under which he exists. Just as we do not violate laws of nature when we use those laws to produce symmetrical rows of corn, neither does God violate laws when he orders them to produce an effect that would not occur under normal ordering. As Brown observes, miracles "represent not the abandonment of all order but the breaking into our present world order of the order of the world to come."[5]

Thus, a miracle in the sense of Scripture may be defined as "a supernatural intervention in the natural, three-dimensional world by a deliberate, intelligent act which produces a result that otherwise would not have occurred at a given place or moment." As Nash explains, the Christian point of view is that "God can act in ways that appear out of the ordinary, as we see things. But such an extraordinary action should not be regarded as a violation of any law of nature."[6]

Admitting the Possibility of the Miraculous

Given this understanding, can we accept the possibility of the miraculous in history? I believe we can.

Simply put, if one accepts the possibility of a supernatural being, no convincing impasse bars the possibility of that being reordering the natural world. McDowell correctly notes, "the whole question depends ultimately on the existence of God."[7] For those willing to candidly scrutinize the available proof, sufficient evidence can be found to concede the possibility that such a being exists.[8]

Unfortunately, many reject the evidence out-of-hand, refusing to consider any evidence. Meier's incisive comments explain the obstacles to dialogue encountered by many Christian scholars as an "academic sneer factor." He writes,

> If a full debate on the possibility and reality of miracles were to take place on American university campuses today—a highly unlikely event—such a debate would be tolerated in many quarters only with a strained smile that could hardly mask a sneer. Before any positions were articulated or discussed, the solemn creed of many university professors, especially in religion departments, would be recited sotto voce: "No modern educated person can accept the possibility of miracles."[9]

Meier, an erudite professor of New Testament at the Catholic University of America in Washington, D.C., and former editor of the *Catholic Biblical Quarterly*, questions such closed-mindedness. Recalling surveys that show that "only 6 percent of all Americans polled by Gallup completely disagreed with the proposition that even today God works miracles," Meier adds,

> If Bultmann and his intellectual disciples are correct in their view on miracles and the modern mind, then it follows that only 6 percent of Americans completely qualify as truly modern persons. A more plausible conclusion is that only 6 percent of Americans share the mind-set of some German university professors.[10]

As to the philosophical sparring generated by David Hume's denial of the possibility of the miraculous, the reader is referred to numerous critiques of that philosophy.[11] Again, Brown's summary is apropos. After reviewing arguments against the possibility of the miraculous, he writes,

Neither science nor philosophy can disprove the possibility of miracles. The most they can do is declare their improbability, when viewed within the frame of reference supplied by our normal experience. But from this standpoint no one has ever imagined that miracles were anything other than improbable. The question of whether they are feasible is another matter. We cannot understand miracles. But we can grasp something of their possibility and purpose when we approach them within the context of a worldview that sees God as the sovereign, personal Creator and Sustainer of the universe. The question whether such a personal God has ever miraculously intervened in the normal order of the world can be decided only by examining the evidence in the light of our fundamental convictions about the nature of God and reality.[12]

Thus, we turn to the evidence.

The Old Testament Prediction of the Messiah's Miracles

Scattered through the Old Testament, several clues of a miracle-worker-to-come infiltrate the mosaic produced by the prophets. The author of Deuteronomy (18:15) explains that the one to come will "be a prophet like Moses." Moses' life and mission were peppered with the miraculous. From the plagues to the crossing of the Red Sea to the provision of food in the wilderness, Moses electrified a nation of slaves through the demonstration of signs and wonders. A prophet similar to Moses needed to demonstrate the miraculous as well.

Even more specific is the prophecy of Isaiah (35:5-6). It was this prophecy to which Jesus alluded in the earlier portion of his ministry (Matt. 11:1-6; Luke 7:18-35) when Herod imprisoned John the Baptist. Facing certain death, John—the cousin of Jesus, the one who had received a special communication from God at Jesus' baptism announcing him as the son of God—began to question his earlier beliefs. Was Jesus of Nazareth really "he that should come?" or should they "look for another?" John's disciples carried the questions and concerns to Jesus.

Jesus' response draws from Isaiah: "Go back and report to John what you hear and see. The blind receive sight, the lame walk, those who have leprosy are cured, the deaf hear, the dead are raised, and the good news is preached to the poor" (Matt. 11:4-5). Once again, Brown's observations are on track:

> ... in the New Testament itself miracles and prophecy were not two independent and unrelated tracks of arguments. Moreover, the miracles of Jesus were not simply to be differentiated from those of others by being bigger, better, and more authentic. ... the miracles of Jesus ... were signs that fulfilled messianic prophecy and works that accomplished the work of the

Father. ... that the miracles of Jesus were the fulfillment of messianic prophecy is central to the message of the Synoptic Gospels.[13]

Jesus performed many of his miracles in the city of Capernaum on the shores of the scenic Sea of Galilee. This synagogue is built over the ruins of another synagogue used in the time of Jesus. His miracles were set in real places among real people. (Photo courtesy, Mr. Lawrence Williams.)

Evidence that Jesus of Nazareth Performed Miracles

To predict miracles is one thing. To verify their occurrence is another. Is there reliable evidence outside the Scriptures that Jesus of Nazareth produced "signs and wonders?" The answer is "yes."

Evidence from Josephus

Joseph ben Matthias, or, as he is more commonly known, Flavius Josephus, was born in Galilee in 37/38 A.D. He was highly educated, a priest, and a Pharisee. When the continual confrontation with Rome erupted in open warfare in 66 A.D., he found himself in charge of defending Galilee. After that defense abruptly crumbled, he ingratiated himself to his captors and successfully predicted Vespasian's succession as Caesar. He was then given an opportunity to author a detailed history of the Jewish nation. Of his four surviving works, the one germane to our current study is the twenty-volume *Antiquities of the Jews* published near the close of the first century.

One key section, known as the Testimonium Flavianum, contains a brief, but detailed, discussion of Jesus of Nazareth.[14] Included is a reference that Jesus "wrought surprising feats."[15] Since Josephus was not a Christian, his reference, at the least, lends credibility to gospel accounts that depict Jesus as demonstrating "signs and wonders." Indeed, Otto Betz, the distinguished professor of New Testament studies at Tubingen University in Germany and at the Chicago Theological Seminary, observed:

> According to the famous and much debated Testimonium Flavianum ... the so-called Christ was "a performer of marvelous deeds. ..." This must refer to the miracles of Jesus and certainly does not betray the language of Christian tradition.[16]

While tacitly approving the "marvelous deeds" of Jesus, Josephus categorically denies the validity of "marvels and signs" offered by others in the first century who claimed the role of deliverer.[17] On some occasions, he even questions the accuracy of miracles recorded in the Old Testament. His uncritical referral to Jesus' miracles offers reputable evidence that this man of Nazareth did, in fact, produce some extraordinary feats.

In his evaluation of the passage regarding Jesus in *The Antiquities*, Meier observes that, as far as the 1st century is concerned, Josephus never attributes miraculous deeds to any human, other than Jesus. "Thus, Jesus of Nazareth stands out as a relative exception ... in that he is a named figure in 1st-century Jewish Palestine to whom Josephus is willing to attribute a number of miraculous deeds."[18] Finally, the term translated "surprising feats," which Josephus applies to Jesus comes from the Greek *paradoxa* — the same word he uses to describe miracles by the prophet Elisha.[19]

Evidence from Hostile Jewish Sources

Testimony from hostile witnesses generally provides extremely reliable evidence. In the first century, with the flames of Christianity darting through the Roman Empire, Jewish resentment of what they widely regarded as "blasphemy" simmered, boiled, then erupted in waves of persecution against the fledgling religion. As a result, the few passing references in rabbinical literature during the early centuries of the Christian era are usually considered of little historical value because "they partake rather of the nature of vituperation and polemic against the founder of a hated party, than of objective accounts of historical value."[20]

However, comments from ancient Jewish sources do lend additional credence to miracle claims in the Gospels because they certify the occurrence of mysterious events associated with the ministry of Jesus. Moreover, the few details exacted from these hostile sources align themselves in perfect symmetry with stories expounded in the Gospels and in the writings of early Christians.

The first morsel of evidence appears in a passage from the Babylonian Talmud (Sanh. 43a)[21] which is generally accepted as an authentic early commentary on Jewish teachings.[22] This passage, possibly composed as early as the second century, announces that *"Yeshu"* (= "Jesus", in some early manuscripts *"Yeshu"* the Nazarene") was executed on the eve of the Passover because he "practiced sorcery and enticed and led Israel astray." Significantly, this manner of explaining the miracles of Jesus is precisely how Gospel writers describe Jewish reactions to his "signs and wonders." Meier summarizes: "This (reference) agrees with the whole tendency of ancient Jewish sources, which do not deny the existence and execution of Jesus. Indeed, not even the miracles of Jesus are denied, but are rather interpreted as acts of sorcery."[23]

Second, the assault on Christianity advanced by Trypho contains identical charges: Jesus performed his miracles through magic. Responding to the challenge, Justin (110-165 A.D.) replies:

> ... this Christ, who also appeared in your nation, and healed those who were maimed, and deaf, and lame in body from their birth. ... And having raised the dead, and causing them to live, by His deeds He compelled the men who lived at that time to recognize Him. But though they saw such works, they asserted it was magical art.[24]

Obviously, Jewish apologists made no effort to deny miraculous feats associated with Jesus. Realizing they deny miracles associated with others, is it possible that substantial and widespread eyewitness accounts made it awkward to openly deny their occurrence in regard to Jesus? R. T. France concludes

> ... it seems clear that by at least the early second century Jesus was known and abominated as a wonder-worker and teacher who had gained a large following and had been duly executed as 'one who led Israel astray.' Uncomplimentary as it is, this is at least, in a distorted way, evidence for the impact Jesus' miracles and teaching made.[25]

Evidence from Early Christian Sources

A brief excursion into the writings of early Christians completes our discussion of non-biblical materials. Were these disciples convinced that Jesus was a "miracle worker"? Were miracles merely isolated events that played only a minimal part in the rise and spread of Christianity, or were they, from the beginning, such an integral part of the story that it is impossible to grasp Jesus' ministry without them? Two references will serve our purpose.

Among the earliest uncontested documents of early Christianity are four fragments of papyrus that "can be dated with some confidence before 150 C.E. on the basis of the script."[26] Known as the Egerton Papyrus 2, they were a small part of a group of Egyptian papyri purchased by the British Museum in 1934.[27] One of the two fragments clearly describes Jesus healing a leper. The story is reminiscent of an account found in the synoptic gospels (Matt. 8:2-3; Mark 1:40-42; Luke 5:12-13; 17:14).

A second fragment alludes to another, previously unknown, miracle. This fragment "is too uncertain to allow more than a hopeful guess, but this may well have been an account of a nature miracle involving the instantaneous growth and fruiting of some plant."[28] The portion insinuating the miraculous reads,

> But when they were perplexed by his strange question, Jesus as he walked stood still on the bank of the River Jordan, stretched out his right hand ... and sowed on the ... and then ... water ... and ... before them produced fruit ... much ... to the (joy?) ...[29]

Another early record also deserves attention. In 1945, Hebrew University professor E. L. Sukenik discovered graffiti scribbled on the walls of a tomb at Talpioth, near Jerusalem. Sukenik labeled these inscriptions, which have been dated to approximately 50 A.D., as the "earliest records of Christianity."[30] A later evaluation revealed that the markings were pleas addressed to Jesus for help (healing?) and resurrection.[31] With these inscriptions, stories connecting Jesus with the miraculous can be traced to within twenty years of his death.

The point is simple. The earliest records of Christianity confirm that the story of Jesus was inseparably connected with the miraculous. While these fragments do not prove Jesus of Nazareth worked miracles, they do confirm that the earliest Christian records made that claim.

Evidence from the Gospels

One final piece of evidence—the testimony of New Testament authors—corroborates the miracle claims. Here the argument over who actually transcribed the words on the scrolls is moot. And while this writer is firmly convinced that the New Testament manuscripts were composed (either by transmitting the material in oral fashion to another or by actual writing), under divine guidance, by the apostles or those closely related to them, prior to 70 A.D., these beliefs are not applicable to the issue at hand.

The real issue remains, "can we believe the New Testament records of Jesus' miracles to be sincere, knowledgeable, trustworthy renderings of actual events?" I believe we can. In fact, an enormous range of evidence endorses their credibility.[32]

The Natural Fit to the Total Narrative. Early Christians—the apostles, church leaders, and those in the forefront of promoting Christianity, either in oral or written form—gladly offered their lives as evidence of their beliefs. While their sacrificial zealotry centered on the greatest miracle—the resurrection of Jesus—that belief would make little sense isolated from the rest of gospel story. The resurrection is incomprehensible aside from the reason people followed Jesus in the first place. It assumes an understanding of the reasons why Jesus suffered a Roman execution. The world's greatest miracle would be unthinkable apart from the claim that Jesus was able to produce other, less dramatic, miracles.

Remove the miraculous and one is hard-pressed to explain why first century followers bothered with Jesus at all. The introductory comments from Meier's epochal study strike home. He ponders,

> To be blunt, without miracles, one wonders how much popularity this particular Jewish preacher and teacher would have enjoyed. Without miracles, many Palestinian Jews might have seen Jesus merely as a more "upbeat" version of John the Baptist, an echo of his former master but lacking the master's striking asceticism and stark venue. Without miracles, the figure, fame, and fate of Jesus would have been quite different and probably quite diminished. Without miracles, one is left with the paper cutout manufactured by Thomas Jefferson and all subsequent questers for a reasonable Jesus.

To more fully understand how completely intertwined are the Gospel records of Jesus and his ability to work miracles, Richardson undertook a verse-by-verse survey of the Gospel of Mark. Of the 660 verses (through Mark 16:8), he noted that 209, or 31 percent, include elements of the miraculous.

The Integrity of the Authors. Another key to the integrity of the record is the depth of sincere belief demonstrated by those who propagated the miracle stories. They were unflappable in their proclamation of the total gospel message. Dr. Simon Greenleaf, one of the great legal minds of an earlier generation, argued

> ... the annals of military warfare afford scarcely an example of the like heroic constancy, patience, and unflinching courage. They had every possible motive to review carefully the grounds of their faith, and the evidences of the great facts and truths which they asserted.[35]

In a similar vein, Moreland observes,

> It seems clear that the New Testament writers were able and willing to tell the truth. They had very little to gain and much to lose for their efforts. For one thing, they were mostly Jewish theists. To change the religion of Israel with its observance of the Mosaic laws, Sabbath keeping, sacrifices, and clear-cut non-Trinitarian monotheism would be to risk the damnation of their own souls to hell. A modern atheist may not worry about such a thing, but members of the early church surely did. For another thing, the apostles lived lives of great hardship, stress, and affliction (see II Cor. 11:23-29) and died martyrs' deaths for their convictions. There is no adequate motive for their labors other than a sincere desire to proclaim what they believed to be the truth.[36]

The Restraint of the Material. The miracle stories are also credible because of their restraint. Harris, for instance, wonders why the number of miracle stories failed to skyrocket during the period immediately following the resurrection account:

> If the stories were fabricated, we should have expected the number of miracles performed by Jesus to have increased markedly once he gained "all power in heaven and on earth" (cf. Mt. 28:18), but in fact only one miracle is recorded as having occurred during a resurrection appearance (viz. Jn. 21:6).[37]

Another scholar, A. E. Harvey, develops a similar theme, noting "the miracle stories in the gospels are unlike anything else in ancient literature. ... They do not exaggerate the miracle or add sensational details. ..." He adds that this occurs to a degree that is "rare in the writings of antiquity."[38]

Even a sketchy expedition into the world of apocryphal miracles instantly reveals the vast difference between the gospel miracles and others. Blomberg cites several prominent examples such as

> ... the child Jesus miraculously lengthening a leg of an imbalanced bed which Joseph is building for a customer (Infancy Gospel of Thomas), all the Roman statues bowing down to Christ during his trial before Pilate (Acts of Pilate 5-6), or John effectively commanding the bedbugs to sleep peacefully in a corner of his room so that he might rest as ease (Acts of John 60-61).[39]

The Impartiality of the Materials. Records of the evangelists acquire further credibility because of their openness in reporting shortcomings and errors among those within their fellowship. Historian Will Durant finds the New Testament reports of "the competition of the apostles for high places in the kingdom, their flight after Jesus' arrest, Peter's denial, the failure of Christ to work miracles in Galilee, the reference of some auditors to his possible insanity," and other examples as strong evidence of their accuracy.[40] Buell and Hyder concur: "The New Testament writers give evidence of a high sense of integrity, frequently conveying to the reader elements in their reports that reflect quite negatively upon themselves. This is almost unheard of among chroniclers of any sort in any age."[41]

Internal Evidence of Accuracy. Strong internal evidence in the gospels implies the presence of eyewitnesses at the various miracle events. Following the lead of John A. T. Robinson[42] and Stephen Smalley,[43] Erickson argues forcefully that the Gospel of John was written by an eyewitness to the events under discussion. He finds numerous references in the book connote a strong understanding of the Jewish background of first century Palestine as well as a unique understanding of the land's topography. Such familiarity, he contends, provides strong circumstantial evidence of the author's actual presence when the events occurred. Erickson concludes, "Recent archaeological study has tended to support the view that the Gospel of John reflects a tradition which knew Palestine intimately. It is evidently the work of someone who was familiar with the places in which the story is set."[44]

Erickson follows his discussion of archaeology by noting numerous internal evidences that are consistent with an eyewitness account which are usually absent otherwise. Among the items he mentions are references to specific times when events occur (1:29, 35, 39, 43; 4:6; 5:2; 18:28; 19:14; 20:19), the inclusion of seemingly insignificant data (2:12), and the consistency of the material in areas that would be almost unnoticeable to anyone but the most astute critics.[45]

Archaeological Discoveries and the Accuracy of the Material. Archaeological discoveries also corroborate the overall trustworthiness of biblical records. While archaeological discoveries, in themselves, can never actually "prove" the Bible to be true, such discoveries do far more to authenticate biblical records than rebut them. Groothuis, in defending the orthodox understanding of Jesus against New Age theology, summarizes:

> Archaeological findings have ... corroborated the pool of Bethesda (cf. Jn. 5:2), discovered in 1888, the existence of Pontius Pilate, mentioned on a fragment of a Latin plaque, the greatness of the Temple during Jesus' time, the kind of tomb Jesus was buried in, many of which have been unearthed in Palestine, and many other items.[46]

Of course, additional clues connecting archaeological discoveries with the Gospels appear throughout contemporary literature.[47] Those discoveries include both major and minor issues. Among minor details, the existence of sycamore trees (Luke 19:1-4) at Jericho during the days of

Jesus is now confirmed after earlier scholars had claimed no such trees could have existed there in that time.[48] Other seemingly insignificant finds produced examples of the phylacteries (Matt. 23:5),[49] remains of Jewish synagogues in Galilee and elsewhere dating from the days of Jesus,[50] and portions of massive stones (Mark 13:1)—larger than any found in the pyramids with one estimated to weigh 415 tons—from Herod's building program.[51]

Major finds relating to the Gospels have been cataloged by several authors, including Charlesworth, who lists such items as the now near-certain discovery of Peter's house in Capernaum (Mark 1:29; Matt. 8:14-16), evidence coinciding with Jesus' clearing the Temple of merchants and traders (John 2), the pool of Bethesda near the old Sheep Gate (John 5:2-9), and the remains of another individual crucified in the area during the first century.[52] In addition, archaeologists believe they have discovered the family tomb of Caiaphas, high priest in Jerusalem at the time of Jesus' crucifixion.[53]

Perhaps the classic example of the results of archaeological research revolves around Englishman Sir William Mitchell Ramsay. Ramsay, inaugurating his archaeological research in Turkey in 1880, at first staunchly denied the veracity of biblical records. Schooled in the skeptical Tubingen philosophy, he trudged dutifully into the region convinced that the author of the Acts "wrote for his contemporaries, not for truth."[54]

Years of research in Asia brought him full circle. Before his death in 1939, the venerable scholar amassed volumes of evidence directly opposing his earlier beliefs. He was amazed. The author of Acts earned his admiration. "I set out to look for truth on the borderland where Greece and Asia meet, and found it there," he wrote. "You may press the words of Luke in a degree beyond any other historian's, and they stand the keenest scrutiny and the hardest treatment."[55] If the evidence points so overwhelmingly to a tenacious search for accuracy in the writing of Acts, should we not also assume his earlier gospel portrays an equal concern?

The conclusion of a cautious Charlesworth bears consideration: "Jesus did exist; and we know more about him than about almost any other Palestinian Jew before 70 C.E. He was a real person who lived in Palestine, growing up in Galilee."[56]

Predicting the Messiah's Suffering, Death and Resurrection

When Charles Dickens' oft-quoted phrase, "It was the best of times, it was the worst of times," danced from his pen into immortality, it tugged at the reality of life. Trouble darkens the brightest of days; hope brightens the darkest of nights. And tucked desperately inside much of first century Judaism danced the glittering hope of a deliverer.

Trouble was no stranger in Palestine. Rome's iron grip tightened around her population. Taxation, often exaggerated by unscrupulous officials, smothered all but the very wealthy. Calloused authorities gleefully used every opportunity to taunt and belittle Jewish religious beliefs. Coupled with natural disasters and poverty, everyday life became a mixture of frustration, depression, and rebellion.

The Impact of Economic Pressure and Taxation

Economic conditions deteriorated rapidly under first, Herodian, then Roman, oppression. Extensive—often opulent—building projects by Herod the Great and his predecessors, plunged the economy into virtual bankruptcy. Besides extensive additions to the temple complex, Herod the Great built a theater, an amphitheater, and a fortified royal palace in Jerusalem, several entire cities (Caesarea Martima, Sebaste, etc.), and another lavish palace near the Dead Sea. To pay for his extravagance, "he placed an immense burden of taxation on the Jewish peasantry (and). ... at his death the country and its people were virtually exhausted economically."[1]

Herod also extracted resources from his people to buy friends and influence people. He made "generous gifts" to cities outside Palestine such as "Athens and major Greek cities bordering on the Aegean Sea. ... The Greeks held Herod in such high esteem (because of his gifts) that they selected him to be the honorary president of the Olympic Games."[2]

In addition to Herod's burdensome taxes came the required religious taxes. Jews were expected to offer a voluntary tithe (10 percent) to the Lord. Also, an extra tax was assessed to assure the availability of adequate operating funds for the temple.

To these Jewish taxes, Rome imposed an even more onerous system. For many, the tax burden drained a minimum of half their yearly production.[3] Nor was any leniency forthcoming. Taxes had to be paid on time, or severe consequences became inevitable. Cities tardy in paying found their populations reduced to slavery.[4]

Unable to eke out even a bare subsistence, the vast underclass first plummeted into a debtor state from which they could not recover, then lost their land and property to wealthy estate builders. Reduced to the role of day-laborers waiting in the markets for jobs (Mt. 20:1-16; Mark 12:1-9) paying barely enough to buy food for a single person, poverty and taxation crushed average citizens who lived lives that were "frugal at best and could easily slide off into grinding, impoverished misery."[5] As Daniel-Rops observes,

> The great mass of the people of Israel ... were poor, and even very poor: S. W. Baron goes so far as to say "of a horrifying poverty," but perhaps this may be a little too strong. And yet in reading the Gospels one has the impression of great economic stringency: the woman who has lost a piece of silver spends hours searching the house for it. ... The poverty of the Jews was even a stock subject for mirth in the pagan comedies, in which they were shown as beggars, with only one shirt apiece, obliged to feed themselves on carobs. "The daughters of Israel are beautiful," said one rabbi sadly, "it is a pity that they should be made ugly by poverty."[6]

The Impact of Military Devastation and Slavery

Judging from history, one would think Palestine was filled with gold or diamond mines, oil fields, or other extraordinary natural resources. Though small geographically, her history is littered with nations intent on controlling her territory and subjugating her people. Maier explains:

> Palestine has the glory of being located at the juncture of two continents— Africa and Asia—and so served as the crossroads of antiquity. But this strategic location also proved a heavy burden. The armies of the ancient world, even if they had no quarrel with the people of Palestine, regularly used the land as a causeway en route to attacking one another, ravaging Palestine in the process. The inhabitants had as much safety as would a flock of sparrows that chose to build their nests on a superhighway.[7]

Unfortunately, the Roman occupation in the first century exceeded all others in barbarism and brutality.

Oppression from Herod

Herod the Great held the throne in Israel (37-4 B.C.) only because Rome legitimatized his rule. Highly unpopular and openly paranoid about the loss of his throne, he bought his security with an army of Germanic, Gaulish, Galatian, and Thracian mercenaries. Coupled with near-by Roman legions, capable of intervening on short notice, and a massive network of well-paid "secret police," he maintained a ruthless hold on the populace:

> His police were everywhere: everything was under their supervision. It is said that he did not scorn to make his own investigations: walking unknown through the streets one day, he asked a passer-by what the people of his quarter thought of King Herod; the man, a knowing fellow, replied by quoting Ecclesiastes, "Of the king, no treasonable thought ... the very birds in heaven will catch the echoes of it, and fly off to betray thy secret."[8]

Realizing his unpopularity with the people, this non-Jew on a Jewish throne, gave in to extreme paranoia and lashed out against all perceived opponents with relentless cruelty. He had no scruples against killing his own children, and he did so. He ordered the execution of seven of his ten sons and the only wife—he had ten—he ever loved.[9] After news of one such execution reached the ears of Augustus, the Roman is said to have remarked, "I would rather be Herod's pig than his son."[10] The Jews' ruling body, the seventy-one-member Sanhedrin, felt Herod's deadly sting as well. Forty-five members were executed on a single occasion.[11]

Even at the edge of eternity, Herod's madness intensified. Convinced his death would be greeted with excitement and celebration rather than mourning, he

> ... proceeded to attempt a horrid wickedness; for he got together the most illustrious men of the whole Jewish nation, out of every village, into a place called the Hippodrome, and there shut them in. He then called for his sister Salome, and her husband Alexas, and made his speech to them: — "I know well enough that the Jews will keep a festival upon my death; however, it is in my power to be mourned for on other accounts, and to have a splendid funeral. ... Do you but take care to send soldiers to encompass these men that are now in custody, and slay them immediately upon my death, and then will all Judea ... weep at it whether they will or no."[12]

Happily, the command was never carried out.

Unfortunately, Herod's death did little to ease the burden. His kingdom was divided among three surviving sons with Archaelaus ruling Judea and Antipas taking control of Galilee.[13] Archaelaus' first act as king led to a vicious riot and the death of over 3,000 Jews.[14] Twice, Roman legions entered Judea in an attempt to quell the violence. Antipas fared no better in Galilee. Roman legions under Varus finally smothered a budding insurrection by crucifying 2,000 Jews at Sepphoris, only a short distance from Nazareth.[15] Constant tension and periodic rebellions followed.[16]

The first monumental inscription to confirm Pilate as the "prefect of Judea" was uncovered at Caesarea Maritima in 1960. The find further confirms the accuracy of biblical accounts regarding people, places, and events. (Photo courtesy, Mr. Lawrence Williams.)

Oppression from Pilate

Angered and frustrated by the continual disturbances, Roman animosity toward the Jews heightened to the point that they began creating confrontations. Fredriksen complains, "Roman insensitivity to Jewish religious feeling in this period, particularly on the issue of introducing images into Jerusalem, seems to have bordered on deliberate provocation."[17]

Such provocations escalated rapidly during the rule of Pontius Pilate (26-36 A.D.). His actions constantly inflamed the people.[18] Philo's characterization of Pilate as "inflexible, stubborn, and cruel" and of his government as filled with "venality, thefts, abusive behavior ... (and) frequent murders of untried prisoners"[19] explains the deep-seated bitterness toward him so evident in early texts.[20] Pilate's activities left many Jews, especially those in the religious community, seething in anger.

Oppression from Jewish Sources

Unfortunately, repression was not limited to that initiated by Herod and the Roman occupation. It arose from within the Jewish community as well. Various factions vied with one another for political control of the country and its people. As Horsley recognized,

> The high priestly families, Herodians, and much of the wealthy aristocracy, of course, were engaged in a mutually beneficial collaboration with the Roman imperial system in maintaining control in Jewish Palestine. As the social order began to crumble, the ruling elite not only made no attempt to represent the interests of the people, but contributed to the breakdown of the society in a violently predatory manner, yielding virtual "class warfare."[21]

Though such conditions were more severe nearer the end of the Jewish state (50-70 A.D.), problems occurred during the early years of the first century as well.

Remains of what many scholars consider the ruins of the house of Caiaphas in Jerusalem have been supplemented by recent discoveries of the tomb of the high priest's family. Both help solidify the Gospel accounts of Jesus' trial as based on accurate information. (Photo courtesy, Mr. Lawrence Williams.)

Rising Expectations of a Deliverer

With excruciating conditions pressing from all sides, the common people craved relief. As in the past, they turned to their heritage and the God of their fathers. After all, had He not swept aside the mighty Egyptian military in the deluge at the Red Sea (Exo. 14)? Had He not delivered their forefathers from many enemies during the period of the judges? Had He not brought them safely back into the land after enslavement in Babylon? Surely, He would not turn His back on them. They delved into the prophets for comfort.

But the diversity of the prophetic writings made a clear picture difficult. They spoke of a future prophet "like unto Moses" (Deut. 18:15-18) who would appear "suddenly" in the last days.[22] They described a coming Davidic king (II Sam. 7:11-14; Psa. 68, 72, 89, 132; Isa. 16:5, 33:17; Jer. 23:5-6; Hos. 3:5). They pointed to a future priest who would serve as a unique priest-king (Psa. 110; Zech. 3:8-10, 6:12-13).

Other, more foreboding, predictions stained the writings. A mysterious insertion in Psalm 110:22 intimated the rejection of God's chosen.[23] A prominent but innocent sufferer pictured in Psalm 22, and often understood as the Messiah, lamented his pain, found his voice silenced by death, and afterward joined in a celebration of praise.[24] A rejected and smitten shepherd/leader emerged in Zechariah (11-13). Isaiah's grieving portrayal of "God's servant" (52:13-53:12) clearly conveyed a future of suffering and rejection.

A Leader Who Would Suffer with the People

Examples of benevolent leaders are one of history's rarest commodities. The old dictum, "Power corrupts, and absolute power corrupts absolutely," has been proven time and again. Perhaps that's why many failed to blend the contrasting Messianic currents into a single portrait. Perhaps that's why the religious community at Qumran looked for at least two, possibly three, Messianic figures—one a king, another a priest.[25]

But kings and priests seldom empathize with the common folk of the world. Insulated from the suffering around them by wealth and an intricate infrastructure of power, ignoring the needs of the masses becomes commonplace, even for those with the best intentions.

The Predicted Rejection and Death of the Messiah

No portion of Scripture more majestically anticipates the New Testament storyline than Isaiah's Fourth Servant Song (52:13-53:12):

> See, my servant will act wisely; he will be raised up and lifted up and highly exalted. Just as there were many who were appalled at him—his appearance was so disfigured beyond that of any man and his form marred beyond human likeness—so will he sprinkle many nations, and kings will shut their mouths because of him. For what they were no told, they will see, and what they have not heard, they will understand. Who has believed our message and to whom has the arm of the Lord been revealed? He grew up before him like a tender shoot, and like a root out of dry ground. He had no beauty or majesty to attract us to him, nothing in his appearance that we should desire him. He was despised and rejected by men, a man of sorrows and familiar with suffering. Like one from whom men hide their faces he

was despised, and we esteemed him not. Surely he took up our infirmities and carried our sorrows, yet we considered him stricken by God, smitten by him, and afflicted. But he was pierced for our transgressions, he was crushed for our iniquities; the punishment that brought us peace was upon him, and by his wounds we are healed. We all, like sheep, have gone astray, each one of us has turned to his own way; and the Lord has laid on him the iniquity of us all. He was oppressed and afflicted, yet he did not open his mouth; he was led like a lamb to the slaughter, and as a sheep before her shearers is silent, so he did not open his mouth. By oppression and judgment he was taken away. And who can speak of his descendants? For he was cut off from the land of the living; for the transgression of my people he was stricken. He was assigned a grave with the wicked, and with the rich in his death, though he had done no violence, nor was any deceit in his mouth. Yet it was the Lord's will to crush him and cause him to suffer, and though the Lord makes his life a guilt offering, he will see his offspring and prolong his days, and the will of the Lord will prosper in his hand. After the suffering of his soul, he will see the light of life and be satisfied; by his knowledge my righteous servant will justify many, and he will bear their iniquities. Therefore I will give him a portion among the great, and he will divide the spoils with the strong, because he poured out his life unto death, and was numbered with the transgressors. For he bore the sin of many, and made intercession for the transgressors.

Countless books and articles bask in the glow of Isaiah's elegant prophecy.[26] Others dissect its words and symbols until only a gutted shell remains. To those far more learned, I leave the erudite squabbling over peripheral concerns. Still, one major theme is easily discerned: God's Servant, according to the text, would suffer for his people.[27]

As Van Groningen observes concerning the passage, "Isaiah proclaims ... the covenental Seed, the anointed One of the Davidic house, called and assigned to be Yahweh's Servant who, while serving, is to experience humiliating and severe suffering on behalf of Yahweh's people."[28] Contrary to the assertions by liberal scholars, that interpretation exists in many Jewish sources. In fact, for more than 1,700 years, Jewish rabbis examined and interpreted the passage as referring to the Messiah.[29] Similar conclusions were reached in the pivotal survey by Ernst Hengstenberg.[30] It was only after the use of the passage by Christian apologists that other explanations were sought.[31]

Finally, the main reason many modern scholars refuse to allow Isaiah 53 to refer to the Messiah remains a deep-seated personal bias. Van Groningen notes that critical views are "controlled, to a large extent, by a number of unscriptural assumptions" and quotes one well-known author who states that his study is determined by "an outright rejection of the Scripture's own testimony to its inspiration by the Holy Spirit."[32]

In other words, these scholars assume predictive prophecy cannot occur. They refuse to consider evidence to the contrary.[33]

The Predicted Resurrection of the Messiah

No one in the first century inundated himself more completely in Judaism and its scriptures than did Saul of Tarsus. By his account he "was advancing in Judaism beyond many of my contemporaries among my countrymen, being more extremely zealous for my ancestral traditions" (Gal. 1:14). He studied in the school of Gamaliel with hopes of becoming a rabbi (Acts 22:3). Some scholars believe he even held membership in the Sanhedrin, his nation's central governing body.[34] His account of his background reads, "I (was) ... circumcised on the eighth day, of the people of Israel, of the tribe of Benjamin, a Hebrew of Hebrews; in regard to the law, a Pharisee; as for zeal, persecuting the church; as for legalistic righteousness, faultless (Phil. 3:5-6).

When Paul speaks in defense of the resurrection to the congregation of believers at Corinth, his writing rings with authority: "... what I received I passed on to you ... that Christ died for our sins according to the Scriptures, that he was buried, that he was raised on the third day according to the Scriptures ... (I Cor. 15:3)." Here, "the Scriptures" to which Paul refers are the Old Testament writings.

Isaiah 53 emphatically conveys a future resurrection of God's Anointed. In the final stanza of Isaiah's Fourth Servant Song (53:10-12), the prophet follows a description of suffering and death ("he was cut off from the land of the living," "He was assigned a grave" (53:8-9) by exclaiming, "After the suffering of his soul, he will see the light of life" (53:11). As Harris observes, "resurrection is clearly presupposed."[35]

Evidence Supporting Jesus' Resurrection

No event in history musters more debate than the resurrection of Jesus of Nazareth. Philosophers, historians, theologians, and common folk rehash the arguments, scrutinize the evidence, and advance their opinions regarding the believability of the biblical account.

Evidence of the Empty Tomb

No one—save a few bedazzled Roman guards—witnessed the events at the garden tomb on that Sunday morning two millennia ago. We do not have their testimony of what occurred as dawn crept toward Judea's eastern hills. Yet, no one since that morning has offered a more rational assessment than that Jesus of Nazareth, without human assistance, startled the world by emerging alive from the dampness of the tomb, none the worse for his experience. And the empty tomb makes the story far more than an endnote in the memoirs of the carpenter from Nazareth. A wealth of evidence and reasoning validates the claim. First, the vigorous testimony of the New Testament eyewitnesses provides potent confirmation of the story. The believability of those records has already been established.[36]

Second, no early Jewish source denies the claim of an empty tomb. The authorities evidently chose as their line of argument that the body was stolen (Matt. 28:11-15). An anti-Christian tract, Toledoth Yeshu, composed by Jewish sources perhaps as early as the fifth century, proposes such a theory. Scholars assume that the material comes from "early and late Talmudic and Midrashic legends and sayings concerning Jesus."[37] In other words, external sources provide an independent corroboration of Matthew's statement. Moreland's comments are worth examining:

> ... the fact of the empty tomb was common ground between believers and unbelievers. ... the fact of the empty tomb was not in dispute and thus it was not at issue. The main debate was over why it was empty, not whether it was empty. In Acts 2:29, Peter makes a reference to the fact that David's tomb was still with them. The implication seems to be that David was buried and remained in his tomb, but by contrast, Jesus did not remain in his tomb, as anyone listening to the speech could verify for himself.[39]

Third, much of the populace seemed to view Jesus as, at least, a prophet. Yet, in the first century, tombs of deceased Jewish prophets were revered. Yamauchi indicates that, in Jesus' time, tombs of approximately fifty prophets and religious leaders served as locations of worship and adoration.[40] Moreland's reasoning is relevant: "... there is no good evidence that such a practice was ever associated with Jesus' tomb. Since this was customary, and since Jesus was a fitting object of veneration, why were such religious practices not conducted at his tomb?" He concludes, "The most reasonable answer must be that Jesus' body was not in his tomb, and thus the tomb was not regarded as an appropriate site for such veneration."[41]

Fourth, even radical skeptics usually concede the historicity of biblical accounts of Jesus' burial. Rudolf Bultmann, who seldom accepts anything in Scripture as historical, acknowledges that Mark (15:42-47) "is an historical account which creates no impression of being a legend."[42] In so doing he recognized the overwhelming preponderance of evidence supporting the biblical narrative.

Craig lists ten independent items that imply that the account drew from historical fact rather than fancy.[43] A brief examination of two items will suffice. Initially, he notes that Mark names Joseph of Arimathea, a member of the Sanhedrin, as the one responsible for the burial. If he were not a member of that body, the account would have been quickly torpedoed by a Jewish response. No denials of Joseph's membership in the Sanhedrin have ever surfaced. Also, if he was known to be responsible for the burial, most other details could be easily confirmed or denied. The location of Joseph's tomb also would have been well-known and a simple stroll outside the walls could quickly confirm or deny whether it was occupied.

Craig[44] and other authors[45] also argue that the inclusion of women in the story would have been unlikely if the account had been fabricated. Moreland explains:

> ... if someone were going to make up an account of the first witnesses to the empty tomb and the risen Christ, why would women be chosen instead of the disciples? This serves only to make the disciples look cowardly and the women look courageous. This would hardly enhance the leadership of the disciples in the early church. ... (But) perhaps (the) most important fact is that in first-century Judaism, a woman's testimony was virtually worthless. A woman was not allowed to give testimony in a court of law except on rare occasions. ... The presence of the women was an embarrassment.[46]

Two ancient texts speak of the low esteem in which women were held: "Sooner let the words of the law be burnt than delivered to women."[47] "Happy is he whose children are male, and alas for him whose children are female."[48] There is no reason that forgers would have given women such a prominent part.

One final note. From earliest times, two competing accounts attempt to explain what happened to the body of Jesus. The Christian account claims resurrection. The Jewish counterattack asserts that the body was stolen. On the other hand, only one burial story appears. Moreland finds that significant:

> If the burial account in the New Testament is not reliable, then it is surprising that other accounts are nowhere to be found. Why were there not several different accounts which tried to specify the details of the burial? No conflicting account is found anywhere, even among Jewish writings, where one would expect to find an alternate account. Further, if the New Testament account is false, why did not some fragment of the true account remain? The presence of just one account of Jesus' burial points to the fact that it must have been known to have been accurate.[49]

Evidence from the Changed Lives of the Apostles

Sweeping changes in the demeanor and lives of the apostles adds more credence to the story circulated by the apostles:

Any theory which competes with the Resurrection must explain what transformed the lives of Christ's apostles around the time of the Resurrection. We know they didn't expect the Resurrection and were skeptical of the first reports from the women. What dispelled the darkness of his tragic death that hung over them like a black cloud? If Christ didn't appear to them, what changed them? What changed Simon Barjona from the coward who dodged the questions of a maid during the trial into Peter the fearless preacher who defied the Sanhedrin by preaching Christ all over Jerusalem? What changed James, the skeptical blood brother of Jesus, into James the Just, a leader of the early Jerusalem church? What changed Saul of Tarsus, the arch-Pharisee, the greatest enemy of the faith, into Paul the Apostle to the Gentiles?[50]

Evidence from the Restraint of the Gospel Records

Another consideration stems from the unusual restraint of the biblical accounts. Ancient writers tend to be notoriously one-sided and imaginative in their presentations. The gospel writers, on the other hand, demonstrate remarkable restraint.

Mark's account (16:1-8), in the opinion of many scholars the earliest written description of the event, exhibits no hype in its concise description. Harris explains the significance of that style:

> If Mark's record were a legendary fabrication, we might have expected the narrative to be adorned with fantastic features befitting an event, which, if true, must from any perspective have been the most stupendous occurrence in human history. Legendary features are clearly evident in ... later Christian writing.[51]

One classic example of the writing to which Harris refers is the Gospel of Peter, a second century document, which offers elaborate extensions to the biblical resurrection story:

> Now in the night in which the Lord's Day dawned, when the soldiers, two by two in every watch, were keeping guard, there rang out a loud voice in heaven, and they saw the heavens opened and two men come down from there in a great brightness and draw nigh to the sepulchre. The stone which had been laid against the entrance started of itself to roll and give way to the side, and the sepulchre was opened, and both the young men entered in. When now those soldiers saw this, they awakened the centurion and the elders—for they also were there to assist at the watch. And whilst they had related what they had seen, they saw again three men come out of the sepulchre, and two of them sustaining the other, and a cross following them, and the heads of the two reaching to heaven, but that of him who was led by the hand overpassing the heavens. And they heard a voice out of the heavens crying, "Thou hast preached to them that sleep," and from the cross there was heard the answer, "Yea." (Gospel of Peter 8:35-42)

Differences between the Gospel of Peter and New Testament records easily leap from the text. Such differences occur throughout apocryphal literature. Another description finds Jesus emerging from the tomb while sitting on the shoulders of the angels Michael and Gabriel (Ascension of Isaiah 3:16). In short, the restraint of biblical accounts offers little evidence of legendary development. It is a simple, straight-forward retelling of an actual, though amazing, event.

In analyzing the resurrection story, the Jewish scholar, Pinchas Lapide, reviewed the restraint with which the four gospels recount the events. He found himself persuaded by their simplicity:

> Nowhere is the event designated as a "miracle," as an event of salvation, or as a deed of God, a fact which tends to support the plausibility of the report for the disinterested reader. We do not read in the first testimonies of an apocalyptic spectacle, exorbitant sensations, or of the transforming impact of a cosmic event.[52]

Sir Norman Anderson also found it difficult to comprehend why anyone forging the accounts later in history would have chosen to use the materials found in Scripture:

> What legend-monger would ascribe the first interview with the risen Christ to Mary Magdalene, a woman of no great standing in the Christian church? Would he not have ascribed such an honour to Peter, the leading apostle; or to John, the "disciple whom Jesus loved"; or—more likely still perhaps—to Mary the mother of our Lord? And who can read the story of the appearance to Mary Magdalene, or the incident in which the risen Christ appeared to two disciples on Easter Day on an afternoon walk to Emmaus, or the episode in which Peter and John raced each other to the tomb, and seriously conclude that these are legends? They are far too dignified and restrained; far too true to life and psychology. The difference between them and the sort of stories recorded in the apocryphal gospels of a century or two later is both striking and significant.[53]

Evidence from the Failure of Counter Theories

The inventiveness and diversity of counter theories concerning the resurrection spans the gamut of human ingenuity. Charles Guignebert argued that Jesus was buried in some unknown tomb and, when the story of the resurrection began to circulate, no one knew where the body was buried.[54] Other statements of the "legend/myth" theory appear in various guises throughout skeptical literature[55] and several modern authors append the biblical stories to myths drawn from other religions.[56] Others argue that the event was always understood to be spiritual in nature.[57] Kirsopp Lake claimed the women who went to the tomb Sunday morning excitedly mistook the real tomb of Jesus for another empty, somewhat similar tomb located nearby.[58]

Other theories accept the empty tomb as fact but argue the body was stolen by his disciples[59] or by Jewish or Roman authorities. One modern appraisal argues that Jesus "passed out" or was "drugged" in such a manner that he appeared to be dead when he was not. He supposedly revived while in the tomb. The theory is a slightly revised version of one advocated by H. E. G. Paulus in 1828. Since each theory finds more than adequate rebuttal elsewhere,[60] one general comment regarding all theories will be noted, then only two will be addressed in detail: (1) the body was removed from the tomb by the disciples, and (2) Jesus did not die on the cross.

Failure of Naturalistic Theories

On May 2-3, 1985, well-known philosopher and atheist Anthony G. N. Flew and Liberty University theologian Gary Habermas engaged in a high-level academic debate regarding the resurrection. In his opening statement, Habermas summarized the problem faced by those who deny the validity of the gospel account:

> ... naturalistic theories have failed to explain away this event, chiefly because each theory is disproven by the known historical facts, as are combinations of theories. One interesting illustration of this failure ... is that they were disproven by the nineteenth-century older liberals themselves, by whom these theories were popularized. These scholars refuted each other's theories, leaving no viable naturalistic hypotheses. For instance, Albert Schweitzer dismissed Reimarus's fraud theory and listed no proponents of the view since 1768. David Strauss delivered the historical death blow to the swoon theory held by Karl Venturini, Heinrich Paulus, and others. On the other hand, Friedrich Schleiermacher and Paulus pointed out errors in Strauss's hallucination theory. The major decimation of the hallucination theory, however, came at the hands of Theodor Keim. Otto Pfleiderer was critical of the legendary or mythological theory, even admitting that it did not explain Jesus' Resurrection.[61]

As Habermas added, many influential modern theologians have recognized the paucity of evidence for the counter-theories.[62]

Failure of the Theory that the Disciples Stole the Body

As far as can be determined, no other theory gained credence in antiquity. Either the disciples removed the body from the tomb or Jesus arose from the dead. Given information currently available, the former explanation defies logical reasoning.

First, no motive exists. Reimarus claimed the apostles removed the body in hopes of gaining wealth and political power. The argument was so preposterous even Albert Schweitzer rejected it. They never came close to obtaining either.

Second, their lives offer eloquent testimony to their sincerity. Every ancient record available—Christian, Jewish, or secular—delineates the extreme suffering these early proponents of Christianity were forced to endure. They gallantly faced beatings, floggings, stonings, flayings, crucifixions, and every other brutality at the disposal of their tormentors. Not once did they break under the pressure. Allow the record to speak.

Herod beheaded James, the brother of John, and attempted to do the same to Peter (Acts 12). Andrew accepted crucifixion in the Achaian city of Patras.[63] Bartholomew (usually understood to be another designation of Nathaniel) suffered a brutal scourging and was beheaded in India.[64] Also in India, where he had been taken as a slave, Thomas was "run through" with spears.[65] Likewise, apocryphal records describe brutal deaths of Matthew, Philip, James the son of Alphaeus, Simon the zealot, and Thaddeus. Angry Jewish leaders hurled James, the brother of Jesus, from the precipice of the temple. When the fall left him clinging to life, his accusers pelted him with stones until he died.

Nero executed both Peter and Paul—Peter by crucifixion, Paul by beheading.[66] John's miraculous reprieve from the hands of Nero,[67] who attempted to have him boiled alive in a vat of oil, landed him instead in the miserable prison colony on Patmos. There, on the barren and desolate Roman rock quarry, the apostle labored under a Roman banishment that many viewed a worse fate than death. As Marlin explains, John's banishment would be "preceded by scourging, marked by perpetual fetters, scanty clothing, insufficient food, sleep on the bare ground, and dark prison work under the lash of the military overseer."[68]

Given such information, the assertion that these men removed a dead man from a Jerusalem tomb, then pranced glibly through the Roman Empire proclaiming a lie they knew would cause them extensive suffering, is still-born. The words of Pascal provide an apt summary:

> The heart of man is strangely given to fickleness and change; it is swayed by promises, tempted by material things. If any one of these men had yielded to temptations so alluring, or given way to the more compelling arguments of prison, torture, they would have all been lost.[69]

Dr. J. N. D. Anderson, former dean of the faculty of law and director of the Institute for Advanced Legal Studies at the University of London, adds that naturalism's attempted refutation of the resurrection

> ... would run totally contrary to all we know of the disciples: their ethical teaching, the quality of their lives, their steadfastness in suffering and

persecution. Nor would it begin to explain their dramatic transformation from dejected and dispirited escapists into witnesses whom no opposition could muzzle.[70]

Third, the morality taught and lived out in the lives of the apostles denies such allegations. Respected historian Edward Gibbon's acclaimed discussion of the deteriorating Roman Empire[71] lists the "purer ... austere morality" of the early Christians/ apostles as one of five key ingredients why the new religion survived. No available evidence suggests that Christianity's earliest proponents were anything other than highly moral individuals.

Fourth, evidence for the historicity of the burial adds credence to the story of the resurrection. If details of the burial are recorded accurately, then the location of the tomb was well-known as were those who placed the body there. And the evidence for the historicity of the burial accounts is exceptionally strong. While the reader may wish to examine the many details described in other materials more closely,[72] this survey will center on only a few generalizations.

The incidental, but detailed, description of the tomb in which the body was placed (Matt. 27:57-28:2; Mark 15:42-16:8; Luke 23:50-24:12; John

This acrosolia tomb would have been similar to the one in which Joseph of Arimathea is said to have buried Jesus. The accuracy of the biblical description of the tomb and the burial lends credence to the overall story. (Photo courtesy, Mr. Lawrence Williams.)

19:38-20:18) perfectly coincides with that of an acrosolia tomb. Such tombs were hewn from rock and closed by rolling a huge stone (3-4,000 pounds) into a groove at the opening of the entrance. Further, use of acrosolia tombs in Jerusalem is limited to the precise time period involved, was reserved for wealthy members of the Sanhedrin, and was located in an area that might be termed a "garden" district. Finally, the record indicates the tomb was "new," which accurately reflects the law of the time forbidding the burial of convicted criminals with other bodies.

Fifth, the changed lives of the apostles described above argues forcefully against the theory.

Sixth, a slab of white marble, now located in a Paris museum, and dating either to the time of Tiberius (14-37) or, more probably, Claudius (41-54), bears a pointed warning to grave robbers: a mandatory death penalty. Until this time, similar infractions faced only a fine.[73] Yet, the slab announced a sharp escalation in the prescribed penalty. Obviously, something caused this major shift in policy. The inscription on the slab reads:

> Decree of Caesar. It is my pleasure that sepulchres and tombs, which have been solemn memorials of ancestors or children or relatives, shall remain undisturbed in perpetuity. If it be shown that anyone has either destroyed them or otherwise thrown out the bodies which have been buried there or removed them with malicious intent to another place, thus committing a crime against those buried there, or removed the headstones or other stones, I command that against such person the same sentence be passed in respect of solemn memorials of men as is laid down in respect of the gods. Much rather must one pay respect to those who are buried. Let no one disturb them on any account. Otherwise it is my will that capital sentence be passed upon such person for the crime of tomb-spoliation.[74]

It is believed this edict did not apply to the entire empire until late in the third century. So, one must ask, "why did Claudius lay down such a severe penalty for only one segment of the empire—significantly the part to which Jesus had belonged?"[75]

Seventh, the actual presence of a guard unit at the site of the burial makes the act of stealing the body extremely difficult to achieve. Here scholars often become bogged down in quibbling over whether the guard was a Roman unit provided by Pilate or merely the Sanhedrin's own Temple Guards. In the long term, the issue is moot. Guards surrounded the tomb and became material witnesses to the events of Easter morning. Remembering the size of the stone and the rocks against which it reclined, no guard unit could have avoided hearing—even had they been asleep—the discordant scraping of rock against rock in the otherwise quiet of the morning.

Evidence Favoring a Roman Guard

Several reasons suggest a Roman rather than a Jewish guard. For instance, many incidental facts disclosed in the text become garbled if a Jewish unit is intended: (1) If a Roman seal was placed on the tomb, it is highly unlikely Pilate would have assigned a Jewish guard to police Roman affairs. If no seal was placed at the tomb, there would have been no reason for Jewish leadership to request of Pilate that their guards be allowed at the tomb. (2) If the Sanhedrin controlled the guard, no cogent reason explains why Jewish officials needed to bribe those under their command.

Why a Roman Guard Makes the Stealing of the Body Unlikely

The first century world knew Rome's military discipline. To assert that Jesus's disciples removed his body from a tomb guarded by Roman soldiers asks too much. A breach of discipline, such as sleeping on duty, was punishable by death—the death of the entire unit. Dr. George Currie, an accomplished scholar of Roman military justice, scoffed at the idea that the body could be spirited from the tomb by the disciples. He wrote that fear of punishment/discipline among the soldiers "produced flawless attention to duty, especially in the night watches."[76] In the early empire, military discipline gained such notoriety that Roman military historian Flavius Vegitius Renatus, over three centuries later, wrote a manual to the Roman Emperor Valentinian to encourage him to install the methods of offensive and defensive warfare used by Romans during the time of Christ.[77]

Even assuming the entire unit fell asleep, the case is hardly strengthened. (1) If the guard was asleep, they could offer no proof, either way, of what happened to the body. Besides, the seal remained and could be tampered with only under penalty of death. (2) If one shred of evidence connected the disciples with theft of the body, Roman authorities—whose proclivity toward execution of Jews needs little documentation would have put to death those involved. A Roman guard makes the stolen body hypothesis appear humorous.

Would Temple Guards Have Permitted the Disciples to Steal the Body?

Some authorities think the presence of a Temple Guard rather than a Roman unit would multiply the likelihood that zealous disciples could pull off a heist. Why that should be the case is a mystery.

Temple Guards were just as disciplined at their posts as were the Romans. McDowell notes, "... at night, if the captain approached a guard member who was asleep, he was beaten and burned with his clothes. A member of the guard also was forbidden to sit down or to lean against something when he was on duty."[78] Moreover, temple guards understood more completely the gravity of the situation.

Failure of the Theory that Jesus Did Not Die

Only one other counter theory merits consideration: The so-called swoon theory and its variants. Again, an abundance of evidence disputes the theory.

First, routine events leading up to crucifixion make survival improbable. Candidates for crucifixion struggled through an infamous Roman scourging.[79] Inflicted by a type of whip known as the flagrum that included leather thongs with embedded balls of lead and sharpened pieces of bone and metal, the many blows to the body intended to push the victim to the verge of death.[80]

One widely recognized description of scourging appeared in 1965 in the journal *Arizona Medicine*. There, Dr. Truman Davis visualized the event:

> The heavy whip is brought down with full force again and again across [the victim's] shoulders, back and legs. At first the heavy thongs cut through the skin only. Then, as the blows continue, they cut deeper into the subcutaneous tissues, producing first an oozing of the blood from the capillaries and veins of the skin, and finally spurting arterial bleeding from vessels in the underlying muscles. The small balls of lead first produce large, deep bruises which are broken open by subsequent blows. Finally, the skin of the back is hanging in long ribbons, and the entire area is an unrecognizable mass of torn, bleeding tissue. When it is determined by the centurion in charge that the prisoner is near death, the beating is finally stopped.[81]

Eusebius, himself a witness of scourgings, provides an apt description of the result: "The sufferer's veins were laid bare, and the very muscles, sinews, and bowels of the victim were open to exposure."[82] Coupled with the emasculating effects of the crucifixion that followed, survival was unthinkable.

Second, only once, in literature from Roman times, did a victim manage to survive crucifixion and its accompanying torture. Maier recounts,

> ... there is a recorded instance of a victim being taken down from a cross and surviving. ... Josephus, who had gone over to the Roman side in the rebellion of 66 A.D., discovered three of his friends being crucified. He asked the Roman general Titus to reprieve them, and they were immediately removed from their crosses. Still, two of the three died anyway, even though they apparently had been crucified only a short time. ... Romans were grimly efficient about crucifixions: Victims did not escape with their lives.[83]

Third, massive distinctions separate survivors and those resurrected from the dead. This factor alone led skeptic David Strauss to jettison the swoon theory as a viable explanation for events in first-century Jerusalem. He wrote:

> It is impossible that a being who had stolen half-dead out of the sepulchre, who crept about weak and ill, wanting medical treatment, who required bandaging, strengthening, and indulgence, and who still at last yielded to his sufferings, could have given the disciples the impression that he was a conqueror over death and the grave, the Prince of Life: an impression which lay at the bottom of their future ministry.[84]

Fourth, even if Jesus barely clung to life when placed in the tomb, conditions made it far more likely his condition would deteriorate rather than improve. For instance, medical science informs us that those near death struggle for oxygen. To seal Jesus hermetically inside a rock grave with nearly 100 pounds of aromatic spices, such as myrrh, would kill an individual whose brain was already barely functioning. In addition, "the contact of the body with the cold stone of the sepulchre would have been enough to bring on a syncope through the congelation of the blood, owing to the fact that the regular circulation was already checked."[85]

Fifth, the theory assumes the credulity of the Romans in charge of the crucifixion. Yet, as Michael Green observes, "These soldiers were experienced at their grisly task: crucifixions were not uncommon in Palestine. They knew a dead man when they saw one."[86] Coupled with the severe discipline imposed on soldiers who failed to carry out their assignments, the unlikeliness of Jesus' body being removed from the cross when there was any chance he remained alive becomes obvious.

Alleged Contradictions in the Resurrection Accounts

Some feel that contradictions in various gospel accounts prove the resurrection false. Amazingly, they prove exactly the opposite. First, the variations that one encounters in the records should be expected. Different people, from different backgrounds, with different purposes for writing, emphasize different details. As Maier notes, "even eyewitnesses can report the same event differently."[87] He further contends that because the variations were not edited out or harmonized shows "the honesty of the Early Church."[88]

Second, it is possible to harmonize all the diverse strands into one account. John Wenham's *Easter Enigma* (1984) provides one excellent effort in that direction. After nearly four decades of research, he concluded, "these resurrection stories exhibit in a remarkable way the well-known characteristics of accurate and independent reporting, for superficially they show great disharmony, but on close examination the details gradually fall into place."[89]

Third, and finally, even if real contradictions do exist between the eyewitness accounts, that would not be sufficient ground to overcome the other evidence:

> The earliest sources telling of the great fire of Rome, for example, offer far more serious conflicts on who or what started the blaze and how far it spread, some claiming that the whole city was scorched while others insist that only three sectors were reduced to ash. Yet the fire itself is historical: it actually happened.[90]

Predicting
Israel's Future

Humanity often pays lip service to the law of graduated responsibility. The law says that we expect and require little of those with mediocre talents and abilities, while we expect much from those with considerable talents and abilities. Thus, those whose physical prowess gives them exceptional strength must protect the weak. Those with exceptional skills and reasoning abilities must guide and counsel those who struggle with their decisions. When those so honored fail to live up to such expectations and responsibilities, shame, disgrace, and death often follow.

From a biblical perspective, expectations of Israel far outstripped the expectations of her neighbors. Israel's storehouse swelled. Rivers of blessings cascaded from the ridges of eternity to fill her reservoirs.

Her armies fought superior enemies with weapons that should never have been effective, in locales where they should never have engaged opposing forces. Yet, despite overwhelming odds, and to the dismay of her opponents, time and again her armies returned in triumph. Against a backdrop of humanly inexplicable events, Israel marched out of slavery and away from the world's most powerful army. Amidst human giants and immense physical obstacles, her people conquered and settled a rich and wild land.

Her laws and ethical teachings blazed a trail toward wellness and lofty conduct. Over 3,000 years later, at the doorstep of the 21st century, they could still eliminate the vast majority of the world's misery and suffering.[1] Even today, her directives regarding compassion, justice, dignity, and human worth stand alone, silent sentinels on the mountain peak of true humanism.

But, like the rich fool who greedily hoarded his goods, Israel refused to share her bounty. She squandered her blessings and opportunities. She turned a deaf ear to her responsibilities. Setbacks plagued her battlefields. Temporary enslavements became more frequent. Warnings boomed from the prophets. And when the people ignored their warnings, the prophets offered a dark future.

Hosea (8:7) exclaimed: "They sow the wind and reap the whirlwind." After viewing a vision of Israel's doom, Isaiah (24:11) grieved, "All joy turns to gloom, all gaiety is banished from the earth." For Jeremiah, Israel's abdication of her responsibility demanded a shroud, not a blanket. There would be no balm in Gilead, no healing of the nation's wound. "Disaster follows disaster," he lamented (Jer. 4:20). "The whole land lies in ruins." Zephaniah's (1:13) conclusion was no different: "Their wealth will be plundered, their houses demolished. They will build houses but not live in them; they will plant vineyards but not drink the wine."

More than a thousand verses outline the decline and fall of the Israelite nation. Obviously, a discussion of each is well beyond the scope of this study. This survey can address only broad generalizations.

Predicting Israel's Dispersion among the Nations

Perhaps the most widely recognized prediction regarding ancient Israel relates to her persecution and scattering among the nations. After they gained their freedom from Egyptian bondage, Moses warned (Lev. 26:33) that, if Israel lived in disobedience, God "will scatter you among the nations and will draw out (His) sword and pursue (you)." In the centuries after Moses' prediction, the Jews have found often themselves scattered throughout the nations.

As early as the period of the judges, invading armies spirited away segments of the population. During the monarchy, the Assyrians and Babylonians carried out wholesale deportations. Slave traders tore smaller groups from the land during the Hellenistic period. Two vicious wars with Rome sent Jews scurrying for safety far from Palestine. The trend continued until the establishment of the modern Jewish state in 1947. Even with the modern nation in place, Jews continue to be dispersed throughout the world. No prophecy has ever seen a more indisputable fulfillment.

Hidden within the many scriptures predicting a scattering of Israel, a far more imposing prophecy appears. Though persecution would scatter her among the nations, the people of Israel would retain their national and cultural identity. Moses' prophecy (Lev. 26:44) concluded: "When they are in the land of their enemies, I will not reject them or abhor them so as to destroy them completely." Invading armies uprooted from their respective homelands many nations similar to Israel. Edomites, Ammonites, Amorites, Moabites, and Philistines faced corresponding deportations. Only Israel survived, distinguished by what some believe to be merely a long string of fortuitous coincidences.

Predicting the Desolation of Israel's Cities

Because of Israel's disobedience, prophetic warnings of impending doom painted a ghastly picture of the nation's future. While admitting a remnant would persevere through God's looming judgments, the prophets foretold that the land would be deserted and the cities would lie in ruins. Moses finished his prophecy (Lev. 26:33) by declaring a warning for those disobedient to God's instructions: "Your land will be laid waste and your cities will lie in ruins."

Later, when Isaiah (6:11-12) remembered his call to the prophetic office, he recounted his instructions to echo Moses' decree. Asking how long he should continue the warnings, he was told, "until the cities lie ruined and without inhabitant, until the houses are left deserted and the fields ruined and ravaged, until the Lord has sent everyone far away and the land is utterly forsaken." The theme of deserted cities appears throughout the prophetic writings. Jeremiah (4:29) wrote of a future Israel where "all the towns are deserted; no one lives in them" while Ezekiel (7:11) added, "none of the people will be left."

Complete desolation of Israel's cities was no simple task. Moses deeded to the half-tribe of Manasseh, which remained east of the Jordan, "sixty cities" that were "fortified with high walls and with gates and bars" with "a great many unwalled cities" (Deut. 3:4-5). Also, when Joshua (15:20-63) first led the fledgling nation into the "promised land," he recorded that 112 cities and unnumbered hamlets existed in the region allotted to the tribe of Judah. He implied that such conditions existed throughout the land.

Of course, some deny that Israel served as home to an extensive population. Years ago, the noted French atheist Voltaire declared Israel to be such a poor country that biblical references to a large population base and many cities could not possibly be accurate.[2] Modern critics often parrot his conclusions.

Yet, historical and archaeological facts coincide with biblical records. Rome's famed chronicler Tacitus described Judea as "being overspread with villages."[3] Dion Cassius, in writing of the blitzkrieg that overwhelmed Israel between 66-70 A.D., claimed Roman legions decimated "five hundred strongly fortified citadels and 985 villages."[4] Josephus spoke of Galilee as thickly populated with villages and cities.[5] Dr. Eli Smith's intensive research in the region surrounding Hebron, uncovered remains of 103 ruined villages.[6] Extensive populations—up to 15,000—

may have inhabited the larger villages.[7] All 103 villages lay in silent devastation.

Similar ruins exist throughout Palestine: sixty-four village ruins surround the site of ancient Jerusalem; thirty-nine deserted villages lie near Lydda; thirty ruins are near Nablus; to the east of the Jordan, 345 former villages, dating to Bible times, have been identified.[8] The haunting accuracy of Isaiah's prophecy (27:10) cannot be exorcised: "The fortified city stands desolate, an abandoned settlement, forsaken, like the desert; there the cattle graze, there they lie down; they strip its branches bare."

Even the return of a large population base during the last five decades of this century has helped set in motion activities that confirm the accuracy of the prophets' warnings. With the creation of the modern state of Israel in 1947, interested in the land's history surged. From one border to another, the shovels of archaeologists have unearthed the ruins of once-proud cities.

Those ruins demonstrate conclusively that, on three or four separate occasions, enemies have voided Israel of her population base: (1) in the years immediately following the Babylonian conquest, (2) after both Roman conquests in 70 A.D. and 132 A.D., and (3) during much of the Middle Ages. Relying on ancient records, Josephus wrote of the period following Babylon's victory, "all Judea and Jerusalem, and the temple, continued to be a desert for seventy years."[9]

Predicting the Future of Samaria

Unlike predictions applicable to all Israelite cities and towns, Samaria, the well-fortified capital of the northern kingdom, drew exclusive attention from the prophets. To understand the reasons, a brief knowledge of the city's history is necessary.

Early Attempts to Locate a Capital for the Northern Kingdom

When the ten northern and eastern tribes dissolved political and religious ties with the southern kingdom nearly a millennium before the days of Jesus, they needed a suitable seat of government. For years, no permanent site could be found upon which they agreed.

Political and religious reasons prompted Jereboam I to name the city of Shechem as the kingdom's first capital.[10] Both Abraham (Gen. 12:6) and Joseph (Gen. 37:14) could be intimately connected to Shechem and Jereboam desperately needed some way to legitimatize his claim to the throne. Evidently he believed that connecting his capital to deeply patriotic/nationalistic memories would do that. Besides the city's connection with the patriarchs, the city also gained prominence during the time of

Joshua (24:32) and the judges (Judg. 9). Two mountains of importance to the Hebrews, Gerizim and Ebal, also can be found nearby.

Ultimately, Shechem proved unsatisfactory as a site for Israel's capital. Nearby Penuel soon replaced Shechem (I Kings 12:25). That location proved unsuitable as well. Two years after Jereboam's son, Nadab, succeeded him on the throne, assassination claimed his life, and Baasha usurped the throne. In the purge following the assassination, Baasha tried to distance himself from everything associated with the prior monarchy. One of his first directives moved the capital to Tirzah, where it remained throughout his 24-year reign.

Ironically, two years into the reign of Baasha's son, Elah, history duplicated itself. Elah, like Jereboam's son Nadab, fell victim to a group of assassins. Zimri, the leader of the conspiracy, seized the throne. Holding the throne proved far more difficult than seizing it. Seven days into his reign, the commander of Israel's army, Omri, surrounded Tirzah. Recognizing his hopeless position, Zimri ordered the burning of his palace and committed suicide (I Kings 16:18).

The Choice of Samaria as Capital

Following Omri's ascension as king (I Kings 16:15-18), he began an intensive search for yet another capital. This time, rather than using an existing city, the king decided to construct a capital from scratch. The hill

Ruins of Omri's palace at the site of ancient Samaria. (Photo courtesy, Fon Scofield Collection, E. C. Dargan Research Library of the Sunday School Board, SBC.)

The choice of the hill of Samaria as the site for the capital of the northern kingdom was based on important military factors. The site offered a commanding view of surrounding areas. (Photo courtesy, Dr. Marlin Connelly.)

of Samaria, some nine miles west of Tirzah, met Omri's criteria and a new city emerged on the hillside. The choice appeared to be an excellent one.

It dominated the high road which led from Jerusalem to Damascus and the cities of Phoenicia. Communications eastward with the lands beyond Jordan were not difficult. ... An easy road led to the sea which is only about twenty-five miles away, and from his palace windows the king could watch Phoenician galleys sailing along the coast. The surrounding country was rich: Isaiah speaks of Samaria as the glorious beauty which is on the head of a fat valley, and the sides of the valley north of the hill are still covered with groves of olive trees and vineyards and terraced gardens planted with fruit trees.[11]

Samaria's location also made it easily defensible. The hill is described as "a round and isolated mass from three hundred to four hundred feet above the valley (which) could offer a stubborn resistance to the best organized armies."[12] A. Van Selms writes of the site,

The spot was well chosen: a nearly isolated hill surrounded by a fertile valley ... The location justifies the name someron, which can be rendered "watching point." A stronghold on top of the hill could be easily defended, and it controlled the whole surrounding area, including caravan roads to the north, west, and south.[13]

Having made his choice, Omri set out to construct a powerful city. He succeeded.

Population of the City. Omri and the rulers that followed him to Israel's throne never visualized Samaria as an ancient population hub. As Crowfoot, Kenyon, and Sukenik observed, "The size of the hill and its contours were not favorable to vast expansion."[14] Only so many people could be packed onto the hill. In addition, a dearth of usable water limited the population. The researchers continued, "the nearest good springs are a mile away on the far side of a deep valley. ... the cisterns inside the walls could not have been sufficient for many thousand inhabitants plus their horses and donkeys."[15]

It is unlikely the city ever held more than a few thousand inhabitants. The only population figures from antiquity show that Ahab numbered 7,232 Israelites among its citizenry (I Kings 20:15), while Sargon claimed to have carried more than 27,000 into slavery when the Assyrians captured the city and its environs around 722 B.C.[16]

Samaria's Wealthy Clientele. Samaria's size underscored her exclusivity. Insufficiently large to house a large population, she evidently served as an oasis of luxury for government officials. Commoners found themselves relegated to villages and hovels in the surrounding countryside while Samaria's leaders accumulated vast sums of wealth from the people. Archaeological digs at the site confirm that "it has yet to be shown that any common dwelling existed at Samaria during the Israelite period."[17]

The city's affluence is described in the writings of Amos (6:4,6), who describes its citizenry as people who "lie on beds inlaid with ivory and lounge on your couches. You dine on choice lambs and fattened calves. ... You drink wine by the bowlful and use the finest lotions." Of the city's leaders, he declared (2:6-7), "they sell the righteous for silver, and the needy for a pair of sandals. They trample on the heads of the poor as upon the dust of the ground and deny justice to the oppressed."

Significant archaeological discoveries concur with the prophetic description of the city. Researchers have recovered many ivory inlays from the ruins. Moreover, since Assyrians later sacked the site in 722 B.C., it is worth noting that ivories similar to those found among the ruins of Samaria have also been uncovered in Assyrian ruins.[18]

Predictions Regarding Samaria

The prophets denounced the Samaritans because of their inordinate lust for material possessions and power, their willingness to exploit people, and their religious apostasy. Amos (6:1-7) caustically warned those who felt "secure on Mount Samaria" that all her defensive advantages would be of no value. She would be delivered into slavery unless she repented. Specifically, the prophets alleged that (1) the city would be violently destroyed, (2) the stones from her buildings would be rolled into the surrounding valleys, (3) her site would be covered with vineyards, and (4) her foundations would be rediscovered (Micah 1:6; Hosea 13:16).

The Violent Destructions of the City

Samaria's fortifications and strong defensive ability lulled her inhabitants into thinking they could withstand attack. If man could build a defensible city, it was Samaria. As Barnes noted,

> Samaria was chosen with much human wisdom. ... Embedded in mountains ... it lay a mountain-fortress in a rich valley. ... The way to Samaria lay, every way, through deep and often narrowing valleys, down which the armies of Samaria might readily pour, but which, like Thermopylae, might be held by a handful of men against a large host. (Samaria was) well nigh impregnable, except by famine.[19]

Samaria's first violent confrontation came when mighty Assyrian armies under Shalmaneser and Sargon easily overran most of the northern kingdom. The little resistance that existed in many cities and towns

John Hyrcanus used water from pools to fulfill one of Micah's prophecies concerning the destruction of Samaria. (Photo courtesy, Dr. Marlin Connelly.)

withered like straw in a furnace. Only Samaria withstood the initial shock. Protected by terrain and strong fortifications, she held out for three years. In the end, her defenses merely prolonged the inevitable. A bloody confrontation followed as Assyrian forces

> ... ruthlessly butchered the majority of the population, burned, looted, and demolished their cities, destroyed their fortresses, and carried into slavery more than 27,000 ... whose youth, strength, and ability would make them profitable as slaves. Children too young to work were destroyed. The nobility ... the aged, infirm, or disabled were killed.[20]

After capturing Samaria, Assyria deported her citizenry and resettled them in other areas of their Empire, then repopulated the region with conquered peoples from other lands (II Kings 17:24). According to Sargon's boast, he rebuilt Samaria "better than before."[21]

The city seems to have weathered the transition to Babylonian, then Persian, control without difficulty. The same cannot be said for the days of Alexander. As Rowell reports, "Evidently the Samaritans revolted against Alexander, who, on his return from Egypt, destroyed Samaria, annihilated the leaders, expelled the rest of the inhabitants, and resettled Samaria with Macedonians."[22]

Stones Rolled into the Valleys. During the last third of the second century, B.C., Samaria again felt the full sting of prophecy. John Hyrcanus and his army besieged the city for a year, "demolished it entirely ... and took away the very marks that there had ever been a city there."[23] After his victory, he hoped to make the site uninhabitable for future generations.

To accomplish his purpose, Hyrcanus ordered that water be diverted around the walls to undermine the foundations. The force of the water helped roll the stones into the valley. Amazingly, the very terms employed by the prophets hundreds of years before implied just that. Micah (1:6) predicted that the city's stones would be "poured" down into the valley. In Hebrew literature, the term is consistently used of water racing in torrents over a waterfall. But, how could it be possible for someone to predict that Samaria, aloof from all natural watercourses, would find her stones rolled down the hillsides by rushing water?

Yet, travelers to Samaria in the nineteenth century dutifully observed that the "stones of the temples and palaces ... have been carefully removed from the rich soil, thrown together in heaps, built up in the rude walls of terraces, and rolled down into the valley below."[24]

Herod the Great frustrated plans that no city would ever again sit on the hill of Samaria when he ordered the city rebuilt nearly a century afterward. It bore the name Sebaste (Greek for "Augustus") and became an important Roman city. Even Herod's fortress city did not survive. It, too, was destroyed during the Jewish revolt (66-70 A.D.) when it was burned by rebel forces. The city was rebuilt yet again by the Roman emperor Severus. That city lies in ruins as well. Still, even with all the rebuilding, the Israelite city had been destroyed exactly as Micah and Amos predicted.

Samaria's Return to Vineyards. As Western travelers entered the region again in the nineteenth century, they found the hillsides of Samaria serving as plots for vineyards. Porter described "the whole hill" as "cultivated in terraces."[25] Van de Velde calls the remains of the city "a huge heap of stones! her foundations discovered, her streets ploughed up, and covered with corn fields and olive gardens."[26]

The Discovery of Samaria's Foundations. Biblical prophets also described an eventual discovery of the "foundations" of the old Israelite capital. That prophecy, too, reveals a haunting accuracy. As city after city supplanted the original, remains of everything except the foundations disappeared. Thanks, in part, to the modern fascination with archaeology, those original foundations are exposed again.[27] Jack's captivating description of ongoing archaeological research at the site corresponds beautifully:

> Before archaeologists began their work, the hill of Samaria was covered with soil under cultivation. As a result of the wars, treasure searches, removal of building stones, quarrying, and agricultural labors during the last twenty centuries, the ancient Israelite and other walls ... lay buried in the depths. The only vestiges of antiquity visible were some of the towers and columns of the Herodian period.[28]

Another, earlier writer, noted, "Samaria has been destroyed, but her rubbish has been thrown down into the valley; her foundation stones, those grayish ancient quadrangular stones of the time of Omri and Ahab, are discovered, and lie scattered about the slope of the hill."[29]

The biblical prophets painted a remarkably accurate portrait of Samaria's future. The detail in their brush strokes are as precise as those of Michelangelo.

Predicting
the Catastrophe
of 70 A.D.

Jerusalem represented both the good and the bad in Judaism. Home to Herod's Second Temple as well as to scribes who laboriously studied the Scriptures, she personified hypocrisy. Her greed and injustice overshadowed her professions of religion. Though she housed the palaces of kings and became the focal point of Jewish nationalism, she also functioned as the center of usury and political expediency.

Jerusalem's rugged individualism allowed her to thumb her nose at authority and dare anyone to regulate her license to do as she pleased. Laws originating at Sinai were obeyed only if convenient. Newer laws and regulations proved overwhelmingly burdensome. Hopelessly subjective, they were often imposed to give one person or group an advantage over another. The unfolding events appeared remarkably similar to others centuries earlier.

Seventh century prophets incessantly warned Jerusalem of impending doom. They foretold the ascendancy of Babylon. They warned of the impotency of relying on Egyptian intervention. They forewarned the populace that Nebuchadnezzar's armies would devour the city and reduce it to ashes. They cautioned against rebellion. Few listened.

Some seven centuries later, history prepared to repeat itself. This time, instead of Babylonian, Roman armies stood poised to deliver the crushing blow. By the spring of 70 A.D., the hounds of destruction reared their heads on the horizon. The story, however, begins four decades earlier when a prophet accurately described the rapidly unfolding events. His name was Jesus.

New Testament Prophecies Will Be Given Top Priority

To imply that prophecies of doom for Jerusalem appeared only in Jesus' pronouncements would be terribly misleading. Old Testament prophets integrate many allusions to this cataclysm into their materials.

However, this study focuses on predictions of the events that appear in New Testament writings.

This approach was chosen for two reasons. First, earlier chapters discuss the prophetic accuracy of the older writings in sufficient detail to establish a pattern of prophetic reliability. To avoid the impression that only these writings provide evidence of supernatural guidance, it is necessary to evaluate the predictive abilities of the New Testament personalities as well. Second, the later predictions are so detailed that they provide an excellent check on the validity of the prophecy.

A Description of First-Century Jerusalem

The Population of the City

First-century Jerusalem bore all the marks of an urban center. A bustling metropolis and a noted center of learning and culture, she also served as home to thousands of people. Though the exact population of the city during the years 66-70 A.D. cannot be determined, all ancient sources agree that the numbers present in the city and its immediate suburbs during the great feasts swelled into the tens of thousands, perhaps into the hundreds of thousands.[1] According to reliable witnesses, the Passover alone required the services of 17,000 priests and Levites.[2]

While some modern writers reject these figures, the unanimous testimony of first-century writers and eyewitnesses is intimately more believable than unsupported assertions from authors twenty centuries removed. Moreover, the claim is not that hundreds of thousands lived year-round inside the walls of Jerusalem, but that these numbers crowded into the immediate area during the feasts.[3]

The Economic Status of Those in the City

Economically, Jerusalem portrayed a schizophrenic character. Among her citizenry, she claimed both the very wealthy and the very poor. Some of the wealthiest rulers, merchants, landowners, tax-farmers, and bankers strode through her streets. Their legendary wealth circulated through much of the ancient world. During the Feast of the Tabernacles, some used golden thread to tie bundles of branches to trees.[4] Others gave opulent banquets.[5] Still another carpeted the walkway from her house to the temple so that she would have no difficulty in walking barefoot to ceremonies on the Day of Atonement.[6]

On the other hand, multitudes of the poor, crushed under years of oppression, trod the streets of Jerusalem begging alms. Barely eking out a minimal existence, they cluttered the alleyways of the old city.

The Majesty of the Temple Complex

Jerusalem boasted exquisite public and private buildings. Herod's massive extensions of the Second Temple required a half-century to complete (John 2:20) and transformed the structure into one of the recognized wonders of the Roman world.[7] Huge slabs of alabaster, stibium, and marble buttressed the sanctuary. Its majesty dominated the Judean landscape. Even the apostles stood in awe (Matt. 24:1). Josephus wrote:

> The exterior of the building wanted nothing that could astound either mind or eye. For, being covered on all sides with massive plates of gold, the sun was no sooner up than it radiated so fiery a flash that persons straining to look at it were compelled to avert their eyes, as from the solar rays. To approaching strangers it appeared from a distance like a snow-clad mountain; for all that was not overlaid with gold was of purest white. Some of the stones in the building were forty-five cubits in length, five in height, and six in width.[8]

This model of the first-century city, and especially the area surrounding Herod's Palace, on the grounds of the Holy Land Hotel in Jerusalem, depicts its grandeur during the days of Jesus. (Photo courtesy, Dr. Marlin Connelly.)

The stones approximated the size of railroad boxcars.[9] No wonder one of Jesus' disciples, overwhelmed with the immensity of it all, stopped him as he emerged from the temple complex, and blurted out (Mark 13:1), "Look, teacher! What massive stones! What magnificent buildings!"

Polished stones paved the courtyards.[10] Passageways overlaid with gold and silver lined every entrance to the complex.[11] Golden plates cov-

Portions of the old city of Jerusalem can still be seen in ruins near the "Dome of the Rock." (Photo courtesy, Dr. Marlin Connelly.)

ered the 150-foot square temple building as well as the entrance between the sanctuary and the porch.[12] Sharp, golden spikes crowned the roof of the sanctuary, designed to prevent birds from landing on the holy shrine.[13] Tables, lamps, bowls, chains, and other vessels of gold and marble garnished the courtyards.[14]

As Lane discloses, "This complex of stone was one of the most impressive sights in the ancient world, and was regarded as an architectural wonder." It became "a mountain of white marble, decorated with gold" and "dominated the Kidron gorge as an object of dazzling beauty."[15] Jewish pride in the temple complex shows through in several surviving documents. The rabbis taught, "he who has not seen Jerusalem in her splendor has never seen a desirable city in his life. He who has not seen the temple in its full construction has never seen a glorious building in his life."[16] So much gold adorned the templex and its outlying buildings that Josephus reports the gold standard in Syria plummeted when Jerusalem fell because so much gold glutted the market.[17] Even Pliny described the city as "the most famous city of the East."[18]

Other Exceptional Buildings in the City

Besides the temple complex, other ornate structures graced Jerusalem. Slightly north and west of the temple area, the Fortress Antonia rose ominously over the city. Named in honor of Marc Antony, Antonia resembled a fortified town with "courts, porticoes, barracks, a parade ground, baths, and royal apartments. Four corner towers, the tallest rising more than a hundred feet (offered) a commanding view of the temple courts and the city."[19] Tunnels connected the fortress with the temple.[20]

South of the temple mount, Herod built a huge hippodrome where chariot races could excite the imagination of his more well-to-do clients. He also added both a theater and an amphitheater. Batey describes a typical scene in Jesus' day:

> In the (amphitheater) trained gladiators fight to the end before excited, blood-thirsty mobs. Wild animals, many imported from Africa, are pitted against one another in mortal combat. Slaves and condemned prisoners fight with wild beasts while spectators place their bets and cheer on their favorites. Most Jews are incensed by these gory spectacles in which human life is sacrificed for public entertainment, but some attend, desiring to be fashionable, as well as enjoying the cruelty.[21]

Still, Herod's building continued. He added a zoo.[22] Later, his crowning achievement came in the construction of his palace located on the city's western ridge. The surrounding wall of huge stones rose forty-five feet above the streets. Three massive towers, even higher than those at the Antonia, jutted skyward. Batey, again, visualizes the scene:

> The main palace, surrounded by verdant lawns and trees watered by fountains and pools, is a paragon of oriental extravagances. The royal apartments, with imported marble walls and huge carved cedar ceiling beams, are appointed with sculptures, paintings, and furnishings of gold and silver. Two cavernous halls, named appropriately Augustus and Agrippa, are each ample enough to sleep a hundred guests.[23]

The City's Defenses

Fun and games found themselves tempered with reality. Warfare still ruled the region. Except for the period known as the Pax Romana, defense often overshadowed culture. Herod intended that Jerusalem have as strong a defense as he could provide. The city became a veritable fortress. Walls that Josephus describes as "practically impregnable" surrounded the city.[24]

Jerusalem's citizenry felt smug and secure. No doubt inhabitants of the day echoed their ancestors (Isa. 26:1) when they bragged, "A strong city have we." Perhaps they quoted the Psalmist (48:13-14): "Walk about Jerusalem, make the round, count her towers. Consider her ramparts, examine her castles."

Jesus Predicts the Future of Jerusalem

Against this backdrop, Jesus offered twelve distinct predictions. All three synoptic gospels record at least a portion of what he had to say. He foretold that (1) some people listening to his words would literally see them happen (Matt. 24:34; Luke 21:32), and that (2) Jerusalem and its temple would be obliterated (Matt. 24:2; Luke 19:44). This devastation would be preceded (3) by wars and rumors of wars (Matt. 24:6), (4) by the appearance of false Messiahs (Matt. 24:5,24; Mark 13:6; Luke 21:9), (5) by a proliferation of natural disasters (Matt. 24:7; Mark 13:8; Luke 21:11), (6) by the beginning of persecution against the church (Matt. 24:9-10; Mark 13:9-11; Luke 21:12,16-17); and (7) by the appearance of teachers who would stray from the teachings of the apostles (Matt. 24:11; Mark 13:22).

Jerusalem's destruction would be signaled (8) by "the abomination of desolation spoken of by Daniel the prophet ... standing in the Holy Place" and by the city being "compassed with armies" (Matt. 24:15; Luke 21:20). After this sign, (9) Christians were to flee the city immediately and go to the mountains (Matt. 24:16; Mark 13:14; Luke 21:21). After their escape, (10) the city would suffer "great tribulation" during which time (11) more false Messiahs would appear (Matt. 24:21,24). Finally, (12) the approaching doom would be signaled by special portents in the skies (Luke 21:25).

Interpreting the Predictions

F. LaGard Smith's introduction to these passages provides a masterful short summation of the three diverse interpretations:

> There is general agreement regarding Jesus' reference to the destruction of the temple. ... Most would agree that Jesus describes events which precede that destruction. Some feel that Jesus' entire discourse is made with reference to Jerusalem's destruction by the Romans, while others see in it additional apocalyptic prophecy concerning future events. Still others view it as one prophecy having a dual significance.[25]

Though many contend these predictions speak of the end of the world, every item occurred during the confrontation between the Jews and Romans. Whether similar events will occur in the future as well bears no relevancy to their apologetic value.

Reviewing the Context of the Prophecy

Before discussing each prediction, we should first study the context in which they appear. Truly, "no scripture is spoken in a vacuum. Every passage must be viewed in ... context."[26]

When Jesus uttered the prophecies, his earthly mission was rapidly drawing to an end. As it did, the inevitable clash with the religious establishment gushed to the forefront. The clash escalated quickly as the leadership, already plotting his death, denied his miracles and verbally abused those he healed. They refused to examine his claims. Their questioning belied motives of poorly concealed entrapment. Finally, the inevitable revulsion exploded (Matt. 23). His scathing response tersely set the stage for what would follow:

> Woe unto you, teachers of the law and Pharisees, you hypocrites! ... Fill up, then, the measure of the sin of your forefathers! You snakes! You brood of vipers! How will you escape being condemned to hell? ... upon you will come all the righteous blood that has been shed on earth ... I tell you the truth, all this will come upon this generation (Matt. 23: 29,32-33,35-36).

Immediately before these events, one of Jesus' final parables focused on the marriage of a king's son and the refusal of the king's subjects to attend the wedding feast. It pictures Jesus' rejection by the Jewish leadership. The conclusion of the parable clarifies about whom he had been speaking: "The king was enraged. He sent his army and destroyed those murderers and burned their city" (Matt. 22:7).

Fulfilling the Predictions

Understanding the context, the question to be addressed is simple: "How accurate were the predictions?" In fact, their accuracy is so arresting that some refuse to accept them as predictions, claiming they appeared many decades after the events. That issue will be considered later. We now examine the predictions.

The Events Would Happen While Many Listeners Still Lived. Fewer than forty years passed between Jesus' original prophecy and the decimation of the Jewish state. All sources agree that John was still alive. Others among Jesus' followers survived to this point as well.

The Temple Would be Destroyed. That Roman armies accomplished this in 70 A.D. stands as one of the most well-authenticated facts of history. Archaeologists confirm the destruction through scattered remains. Simons notes that whether Jesus' prophecy "referred to the temple proper or to the entire block of buildings within the outer enclosure, no prophecy has been fulfilled more literally, since the very site of the sacred edifice and the disposition of all the accessory buildings have become matters of discussion."[28]

From our vantage point in history, the prediction of Jerusalem's fall seems almost a foredrawn conclusion. Nothing could be less factual.

Were it not for a totally out-of-character, inexplicable decision by a Roman general, the rebellion would have been squashed without the devastation of the city and its sacred precincts.

The story begins in November, 66 A.D., at the outset of hostilities. The Roman general Cestius Gallus with lightning rapidity, stuck a dagger in the heart of the rebellion. Accompanied by Rome's powerful Twelfth Legion that had been stationed in Syria, he easily brushed aside all opposition in Galilee and Judea and quickly reached the outer fringes of Jerusalem.

Gallus maneuvered his troops into perfect position. They routed the defenders of the suburbs, squeezed the multitudes present for the Feast of the Tabernacles behind the city walls, undermined the walls, and stood poised to deliver the fatal blow to the rebellion. Inside the city, an arrogant but jubilant atmosphere quickly faded. In its place, a pall of gloom settled over the rebels. Josephus believed the city teetered on the verge of surrender:

> Cestius ... put the Jews to flight, and pursued them to Jerusalem. He then pitched his camp upon ... Scopus ... put his army in array (and) brought it into the city ... And when Cestius was come ... into the upper city, (he) pitched his camp over against the royal palace. ... (And) Cestius took a great army of his choicest men ... undermined the wall, without themselves being hurt, and got all things ready for setting fire to the gate of the temple.[29]

With the rebellion in its death throes and the once impertinent rebels quivering on the verge of surrender, Gallus managed the unthinkable. He ordered a retreat. Josephus, an eyewitness to the events, was dumbfounded. "Had he at this time attempted to get in the walls by force, he had won the city presently, and the war had been put to an end at once"[30] because "a horrid fear seized upon the seditious insomuch that many of them ran out of the city, as though it were to be taken immediately."[31] Yet, Cestius "retired from the city without any reason in the world."[32]

Bemused, and with a new surge of confidence, the Jews poured from the city, inflicting heavy casualties on the fleeing Romans. Nearly 6,000 died during the retreat. This one event, more than any other, encouraged the rebellion. Had Cestius behaved normally, it would have been extinguished with the city and its temple intact.

Wars and Rumors of War. Jesus' predictions came during the renowned Pax Romana ("Peace of Rome")—a period when the unquestioned military superiority of the Roman legions held rebellions in check. Will Durant's study, though now a quarter of a century old, bears reviewing. In 1968, he wrote: "War is one of the constants of history, and has not diminished with civilization and democracy. In the last 3,421 years of recorded history, only 268 have seen no war."[33] Though not totally absent during this period, history records a dearth of wars and insurrections. Even rebellion-plagued Judea endured an uneasy peace with Imperial Rome. Yet, soon after Jesus' death, Palestine reverberated with an ever-increasing crescendo of "wars and rumors of wars."

A brief survey of Roman authors who wrote concerning the period (40-65 A.D.) reveals many descriptive terms such as "war," "insurrections," "rebellion," "commotions," and "conflicts." Strife in Palestine erupted at a moment's notice. "An uprising in Caesarea cost the lives of 20,000 Jews; at Scythopolis, soldiers slaughtered 13,000 Jews; in Alexandria, an uprising cost the Jews 50,000 slain; another 10,000 died in Damascus."[34]

Josephus and other writers describe an intense confrontation with Caligula over whether his statue would be allowed in the temple.[35] Every proposed compromise failed. Caligula ordered "an invasion" of Judea with instructions that if the Jews would not allow his statue in their temple "willingly" they should be "conquered by war."[36] Convinced of the inevitability of war, the citizenry refused to prepare their lands for the spring planting.

Only a last-minute reprieve averted all-out war. Tacitus claims the key was the assassination of Caligula in January, 41 A.D.[37] Josephus reports that Caligula relented because of the intercession of Petronius and King Agrippa.[38]

False Messiahs by the Dozens. As for pretenders to the Messiahship, both religious and secular writers testify to their frequent appearances. Luke (and Josephus[39]) speaks of Theudas (Acts 5) as gaining a large following; Simon Magnus, before his conversion, advanced similar claims (Acts 8); Bar-Jesus also claimed great power for himself (Acts 13). Secular sources describe many more. Josephus even states that, during the rule of Felix, "the country was filled with ... impostors who deluded the multitude. ... Yet did Felix catch and put to death many of these impostors every day."[40] Origen and Jerome offer the names of additional impostors.[41]

Natural Disasters. Widespread disaster swept the far reaches of the Empire in record numbers. Josephus recounts a severe famine in Judea during the years 44-46 A.D. when "many people died for want of what was necessary to procure food."[42] Other sources list three other major famines during the reign of Claudius alone.[43] Tacitus explains the severity of the famine prompted an angry mob to pelt the emperor with scraps of bread during an appearance at the Forum. This famine, described in detail by Josephus,[44] triggered Paul's special relief efforts (Acts 11:27-30; II Cor. 8:1-9:15).

As for the "pestilence," Suetonius describes one outbreak during the time of Nero that became so severe that 30,000 people died within a matter of weeks.[45] Earthquakes also disturbed the Empire. Tacitus, Seneca, Suetonius, and Josephus all describe their devastation. Josephus describes one major quake that shook Jerusalem just before the final conflagration:

... there broke out a prodigious storm in the night, with the utmost violence, and very strong winds, with the largest showers of rain, and continual lightnings, terrible thunderings, and amazing concussions ... of the earth ... in an earthquake. These ... were a manifest indication that some destruction was coming upon men ... and anyone would guess that these wonders foreshewed grand calamities that were coming.[46]

Additional earthquakes occurred during the days of Caligula, Claudius, and Nero on Crete, in the cities of Laodicea, Hierapolis, Colossae, Pompeii, Paphos, Smyrna, Miletus, and Rome.[47]

Proliferation of False Teachers. The period from 40-70 A.D. saw increasing troubles in the church over false teachers. The book of Acts and the New Testament epistles abound with warnings and examples.

Appearance of "the Abomination of Desolation." Perhaps the most controversial fulfillment relates to the identification of Daniel's predicted "abomination." In referring to the prophet's words, Matthew (24:15-16) writes, "So when you see standing in the holy place 'the abomination that causes desolation,' spoken of through the prophet Daniel ... then let those who are in Judea flee to the mountains." The full context of the passage suggests (1) an "abomination" that desecrates, or causes to be desecrated, will appear in or near the temple or in the area of Jerusalem, (2) when the "abomination" appears, Christians are to flee immediately to "the mountains," and, (3) for those who remain an horrific tribulation will soon follow. A valid interpretation of Daniel's "abomination" must account for the factors that follow as well.

Through the centuries, translators have struggled with Daniel's statement (9:27; 11:31; 12:11). As Lane observes, "The language ... is cryptic and difficult. Yet, its interpretation is crucial to the understanding of the discourse."[48] Specifically, the language can refer equally to an object that desecrates or becomes a sacrilege or to an individual who causes desecration.

Many commentaries see in the phrase the atrocities committed by the Seleucid ruler Antiochus IV Epiphanes during the second century B.C. After overpowering the Jews, he built an altar to Zeus over the altar of burnt offering, offered a pig on the altar, sprinkled the broth throughout the temple complex, and declared the practice of Judaism a capital offense. I Maccabees interpreted Daniel's prophecy in light of both Antiochus and his actions (I Mac. 1:54-59; 6:7). This interpretation, common in antiquity, is still held in high regard today.[49]

Though many of his contemporaries applied Daniel's prediction to Antiochus, Jesus used their familiarity with the passage to point to a future "act of profanation so appalling that the Temple would be rejected by God as the locus of his glory (cf. Ezek. 7:14-23)."[50] Though difficult to imagine anything more repulsive than the actions of Antiochus, at least two distinct possibilities emerge.

First, Josephus finds actions by the Zealots before the final Roman siege to be acts capable of profaning the temple. He reminds his readers that the Zealots used the temple as a base for their campaign of murder, pillage, and rape.[51] While Antiochus shed the blood of a pig in the sacred precincts, the zealots shed human blood.[52] Moreover, criminals and murderers roamed freely in the Holy of Holies, an area to be reserved for the high priest.[53] No longer used for its intended purpose, Yahweh's temple stood condemned.

Lane concludes that these "acts of sacrilege were climaxed in the winter of 67-68 by the farcical investiture of the clown Phanni as high priest,"[54] an act over which the retired high priest Ananus wept bitterly. Josephus records Ananus' lament: "It would have been far better for me to have died before I had seen the house of God laden with such abominations and its unapproachable and hallowed places crowded with the feet of murderers."[55] Profane people occupied the temple precincts. Finally, the zealots opened Jerusalem to an army of brigands, thieves, and cutthroats who used the temple area as a base for unspeakable crimes of barbarity. For Lane and others, then, the "abomination" must have been either the parody of a high priest, the army of brigands, the Zealots, or their actions.

Second, others argue that Daniel's "abomination" describes the Roman invasion and destruction of the city. Kimball sees the approaching Roman army as the culprit: "Nothing could be more detestable to the Jews," he writes, "than the realization that an idolatrous Gentile army was advancing to destroy their beloved city and holy sanctuary."[56] For Kimball, Luke supplies (21:20) a key indicator for his interpretation when he adds to Jesus' prediction the words, "When you see Jerusalem surrounded by armies, you will know that its desolation is near." Luke's account generally parallels those of Matthew and Mark except that he substitutes "Jerusalem surrounded by armies" for "the abomination that causes desolation."

Kimball's interpretation also fits snugly with explanatory notes offered by Daniel: "The people of the ruler who will come will destroy the city and the sanctuary," (Dan. 9:26) and "His armed forces will rise up to desecrate the temple fortress and will abolish the daily sacrifice. Then they will set up the abomination that causes desolation" (Dan. 11:31). Both agree with Mark's description (13:14) of "the abomination that causes desolation, standing where it does not belong."

A sense of urgency pervaded the remainder of Jesus' warning: "When you see Jerusalem surrounded by armies, you will know that its desolation is near. Then let those who are in Judea flee to the mountains, let those in the city get out, and let those in the country not enter the city" (Luke 21:20-21). A parallel passage (Matt. 24:16-25) adds: (1) the siege was to be shortened for the sake of Christians; (2) the lifting of the siege would only be temporary; (3) false prophets would appear in the desert and in the temple, claiming to be the Messiah; and (4) great tribulation would follow when the siege resumed.

Directions for Christians to Flee the City. Exactly when Jerusalem's Christian population streamed out of the city heading for the mountains east of the Jordan cannot be determined with precision. That they did is an accepted historical fact. Eusebius, the fourth-century historian, describes what happened:

> But before the war, the people of the Church of Jerusalem were bidden in an oracle given by revelation to men worthy of it to depart from the city and to dwell in a city of Perea called Pella. To it those who believed in Christ migrated to from Jerusalem. Once the holy men had completely left the Jews and all Judea, the justice of God at last overtook them, since they had committed such transgressions against Christ and his apostles. Divine justice completely blotted out that impious generation from among men.[57]

Christians twice had the opportunity to flee the city. First, they could have left when the Roman general Gallus began his inexplicable retreat. If the the presence of Roman armies surrounding the city signaled an imminent crisis, an opportunity to leave came immediately after the ill-advised Roman retreat. Though not naming Christians specifically, Josephus notes that people fled the city in droves at that point.[58]

A second, brief, opportunity to leave came after the zealots seized the temple area for their campaign of terror and invested as high priest one who lacked the right to the position. Lane believes Christians fled the city at precisely this period.[59] Soon afterward, the zealots sealed off the city, refusing to allow anyone to leave.[60]

The Great Tribulation. In due time, the Roman juggernaut, under Titus, stalked into position for the final battle. So wretched did conditions become inside the city and its surrounding countryside, it would prove difficult to imagine worse. Roving bands of marauders and murderers swept through the city. Terrorism, treachery, civil disturbances, and armed confrontations inside the walls exterminated tens of thousands. One of Josephus' most sobering commentaries speaks of the factious battles: "They agreed in nothing but this, to kill those that were innocent."[61] He concluded that the sound of battle from the interior of Jerusalem "was incessant, both by day and by night; but the lamentations of those that mourned exceeded the noise of the fighting. ... (for they) omitted no method of torment or of barbarity."[62]

A Roman siege bank tightened the noose around the city as the Romans settled back to wait for the inhabitants to surrender or starve. Many starved. Famine inside the walls reached gargantuan proportions. Many would have surrendered had the zealots allowed it. They would not. Anyone suspected of plotting an escape faced certain torture. Unthinkable atrocities followed:

> A deep silence ... and a kind of deadly night had seized upon the city; while yet the robbers were still more terrible than these miseries were themselves; for they broke open those houses which were no other than graves of dead bodies, and plundered them of what they had; and carrying off the coverings of their bodies, went out laughing, and tried the points of their swords on their dead bodies; and ... thrust some of those through that still lay alive upon the ground.[63]

Famine within the walls intensified and the Romans baited the city's inhabitants by showing them the great quantity of food they possessed. The mere sight of food led many to leave the city under the guise of attacking the Romans. Some were wealthy Jews, looking for an opportunity to escape, but unwilling to leave their wealth behind. As repulsive as it sounds, these often swallowed gold, hoping to recover it from their excrement after their surrender:

> But when this contrivance was discovered ... the fame of it filled their several camps. ... So the multitude of the Arabians, with the Syrians, cut up those that came ... and searched their bellies. Nor does it seem ... that any misery that befell the Jews was more terrible than this, since in one night about two thousand of these deserters were thus dissected.[64]

Still, Jerusalem's demented defenders refused to surrender. Blood, both Jewish and Roman, purchased every inch of ground. When a wall crumbled under the battering of the machines of war, Rome's soldiers found yet another hastily constructed behind the first.

Through it all, famine's forces stormed in a frenzy throughout the population, claiming her victims by the hundreds in scenes reminiscent of the living skeletons who survived Hitler's onslaught during the holocaust. Jewish soldiers ate their shoes and their clothing along with the leather from their shields. Fathers ripped food from the mouths of their children. The most revolting story describes a mother killing and eating her son.[65]

This close-up of a scene from the famous Arch of Titus in Rome shows Roman soldiers carrying away treasures from the temple area. (Photo courtesy, Dr. Marlin Connelly.)

Eventually, Rome's power prevailed. Defenses crumbled. The temple precincts fell under Roman domination. Smoke from sacrifices to Caesar drifted over the eastern edges of Jerusalem. Still, the fighting continued. Portions of the Upper City (Mt. Zion) remained unconquered. A fire, started in disobedience to a direct command from Titus, gutted the temple. Roman banners, crowned with the symbolic Roman eagles, claimed the city's skyline. Finally, the rebellion collapsed and Roman soldiers streamed into the last bastion of the defenses. Again, Josephus provides a vivid description of the Roman soldiers who "slew those whom they overtook without mercy ... (and) obstructed the very lanes with their dead bodies, and made the whole city run down with blood, to such a degree that the fire ... was quenched ... with blood."[66]

When the butchery ceased, Josephus tells us more than one million Jews had died. Another 97,000 trudged into Egypt to serve as slaves in Roman mines.[67] The words of Hosea (8:13-14) provide an excellent backdrop: "... the Lord ... will ... remember their iniquity, and visit their sins: they shall return to Egypt. For Israel hath forgotten his Maker."

Strange Events in the Heavens. Lastly, Jesus refers to astronomical phenomena visible during the interim period between his prediction and the final desolation. Josephus records those as well:

> ... there was a star resembling a sword, which stood over the city, and a comet, that continued a whole year. ... When the people came in great crowds to the feast of unleavened bread (just prior to the war) ... at the ninth hour of the night, so great a light shone round the altar and the holy house, that it appeared to be bright day-time; which light lasted for half an hour. ... and a few days after that feast ... before sunsetting, chariots and troops of soldiers in their armor were seen running about among the clouds.[68]

Jesus' predictions must be labeled "remarkable." The evidence suggests that he saw the future. He then warned his disciples, providing them with a detailed account of what to expect. His words ring through the ages: "See, I have told you ahead of time" (Matt. 24:25).

18

Deficiencies
of the
Greek Oracles

They stalked the future for a fee.

Known as "oracles," they stood astride the entrance to the future, claiming to pry information from both the dead and the gods. Along the way, vast sums of wealth tumbled into their treasuries. Power, prestige, and influence filled their egos as rapidly as silver and gold lined their pockets.

Ruins of the Temple of Apollo at Didyma in Turkey. Here, one of antiquity's most well-known oracles offered advice for the future. (Photo courtesy, Fon Scofield Collection, E. C. Dargan Research Library of the Sunday School Board, SBC.)

Their pronouncements created and legitimatized rulers and empires. Their words called armies into battle. Their flair for the spectacular charmed both kings and peasants. If anyone could compete with the biblical prophets in influence and predictions, surely the oracles had the best opportunity. For the serious student of prophecy, no trek across history would be complete without a tour of the oracular museum. Our tour opens in the world of the Greeks.

From the eighth century B.C. onward, clients by the thousands—rulers and peasants, the rich and the poor, politicians and lovers—crowded the dusty highways to sites like Delphi, Olympia, Dodona, Didyma, Lebadea, Oropus, and Ephyra. They came to learn the future and how to pattern their lives accordingly.

In each of these locations, like many others, representatives of the gods were thought to possess the gift of prophecy. Some prophets were men; some were women. Some were young; some were old. Some prophesied by interpreting dreams; some studied the entrails of animals. Some worked themselves into a frenzy; some prepared by consuming blood. Some used clever deceptions in their work; some seem to have been devoutly honest. Some were well-known; others were obscure. Yet, whatever the input, available evidence supplies no proof that any held a hot-line to the supernatural.

A wealth of information concerning the oracles beckons today's scholars. Sites where many oracles offered their predictions stand open for investigation. Writings of ancient historians bubble with rich, detailed information. Archaeology also adds to the lore of these ancient prophets. The resulting mosaic paints a familiar picture of deceit and fraud. Scandals in the name of religion infested ancient religion as easily as they do today.

While this investigation cannot focus on every oracle, the chosen examples are not atypical. Instead, like a well-fitting jigsaw puzzle, an insightful pattern emerges: Greek oracular establishments mastered the art of deception.

Examples of Prophetic Fraud

Our investigation opens on the shore of the Bay of Naples near ancient Baiae. There, in the 1960s, not far from the site of another famous oracle at Cumae, researchers Robert Paget and Keith Jones discovered the location of the Oracle of the Dead.[1] The oracle held a prominent place in the Geography of Strabo (63 B.C. - 25 A.D.)[2] who remembered that Ulysses visited here in search of the future. Though the oracle no longer existed in Strabo's day, the Greek geographer did learn that the oracle lived "far below" the surface and that oracular priests used a series of subterranean passageways.

Another celebrated writer, the poet Virgil (70 - 19 B.C.), describes the oracle and the site at Cumae in vivid detail. In his epic poem, Aeneid, Aeneas, the poem's hero, flees Troy to establish a new city in Italy.

Anxious to know the fate of his adventures, Aeneas consults the oracle. In light of recent archaeological discoveries, Virgil's vivid description of the site is hauntingly accurate.

Using historical and archaeological data, researchers established several facts: (1) Inquirers visited the oracle at a complex underground location. (2) Before presenting an inquiry, visitors faced a month of mind-altering experiences. These included solitary confinement in a room plastered with dreadful pictorial representations of the underworld. (3) Visitors lived for a month in extremely cramped quarters, shut off from natural light. (4) The only light came from lamps probably burning hashish. The psychological setting, coupled with the inhalation of vast amounts of hashish, possible bathing in drugged water, and ingestion of drugs by various mechanisms, guaranteed vivid, strong, and repeated hallucinations.

Preparation for Consulting Oracles

Consulting an oracle was never simple. Before beginning their descent underground to meet the dead, inquirers endured up to a month of grueling preparation.

Sensory Deprivation. Step one involved extensive use of sensory deprivation. Priests guided their subjects into a small room. There, isolated from outside influences, the priests began their routine. The room measured less than 200 square feet with only a small torch or oil lamp for lighting.[3] What followed often proved fatal. Merely the month of solitary confinement robbed many of their senses. Modern military brainwashing efforts focus on such deprivation. Prisoners are forced to live "in cramped circumstances, undergoing physical hardship and a boring routine existence, always surrounded by the uncertainty of his fate and having to obey" those in control.[4]

Use of Hallucinogens. Much more than sensory deprivation awaited. Next, the priests turned to hallucinogenic drugs.

At Baiae, researchers Paget and Jones encountered what they termed the "Painted Room" into which priests eventually ushered their subjects.[5] Upon entering this room, Virgil's Aeneas recoiled from its paintings. Startled, he drew his sword to confront the menacing artistry.[6] On the walls Aeneas saw

> ... horrifying paintings which portrayed various Diseases, Old Age, Fear, War, Poverty, Sleep, "Joy of Sinning," Hunger, Strife, Insanity, and the "Counsellor of Evil." The enquirer would have plenty of time to dwell on these sobering and graphic pictures, for he seems to have stayed alone in the Painted Room for three whole days with no other amusement. He would come to know every detail of the gruesome visages before him in his isolated room, and how marked would be their effect on his narrowed attention![7]

While we might be tempted to snicker at the idea that a hero such as Aeneas could be startled by mere paintings, we would do well to refrain. Powerful hallucinogens were at work. Archaeologist Sotiris Dakaris, whose pioneer excavations first located the oracle's remains at Ephyra in northern Greece, uncovered extensive use of hashish.[8] The properties of hashish likely lulled many inquirers into the incubatio, or temple sleep, so common in antiquity.

In the cramped, nearly air-tight, enclosures, simply breathing the stale air would become laborious. Fumes from oil lamps or torches aggravated the process. If fumes and ashes from burning hashish or other hallucinogenic substances joined the mix, even the strongest subject soon became putty in the hands of the priests. Henbane, one hallucinogen available in antiquity, proved especially potent. Temple explains, "If you pull up a henbane plant and throw it on the bonfire, and then inhale the smoke, you may go insane or die, or at least become unconscious for a couple of days. Even the ashes are poisonous!"[9]

Besides inhaling hallucinogenic fumes, many scholars believe inquirers unknowingly ingested massive doses of other hallucinogens. French parliamentarian Eusebe Salverte devoted much of his life to a study of ancient wonders. He carefully inspected accounts from classical authors about those who visited oracles. He was convinced that their behavior corresponded perfectly with that of those under the influence of strong hallucinogens. One description by Plutarch appeared especially convincing:

> Plutarch has preserved to us a description of the mysteries of Trophonios, related by a man who had passed two nights and a day in the grotto. They appear to be rather the dreams of a person intoxicated by a powerful narcotic than the description of a real spectacle. Timarchus ... experienced a violent head-ache when the apparitions commenced; that is to say, when the drugs began to affect his senses, and when the apparitions vanished and he awoke from this delirious slumber, the same pain was as keenly felt. Timarchus died three months after his visit to the grotto; the priests no doubt having made use of very powerful drugs. It is said that those who had once consulted the oracle acquired a melancholy which lasted all their lives, the natural consequence, no doubt, of all the serious shocks to their health from the potions administered to them.[10]

Dr. Jane Harrison also notes strong evidence for the use of drugs in her extensive study of Greek religion. After evaluating Plutarch's account, she wrote, "The whole ecstatic mystic account beginning with the sensation of a blow on the head and the sense of the soul escaping, reads like a trance-like experience or like the revelation experienced under an anesthetic."[11]

Another account from Pausanias fuels the theory. The Greek author and traveler of the second century A.D. explains:

> When a man comes up from Trophonios the priests take him over again and sit him on the throne of Memory, which is not far from the holy place, to ask him what he saw and discovered. When they know this they turn him over to his friends, who pick him up and carry him to the building where he lived before with the Good Spirit and Fortune. He is still possessed with terror and hardly knows himself or anything around him. ... I am not writing this from hearsay, as I have consulted Trophonios and seen others do so.[12]

Gaius Plinius Secundus, or simply Pliny, wrote thirty-seven books of natural history. In one he notes that hallucinogenic henbane is named apollinaris (Apollo). Apollo served as the primary God of prophecy and divination. This famed Roman author further explains that those practicing divination made extensive use of hellbore, another hallucinogenic plant.[13]

Another method of administering hallucinogens came through oils or ointments absorbed through the skin. Modern medical techniques only recently are rediscovering the value of skin patches in dispensing medicines. Absorbing medicines through skin patches treats a diversity of patients from those suffering from heart disease to those wishing to stop smoking. Yet, both the rapidity and effectiveness of the skin in absorbing drugs seem to have been well understood in antiquity. Can it be mere coincidence that those consulting oracles bathed in specially-prepared waters or were rubbed with lotions and oils just before their consultations? Consider the testimony of Philostratus. This third century A.D. author explains that oracles "concocted and adapted different drugs" such as oils and lotions for use in their work.[14]

Using such information, Temple concludes:

> The visitor to the Oracle ate for some days only what the priests gave him, which may have contained drugs, drank of two special "waters" before the consultation, almost certainly drugged, and was anointed with olive oil before entering the cavern. This oil also probably contained drugs which were absorbed directly through the skin. There were thus four possible sources of hallucinogenic stimulus for the visitor, and they were probably all used.[15]

Utilization of Dramatics

After extensive preparations, and while their subjects still floated in and out of reality, the priests added their final step: a vivid, imaginative dramatic presentation. Convinced they were about to descend into Hell, inquirers at Baiae followed chanting priests through a narrow, circular hole in the earth. An eight-foot descent down a ladder brought the subjects into a circular room with a tunnel sloping obviously downward into the earth. The tunnel would lead the inquirers 600 feet from the entrance and 140 feet underground. Smoke, fumes, and light from over 500 oil lamps added to the illusion of a trip into Hell.[16]

Slowly, the priests led the subjects into a labyrinth of tiny rooms, secured by iron-mounted doors. Moving from one room to another, visitors would experience a steadily increasing trauma as they edged closer and closer to the pits of hell and the abode of the dead. At Baiae, an underwater stream, heated by hot springs and large enough in antiquity to float a small boat, lay ominously between the subjects and their final destination. The scene easily brought to mind the story of the fearful ferryman Charon who escorted souls across the River Styx into Hades.[17]

Disembarking on the other side of the steaming waters, the oracle and subject would join another group of priests and move toward a foreboding, dark opening in the earth. This was Hades. Completing a sacrifice, the enquirer poured blood into the abyss and awaited a response.[18]

Though what happened next remains conjecture, enough evidence exists to piece together a plausible theory. At Ephyra, deep in caves used by the oracle, archaeologists discovered an ingenuous pulley system and the remains of a large bronze cauldron capable of concealing an adult. Use of these items would allow priests to "stage" an appearance of the dead. Vandenberg imagines the apparition would have been accompanied by loud, eerie noises, hypnotic-like chants from the priests, and the necessary special effects.

Ephyra's oracle proved to be creative and an excellent dramatist if not supernatural. True prophets do not require cauldrons, pulleys, hallucinogenic drugs, or clever tricks.

Use of Evasive Answers

Yet another trick of the oracles can be found in their evasive and ambiguous responses. Many oracles only answered "yes" or "no" to the inquiries of their clients. If someone quizzed the oracle, and the oracle responded "yes," the oracle could never be shown to be in error. A million mitigating circumstances could be invented to "explain away" failures. Under these circumstances, no one could ever prove the oracle wrong.

Even when oracles offered more than a single-word response, we know that responses were often garbled, capable of multiple meanings, and easily misinterpreted. Perhaps the most famous oracular response of all time came from Apollo's Oracle at Delphi in response to an inquiry by Lydia's King Croessus. When Croessus attempted to learn the outcome of a battle with Persians, he was informed that such a war would destroy a great empire.[19] Regardless of the outcome, the Oracle was protected. Croessus did attack. He was defeated.

Monetary Motives

One other matter looms as important. A strong monetary motive overshadowed the oracular culture. Unlike biblical prophets who gained little if anything financially from their predictions, the classical oracles built a thriving monetary empire through their work. Their lifestyle, and it was often plush, depended upon their success. One example of the enormous economic power they possessed comes from the story of Croessus.

Croessus Invests His Wealth. Croessus modeled his life and decisions around advice from oracles. Unlike others, however, his measureless wealth allowed him to consult as many as he desired. One indication of his wealth appears in the tribute he paid for information from the Oracle at Delphi. It cost a fortune.

Herodotus describes the sacrifices offered by Croessus in an attempt to curry favor with the oracle:

> Of every kind of appropriate animal he slaughtered three thousand; he burnt in a huge pile a number of precious objects — couches overlaid with gold or silver, golden cups, tunics, and other richly colored garments — in the hope of binding the god more closely to his interest; and he issued a command that

Set in the rugged Greek mountainside, the location of the Temple of Apollo at Delphi added to the oracle's mystique. (Photo courtesy, Fon Scofield Collection, E. C. Dargan Research Library of the Sunday School Board, SBC.)

Ruins of the "Round Temple" at Delphi. The site of antiquity's most widely respected oracle was adorned with small temples and monuments dedicated by those who had come to consult the gods. (Photo courtesy, Fon Scofield Collection, E. C. Dargan Research Library of the Sunday School Board, SBC.)

every Lydian was also to offer a sacrifice according to his means. After this ceremony he melted down an enormous quantity of gold into one hundred and seventeen ingots about eighteen inches long, nine inches wide, and three inches thick; four of the ingots were of refined gold weighing approximately a hundred and forty-two pounds each; the rest were alloyed and weighed about a hundred and fourteen pounds. He also caused the image of a lion to be made of refined gold, in weight some five hundred and seventy pounds. ... This was by no means all that Croessus sent to Delphi; there were also two huge mixing-bowls, one of gold ... the other of silver. ... the golden one weighs nearly a quarter of a ton ... and the silver one holds over five thousand gallons.[20]

Aeneas' Consultation Proves Expensive. Although Croessus provided the oracle's biggest monetary offering, others consulting the oracles paid dearly for information. In the Aeneid, Aeneas provided seven bullocks and seven ewes for the Sibyl at Cuma. He later purchased and sacrificed four bullocks, a lamb, a ram, a cow, and several gigantic bull oxen — all to be basted with expensive olive oil as they roasted — before consulting the oracle at Baiae. As Temple explains, entire communities profited from "the oracle business," much like many who exploit religion for profit today.

Since only small portions of these sacrifices were actually made as offerings to the deities, (the sacrifices) would provide enough meat, fat, offal, hides and even wool to make life comfortable for these religious officials at Cuma for a considerable period. In addition, the beasts would have been purchased by the visiting enquirer from the same officials, thus filling the priests' pockets with ready money at the same time. Vast quantities of the best olive oil had to be purchased to pour over the carcasses as they roasted, and we can be sure that many jars were left over for the priests' use afterwards.[21]

Willingness to Kill to Preserve Their Lifestyle. The success of the oracles involved more than mere prestige. It involved the livelihood of scores of families. Many of those enriched in the process would be willing to do whatever was necessary to protect their investment. The famous fable-writer Aesop made the mistake of belittling the profiteering at Delphi. His criticism was not well received. The priests "slipped a gold dish ... into his traveling pack, and spread the rumor that the Temple of Apollo had been robbed. The dish was found, and Aesop punished with death. The priests threw him from the Hyampeian cliff."[22]

Aesop's treatment reminds us of Paul's encounter with a "fortune-teller" in Philippi (Acts 16:16-24). Luke tells us that the young girl "earned a great deal of money for her owners." Pollock is convinced that the young girl came from Delphi. He writes that

> Luke found that the girl was a slave, a "Pythoness" from Delphi or Pytho the world-famous shrine of Apollo on the southern slope of Mount Parnassus overlooking the Gulf of Corinth. The Delphic Oracle was consulted by statesmen and ambassadors; a girl controlled by whatever strange force of evil lay at the back of it would be in much demand by men and women wanting to peer into the future. She was so valuable that she had been bought by a syndicate, not by an individual.[23]

Testing the Oracles

Many diverse oracles plied their wares in the classical world. All claimed authenticity. How could inquirers choose between them? Given the sizable monetary investment he would make, Croessus devised a careful test. Perhaps he felt that in times of crisis he would have time to consult only one of many oracles available and wanted to know which could be trusted. Perhaps he entertained doubts about the trustworthiness of all oracles. That he anticipated difficult times were rapidly approaching for his kingdom made his search more urgent: Menacing Persian armies gathered on the horizon and cast greedy eyes at the wealth of Lydia and Asia Minor. Moreover, Croessus' second son, his heir apparent, lost his life on a hunting trip. Succession to the throne became uncertain.

Croessus definitely needed wise counsel. To his credit, he attempted to check the validity of the information he received. Eventually, he proposed a challenge.[24] Couriers were dispatched to seven of antiquity's leading oracles.[25] They were to consult the oracles 100 days after leaving Sardis and inquire as to what Croessus was doing at that moment in his palace. The king had carved a tortoise and a lamb with his own hands and boiled them in a bronze cauldron with a bronze lid.

Only the Oracle at Delphi accurately answered the couriers. Croessus was convinced. The Oracle at Delphi became his chief adviser.

Failure of Most Oracles

At the least, Croessus' cunning test easily established the ineffectiveness of most oracles. Though they offered responses, Croessus found them in error. Had they possessed supernatural powers, they could have answered the king correctly. Instead, they accepted a challenge and lost.

Explaining Delphi's Success

Now to examine the one success story. How was Apollo's Oracle at Delphi able to correctly answer the king? Admittedly, we can never be certain. We can offer several suggestions.

Methods Used by Apollo's Oracle. Pronouncements from Apollo at Delphi came through a prophetess known as the Pythia. On the seventh day of each month (except in winter), she weaved her way into the sacred precincts of Apollo's temple. There, while seated on a tripod, she claimed to reveal the future.

Long before she entered the temple area, however, hundreds of emissaries and inquirers gathered around the temple in hopes their questions would be answered. The Pythia was not required to answer anyone. Even on the specified seventh day, many factors could intervene and postpone or cancel her prophetic activities. So, when the Pythia reached the altar of Hestia, she paused. Here, the priests brought a young goat, placed it on the marble floor and sprinkled it with ice-cold water. If the animal trembled, the activities continued. If not, the proceedings came to an abrupt end. Moreover, since these events took place in complete secrecy, priests could delay an answer almost indefinitely.

Even assuming everything proceeded as planned, the multitude of petitioners made it impossible for the Oracle to answer each one. Some simply had to wait until the next month. Thus, if the priests wished to stall an answer to a question, that was accomplished easily.

In the case of Croessus, from the time his emissaries arrived, the priests would have had many opportunities to determine the reason for their visit. It is possible that the oracular priests knew Croessus' question days or weeks before it was presented. Two possibilities then arise. First, the priests could attempt to learn the king's plans in advance, or, second, they could delay the inquiry until after the events, then attempt to learn of their occurrence after the fact. But, would such be possible? The answer is "yes."

A Large Spy Network. Delphi's Oracle is suspected of developing one of the more intricate information-gathering networks in antiquity. Vandenberg is convinced that Delphi's priests possessed both the motives (respectability of the oracle, defense of their livelihood, future economic security, willingness to kill to protect the oracle) and the means (tremendous wealth) to sustain a wide-ranging spy network.[26]

Coupled with the information-gathering services, a sizable body of evidence implies that many oracles employed carrier pigeons in order to speed messages throughout the empire.[27] Since these birds fly hundreds of miles in a day, a carefully placed spy, watching events unfold at Sardis, could easily provide the oracle center at Delphi with an account of the events in a relatively short time.

Of course, all this is mere conjecture. And while we know more about the Oracle at Delphi than any other in antiquity, we really know very little.

Comparing Oracles and Biblical Prophets

Without denying a number of minor similarities between the fabled oracles and the biblical prophets, even the casual observer can catalog the major differences. While we possess sizable information regarding the oracles, we lack the knowledge necessary to posit their supernatural origin. Moreover, the circumstantial evidence we do possess argues against a supernatural connection.

Opportunities for Collusion and Subterfuge

The oracles could have gained information used in their predictions through subterfuge. The use of narcotic agents, numerous opportunities for inquisition by the oracle priests, and almost certain "spy" networks capable of using sophisticated communication systems monopolized the oracular scene. Any of these allow room for substantial collusion. The use of more than one would virtually guarantee it. By contrast, no reliable evidence connects biblical prophets to such devices. Moreover, many of their predictions were years removed from their fulfillment. Differences are substantial.

Timing of the Prophecies

None of the oracular predictions are sufficiently removed from events that follow to assure the absence of collusion. Many questions that they addressed concerned events in their immediate future. Few, if any, oracular concerns dealt with events years removed from the date of the prediction. Again, differences are sizable. Many predictions of the biblical prophets dealt with events in their distant future. Prophecies of the coming Messiah preceded their fulfillment by centuries. Predictions of the future of Tyre tumbled from the prophets long before the actual events. And while a number of prophecies from the biblical prophets dealt with current events, the more amazing did not.

Concern with the Mundane

Most inquiries of the oracles dealt with issues and events totally isolated from the arena of apologetics. They found themselves answering questions regarding everything from the faithfulness of a spouse to the success of certain business ventures.

From a strictly human perspective, it is impossible to determine whether a particular course in politics or romance should be pursued. Suppose an oracle was quizzed as to whether or not a man should take a certain young woman to be his wife. Suppose the oracle answers in the affirmative. Suppose, then, that after two years of marriage the wife poisons her husband. Would that prove the oracle to have made an error? Hardly. The oracle could easily respond that had the man not married the woman he would have been traveling three months after the marriage and met with a fatal accident. Under these conditions, the marriage actually prolonged his life by twenty-one months. In fact, because the majority of oracular concerns focused on issues such as these, no one could demonstrate that their predictions were valid or not. They simply lack evidential value. Biblical prophecies, on the other hand, often dealt with major events unlikely to occur and easily verified.

Ambiguity of Answers

Ambiguity of answers from many oracles, especially the famed Delphic Oracle, further implies a conscious attempt to deceive. When blended with an extensive use of hallucinogens, mind games, and theatrics, the preponderance of evidence denies a supernatural element among the oracles.

Failures of
Divination and Astrology

While the ancient oracles earned their share of press clippings throughout antiquity, divination, omens, and astrology comprised the real workhorses of prediction. Thousands consulted the oracles. Tens of thousands patterned their lives by the pronouncements of diviners.

Even oracles intermeshed their work with that of diviners. Apollo's oracle at Delphi used divination before deciding whether to prophesy.[1] Moreover, since the oracle's fame prompted a deluge of inquiries, divination by lots was used to answer the more mundane questions.[2] The oracle of Zeus at Dodona followed a similar pattern.[3] Divination dominated the prophetic stage.

Definition and Types of Divination

Because of the close connection between divination and the consultation of oracles, the distinction between the two is often ambiguous. At this point, Aune's dissection of oracles and divination proves both simple and reliable. For Aune, "Divination may be defined as the art or science of interpreting symbolic messages from the gods" while oracles "are messages from the gods in human language, received as statements from a god, usually in response to inquiries."[4]

Diviners, then, were interpreters. Since a variety of symbolic messages supposedly emanated from the gods, their job was to uncover and decipher them. Aune identifies the more widely-known sources as

> ... (1) the casting of lots (kleromancy), (2) the flight and behavior of birds (ornithomancy), (3) the condition and behavior of sacrificial animals, or their vital organs, before and after sacrifice (hepatascopy, hieromancy, pyromancy), (4) various omens or sounds (cledonomancy), and (5) dreams (oneiromancy).[5]

To Aune's list, we can add the movement of oil and water in a bowl (hydromancy or lecanomancy), the movement of smoke patterns (libanomancy), the shaking of arrows (belomancy), the use of a rod or staff (rhabdomancy), and the location and movement of astronomical bodies (astrology). This study will not attempt an in-depth discussion of each. Rather, we will turn our attention to two of the more widely known methods — hepatascopy and astrology.

Hepatascopy: A Unique Form of Divination

Among ancient forms of divining, none proves more intriguing than predicting the future through the inspection of animal entrails (exticpicy), especially the liver (hepatascopy). Born amid the gentle Tigris and Euphrates valleys, this method of inquiry quickly became the predictor of choice for the Hellenized world. By the first century B.C., Cicero could lament that "the whole Etruscan nation has gone stark mad on the subject of entrails."[6] Any foray into history easily confirms Cicero's dictum. If anything, the fabled Roman probably understated its significance.

Recent evidence shows that, "for thousands of years," it served as "the leading form of divination" for "the cultures of ancient Greece, Rome, the Etruscans or, especially, Babylonia and Assyria."[7] Dr. Morris Jastrow, one of history's most respected experts in the area of Mesopotamian divination, concluded,

> From the earliest period down to the days of the last king of Babylonia, [it] continued in force as the official method of divining the future; and while other methods were resorted to, none equaled in importance and scope the system of divination through the liver.[8]

To appreciate its pervasiveness in daily life, one need only read ancient biographies of Alexander or the adventure of the famous Greek mercenary, Xenophon.

Divination in the Life of Alexander of Macedon

Alexander of Macedon, easily one of history's more colorful characters, set the course of his life around his belief in fate. That fate, he was convinced, could be known through astrology, omens, and divination. One story about the birth of the young prince declared that when his mother, Olympias,

> was about to give birth to Alexander ... Nectanebus stood by her making observations of the heavenly bodies, and from time to time he besought her to restrain herself until the auspicious hour had arrived; and it was not until he saw a certain splendor in the sky and knew that all the heavenly bodies were in a favorable position that he permitted her to bring forth her child.[9]

With this emphasis on astrology and omens surrounding his birth and most of his culture, Alexander's staunch belief in their validity is hardly surprising. In fact, throughout his life, Alexander's biographers constantly refer to his consultation of oracles, astrologers, and diviners. Still, no consultations proved more succinct than the warnings he received in the last year of his life. After calling an end to the relentless eastward march of his armies that had carried them to the borders of India, he turned westward toward Babylon.

As Alexander approached the city, both Arrian[10] and Plutarch[11] record that he became openly disturbed by reports from diviners that tragedy awaited. They reported that inspection of the liver of a sacrificial animal used to inquire about his future had revealed a missing lobe in the animal's liver. When Alexander asked how that should be interpreted, one diviner (Pythagoras) responded, "Something of the utmost gravity."[12] From that point, Alexander's fortunes plunged as he stewed over the prediction. Temple notes that he sank "into a superstitious torpor and a terror of omens. He succumbed to the portents in a spell of self-destructive gloom. He had lost all bearings, and is a terrible witness to the maxim that those whom the gods would destroy they first make mad."[13]

History fails to establish the exact cause of Alexander's death, though poisoning is one possibility.[14] Whatever the cause, Alexander's unflagging belief in omens, divination, and oracular consultation set the table. If poisoned, his egotism and increasingly eccentric behavior, laced with depression over the diviner's pronouncements, led many around him to fear his future actions. If he died of natural causes, his excessive drinking binges, depression, and bizarre lifestyle played major roles in his death. These owed their power over his life to his deeply rooted belief in diviners and oracles.

Divination in the Adventures of Xenophon

Divination also played an important role in the life of one of history's more well-known characters. It totally enslaved Xenophon, the Athenian mercenary and disciple of Socrates. Xenophon, who lived in the fourth century B.C., traveled to Persia seeking adventure. He found all he could handle as he and 10,000 Greek mercenaries joined a failed revolt and endured one terrifying experience after another in their attempt to return to Greece. Fifteen months and 3,400 miles after his adventures began, he and a fraction of his compatriots struggled home. Upon arrival, Xenophon recorded his adventures for posterity.[15]

Though his adventures still provoke interest among historians, the average reader sits in awe at a multitude of references to divination by entrails. Before breaking camp, his augurs consulted entrails. Before allowing battle, he consulted the augurs. In fact, before making any decision, he consulted the augurs. Xenophon and his forces even refused to move without favorable omens. Perhaps the most extreme example occurred when remnants of his force found themselves in imminent danger of starvation. With precious little food and only a few pack animals remaining, Xenophon provided one of the animals for diviners to inspect its entrails before allowing the soldiers to leave camp in search of food.[16]

Divination in Mesopotamia

Long before exticpicy prompted unyielding reverence from Alexander and Xenophon, it took Mesopotamia by storm. It also is the oldest form of divination with roots reaching into the region's earliest records.[17] No ancient cultures prized exticpicy more than those of the "Fertile Crescent." For the Hittites, Assyrians, and Babylonians, "looking into the liver," became as common as reading a daily horoscope in the newspaper.

So widespread did its use become that models of livers used in divining have been uncovered by the hundreds throughout Mesopotamia. Some were extremely expensive, made from pure gold. Others were modeled from clay.[18] Accompanied by many handbooks, these were intended to help the diviners in their work of prediction. The handbooks, compendiums, and encyclopedias cataloged large numbers of liver descriptions and attempted to cross-reference them to actual events. Gurney lists a few of the surviving references:

> If there is a cross drawn on the "strong point" of the liver, an important person will kill his lord.
> If there are two "roads" on the liver, a traveler will reach his goal.
> If the lung is red on the right and left, there will be a conflagration.
> If on the right of the liver there are two "fingers," it is the omen "Who is king? Who is not king?", i.e. of rival pretenders.[19]

With the development of an extensive bureaucracy, inquiry soon proved expensive. Sacrificial animals, usually sheep, had to be secured. That alone limited use to the wealthier classes.[20] Besides, the examination of a single animal seldom proved sufficient. Gurney explains that some enquiries "might entail as many as 34 inspections of the entrails, presumably of sheep, and 20 of cave birds, each, one may suppose, requiring a fresh victim." He concluded, "Small wonder that exticpicy was an art reserved for royalty and affairs of state."[21]

Yet, besides the phenomenon of the self-fulfilling prophecy, there is no evidence that either exticpicy, in general, or hepatascopy, in particular, could ever foretell future events. An unbridgeable chasm separates either from the clarity, detail, and accuracy of biblical prophecies.

Astrology: The Divination of Choice

Astrology gradually overshadowed exticpicy as the "divination of choice" by the majority of the populace. Once accepted, it outlasted every attempt to purge its hold on humanity. Even today a sizable majority remains committed to its tenets. The respected *Encyclopedia Britannica* notes in its latest edition that astrology's influence has been "extensive" in modern as well as ancient cultures.[22] In China and India alone, the world's two most populous nations, virtually the entire population accepts it in one form or another.[23] Astrological influence in the United States, even at the highest levels of government, has rebounded dramatically in recent years. Donald Ragan's shocking expose of the popular Ronald Reagan presidency revealed that "virtually every major move and decision" the president and his wife Nancy made followed the advice of their personal astrologer, Joan Quigley.[24]

Astrology Fails Attempts at Verification

For all its bluster and popularity, astrology fails every effort at verifying its powers. Our current study touches only a few of the more prominent efforts.[25] During the 1970s, two astronomers, R. B. Culver and P. A. Ianna, carefully examined more than 3,000 predictions by well-known astrologers. The predictions appeared in leading, and easily-accessible, astrological magazines. Even when the two scientists numbered as "successful" those predictions that might just as easily have been made by educated non-astrologers, the "failure" rate exceeded 90 percent. Culver and Ianna concluded, "The results ... paint a dismal picture indeed for the traditional astrological claim that 'astrology works'."[26]

Failure in Earthquake Prediction

Findings similar to those of Culver and Ianna are common. A quick perusal of astrological predictions in magazines and national tabloids reveals a penchant for forecasting earthquakes. Quakes are so common that any amateur can easily predict that one or more major ones will occur in a given year. Since some areas are more prone to these seismic events, educated observers can even specify a region of the world where a quake will strike and be somewhat sure of success. So, because of the extraordinary attention afforded earthquakes by astrologers, scientists from the U. S. Geological Survey analyzed 240 astrological predictions regarding earthquakes from nearly thirty leading astrologers. They found their accuracy rate was worse than mere guessing.[27]

Failure to Predict World Events

Another study of 105 major world events in 1965 revealed a nearly unanimous failure rate. The study concluded, "what was announced did not happen, what happened was not announced."[28] Unfortunately for astrologers, the list of major errors in recent years becomes almost laughable. Consider the following blunders:

Failures Regarding Hitler. On August 27, 1939, astrologers confidently announced that Hitler would not invade Poland. Another psychic proclaimed that Hitler's horoscope was not a "war horoscope." Four days later, Hitler's invasion touched off World War II.[29]

Disastrous Stock Market Predictions. Astrologers termed the week of October 18-24, 1987, as the week for a "strong rally" on Wall Street that might last for months. October 19, 1987, wears the label of "Black Monday."[30] The worst market crash in history saw the Dow plummet more than 500 points on October 19, 1987.

Political Blunders. Noted Hindu astrologer James Braha confidently announced in 1986 that U. S. Senator John Glenn of Ohio would be elected president in 1988.[31] The senator never entered the race.

Failed Wedding Predictions. During most of 1968, astrologers around the world insisted that Mrs. Jacqueline Kennedy, widow of the late president, would not marry.[32] Her wedding to Greek tycoon Aristotle Onassis occurred October 20, 1968.

Failure to Predict Kennedy's Death. Several internationally-known astrologers predicted in 1963 President John F. Kennedy's reelection in 1964.[33] Kennedy was assassinated in Dallas in November 1963. Only one astrologer, Jeanne Dixon, supposedly predicted the president's untimely death. That she alone could offer such a claim says much of the profession as a whole. Why did thousands of other psychics and astrologers fail to see the inevitable? Although Mrs. Dixon proclaimed at one point the assassination of a young, blue-eyed Democrat elected president in 1960, in August 1960 she predicted that Richard Nixon would be elected president.[34]

That Mrs. Dixon has generated little excitement in the general population since her 1963 prediction, speaks volumes regarding her total prophetic abilities. In fact, many of her more notable post-1963 predictions fail miserably. She predicted that Walter Reuther would be the 1964 Democratic nominee for president. He never ran. His supposed opponent was to have been Richard Nixon. It was Barry Goldwater. She prophesied that Lyndon Johnson would be the Democratic nominee for president in 1968. He bowed out in humiliation over his handling of the Vietnam War. The day prior to Mrs. Jacqueline Kennedy's marriage to Aristotle Onassis, she confidently proclaimed there would be no marriage. On May 7, 1966, while speaking at the University of Southern California, one questioner asked the length of the Vietnam War. She responded that the war would end in ninety days. Perhaps her most ignominious forecast predicted a new job for Bishop James Pike. He died while the book containing her prediction was being printed.[35]

The conclusion? Ankerberg and Weldon state it simply: "The evidence shows that astrologers consistently miss predicting major disasters or events, not only in weather and economics, but in politics, science, medicine, and every other field."[36]

Imperfections of Modern Visionaries: Failing to Predict Doomsday and the Millennium

Modern society can assert no immunity from prophetic claims. They occur constantly. Most attempt to set the date for the end of civilization. So far, every one has failed.[1] Among the more influential of the doomsday prophets is Michel de Nostredame (Nostradamus).

Nostradamus' Failure as a Prophet

Deservedly or not, Nostradamus owns the title as the most celebrated secular prophet of modern times. Born in 1503 in Saint-Remy, France, he became "the very synonym for successful prognostication." His status is backed by "a multitude of ardent propagandists, the like of which no other prophet has been blessed with."[2] Given his popularity, an important question must be raised. Is there sufficient evidence that this French Jew received Divine assistance in forecasting the future? He certainly claimed it.[3]

Before answering the question, we must understand what brought Nostradamus his celebrated status. Around 1558, Nostradamus published an unusual book of quatrains known simply as *The Centuries*. These veiled statements supposedly revealed the future of humanity through the year 3797. He covered at least seven centuries in the early edition and, though later versions contain ten centuries, no one can prove that these additions were his work.[4] Whether he wrote the additional material is of no concern. The validity of the predictions — not the authorship — is the major priority.

Disciples of Nostradamus claim his quatrains correctly predicted future events such as the rise and fall of Napoleon, the birth and work of Pasteur, the rise and uncertain end of Adolf Hitler, the appearance of many world leaders and popes, many wars, and assorted disasters. His followers also claim he predicted the opening of his grave in 1700.[5] Without engaging in a detailed refutation of hundreds of quatrains, it is possible to suggest that Nostradamus, though creative and perhaps insane, received no supernatural guidance. His writings belie his humanity, not his inspiration.

The Ambiguity of the Writings

Nostradamus' quatrains are uniformly ambiguous. Critics throughout the centuries caution that his references are "obscure and enigmatic,"[6] "an enigma ... ambiguous ... concealing ... a pell-mell, universal mass of confusion."[7] Generally, modern critics agree.[8] There simply is no way to test the validity of his predictions. Even Nostradamus admitted his verse to be "deliberately obscured ... and veiled ... as heavily as possible."[9] As Leoni noted, "No one could rightly claim that the meaning of the quatrains is always readily apparent. ... The common view (is) that they either have no meaning at all, or have a meaning so equivocal that they can be applied to almost anything."[10] In short, anyone taking time to read the quatrains will quickly see there are no obvious predictions and fulfillments.

Nostradamus and Plagiarism

Though claiming the material as his own, scholars now know that Nostradamus plagiarized extensively from the writings of a fourth century philosopher named Jamblichus.[11] Why an inspired prophet should be forced to copy from another writer raises eyebrows. It should. If much of his material originated in a setting a thousand years before his time, the modern "interpretations" are shredded. They speak of events beginning soon after their origin. In addition, when Nostradamus lied about his plagiarism, he committed an unpardonable error. He admitted he needed to conceal information about his materials in order to make them believable.

Obvious Errors Occur in His Writings

Even in an enigmatic sense, Nostradamus never approached perfection. When his predictions do become understandable, they are often wrong. For instance, he predicted he would die in November 1567. He did not. His death came in July 1566, nearly seventeen months before the date he predicted.[12] He told Queen Catherine de' Medici that all her sons would serve as kings. They did not.[13]

Further, a prose outline, written by Nostradamus, explains the meanings of some of his quatrains. With this information, scholars gain insight into his predictions. The outline also serves as the best evidence against the self-proclaimed prophet. Using the outline as his guide, Leoni reconstructed the probable meaning of *The Centuries* and concluded, "... in the huge mass of predictions that can be found in the prose outline, there is not a single successful prophecy. The dating of two calamities serves to discredit him completely. ... some quite clear predictions ... were never realized."[14] No, Nostradamus was not a prophet.

Joseph Smith, Jr.'s Failure as a Prophet

Another widely acclaimed modern prophet is Joseph Smith, Jr., the founder of the Church of Jesus Christ of Latter Day Saints — the Mormons. Smith's followers adamantly insist that God helped him see the future. According to the *Doctrine and Covenants*, he is "a seer, a revelator, a translator, and a prophet."[15] Members of the church he founded call him "The Prophet." Amid such claims, an evaluation is in order. Is there sufficient evidence that Joseph Smith, Jr. received supernatural guidance in composing his predictive scriptures? The evidence fails to suggest that he did.

Smith's Predictions Were Often Wrong

The key test for validity of predictive prophecy must be the accuracy of the predictions. In this arena, far too many blatant errors occur for us to overlook. Unlike biblical prophecies that are clothed in conditionality, no such conditions appear in Smith's writings.

Failed Prediction of Christ's Return. According to the Mormon prophet, Jesus Christ would return to earth before the close of 1891. The official church record noted that on February 14, 1835, "President Smith then stated ... the coming of the Lord was nigh — even fifty-six years should wind up the scene."[16] Fifty-six years added to 1835 brings one to the year 1891. Christ did not return in 1891. Smith was in error. Modern Mormon apologists often assert that Smith made no such prophecy. Evidence easily disproves that assertion.

Many parallel references prove he fully intended to predict Christ's return. More than once he told his followers, "There are those of the rising generation who shall not taste death till Christ comes."[17] He told several church leaders — including Lyman E. Johnson, Heber C. Kimball, Orson Hyde, and William Smith — that they would live until Christ returned.[18] His diary, dated April 6, 1843, reported, "I prophecy (sic) in the name of the Lord God — & let it be written: that the Son of Man will not come in the heavens till I am 85 years old, 48 years hence, or about 1890."[19] Church officials removed the last six words of the prophecy from modern versions of the diary. The revisions also add the word "if" at the beginning of the prophecy. Yet, the original diary shows that no such conditional statement existed either during Smith's lifetime or for years afterward.

Another Mormon writer records that Smith told a group of followers in 1831, "Some of you shall live to see it (the second advent of Christ and the establishment of an earthly kingdom) come."[20] Further, on January 23, 1833, Smith added that his father had told him (through supernatural inspiration) "in the name of Jesus Christ ... that I should continue in the Priest's office until Christ comes."[21] Oliver Cowdery, an original witness for the Book of Mormon's authenticity, wrote in 1839 of Smith's "frequent prediction that he himself shall tarry on the earth till Christ shall come in glory, and that neither the rage of devils nor the malice of men shall ever cause him to fall by the hand of his enemies until he has seen Christ in the flesh at his final coming."[22]

Early Mormons also understood Smith's prophecy to refer to the end of the world in 1890-91. One writer admits, "in 1890 there was a widespread belief among church members that Joseph Smith's prediction of 1835, that fifty-six years would 'wind up the scene,' would be fulfilled."[23] So strong did the belief become that Parley P. Pratt, a leading member of the church, said in 1838, "I will prophesy, that there will not be an unbelieving Gentile upon this continent 50 years hence; and if they are not greatly scourged, and in a great measure overthrown, within five or ten years from this date, then the Book of Mormon will have proved itself false."[24] When the church reprinted Pratt's writings in 1952, they ordered the statement removed.

Failed Prediction of the Great Temple in Independence, Missouri. Another failed prediction concerns the building of a massive temple for the faithful in Independence, Missouri, during the lifetime of the "generation" then living.[25] Even today no temple stands on the site. Though apologists now assert that "generation" really means "dispensation," other collateral references easily show that Smith meant the temple to be completed before Christ's return in 1891. Another prophecy predicted the "Gathering" of Smith's followers during the lives of "the generation then living" in Jackson County, Missouri. His prediction drew staunch defense in the early church.[28] Today, the idea of a "Gathering" lies abandoned,[29] an embarrassment to those who attempt to prove Smith received "revelations" from God.

Failed Prediction Regarding His Son. Smith also prophesied that his son, Joseph Smith III, would follow him as leader of the Saints.[30] The predicted succession failed after Smith's assassination in 1844. With the assassination, and at the insistence of Brigham Young, most Mormons left Missouri and traveled to Utah. There, Young, and not young Smith, had himself proclaimed prophetic successor. As Crouch concluded,

> ... a greater weight of testimony exists to establish that Smith did bless his son and ordain him to be his successor than exists to establish the reality of the plates from which the Book of Mormon is said to be translated. ... When

the Mormons accepted Brigham Young as the "prophet, seer, and revelator" of the church it constituted a weighty indictment against the claim that Joseph Smith, Jr. was a prophet of God.[31]

At first, apologists denied Smith gave the prophecy. Those efforts stopped a few years ago when sources revealed the existence of a handwritten blessing of Joseph Smith, Jr. that included his son's right to succeed his father as head of the Saints.[32]

Brigham Young, like his predecessor Joseph Smith, Jr. made numerous predictions which were never fulfilled.

Prophecies Against Government. Conflict with government characterizes much of the life of Joseph Smith, Jr. Issues promoting the conflict included polygamy, the group's militant, armed stance, and efforts to go around or co-opt local authorities. In May 1843, Smith lashed out at the federal government. He claimed that if it did not redress the wrongs perpetrated by Missouri upon the Mormons, "in a few years the government will be overthrown and wasted, and there will not be so much as a potsherd left."[33] Smith's language became more abrasive in December when he petitioned Congress again. If Congress refused, he claimed, "God shall damn them, and there shall be nothing left of them — not even a grease spot."[34] His language in a letter to John C. Calhoun was even more expressive.[35] Neither the strong language nor the threats helped. No petition was granted. None of the predicted calamities followed.

Finally, a collateral prophecy by Orson Pratt also failed. He wrote regarding New York City:

> The great, powerful, and populous city of New York ... will in a few years become a mass of ruins ... there are some in this congregation who

will live to behold the fulfillment of these and other things, and will visit the ruins of mighty towns and cities scattered and desolate of inhabitants."[36]

Other Failed Predictions

Perhaps the most unusual of Smith's predictions appears in the journal of Oliver B. Huntington. Huntingdon had become one of Smith's most devoted disciples. He recorded that Smith predicted there were people living on the moon who grew to be approximately six feet tall, dressed like Quakers, and lived to be 1,000 years old.[37] When American astronauts landed on the moon in 1969, no such people appeared.

At the outset of his work in 1830, Smith prophesied that the Lord had told him a copyright of the Book of Mormon would be sold in Canada in the 1830s.[38] It was not. He told his followers that a "revelation" from God informed him that he and his followers would receive great wealth and many more disciples in Salem, Massachusetts.[39] Neither occurred. Smith also announced that a "revelation" informed him that he would never be harmed.[40] Assassins murdered him in Nauvoo, Illinois.

Another prophecy, relating to David W. Patten, one of Smith's early followers, ended in similar disaster. On April 17, 1838, Smith wrote, "Verily, thus saith the Lord ... David W. Patten ... will testify of my name and bear glad tidings unto all the world."[41] He died of gunshot wounds on October 25, 1838. McElveen summarized the obvious: "God, who knows the future, would not call a man to go on a mission and have it predicted and recorded if He knew the man would die before the time of the mission."[42]

One prophecy that Smith's followers assert establish his claim as a prophet is his prediction of an impending Civil War to begin in South Carolina.[43] Smith claimed to receive the prophecy on December 25, 1832. If true, it is surprising that it fails to appear in the 1835 edition of the *Doctrine & Covenants*. In fact, it did not appear in print until July 1851.

Still, the actual date is unimportant. In both fall 1832 and summer 1851 war clouds darkened the nation. At both times, many authorities openly predicted civil war to be imminent. In 1832 South Carolina stood in virtual rebellion against President Andrew Jackson and the Union over the issue of tariffs. The rift became volatile when Carolina, backed by much of the South, declared the tariffs "null" and threatened separation from the Union.[44] The action incensed Jackson. A warship and "seven revenue cutters" entered Charleston Harbor. Federal authorities hurriedly reinforced area garrisons. Should war come, Jackson — the hero of New Orleans and the Creek Wars — stated he would personally assume control of the troops. After several tense months, the crisis passed.

If Smith offered his prophecy on December 25, 1832, he merely reflected widespread public opinion. Worthy of note was a front-page editorial in the *Painesville Telegraph and the Geauga Free Press*, a newspaper published only a few miles from Smith's temporary home in Kirtland, Ohio. Four days before Smith's prophecy, the paper criticized Georgia and South Carolina, noting their action "aims at once at armed rebellion and civil war."[45] Thus, as Jonas explains, "At the time Smith made his prophecy, the nation expected a war between North and South to begin at the rebellion of South Carolina."[46]

By 1835, when Smith first published his *Doctrine & Covenants*, the crisis had subsided. If the prophecy was deliberately left out of the first edition, one plausible reason for the "oversight" is that Smith spoke of the altercation in 1832 and felt the prophecy no longer valid. Later, in 1851, the crisis seethed again, and the prophecy reappeared. Again, many authorities predicted war. On May 5, 1851, the Southern Rights Association held its convention in Charleston and openly affirmed the right of secession.[47] So, whether the prophecy originated in 1832 or 1851, Smith or some unnamed prophet merely reflected popular opinion.

Yet another discovery supports the theory. A handwritten copy of the revelation, suppressed for years by the church, reveals an additional 300 words. These extra "words" in the revelation are found in Joseph Smith's diary for March 11 and April 2, 1843. The March 11 entry describes a dream in which an old man asks for Smith's help in escaping an armed mob. He supposedly tells Smith that large numbers of men would be placed under his command. Just before the April 2 revelation, editors provide us with an interpretation of the March 11 dream. It reads in part, "old man. government of these United States, who will be invaded by a foreign (sic) foe, probably England. U. S. Government will call on Gen. Smith to defend probably all this western territory and offer him any amount of men he shall desire."[48] They explain:

> The reason that it was suppressed is obvious: Joseph Smith was dead by the time the Civil War started, and therefore the interpretation could not be fulfilled. In his first account of the prophecy on the Civil War, Doctrine & Covenants 87:3, Joseph Smith had predicted that England would come into the war and that the war would spread until it "shall be poured out upon all nations." The war did not spread to "all nations" as Smith had predicted, and the U.S. government certainly did not call upon Joseph Smith to protect it from England or any other country.[49]

Though Smith predicted war would begin in South Carolina, he also said it would "be poured out on all nations;" it was not. He predicted Great Britain and other nations would enter the conflict; they did not. He said new

alliances would form as a direct result of the war; they did not. He predicted a rebellion of slaves because of the conflict; no rebellion followed. He
predicted Indians would rise to oppose the people; they did not. He predicted in a letter to N. E. Seaton, on January 4, 1833, that all the wicked of his
generation would soon be destroyed in civil conflict;[50] they were not. The
Civil War prophecy hardly establishes Smith as one able to see the future.[51]

Failures of the "End-Time" Doomsayers

No evaluation of modern prophecy would be complete without a brief
review of the failure of a series of self-styled prophets. These "doomsay-
ers" struggled to set the date for Armageddon. They appear in every generation. Ignoring the plain statement of Jesus that even he did not know
the timing of his return, these zealous "prophets" offer their predictions
of humanity's terminal point.

That Christians expect Christ's return is undeniable. That is taught
plainly in Scripture. That Christians in the first century prayed for, and
longed for, his return is equally certain. That some first-century
Christians believed that Jesus stood poised to return at any moment is
also undeniable. Yet, Jesus charged his followers to "keep watch,
because you do not know on what day your Lord will come" (Matt.
24:42). Earlier, he explained,

> As it ways in the days of Noah, so it will be at the coming of the Son of
> Man. For in the days before the flood, people were eating and drinking, mar-
> rying, and giving in marriage, up to the day Noah entered the ark; and they
> knew nothing about what would happen until the flood came and they knew
> nothing about what would happen until the flood came and took them all
> away (Matt. 24:37-39).

Montanus and "End Times" in Central Turkey

Unfounded speculation and claims constantly display their seductive
goods to anyone willing to look. In the middle of the second century,
Montanus declared himself a "prophet" and announced the "new
Jerusalem" would soon "descend from heaven" and take root in Central
Turkey (ancient Phrygia). Christians throughout the Roman world were
ordered to move to the region to await the coming of the Messiah.
Montanus was wrong.[52]

The Surge of Speculation near 1000 A.D.

As the old millennium drew to a close, predictions of the "end" proliferated. Even the normally staid Catholic Church jumped into the fray.

Brookes explains: "Intense excitement prevailed throughout a large part of Europe." They believed Christ would return after the "first thousand years of the Christian era. ... Multitudes sold their estates to unbelievers and gave away the proceeds in charities, business was neglected, the fields were left uncultivated, and for some years the wildest confusion and terror reigned."[53] Again, the "seers" failed in their efforts.

Other Attempts at Predicting the End

Throughout the second millennia of the Christian Era, many self-proclaimed prophets appeared briefly on the doomsday stage.[54] Their success rate remains at zero. One typical effort came from German bookbinder Hans Nut in 1527. Declaring himself a prophet and announcing the end of time as 1528, he predicted a thousand years of free food, love, and free sex.[55] Nut's escapades led him afoul of authorities. They captured him in 1527. Shortly afterward, in an attempt to flee Augsburg Prison, Nut lost his life.

William Miller's end-time prophecy regarding 1844 stirred large sections of the country. When the judgment failed to materialize, Miller lost credibility as God's spokesman.

Failed Prophecies in 1844

The first major prophetic revival of the modern era came in the nineteenth century when William Miller set the period from March 21, 1843, to March 21, 1844, as the year Christ would finally return. Miller's followers numbered at least 50,000, mostly in upstate New York and New England. So assured were they of the date set by Miller, they sold their property, refused to plow their fields, gave away their possessions, donned "white ascension robes," and climbed to the tops of trees and houses to await Jesus' reentry. Four times he set specific dates. Four times, he failed. The last effort — October 22, 1844 — collapsed his prestige and believability. It would soon be resurrected by another. To

his credit, he publicly acknowledged his error and never again set another date. The damage had already been done.
A later review of the movement describes the reaction:

> The world made merry over the old prophet's predicament. The taunts and jeers of the "scoffers" were well-nigh unbearable. If any of Miller's followers walked abroad, they ran the gauntlet of merciless ridicule.
> "What — not gone up yet? — We thought you'd gone up! Aren't you going up soon? — Wife didn't go up and leave you to burn, did she?"
> The rowdy element in the community would not leave them alone.[56]

Perennial Failures at Prediction

No organization speculates/prophesies more about "end-times" than does the Jehovah's Witnesses. From the days of their founder, Charles Taze Russell (1852-1916), to the present, the ghostly caravan of failed and decaying prophecies offer mute testimony to the futility of failed prophecy.

Russell Claimed to Be a Prophet. The Witnesses published Volume VII of Russell's *Studies in the Scriptures* series the year following his death. Editors Woodworth and Fisher set forth the following claim:

> He listened to the word direct from the mouth of God, spoken by holy men of old as moved by the Holy Spirit. ... Pastor Russell's warning to Christendom (comes) direct from God. ... He said that he could never have written the books himself. It all came from God, through the enlightenment of the Holy Spirit.[57]

Witnesses also call Russell "the special messenger to the Last Age of the Church"[58] and "the sole steward" of biblical truth.[59] Russell wrote in the September 15, 1910, issue of *The Watchtower* that it was impossible to learn the future from studying the Bible alone. Instead, he stated that reading his (then) six-volume set of *Studies in the Scriptures* would enlighten students far more.[60]

The Witnesses Organization Claims to Serve as a Prophet. *The Watchtower* exclaimed on April 1, 1972, that God's prophet in the present times is "not one man, but a body of men and women. ... Today they are known as Jehovah's Christian witnesses. ... this group acts as a "prophet" of God."[61] Some thirty years earlier, the organization denied being "prophets" in the true sense. At that point they merely declared themselves "interpreters" of "revealed" prophecies.[62] The January 15, 1959, issue of *The Watchtower* raises the question, "Whom has God actually used as his prophet?" The reply follows: "Jehovah's witnesses are deeply grateful today that the plain facts show that God has been pleased to use them."[63]

Double-think abounds in the Witness literature. In George Orwell's best-seller, *Nineteen Eighty-Four*, he describes the government forcing people "to know and not to know, to be conscious of complete truthfulness while telling carefully constructed lies, to hold simultaneously two opinions which canceled out, knowing them to be contradictory and believing in both of them."[64] So, when confronted with being false prophets, Witnesses are taught to respond, "Jehovah's Witnesses do not claim to be inspired prophets."[65] Yet, each issue of *The Watchtower* during the late 1970s and 1980 carried the following note in its masthead: "A WATCHTOWER enables a person to look far into the distance and announce to others what is seen. Also, this magazine, published by Jehovah's Witnesses, aids the reader to see what the future holds."[66] Whether the claim is to inspired prophetdom or inspired interpreters makes no difference. In either case, the claim is to know what no one else knows and to have gained that knowledge through supernatural guidance.

All Repeatedly Failed to Predict End-Time Events. Russell began his "prophetic" tenure by announcing that Christ invisibly returned to earth in 1874. Using this date as a stepping-stone, pointed toward 1914 as the "end" of the world. Russell wrote in volume 2 of his *Studies*: "within the coming twenty-six years all present governments will be overthrown and dissolved."[67] Volume 3 continued the prophecy, adding, that 1914 would usher in "the full establishment of the kingdom of God in the earth."[68] Likewise, the July 15, 1894, *Watchtower* concluded, "1914 is not the date for the beginning, but the end!"[69] So strong did the belief prove, that many faithful "sold all their property, refused to plow their fields, and gave away all their possessions."[70]

The failure of the 1914 prophecy left Russell undaunted. Near the end of the year, he was already speaking of other times. Throughout 1917, Witnesses spoke of 1918 in terms that implied the end of the world.[71] When 1918 didn't usher in the desired occurrences, Witnesses merely changed the date again, this time to 1925. They confidently predicted the "establishment of the kingdom in Palestine"[72] and the visible resurrection of Abraham, Isaac, and Jacob.[73] The 1980 *Yearbook of Jehovah's Witnesses* candidly admits, "A mistake has been made but, as Brother Rutherford stated, this was no reason to stop serving the Lord."[74]

Later years have proven just as unfruitful. In 1940, the Witnesses proclaimed victory by the Nazis over the British.[75] They drastically altered that prediction only a year later. In 1941, Witnesses explained that World War II would not end in victory for either side, that America and England would turn into dictatorships, and that God would rule once the Nazis were defeated.[76] All predictions failed.

Even today, the Witnesses continue to offer their string of implied "end-times." Their latest effort strongly suggested that the world would end in 1975.[77] Clearly, it did not. Gruss concludes, "the pronouncements by the Society since its beginning, should convince any objective researcher that this movement stands guilty of false prophecy."[78]

Contemporary Members of the Date-Setters.

Like the close of the first millennium, the approaching close of the second has given birth to an increasing hodgepodge of end-timers.[79] From somewhat benign predictions that fill the weekly newspapers to often violent confrontation led by men like self-proclaimed Jesus, David Koresh, many religious people have been convinced that the end of the world is near.

David Koresh and the Waco Standoff. Koresh differed from other end-timers in that he refused, at least openly, to set a specific date for the final battle between good and evil. When officers from the Bureau of Alcohol, Tobacco, and Firearms (ATF) attempted to arrest him and his followers on weapons charges, he obviously expected the final scenario to be played out quickly. More than a dozen people lost their lives in the aftermath. Through it all, Koresh preached that he and his followers "should ready themselves for a final battle with the unbelievers."[80] Those who joined him in his Waco, Texas, compound were awaiting "the end of the world."[81]

88 Reasons Why the Rapture Wasn't in '88. Much more benign from the secular perspective were the widespread distractions created by the publication of a short, 56-page booklet by former NASA engineer Edgar C. Whisenant entitled "88 Reasons Why the Rapture will occur in 1988."[82]

Whisenant set September 13-14-15, 1988, as the three days most likely for the Rapture to occur. Over three million copies of his predictions were sold.[83] The year 1988 was to be special. Yet, by the morning of September 16, the world knew Whisenant's calculations were wrong. He recalculated and set a new date for the end on October 3.[84] When that, too, failed, he changed dates again. This time he first choose September,[85] then October 1989. When the last October date fell through, he finally learned not to set exact dates and remarked that "the end would come within the next few weeks."[86]

Allowing the Possibility
of the Supernatural:
The Cosmological Argument

One concern remains. If the case for fulfilled biblical prophecies rests on such solid evidence, why do so many either ignore it or deny its validity?

Many answers are possible.

Some conclude the prophecies were composed after the events had already taken place. Some believe them to be a series of lucky guesses. Some suggest they are the result of educated men making rational deductions based on the available data. Some are concerned about predictions they believe went unfulfilled.

But I suspect most who reject the data, if they are honest with themselves, will admit they do so because they no longer accept the existence of a Supreme Being. If no God exists, it is ludicrous to speak of fulfilled prophecies. Yet, is such a rejection of the supernatural warranted by the evidence? Can modern, rational, scientific humanity still find legitimate reasons to accept the existence of Deity? I answer, "Yes!" Belief in God is at least as rational (I believe the evidence shows it to be far more rational) as the philosophies of atheism.

The Brevity of the Answer

Through the centuries, hundreds of scholars far more learned than I have debated the fine points of God's existence. These arguments march gallantly through the literature of the ages, challenging unbelievers to engage in open, intellectual combat. The battles have often become no-holds-barred engagements with many casualties and few prisoners taken. It is not the intent of this essay to dissect and evaluate these encounters.

What follows is a simplified overview of the basic reasons why countless millions of highly-educated, rational people accept the idea of a God as a reasonable interpretation of available data. Evidence marshaled favoring the existence of God comes from accepted, rational thought processes. It is just as rational to deduce the existence of God from the currently-available data as it is to conclude there is no God. Christians do not have to become intellectual pygmies.

Finally, this essay does not advocate the old Roman adage, "vox populi, vox dei" ("the voice of the people is the voice of God"). Truth can never cower into submission on the basis of a popular vote. That most educated Americans accept the existence of a Supreme Being merely suggests that such a belief can be sustained among educated people. On the pages that follow, we will explain why this is so.

Reason One: The Cosmological Argument for God's Existence

Much of modern society accepts the notion of causality and how it applies to the physical universe. Laws of causality dominate our reasoning. Insurance agents seek "the cause" of an automobile accident. Doctors search for "the cause" of an illness. Coaches view hours upon hours of film looking for "the cause" of an opponent's success. The list is almost inexhaustible. We live and operate by the laws of cause and effect. Even the founder of wave mechanics admits that the "search for causation is an instinctive tendency of the human mind."[1] The vast majority of scholars agree.[2]

The Importance of Cause and Effect in Modern Society

While studying various causes that impact our lives, we easily observe that some causes are far more complex and far-reaching than others. For example, determining the causality of a major earthquake is exceedingly more complex than attempting to find the cause of a flat tire. Yet, we believe causality can be determined in both. Even atheists betray the dichotomy between what they say and how they live. Many smugly assert that religious folk believe in God "because" of dysfunctional homes, schools, churches, and educational institutions. And, while some skeptical philosophers quibble over semantics, no atheist dares to live his/her life in a manner consistent with atheism's explanation. Neither paying lip service to a philosophy nor attempting to smuggle Christian morals into an atheistic setting can overcome the paucity of the atheistic philosophy. At least within our known, physical, universe, everything has a cause. Even noted skeptic David Hume accepted the causal principle. Hume wrote,

> I never asserted so absurd a Proposition as that anything might arise without a cause: I only maintain'd, that our Certainty of the Falsehood of that

Proposition proceeded neither from Intuition nor Demonstration, but from another source.[3]

The Distinction between Primary and Secondary Causes

Our next step evokes considerable controversy. Theists, following the philosophies of Plato and Aristotle, observe that causes exhibit an extremely limited impact when considering the universe at large. As a result, these causes wear the label of "secondary causes." By definition, these secondary causes are those that are, themselves, caused by something else. Another way of describing these causes is to note that anything that cannot explain everything else is a secondary cause. For example, a tree cannot explain the earth and is a secondary cause. A human being living today cannot explain, or be the cause of, another human who lived in 1000 B.C. The earth cannot explain the Milky Way galaxy, and so on.

On the other hand, the primary, or first, cause must meet one of two qualifications: it must either create itself from nothing[4] or it must have always existed. Only two options attempt to identify what this primary cause might be. Some claim God satisfies the description of a primary cause. Others grant that right to the material universe. Since a self-caused entity seems at odds with rational thinking, we will assume the first cause to be eternal, as having always existed.[5]

Time and space limit all physical events that we label as secondary causes. Since these finite events comprise the fabric of the universe, rational beings can conclude that the universe itself is likely to be finite as well. As ancient philosophers argued so ably, an infinite regression of secondary causes is logically improbable.

Scientists Give Dates for the Beginning of the Universe. Most scientists assign some age to the universe. Exact ages are irrelevant. Whether we assign our universe an age of 10,000 years or an age of 100 billion years, it remains that this universe had a beginning. If it had a beginning, it is finite and an unlikely candidate for the primary or first cause.

Big Bang Demands Creative Event. Further, the currently popular theory of the universe's origins, the fabled Big Bang theory, demands some type of creative birth for the universe. Dr. Robert Jastrow, director of NASA's Goddard Institute for Space Studies, in outlining the evidence for the theory, explains:

> Three lines of evidence — the motions of the galaxies, the laws of thermodynamics, and the life story of stars — pointed to one conclusion; all indicated that the Universe had a beginning.[6]

Jastrow later concluded,

> Science has proven that the Universe has exploded into being at a certain moment. It asks, What cause produced this effect? Who or what put the matter and energy into the Universe? Was the Universe created out of nothing, or was it gathered together out of preexisting materials? And science cannot answer these questions, because, according to the astronomers, in the first moments of its existence the Universe was compressed to an extraordinary degree, and consumed by the heat of a fire beyond human imagination. The shock of that instant must have destroyed every particle of evidence that could have yielded a clue to the cause of the great explosion. An entire world, rich in structure and history, may have existed before our Universe appeared; but if it did, science cannot tell what kind of world it was. A sound explanation may exist for the explosive birth of our Universe; but if it does, science cannot find out what the explanation is. The scientist's pursuit of the past ends in the moment of creation. This is an exceedingly strange development, unexpected by all but the theologians. They have always accepted the words of the Bible: In the beginning God created the heavens and the earth.[7]

To believe in the Big Bang is to accept a monstrous creative event.[8] Yet, that is highly disconcerting to atheistic philosophy, for the implication of a creative event is the existence of some force or power behind the universe. British theorist Edward Milne wrote, "As to the first cause of the Universe ... that is left for the reader to insert, but our picture is incomplete without him."[9]

The necessity of this creative act has led some scientists to mutiny. As Jastrow explains,

> ... the astronomical evidence leads to a biblical view of the origin of the world. The details differ, but the essential elements in the astronomical and biblical accounts of Genesis are the same: the chain of events leading to man commenced suddenly and sharply at a definite moment in time, in a flash of light and energy. Some scientists are unhappy with the idea that the world began in this way. ... Theologians generally are delighted with proof that the Universe had a beginning, but astronomers are curiously upset. Their reactions provide an interesting demonstration of the response of the scientific mind — supposedly a very objective mind — when evidence uncovered by science itself leads to a conflict with the articles of faith in our profession. It turns out that the scientist behaves the way the rest of us do when our beliefs are in conflict with the evidence. We become irritated, we pretend the conflict does not exist, or we paper it over with meaningless phrases.[10]

Entropy and the Laws of Thermodynamics Demand a Finite Universe. In the mundane world of practical/pragmatic science, entropy can be best understood in terms of disorder or unusable energy. The Second Law of Thermodynamics incorporates this understanding and concludes that, with the occurrence of every physical event, entropy in the universe always increases.[11] Davies' well describes the law:

> (It) says, roughly speaking, that in any change the Universe becomes a slightly more disorderly place; the entropy goes up; the information content goes down. This natural tendency towards disintegration and chaos is evident all around us: people grow old, cars rust, houses fall down, mountains erode, stars burn out, clocks run down.[12]

Consider a simple example. Suppose you find yourself building a campfire on a crisp evening. Carefully, you pile several logs together. You soak the wood with a flammable liquid. Then, you take a single match and ignite it. Soon, an orange glow testifies to the warmth emanating from the flames. Surrounding objects bask in the warmer temperatures. But the flames soon diminish, then die out altogether.

The Second Law has been in operation. Even the momentary — and highly localized — increase in heat exacted a high price. During the process, vast amounts of energy became unusable. On a grand scale, energy from the sun dissipates throughout space as the temperature of the solar system edges toward uniformity. Without an enormous expenditure of energy from our star, life on earth would be impossible. Yet, much of the energy released from the sun quickly becomes unusable as it scatters into space. On a smaller scale, energy from the campfire dissipates into the surrounding air. This energy, too, becomes unavailable for future uses due to its uniform dissipation. Everywhere we look, the story is repeated. In each event, the amount of unusable energy increases.

Here, we must remember that the First Law of Thermodynamics states that energy can be neither created nor destroyed by known physical processes. So, if the total amount of matter and energy in the universe remains constant, and if more of the energy becomes unavailable for use, it follows that, at some future point, no more energy will be available for use and the universe will grind to a halt. Physicist Paul Davies expresses the argument well:

> If the universe has a finite stock of order, and is changing irreversibly toward disorder — ultimately to thermodynamic equilibrium—two very deep inferences follow immediately. The first is that the universe will eventually die, wallowing, as it were, in its own entropy. This is known among physicists as the "heat death" of the universe. The second is that the universe cannot have existed forever, otherwise it would have reached its equilibrium end state an infinite time ago. Conclusion: the universe did not always exist.[13]

The credibility of the Second Law of Thermodynamics is impeccable. No less an authority than Albert Einstein proclaimed that it was the only law of universal content that would never be overthrown. Noted scientist P. W. Bridgman echoed that thought: "The two laws of thermodynamics are, I suppose, accepted by physicists as perhaps the most secure generalizations from experience that we have."[14] The chemist Harry Bent also confirms Einstein's analysis when he observed that the chance for one tiny reversal of entropy would be equal to the chance that monkeys hitting typewriter keys at random could produce William Shakespeare's work in succession without error.[15] Finally, even an ardent evolutionist at Cal Tech, admitted the strength of the argument. Though his naturalistic biases prevent him from accepting a creation, he wrote, "These laws argue strongly for a created universe."[16]

Thus, the evidence is consistent with a universe limited by both time and space. Given these limits, it will be necessary to look elsewhere for a primary cause. The only remaining alternative is that some force outside the universe is the cause of the universe. Of course, by itself, this argument does not prove that the force is synonymous with the God of the Bible. It does, however, make that alternative far more likely than the one proposed by atheism. And, when combined with the teleological argument that follows, the theistic alternative becomes far more reasonable.

Allowing the Possibility of the Supernatural: The Teleological Argument

The teleological argument centers on what may rationally be inferred as evidence for a plan, design, or purpose that seems to inhere in the universe and its component parts.

Although this argument appears in many forms,[1] it drew its popular appeal from the writings of William Paley. Paley illustrated the idea through what is generally termed "the watchmaker analogy."[2] In his time, the storied complexity of a well-manufactured watch prompted many spirited conversations. Using the watch analogy, the respected logician argued that anyone who chanced upon such a mechanism could not rationally conclude that it was merely the product of a fortunate string of lucky accidents. To the contrary, everything about the watch implied an intelligent maker. We would never expect the various pieces of a watch to be disassembled, placed in a large container, and shook until they reformed the watch.[3]

Yet, as illustrations in this section document, conditions necessary for the formation of life anywhere in the universe are immeasurably more complex than the orderly arrangement of a watch. Surely, if the complexity of a watch demands a planner or a designer, then the complexity of life also demands a planner or designer.[4] Before opening our argumentation, two brief lessons are in order.

Introducing Probabilities and Powers of Ten

Mathematics and big numbers intimidate most folks. They seem ill at ease with numbers surpassing trillions. It's understandable. Few people deal with such figures. Yet, awesomely large numbers play key roles in the argument from design. So, just for a moment, we turn to what scientists and mathematicians label "powers of ten."[5] Powers of ten are written as the number ten followed by an exponent. The exponent tells how many zeros follow the opening number one. The number "10," for instance, would be written as a 10^1. It would be expressed as "ten to the first power." The number "100" would be written as 10^2, or a one followed by two zeros, or "ten to the second power."

The real value of expressing numbers in powers of ten comes with numbers surpassing trillions. For example, writing the number 10000000000000000000000000000 is cumbersome. Yet, it can be expressed easily as 10^{26} or "ten to the 26th power." Besides, once we pass 10^{20} in dealing with numbers we enter a hinterland meaningful to only a few. Consider the following numbers:

10^{26} represents the distance across the known universe when expressed in inches;

10^{49} represents the weight of the universe in tons;[6]

10^{53} represents the estimated number of grains of dust in the Milky Way galaxy.[7]

10^{80} represents the estimated total number of protons, neutrons and electrons in the known universe.[8]

In dealing with such massive numbers, it is easy to lose one's perspective and focus on the number of the exponent rather than what the exponent represents. Remember that the number 10^{80} represents 100000000000000000000000000000000000000000000000000 00000000000000000000000000000 and not the real number, 80.

With large numbers, we also need a simple understanding of probability statistics or laws of chance.[9] Take a simple example such as the tossing of a coin. Since the coin has two sides, we may conclude that there is a somewhat even likelihood that someone flipping a coin at random might come up with "heads" or "tails." The probability of predicting one of the two outcomes in advance is 50-50 or one chance in two. The probability of naming the outcome of random tosses twice in succession is calculated as "one chance in two times one chance in two" or one chance in four. The probability of successive correct predictions becomes one in eight, one in sixteen, one in thirty-two, and so on.

Now, most people understand that betting one's life savings on a horse where the odds are only one in 100 that the horse will win is a foolish choice. It is somewhat akin to betting your house on the Florida Marlins or Colorado Rockies capturing the World Series in their first year of competition. Interestingly, as the odds grow to extreme levels, statisticians observe that they eventually reach a point of no return, a point at which the odds against an event occurring are so decisive that such an event will never happen.[10] On a cosmic scale, noted French mathematician Emile Borel contends that such a point is reached when odds go beyond one chance in ten to the fiftieth (10^{50}) power.[11] Lafont admits that "the impossibility threshold of any chemical phenomenon on earth is a probability of one chance in 10^{100}. [12]

Again, don't be lulled to doubt by the number of the exponent, whether 50 or 100. Remember that the actual number is a one followed by either fifty or one hundred zeros. George Wald's classic treatise, *Time's Arrow*, says that anything that is 99.995% likely should be considered certain. That is, any event with a probability of 9,995 chances in 10,000 of occurring will occur. Conversely, any event with a probability of less than five in 10,000 is extremely unlikely.

Introducing the Complexity of Life and the Universe

Life's amazing complexity defies simple explanations. When Charles Darwin first popularized the theory of macroevolution in his 1859 book, *The Origin of Species*, conventional wisdom viewed the cell as a simple organism. Darwin and his supporters knew nothing of the genetic code. The discovery of DNA and its computer-like "language of life" remained a century away. Yet, in the hundred-plus intervening years, a deluge of discoveries has swamped previous understandings of the cell and its components.

No discovery jolted the scholarly community more than the observed similarity between DNA and information systems. As our knowledge mushroomed, estimates suggested that the DNA in the simple bacterium E. coli contained the same information found on one hundred million pages of the *Encyclopedia Britannica*.[13] Put another way,

> … this would be the same as 10^{12} bits of information. In comparison, the total writings from classical Greek civilization is only 10^9 bits, and the largest libraries in the world: the British Museum, Oxford Bodelian Library, New York Public Library, Harvard Widener Library, and the Moscow Lenin Library have about ten million volumes, or 10^{13} bits.[14]

Nor did the similarity between DNA and a sophisticated computer code pass unnoticed. Even in the smallest organisms DNA's information-like code stretches for billions of lines. Each line, or group of lines, codes for a specific action. Also, randomly altering the code ends in disaster.

Early in the computer age, the Wistar Institute in Philadelphia summoned computer engineers and communication experts to examine the likelihood that information systems such as DNA might arise accidentally through chance combinations.[15] The effort stymied the experts. Random changes devastated all information systems. Murray Eden explained, "No currently existing formal language can tolerate random changes in the symbol sequences that express its sentences. Meaning is invariably destroyed."[16] University of Paris computer expert Marcel P. Schutzenberger simulated random changes in information content in the DNA code to improve gradually the DNA structure. He failed: "... if we try to simulate such a situation by making changes randomly at the typographic level ... we find that we have no chance (i.e., less than $1/10^{1000}$) even to see what the modified program would compute; it just jams."[17]

Further, several scientific studies shatter the idea of a "simple" cell originating through chance interactions of amino acids and proteins. Final numbers in these studies differ substantially because each study operated on widely diverse assumptions. Even so, all concur that a chance origin of life on earth is inconceivable.

No claims suggest that the following research includes anything more than a representative sampling. Also, most of the researchers who produced such statistics do not feel compelled to abandon their faith in nontheistic explanations. Yet, few of those researchers would dare accept such odds in the real world. Still, the results of a chance origin of a living cell or its components stagger the imagination:

Chance of one polypeptide of only ten amino acid units: 1 in 10^{20}. [18]
Chance of one protein: 1 in 10^{160}. [19]
Chance of one protein: 1 in 10^{160}. [20]
Chance of DNA chain necessary to produce one medium protein of 300 amino acids: 1 in 10^{600}. [21]
Chance of one cyctochrome c molecule: 1 in 10^{94}. [22]
Chance of sufficient enzymes for smallest theoretical organism: 1 in $10^{40,000}$. [23]
Chance of smallest theoretical organism: 1 in $10^{2,000,000}$. [24]
Chance of smallest theoretical organism: 1 in $10^{100,000,000,000}$. [25]
Chance of living cell: 1 in $10^{2,999,999,999,986}$. [26]

In reviewing such odds, most scientists admit the odds seem insurmountable. Orgel observed, "The origin of the genetic code is the most baffling aspect of the origins of life."[27] Ambrose added, "We are compelled to conclude that the origin of the first life was a unique event, which cannot be discussed in terms of probability."[28] Monod concluded of life's first appearance on earth that "its a priori probability was virtually zero."[29] Lovell calls the odds "unimaginably small,"[30] and Blum concedes that "the spontaneous formation of a polypeptide the size of the smallest known proteins seems beyond all probability."[31] Hoyle adds, "The notion that ... the operating programme of a living cell could be arrived at by chance in a primordial organic soup here on the Earth is evidently nonsense of a high order."[32]

Of course, even a single, completely functional protein would be useless by itself. Yet, for life to appear, hundreds of functional proteins and enzymes must evolve side by side. For Thorpe, that taxes credulity. He writes, "the simultaneous formation of two or more molecules of any given enzyme purely by chance is fantastically impossible."[33]

Keosian summed up the difficulties: "The simplest heterotrophic cell is an intricate structural and metabolic unit of harmoniously coordinated parts and chemical pathways. Its spontaneous assembly out of the environment, granting the unlikely simultaneous presence of all the parts, is not a believable possibility."[34]

James F. Coppedge, director of the Center for Probability Research in Biology at Northridge, California, graphically illustrates the overwhelming nature of the odds. He writes that an amoeba, traveling at the rate of one inch every 15 billion years, could carry 10^{64} universes, one atom at a time, "across the entire diameter of the known universe during the expected time it would take for one protein molecule to form by chance, under those conditions so favorable to chance."[35] French biophysicist, Lecomte du Nouy, formerly of the Pasteur Institute, reached similar odds. He claimed that the "time needed to form ... one (protein) molecule in a material volume equal to that of our terrestrial globe is about 10^{243} billion years."[36] Finally, consider Hoyle's illustration:

> Imagine a blindfolded person trying to solve the ... Rubik cube. Since he can't see the results of his moves, they must all be at random. ... If our blindfolded subject were to make one random move every second, it would take him on average ... 1,350 billion years to solve the cube. ... These odds are roughly the same as you could give to the idea of just one of our body's proteins having evolved randomly, by chance.[37]

While none of these odds "prove" the existence of Deity in the universe, they do provide a solid foundation for those who choose to accept theistic explanations. They also underscore the rationality of theism.

Seeming Evidence of Design in the Universe

Scholars also point to many examples of planning and design in the physical world.

Less than a quarter century ago, scientists expected varied forms of life to leap from every pothole in the universe. Though SETI (Search for Extraterrestrial Intelligence) programs continue to gobble up billions in tax dollars each year, an increasing number of scientists realize that life treads a razor-thin road between a fragile existence and oblivion. Living organisms simply cannot exist except under ideal conditions. That realization led British scientist Freeman Dyson to muse, "I do not feel like an alien in this universe. The more I examine the universe and study the details of its architecture, the more evidence I find that the universe in some sense must have known that we were coming."[38] Dr. Hugh Ross adds that "much fewer than a trillionth of a trillionth of a percent of all stars will have a planet capable of sustaining advanced life." He concludes, "Considering that the universe contains only about a trillion galaxies, each averaging a hundred billion stars, we can see that not even one planet would be expected, by natural processes alone, to possess the necessary conditions to sustain life."[39]

Conditions Necessary to Sustain Advanced Life.

Ross and others were confronting rapidly-multiplying knowledge that continually identifies the precise conditions on which advanced life-forms are totally dependent. For example, living organisms require heat and light from a single, nearby star. More than a single star would disrupt the delicate orbital balance necessary for life. That star must exist in a narrow belt surrounding a galaxy. The centers of galaxies where most stars appear produce too much radiation and gravitational pressures to allow the formation of life. The star must also emit a specific amount or heat and light regularly over an extended period.

Moreover, the planet must exist at a precise distance from the star. Estimates suggest that merely moving the earth from 1-5% closer to or farther from the sun would spark chaos among the family of living things.[40] The planet must be just large enough to retain an atmosphere. Mercury is too small to retain an atmosphere; the larger outer planets exert far too many gravitational pressures to allow life an opportunity to develop. The planet's electromagnetic field must maintain a meticulous balance. If it were much stronger electromagnetic storms would disrupt any life form on the planet. If it were much weaker, it would be incapable of shielding fragile life-forms from intense and deadly stellar radiation. The atmosphere of the planet must be composed of a delicate mix of gases. More oxygen would prompt excessive fires on the planetary surface. The thickness of the planetary crust must be sufficient to limit volcanic and tectonic activity, yet not so large as to absorb extra oxygen from the atmosphere.

Scientists also observe that the earth-moon system provides an optimum opportunity for life's existence, as does the tilt of the earth on its axis, and the location of most land masses in the northern hemisphere.

And evidence continues to accumulate. The collision of Comet Shoemake-Levy 9 with Jupiter in mid-1994 prompted numerous studies of the likelihood of cometary collisions. The results revealed startling new information—the presence of Jupiter at its exact location in the solar system diverts comets from likely catastrophic collisions with the earth.[41]

Necessity of Unique Molecular Structures.

Not only must larger structures cooperate, life also depends on the precise function of certain elements and molecules. Scientists tell us the unique stability of carbon is crucial to life's existence, as is the unique molecular arrangement of the water molecule.[42] That arrangement creates the necessary properties on which all living things are singularly dependent. Examples such as these and many others even lead evolutionists and atheists to admit the uniqueness of life.

Although their conclusions reject Deity, Barrow and Tipler agree with the uniqueness of life on earth,[43] a conclusion echoed by many scientists.[44] They explain, "there has developed a general consensus among evolutionists that the evolution of intelligent life, comparable in information-processing ability to that of Homo sapiens, is so improbable that it is unlikely to have occurred on any other planet in the entire visible universe."[45] Though this "consensus" is decidedly anti-God, they candidly admit the "improbability" that intelligent life-forms result from random processes.

Evidence of Plan or Design in Living Things.

As impressive as the case may be that the earth and its constituent elements demand a "designer" or "planner," the living world speaks just as clearly. Even the tiny number of examples chosen offer meaningful grounds to suspect an intelligent plan in nature.

Amazing Defenses of the Bombardier Beetle.

An audible "pop." A tiny puff of vapor. For humans, both appear meaningless. Yet, for would be predators like ants, preying mantids, wolf spiders, frogs, and mice, they signal pain and failure. In their search for food, they had stumbled over a bombardier beetle. The hunted has turned back the hunter. In this game of mouse and beetle, it is the beetle that generally emerges victorious.

The secret of the beetle's success lies in a unique defense mechanism. This mechanism produces a vile spray, similar to tear gas, that can disable an attacker long enough for the beetle to scurry to safety. The spray originates in two glands, one producing hydrogen peroxide, the other, hydroquinones. When a beetle feels threatened,

... muscular compression forces these chemicals into a "reaction chamber" containing enzymes that catalyze hydroquinones' oxidation. The reaction products are benzoquinones — odorous and irritating substances — and gaseous oxygen — which propels the spray out of the beetle's abdominal tip.[46]

Also, the beetle's abdominal tip contains two external tubes that can direct the spray, which emerges at approximately 100 degrees centigrade, in any direction. The apparatus defies simple explanations. First, mixing hydrogen peroxide and hydroquinones produces highly explosive conditions. Together, the two prove so volatile that they supply key ingredients for use as rocket fuel. German scientists who first studied the beetle labeled the area where the mixing occurs as a "combustion chamber." Second, the apparatus is valuable to the beetle only when fully functional. Kofahl and Seagraves reason,

> a rational evolutionary explanation for the development of this creature must assign some kind of adaptive advantage to each of the millions of hypothetical intermediate stages in the construction process. But would the stages of one-fourth, one-half, or two-thirds completion, for example, have conferred any advantage? After all, a rifle is useless without all of its parts functioning. One small part missing or malfunctioning renders the rifle useless except, perhaps, as a club.[47]

Similarly, Ginskey argues,

> The creature contains a complex and elaborate system for producing, aiming, and firing an explosive, poisonous mixture of unstable chemicals. The inner compartments containing the two potentially explosive chemicals must have always been securely isolated from the outer reaction chamber containing the special enzymes that initiate the explosion. Unless everything worked perfectly from the very beginning, the bombardier beetle could literally have blown himself into extinction — or at least boiled himself alive. Nor would the ability to produce such mini-explosions of noxious spray have been of much survival value unless the beetle also had the ability to properly aim the resulting spray at a potential predator.[48]

The apparatus is more likely the result of a distinct plan or design than of an indeterminate series of "lucky accidents."

Mysterious Symbiotic Relationships.

Symbiosis, a term fashioned by mycologist Anton deBary from two Greek words meaning "life together" in 1876, refers to "any mutually beneficial association between two or more dissimilar organisms."[49]

Parasitic relationships are not included. While countless examples of relationships exist, some argue strongly for a design or plan.

Consider the relationship between the mimosa tree and a tiny beetle called a mimosa girdler. Mary Batten explains,

> When a female beetle called a mimosa girdler finds a mimosa tree, it climbs up the trunk, crawls out to the end of a limb, cuts a slit in the bark and lays its eggs there. The beetle then crawls back to the middle of the branch and gnaws a girdle around it—digging just deep enough to cut off the limb's circulation. The branch soon dies, falls off the tree, and the beetle's eggs scatter. When the eggs hatch, the young beetles seek out a mimosa tree and the cycle begins again. What's in it for the mimosa? With this pruning, it survives for 40 to 50 years; without it, the tree lives only half as long.[50]

A second incredible example involves the Large Blue Butterfly (Maculinea arion) and Red Ants (Myrmica scabrinoides and Myrmica laevonoides). The story, first understood in 1915, opens when the female lays her eggs on the buds of wild thyme. When the caterpillars appear, they feed on the host's flowers for approximately three weeks. After the original feeding, never again will these insects accept plants for food again.

Upon leaving the thyme, the caterpillar searches for a red ant. When one is located, the ant "strokes the caterpillar with antennae and legs and thus causes sweet fluid to exude from a special gland in the tenth segment[51] of the caterpillar's body."[52] Eventually, the ant picks up the caterpillar in its jaws (as a cat might pick up a kitten) and lugs it back to its underground nest. For the next six weeks, the ants feed the caterpillar their larvae and, in return, milk the caterpillar's sweet fluid. After the feeding has been completed, the caterpillar hibernates until spring in an area specially prepared by the ants.

In the spring, the process resumes and soon the caterpillar spins its chrysalis. Approximately one month later, it emerges as a butterfly. With its wings folded, it is escorted through the nest by the ants and released into the open air. Its wings unfold and dry. Soon afterward, the butterfly wings its way skyward and the cycle begins again. Irishman Geoffrey Taylor concludes, "this complex, eccentric, fairytale adaptation of two different insects to one another can only be a result of final causes, and is clear evidence of intelligent design — involving, of course, an intelligent designer."[53] Amazingly, Perry notes that "all attempts to rear the large blue butterfly artificially without ant grubs ... have failed to produce adult butterflies (because the caterpillar will not pupate). It is therefore assumed that some nutrient within the grubs is essential for the caterpillar to develop."[54]

Finally, cleaning symbioses abound in nature.[55] Scientists recognize that, "it is essential for all creatures to have some method of keeping themselves clean and free from parasites. If they do not, they will probably fall ill from infected wounds or the effects of disease and blood loss."[56] Perhaps two of the more intriguing are the "two species of crabs that remove parasites from land mammals and marine iguanas" and various species of seagull that "pick parasites from the Ocean Sunfish."[57] So crucial are these species that "without the work of all the cleaners of the oceans, the effects of parasites, fungi, and injury would kill many ... species."[58]

Other extraordinary examples include the symbiotic relationships between figs and wasps,[59] certain ants and aphids,[60] the giant cowbird and other birds such as the oropendolas and caciques,[61] the leaf bug (Coptosoma) and certain types of bacteria,[62] and the devilfish (Tremoctopus violaceus) and the Portuguese man-of-war.[63]

Delicate Protection of the Giraffe's Brain

Yet another argument from design follows from some astonishing facets of the neck of the giraffe. The typical Darwinian explanation — that the neck gradually lengthened over many generations as the giraffe stretched to reach dwindling food supplies — hardly satisfies most evolutionists.[64]

The heart of the giraffe's is among the most powerful in the animal kingdom. It has to be. It must pump life-giving blood all the way to the brain. Yet, the brain of the giraffe also ranks among the most delicate in the animal kingdom and cannot tolerate high blood pressure. This creates no difficulties until Africa's tallest bends over to take a drink. At this point, without special mechanisms to control the pressure, the giraffe's brain would be devastated.

Fortunately, as Kofahl and Seagraves point out, three precise features solve the problem:

> In the first place, the giraffe must spread his front legs apart to drink comfortably. This lowers the level of the heart somewhat and thus reduces the difference in height from the heart to the head of the drinking animal, with the result that excess pressure in the brain is less than would be the case if the legs were kept straight. Second, the giraffe has in his jugular veins a series of one-way check valves which immediately close as the head is lowered, thus preventing blood from flowing back down into the brain. But what of the blood flow through the carotid artery from the heart to the brain? A third design feature is the "wonder net," a spongy tissue filled with numerous small blood vessels and located near the base of the brain.[65]

Advanced Radar of the Bat

Perhaps you can remember those sweltering summer evenings just as dusk settled. It was perfect bat feeding time. After watching these flying mammals dart back and forth across the darkening skies, chasing down their insect suppers, you probably did a typical experiment. You stooped over to pick up a small pebble. As a bat swooped into view, you chucked the pebble in its vicinity and waited to see what it would do. At first, the bat started after the airborne missile. Then, just as quickly, it peeled off and returned to hunt its supper. The bat obviously knew the difference between your pebble and a moth though it never came close to the rock. But, how? Bats have poor eyesight.

Scientists now understand that the bat flies in crowded areas and pursues insects during flight by sending out shrill noises that act in the same manner as radar. When the sounds strike something in the bat's path, an echo returns, and the bat brain computes the distance and location of the source. This calculator-like computation continues hundreds of times per second as the bat closes on its prey. Again, such features are more easily explained by design than by a series of fortunate accidents.

Many other features of design add their testimony to the argument from design.[66] Among the more noteworthy are the unique abilities of sight,[67] the reproductive system of the kangaroo,[68] the detailed and well-devised migratory patterns of birds and other animals,[69] the unusual cooling system of the gazelle,[70] the uncanny ability of the mallee to find the temperature in its underground nest,[71] and the singular shock absorber system of the woodpecker.[72]

In each, explaining various ideas, behaviors, and characters through intelligent design serves as a rational, viable option. It answers the "why" queries just as effectively, and just as scientifically, as any atheistic approach. It also leaves unanswered the "how" queries so important to science. Believing in a God no more suppresses research than believing in the existence of UFOs. As Clark concludes,

> Far from hindering progress, the recognition of purpose and design in nature has been generally helpful rather than otherwise in scientific research. In the early days of the scientific era it led to such discoveries as the circulation of blood, Kepler's laws and the principle of least action (Maupertius).[73]

Again, considerable evidence endorses faith in a Supernatural Being. And, while arguments for and against each position outlined above can be added, those who dismiss, out-of-hand, any idea because they refuse to consider the possibility of Deity, are occupying risky ground. To deny the possibility of predictive prophecy because one assumes there is no God is unwarranted.

Dating the
Old Testament Prophecies

For some, granting the probable existence of Deity still fails to provide an adequate basis for the likelihood of fulfilled prophecy. Some assume that no God could possibly be concerned in any meaningful way with a tiny speck tucked away in a corner of an immense universe. Their God sprinkles a few seeds of life throughout space, then withdraws into permanent apathy, content to let his experimental toys run their course. For authors convinced that no God would ever intervene in human history, fulfilled prophecy remains a misnomer.

The Challenge: *Ex Post Facto* Prophecies

When faced with what appear to be accurate predictions, these scholars retreat to their Maginot Line: Fulfilled predictions do not exist, only *ex post facto* forgeries. For such exegetes, Ezekiel's amazingly accurate picture of Alexander's conquest of Tyre is supposed to have eased into the prophet's record sometime after the event, the product of unnamed authors. Likewise, Jesus' detailed account of the fall and devastation of Jerusalem in 70 A.D. slithered into New Testament folklore sometime during the second century.

Critics tell us that the accounts look far too accurate to have been written beforehand. Surely, they reason, the intricate details demand an eyewitness. For these authors, Nahum's denunciation of Nineveh and her people evolved from a few articulated wishes that rabid priests and scribes later embellished for political and religious purposes. Simply, anti-supernatural scholars assume that a web of forgery, deceit, and manipulation entwine all fulfilled predictions.

Thus, a brief excursion into the timing of biblical predictions follows. Before proceeding, I freely admit that a precise dating of many predictions cannot be determined by currently accepted procedures. This ensues whether one assumes the prophecies occurred when the biblical record claims or whether one assumes them to be products from a much later period. All anyone can do is to provide a preponderance of evidence and logical reasoning. From this perspective, older, internal evidences that claim the prophecies sprang from the prophets before the events they predicted possess greater validity.

The Necessity of Considering the Internal Claims

We expect our court system to carefully and objectively weigh both sides of an issue. Suppose, for instance, your uncle names you as the chief beneficiary in his will. Suppose, also, that the will was located in his safety deposit box soon after his death. How would you feel if the court began its proceedings by announcing that the court assumed that the will was in error since it named you to receive most of the estate? Chances are, you would be livid, and rightly so. Yet, most scholars today refuse even to consider the possibilities that the prophets accurately described future events.

To be fair, one should at least consider the claims. As written, they assert the predictions precede the fulfillments. That means Nahum claims to have told the minute details of Nineveh's fall before 612 B.C. That means predictions of Babylon's doom appearing in the writings of Isaiah and Jeremiah first became public before 540 B.C. Further, that means various predictions of the Messiah must have circulated before 25 B.C. and so forth.

In addition, two Old Testament books, generally thought by even critical scholars to have been written before the 2nd century B.C., confirm that materials from earlier "prophets" existed before their own. Zechariah (7:12) speaks of "the law and the words which the Lord of hosts had sent by his Spirit through the former prophets." He obviously expected his readers to be familiar with those materials. Also, Nehemiah (9:30) writes, "For many years you were patient with them. By your Spirit you admonished them through your prophets."

For apologetic purposes, two issues of concern emerge: (1) Do the materials accurately describe events that occurred in history, and (2) Were these materials made public earlier than the actual occurrences? Answers to the initial concern appear earlier in the text. So, the only issue requiring resolution pertains to timing. Since space prevents an encyclopedic study of each prophecy, this investigation focuses on a few representative samples. But, should these predictive claims prove credible, a mantle of trustworthiness will be cast over similar claims from other prophets.

The Response: Prophecies Are True Predictions

Several predictions from the writings of the Old Testament prophets can easily be shown to have been given many centuries before their actual fulfillment.

Isaiah, Jeremiah, Ezekiel and Egypt

The various visions of Egypt's future demise occur throughout the major prophets (Isaiah, Jeremiah, and Ezekiel). Yet, most detailed predictions found fulfillment as late as the Moslem conquest six centuries after Christ. Since no reputable critic, liberal or conservative, denies the books existed in their current form in the days of Jesus, the predictions obviously came well before the actual events. Also, the Isaiah Scroll from Qumran offers definitive proof that the book, with its prophecies, predates the Christian Era.

The site of the original finds of the Dead Sea Scrolls in 1947. Discovery of portions of Old Testament writings, including the famous Isaiah Scroll, provides strong support for those who believe the Old Testament was in written form at least 300 years before the time of Jesus. (Photo courtesy, Fon Scofield Collection, E. C. Dargan Research Library of the Sunday School Board, SBC.)

Predictions regarding the Nile River, its vegetation and fisheries, Egyptian canals and culture, and the future of Thebes and Memphis as well as the loss of royalty and the decline of Egyptian power and her spoilage by foreigners all occurred during the centuries after Jesus' birth. All occurred well after the predictions. All qualify as accurate predictions, and all came from those who claimed to be prophets. At some point, critics must face reality. The books contain predictions of future events. These predictions were fulfilled in an obvious manner. Other predictions in the books make similar claims. The obvious credibility of predictions regarding Egypt lends credibility to the other predictions. If these represent actual fulfilled prophecies, then the existence of additional predictions within the same writings would be expected.

Amos, Jeremiah, and Zephaniah and the Philistines

A diversity of predictions regarding Gaza, Ashkelon, Ekron, and Ashdod and the Philistine nation as a whole cascaded from the prophets. While some fulfillments occurred during the conquests of the Babylonians and the Assyrians, others found fulfillment during the Christian era. Again, these predictions obviously predated the actual events.

Messianic Prophecies in Isaiah and the Minor Prophets

Predictions regarding the Messiah easily appeared in the years and centuries before Jesus' birth. The general time and place of his birth, his character, his use of the miraculous, his death, and his resurrection appear in non-biblical materials completed and publicized well before the first century. Even non-Christian historians document the existence of prophecies. Suetonius explains, "There had spread over all the Orient an old and established belief, that it was fated at that time for men coming from Judea to rule the world."[1] Tacitus, the famous Roman historian, also wrote of the "firm persuasion ... that at this very time ... rulers coming from Judea were to acquire universal empire."[2] Not only did Messianic predictions exist before Jesus' birth, they were widely known.

Further, that Daniel predicted the establishment and character of both the Roman Empire and Christianity and the correct timing for the appearance of the Messiah before the actual events can be confirmed by materials from Qumran. There, at least one manuscript of Daniel dates to 120 B.C.[3] This ancient find offers striking evidence that the book of Daniel existed well before the birth of Jesus and, very likely, before the blossoming of the Roman Empire.

Amazingly, most radical critics force the authorship of Daniel into the Maccabean period. They assert it originated between 168 - 165 B.C. Yet, even if their claims stand scrutiny, one still faces detailed predictions fulfilled over a century later.[4] On Daniel's prediction of the Roman Empire, Archer explains that the fourth empire described in Daniel 2 "clearly pointed forward to the establishment of the Roman Empire (as corroborated by the other symbolic representations of chapter 7)" and notes "it can only follow that we are dealing here with genuine predictive prophecy and not a mere vaticinium ex eventu." He concludes, "... the Roman Empire did not commence (for the Jews at least) until 63 B.C. when Pompey the Great took over that part of the Near East that included Palestine."[5] McDowell adds, "even if Daniel had been written around 165 B.C., the writer could not have foreseen the power and extent of Roman influence unless the visions were of a supernatural origin."[6] The argument becomes more compelling when applied to references that concern the arrival and death of the Messiah.

Dating the New Testament before 65 A.D.

The marvelous accuracy of Gospel predictions regarding Rome's conquest of Judea, Galilee, and Jerusalem leads many to argue that the synoptic Gospels were written after the events in 70 A.D. Yet, evidence for such a late date falters. Wenham's latest study, for instance, concludes that all three synoptic Gospels circulated during the fifth decade of the Christian era. He even places both Matthew and Mark during the early-to-mid 40s.[7] An earlier treatise by the respected scholar John A. T. Robinson[8] reached similar conclusions. Both works show the flimsy, deteriorating foundations on which critical scholars constructed their late-date hypotheses.

Again, no established facts deny the validity of the prophecies. If even one of the three synoptic Gospels circulated before 65 A.D., one cannot deny that it contained some amazingly accurate descriptions of the period from 66-70 A.D.

Dating the Old Testament No Later than 300 B.C.

If one can show that the Old Testament attained its final form somewhere between 400 - 200 B.C., the case for predictions predating fulfillments becomes very credible. It seems highly unlikely that the Jewish religious community would accept any book hurriedly. Given their strong oral traditions and deep appreciation for their roots, an intruder into their religious heritage would have been immediately suspect. Even an early-second century B.C. existence of the combined Old Testament scriptures would point to a much earlier existence of the prophecies.

Before dealing with specific cases, we must first decide when scholars and scribes gathered various scrolls into the Old Testament canon. The term "canon" comes from a Hebrew word (qaneh) that means a "reed" or a "stalk." Since the Hebrews used reeds as measuring devices, "canon" gradually came to mean "a standard of measurement." Thus, regarding scripture, it refers to the set of books that meet the "standard" of inspiration. Most scholars who reject inspiration assert that the first such grouping, or canonization, occurred at the Council of Jamnia around the year 90 A.D. Several factors argue against that position, and Blenkinsopp concludes that the notion is a scholarly myth without historical foundation.[9]

Evidence from the Prologue to Ecclesiasticus. The Prologue, written in 132 B.C., refers to an authoritative grouping of Old Testament scripture. This grouping included three sections, "the Law, the Prophets, and the rest of the books (the Writings)." That tripartite division is identical with the manner in which the oldest known Jewish materials divided the Old Testament writings.[10] It is reasonable, then, to believe that the reference confirms the existence of the Old Testament scriptures. Also, that Jewish leaders accepted these books as authoritative suggests that they must have been known for some time.

The Septuagint. The translation of Jewish scriptures from Hebrew to Greek in the Septuagint Old Testament occurred before the time of Jesus. Traditionally, the process began around 250 B.C. The books of the Law were translated first and the Prophets next.[11] That the translators began at this date offers strong evidence that the collection of books being translated originated many years earlier. R. K. Harrison concludes, "In all its essentials the canon was most probably complete by about 300 B.C."[12]

The Tradition of a Cessation of Classical Prophecy. The existence of a secure tradition that inspired prophecy ceased in Israel after the fifth century B.C. lends additional credibility to the belief that writings from the prophets existed by 300 B.C.[13] Zechariah (13:3) revealed the coming dearth of prophecy when he wrote, "And if anyone still prophesies, his father and mother, to whom he was born, will say to him, 'You must die, because you have told lies in the Lord's name.' When he prophesies, his own parents will stab him." Later, we read of Israel's sorrow because "the prophets ceased to appear to them" (I Maccabees 9:27). Earlier in the same book (4:45-46), we read, "So they tore down the altar, and stored the stones in a convenient place on the temple hill until there should come a prophet to tell what to do with them." Also, the apocryphal book of II Baruch (85:3) laments, "the Prophets have fallen asleep."

Though forms of prophecy continued during the intertestamental period,[14] these forms never gained widespread acceptance among either the populace or the religious establishment. One rabbinical text frequently cited (Tosephta Sotah 13:2) explains, "When the last of the prophets [Haggai, Zechariah, and Malachi] died, the holy spirit ceased in Israel. Despite this they were informed by oracles." Another rabbinical passage (Seder Olam Rabbah 30) adds, "Until then, the prophets prophesied by means of the holy spirit. From then on, give ear and listen to the words of the sages." Though scholars often attribute self-serving motives to authors of these statements, even critics admit that prophecy after Zechariah occurred "in a form considerably different from that of classical Old Testament prophecy."[15] Again, the evidence points to traditions of well-known prophetic literature that existed years before the time of Jesus.

Nehemiah's Library. An early reference (II Maccabees 2:13-14) to Nehemiah suggests that prophetic materials had been collected during his lifetime. The reference explains how Nehemiah "founding a library, gathered together the books about the kings and prophets, and the books of David, and letters of kings about sacred gifts. In like manner Judas (Maccabaeus) also gathered together for us all those writings that had been scattered by reason of the war that befell, and they are still with us."

These traditions merit serious consideration. First, in the days of the Maccabean revolt, Antiochus Epiphanes threatened to destroy all copies of the Hebrew scriptures. That he deemed them a threat speaks volumes for the reverence with which they were held. Such reverence could hardly emerge quickly in Israel. Second, following the successful expulsion of Syrian forces, Judas Maccabaeus "regathered" the materials. In describing what many witnessed firsthand, the writer of II Maccabees explains that Judas merely repeated what Nehemiah had done centuries earlier. The text implies that the book's readers were familiar with the earlier episode that followed the traumatic period of captivity in Babylon.

Critical Assumptions No Longer Convincing. Finally, the assumptions on which critics base their rejection of an early compilation and acceptance of Old Testament prophetic scriptures no longer appear tenable. A detailed examination of these failures appears elsewhere.[16]

Dating the Old Testament Books:
Isaiah and Jeremiah

Even granting that the general corpus of materials we call the Old Testament existed well before the time of Christ, can we be confident individual books and prophecies were written when they claim? Can we be confident they did not contain later additions that altered the meaning of the original text? If we seek absolute physical evidence, the answer is "no". No physical evidence proves that any book in the Old Testament was written at a specific time. Yet, neither can the critics offer contrary proof. All they can provide are fragments of evidence pieced together by highly imaginative theories. Against those fragments and theories stand the claims of the books themselves, other fragments that suggest the books are as old as they state, and fragments of counter evidence that deny the critics' theories.

In the two chapters that follow, a small portion of the arguments regarding the dating and authenticity of Isaiah, Jeremiah, Ezekiel, and Daniel come under scrutiny. Space will not permit an investigation of Lamentations or the Book of the Twelve (minor prophets). Still, the results are transferable. If evidence allows the composition of these major prophetic books at approximately the time they claim, there would be little reason to deny the same to the others. If evidence precludes these books being written until after the events they supposedly predict, there would be little reason to believe otherwise regarding the remaining books.

Throughout the investigation, three issues weave through the material. (1) Many theories dating the books very late are shaped by antisupernatural philosophies. (2) Theories denying biblical claims are beset with inconsistencies and logical fallacies. (3) Evidence offering support for these theories easily can be placed in other scenarios that complement, rather than contradict, traditional biblical dates.

In realms of law and academic debate, original claims or documents are said to possess "presumption."[1] This means they are assumed to be what they claim unless a preponderance of evidence contradicts that claim. Also, when evidence counters the claim, the opposition faces the burden of rebutting or refuting that evidence. In a round of academic debate, judges consider the failure to refute an argument to be a tacit admission that it cannot be refuted.

When dealing with higher criticism, it is often the critics who drop an argument and refuse to deal with issues. For example, critics deny the book of Daniel was written at the time it claims (c. 550-500 B.C.). In denying the internal claim, many reasons are offered in evidence. Each reason has been countered both by presenting additional evidence and by offering alternative explanations. Here, the usual pattern finds the critics refusing (for whatever reason) to answer the counter claims. Instead, they continue to parrot their original position, oblivious to their need to respond. In academic debate, repetition is not considered refutation.

So, in the following chapter, we will glance at several reasons critics reject the "claims" provided in the documents and evaluate their validity. As we attempt to determine the approximate dates when individual manuscripts first appeared, it will become obvious that, often, exact dates simply do not matter.

The bulk of prophetic fulfillments occurs well after the fourth century B.C. Geisler and Brooks explain:

> Even the most liberal critics admit the prophetic books were completed some 400 years before Christ, and the book of Daniel by about 167 B.C. Though there is good evidence to date most of these books much earlier (some of the psalms and earlier prophets were in the eighth and ninth centuries B.C.), what difference would it make? It is just as hard to predict an event 200 years in the future as it is to predict one that is 800 years in the future. Both feats would require nothing less than divine knowledge.[2]

Still, meaningful evidence dates most prophetic literature much earlier than the second century.

Dating the Book of Isaiah

The traditional view among Jews and early Christians places the composition of Isaiah during the prophet's lifetime (in the eighth century B.C.). The superscription (1:1) avows the book to be the inspired product of Isaiah ben Amoz. This view dominated thinking until the nineteenth century. Then, bolstered by a surge of anti-supernatural critics, scholars splintered the book into various strands.[3] They held each to be the work of different authors. The more common scheme attributes much of chapters 1-39 to Isaiah ben Amoz with chapters 40-66 to an unknown later prophet. Others subdivide the second section into "Second Isaiah" (40-55) and "Third Isaiah" (56-66). Still others claim additional editors, or redactors, shared in shaping the final version.

Reasons for Assigning Isaiah a Late Date

Three reasons support the critic's position. First, the times offered safe haven to those who denied the prophets intended to predict future occurrences. Clearly, if the prophets did not foretell events, the highly accurate description of history had to be written after the event.

Second, scholars detected a stylistic distinction between chapters 1-39 and chapters 40-66. They assumed these divergent styles and subjects meant different authors. In recent years, the argument has been bolstered by computer studies. In 1973, for example, Y. T. Radday published results which compared a variety of linguistic features in the two major sections of the book of Isaiah.[4] He concluded that a single author could not have written both sections. A second study arrived at related conclusions.[5]

Third, critics argued "Second Isaiah" often demands a setting during the Babylonian exile while much of the opening chapters demands a setting in Palestine. Again, critics assume the impossibility of "looking into the future."

Reasons for Rejecting a Late Date

Opposing voices countered these theories from the beginning.[6] One area that was vigorously defended — the possibility of a predictive element — has been explained earlier (see chapter three).

As to the distinctive styles, the argument simply does not relate to the date of composition. Two authors could have written simultaneously as easily as at two separate times. Moreover, accepting Isaiah as the source of the material does no disservice to the diversity of styles. Conservative scholars concede the book to be an anthology or compilation of prophecies delivered over many years and under many circumstances. Yet, they argue the anthology easily could have been compiled by Isaiah or by his disciples after his death.[7] The mere existence of an anthology does not demand multiple authors. Stylistic evaluations for most writers yield major differences between earlier materials and those written much later. Since Isaiah's prophetic career touched five decades, differences in his writing style ought to be detectable.

I sense shifts in my style between this book and earlier efforts even though less than five years separate them. In my earlier work,[8] I deliberately altered the style of chapter 25. Paragraphs and sentences are shorter. Documentation is not used. More picturesque language appears. In

short, if the standards applied to biblical prophecies were used to compare the first twenty-four chapters with the twenty-fifth, it is likely that
the study would suggest two different authors. That was not the case.
Oswalt's conclusion summarizes the point: "attribution of authorship on
the basis of style is not a precise science. It is a matter of observation
that different subject matters, as well as different periods in a person's
life produce different styles."[9]

Nor is this conclusion denied by the computer studies. At least for the
present, such results remain inconclusive. First, the instruments used in
the early studies were highly experimental and subject to experimenter
intervention or bias.[10] Second, a wide diversity of results underscore the
problems. While most critics acknowledge the Radday study, few refer
to another computer study, conducted at the same time, that reached
opposite conclusions.[11] Even two studies that reached the same general
result contained glaring inconsistencies in major details.

In summary, there is no need to postulate an "unknown" later prophet
on the basis of a variation in styles. Those who do generally choose the
alternative because of a bias against predictive prophecy or divine intervention in human affairs. Most critical scholars refuse to consider arguments counter to their theories.[12] It is easier to ignore them altogether or
to deny them an opportunity to be heard. Harrison notes that

> ... by the end of the nineteenth century it was considered academically
> bizarre and unrespectable to begin to suggest views that could be interpreted
> as maintaining the unity of the prophecy. In Europe, as in England, the
> appointment to University chairs in Old Testament depended to no small
> extent upon the amount of enthusiasm with which the prospective candidate
> adhered to the "assured findings" of the critical school in both Pentateuchal
> and Isaianic studies, a situation prevalent to a considerable degree also in
> North America.[13]

Today, anti-supernatural scholars trudge doggedly along the same
paths. Oblivious to increasing evidence that the assumptions on which
their arguments rests can no longer be sustained,[14] they continue to pile
more superstructure on old, crumbling foundations. One of their own
candidly warns his readers that ...

> Historical and literary criticism is undeniably useful when working with
> ancient sources, but not only has its limitations, it sometimes leads nowhere.
> One manifest restriction in its application to most biblical material is that the
> historical results hypothesized cannot be corroborated. The speculative char-
> acter of most such results is easily overlooked because the historical method
> is so deeply entrenched in scholarly approaches. With a little distance, we
> can see just how shaky the historical method is. ...The procedure is a dispir-

iting one, dull to read, difficult to follow, and largely illusory given the paucity of results and the conjectured historical realities dotted here and there over a vast span of time. ...E. M. Forster, struck by the cavalier way in which we treat the past, attributed the attitude to the fact that those who lived then are all dead and cannot rise up and protest.[15]

Reasons for Accepting an Early Date

Since the anti-supernatural barrage fails to justify banishing either predictive prophecy or the supernatural from the prophecies of Isaiah, we may now turn to several reliable witnesses who place the manuscript's origin years before many of its predictions came to pass.

The Isaiah Scroll from Qumran

The Isaiah Scroll, found at Qumran and said by most authorities to be a copy of an earlier manuscript of the prophet's work, gives the best evidence on the age of the book. Scholars set 200 B.C. as the earliest verifiable date for the scroll's composition, with 100 B.C. the "best guess."[16] If copies found at Qumran date from the early second century, the original should be much older. Harrison explains:

> Isaiah was in its final form not later than the beginning of the second century B.C. Allowing for the lapse of time necessary to insure knowledge of the work as a whole by responsible scribal authorities, and acceptance of it as a genuine component of the prophetic section of the Hebrew canon by general approval, it would seem necessary to advance the date of the original autograph to the middle of the Persian period at the very latest, as has also been done in connection with certain Psalms that were formerly assigned to the Maccabean period.[17]

Harrison's point strikes home. By the Maccabean period, scribal authorities meticulously poured over each manuscript to preserve them for future study. To introduce a new, previously unknown, document would create immediate, public controversy. The lack of controversy suggests that Jewish religious and scribal authorities knew of and accepted the book/scroll as authoritative long before the work at Qumran.

The Testimony of Early Sources. Early Jewish sources unanimously attribute the book and its contents to Isaiah ben Amoz. Josephus clearly credits the material to the eighth century prophet and argues that the Persian monarch Cyrus read the book.[18] That an old tradition suggests the possibility lends credence to the antiquity of the material. Also, the Jewish Talmud (Baba Bathra 15a) assigns the compilation of the oracles to Isaiah, though it asserts that "Hezekiah and his company" arranged the materials in their current form.

Cave 4 at Qumran yielded important manuscript discoveries that included numerous fragments from the book of Isaiah. Most fragments are dated prior to the time of Christ. (Photo courtesy, Fon Scofield Collection, E. C. Dargan Research Library of the Sunday School Board, SBC.)

Jewish reverence for Isaiah and the book bearing his name makes its vintage nature more believable. Throughout early Jewish literature, Isaiah was considered "as great as Moses."[19] Yet, if true, it is difficult to understand how such a powerful following could arise if much of the material first appeared during the Maccabean period or if the book originally had been limited to chapters 1-39. Obviously, the scribes at Qumran had reason already to consider the complete book worthy of reproduction.

Close Parallels with Other Writings. Much of Isaiah's material closely parallels writings of Amos and Micah,[20] both of whom wrote during the eighth century B.C.[21] When compared to these early prophets, Isaiah plainly shares both a common background and common experiences. Since most scholars accept an early origin for both books, it is contradictory to deny a comparable early origin to Isaiah.[22]

Also, similarities between "II Isaiah" and Nahum and Zephaniah,[23] both early prophets, as well as the total lack of similarity with later, supposedly contemporary writers, such as Ezra, Nehemiah, and Malachi, makes little sense if the last half of the book was written between 400 - 150 B.C. In addition, a growing corpus of evidence suggests that "the book of Kings, completed by the middle of the Exile, used the complete book of Isaiah as a source (and this) favors a pre-exilic date for the writing of the entire book."[24]

Weaknesses in the "Unknown Prophet(s) Theory. Those who deny predictive elements in Isaiah's writings smugly allege that these elements oozed from the pen of some unknown writer or group of writers much later. Although widely accepted, the position remains unproven. Every hypothesis has been countered and alternative explanations presented. Again, Harrison's comments apply:

> ... if this unknown individual had actually been all that was claimed for him ...and is to be regarded as one of the greatest, if not the most notable of the Hebrew prophets, it would indeed be most surprising if every trace of this eminent and talented man had been so completely erased from Hebrew tradition that not even his name had managed to survive. This objection has been raised many times since the days of J. A. Alexander, and over the generations it has gained rather than lost in its cogency. In fact, it is so telling that to date no convincing rebuttal has been forthcoming from critical circles, and in the nature of the case it appears highly improbable that one ever will emerge.[25]

An Unexplainable Position. Scholars representing all theological positions generally agree that chapters 40-66 far exceed chapters 1-39 in both the grandeur of their vision and the elevated nature of their development. Many speak of these chapters as the mountain peaks of Hebrew prophecy. Therein lies another problem:

> Quite aside from the fact that it would be without parallel for the name of such an incomparable individual to pass from human memory, it would also be inconceivable for his work to become the mere appendix to that of an inferior Palestinian prophet, however much the latter may have been admired by the former, and that for two thousand years his writings should have been uniformly regarded by Jewish tradition as being the work of this inferior prophet.[26]

Add to Harrison's comments the total silence in Jewish literature regarding the existence of this "Second Isaiah." No one mentions his/her name. No one even refers to this "unknown" writer. Neither Ezekiel, Daniel, Jeremiah, Ezra, nor Nehemiah hint at his/her presence. Many non-canonical Jewish writings speculate freely about the authors of other Old Testament writings. For Isaiah's unknown prophet, the materials echo with a resounding silence.

Similar Subject Matter. Contrary to the critics, many parallels exist between the two sections of Isaiah both in regard to subject matter and linguistics. For instance, Archer[27] notes a common concern for violence and bloodshed (1:15 and 59:3,7), for falsehood, injustice, and oppression (10:1-2 and 59:4-9), and religious hypocrisy (29:13 and 58:2,4). Likewise, in both sections, idolatrous practices are said to occur near pagan oak groves (1:29 and 57:5). While this does not deny major differences exist, it does note a common thread often winds its way through the differences.

Further, one lengthy passage (44:9-20) speaks of the evils of idolatry as if they were still prevalent in Israel. Other references to idolatry surface as well (57:4,5; 66:17). Idolatry persisted as a major concern before Babylonian captivity. After the exile, its strength vanished. Yet, "II Isaiah" (57:7; 65:2-4) assumes the existence of pagan "high places." These existed before the exile, not afterward. Statements in "II Isaiah" (40:9; 62:6) also imply the existence of Jewish cities. These cities lay in ruins during the Babylonian exile and for years afterward.

Yet another similarity involves the repetition of the phrase, "the Holy One of Israel." It appears almost thirty times in the book of Isaiah with a nearly equal representation in both chapters 1-39 and 40-66. Elsewhere in the Old Testament, the phrase occurs only seven times. If we assume the two parts of Isaiah to be the work of more than one author, a serious difficulty appears. Oswalt explains:

> Thus it becomes necessary to posit a "school" of students of "I Isaiah" who steeped themselves in the style and thought of the "master." It would be out of such a group that "II Isaiah" sprang during the Exile and from which, later still, came the writings which now constitute chs. 56-66. Aside from the fact that there is no other evidence for the existence of this "school," it is hard to imagine how it ever would have come into existence for Isaiah (and not the other prophets) in the first place.[28]

For Oswalt, the problem becomes more acute when one realizes that most modern critics attribute progressively less of chapters 1-39 to Isaiah. He argues,

> It is now argued that what is truly Isaianic is not of much more extent than the material of Amos or Hosea. Yet we are asked to believe that of all the prophets, only Isaiah sparked a movement which would continue for five centuries and eventually produce a book in the "founder's" name that would be some five to six times the volume of the original input.[29]

To these comments, we might add that this marvelously talented "school" supposedly so disguised their activities that they left no trace among their peers and, having finished their key task, disappeared without a trace.

Respected Scholars Find Early Appearance Convincing. No exaggerated claims accompany the following references. I recognize most scholars hold opposing views. Yet, reputable, respected scholars accept the early existence of most Isaianic materials. Their testimony provides solid evidence that the biblical claims can be sustained. A representative sample of those who contend for an early date includes Hill and Walton,[30] Coffman and Coffman,[31] Hayes and Irvine,[32] Bullock,[33] Oswalt,[34] Hailey,[35] McGuiggan,[36] LaSor, Hubbard, and Bush,[37] Willis,[38] Butler,[39] and Archer.[40]

Dating the Book of Jeremiah

The book of Jeremiah is set in the late seventh and early sixth centuries B.C. During these years, Assyrian power teetered, tottered, and crashed. A resurgent Egypt briefly overcame her internal struggles and posted one last bid for leadership. A sudden, generally unexpected, flourish boosted Babylon to the forefront of Western history. These rapid changes left a political quicksand. Backing Assyria meant war with Egypt. Backing Egypt meant war with Babylon. Either way, the tiny kingdom of Judah stood to lose. Alone, she stood little chance of turning back the mammoth military might poised on her borders. To make matters worse, Judah's moral fiber unraveled at every turn. Judah and Jerusalem slipped precipitously toward extinction.

Haplessly, Judah squandered the last opportunity to regain her character and retain her sovereignty. That opportunity surfaced during the reign of Josiah[41] when renovations in the Temple uncovered a "law-book" (II Kings 23:3ff). While no one knows exactly what the book contained, many scholars believe it held all, or part, of the book of Deuteronomy.[42] An old Jewish tradition claims the find included all five "books of the law."[43]

During the years after the discovery, Jeremiah delivered his prophecies. Whether he or someone else compiled the varied materials in the book bearing his name still produces heated debate among scholars. As was true regarding the book of Isaiah, our main concern remains the date of origin, not the specific author.

Reasons for Assigning Jeremiah a Late Date

Varied Writing Styles. The usual reason for assigning a late date to Jeremiah revolves around the work of critic Bernard Duhm.[44] Duhm claimed to isolate three distinct strands of writing in the book. These strands, later described in more detail by Mowinckel,[45] became known as Types A, B, and C. Literary critics designated the poetic speeches (generally attributed to Jeremiah) as Type A, the biographical narratives (often ascribed to Jeremiah's secretary, Baruch) as Type B, and the book's prose (said to be theological overlays by editors who applied the recently found/composed book of Deuteronomy to Jeremiah's prophecies) as Type C.[46]

The Book's Disjointed Chronology. Anyone casually reading through the book of Jeremiah for the first time will easily sense the lack of chronological sequencing.[47] Chapter 52, for example, follows the declaration (51:64), "The words of Jeremiah end here." Either chapter 52 contains a later addition to the original or the material is out of place. **Differences in Old Copies of the Book.** A third reason for assigning the book to a later period turns on differences between the words of the authorized version of the book and a shortened version found in the Greek Septuagint. The Greek translation contains some 2,700 fewer words (approximately 6-7 chapters) than modern translations.[48] Those chapters are often assumed to be the work of later writers. **Close Links to Deuteronomy.** Additional reasoning for a late date centers on a supposed relationship between the prophet and the book of Deuteronomy that is also supposed to have been composed very late.

Reasons for Rejecting the Late Date Theory

Assumptions Remain Unproven. No reason offered as proof for late dating has successfully cleared the necessary logical hurdles. Conservative scholars, without denying the distinct types of writing, normally attribute the book either to Jeremiah or to the prophet and his secretary, Baruch,[49] though some do allow unknown editors a minor role in shaping portions of the book.[50] Again, even the existence of multiple authors does not provide evidence that these authors wrote at different times.

Similarly, lack of chronological sequencing proves no more than the lack of chronological sequencing. No evidence suggests that such styles failed to exist in the seventh century B.C. As to differences between two older manuscripts, no firm conclusions are possible. It is possible the shorter version is the youngest and that a later scribe, for any of several plausible reasons, failed to copy the older manuscript in its entirety. Finally, the assumption of a late date for Deuteronomy itself relies on many unproven, and several disproven, assumptions. Also, the relationship between the two books may be less significant than originally believed.[51]

Evidence for Multiple Authors Relies on Doubtful Assumptions. In recent years, appraisals of both the multiple-authorship and late-date theories raise serious concerns about the assumptions on which these theories rest. Brueggemann, though hardly a conservative writer, explains that "the three-source critical consensus, however, is now open to serious doubt. Scholars no longer agree that the character of the book can be understood according to such a mechanistic literary process."[52] Part of the difficulty lies in a built-in bias that assumes the book to be a purely human process. Bullock writes,

> As a review of modern scholarship on the subject reveals, that process of proof is often subjective and prejudiced against the prophet. Of course, the charge can be made in the other direction, and sometimes justifiably so. Yet the assumptions upon which many critical scholars approach the prophets are based upon those materials that they will allow to these biblical spokesmen. For example, some interpreters will not allow universalism in the preexilic prophets because they assume that idea was a post-exilic belief. Even literary style is an elusive criterion for determining authenticity and must be used cautiously, although it certainly is not an invalid one.[53]

Archaeological Finds. Recent discoveries at ancient Lachish cast further doubt on the earlier consensus. Lachish fell to the Babylonians just before Jerusalem's capture in 587 B.C. When archaeologists excavated the remains from 1932-38, they found twenty-one letters written on broken pieces of pottery. The letters included language nearly identical with that found in Jeremiah along with a veiled reference to "the prophet" whose message was "Beware."[54] Though "the prophet" remains unnamed, even most radical critics admit Jeremiah offered such warnings to the people of his day.

Reasons for Accepting the Early Date

Early Jewish Witness. Like the book of Isaiah, the earliest witnesses to the book unanimously assign it both to the prophet described and to the period implied in the writings. Both Ecclesiasticus (49: 6-7) and Josephus[55] credit materials to Jeremiah. Also, the absence of any counter-tradition must be considered. Why do no ancient authorities seem to perceive the book to be the product of other authors?

Testimony of the Septuagint and the Dead Sea Scrolls. Two additional witnesses lend confidence to those advocating an early date. The Septuagint, though differing from the traditional text, includes Jeremiah. Also, scribal copies of Jeremiah appear among the Dead Sea Scrolls. Both show the antiquity of the writings.

In summary, no insurmountable evidence indicates the book of Jeremiah had to be written by some unknown author or authors at a date that would turn the prophecies into ex post facto pronouncements.

Dating the Old Testament Books: Ezekiel and Daniel

Dating the Book of Ezekiel

The book of Ezekiel bears the name of a young Zadokite priest (Ezek. 1:3) ushered into Babylonian captivity by Nebuchadnezzar. He joined some 10,000 other Hebrew slaves in the 597 B.C. diaspora (II Kings 24:10-17). Settled by his captors alongside the Kebar River/Canal in Babylon, the young priest answered a call to prophesy to his people. His book includes a series of extraordinary visions and messages. From the majestic vision of God's throne (Ezek. 1) to the provocative vision of the Valley of Dry Bones (Ezek. 37), the book exudes an imposing picture of doom and deliverance. One expositor found it so intriguing that he entitled his commentary on the book, *All Things Weird and Wonderful*.[1]

For centuries, critics found little to question about the book of Ezekiel.[2] Its style, though not homogeneous, gives all appearances of being the work of one mind.[3] Yet, by the 1920s, the quiet unanimity dissolved in a quagmire of skeptical assumptions. The most widely-known attacks spewed from the German critic Gustav Holscher.[4] His sharpened assumptions excised all but 170 of the book's 1,273 verses. Holscher claimed sections of elegant poetry could not have come from the same person who wrote the book's mundane prose. During the next fifty years, critics following Holscher dissected the book in many ways. Our interest, however, concerns only those areas related to the time the book first appeared.

Reasons for Assigning a Late Date to Ezekiel

Rejection of the Supernatural. Realistically, the major reason for applying a late date to Ezekiel is the rejection of the supernatural. Every advocate of the critical position denies predictive prophecy and attempts to explain the text without recourse to the supernatural. This study argues that the book originated during the sixth century B.C. and that allowing for the supernatural best explains its amazingly accurate descriptions of future events.

Still impressive even in their broken condition, temples at Luxor and Karnak reflect the accuracy of Ezekiel's predictions. (Photos courtesy, Dr. Marlin Connelly.)

Jehoiakim and Problems of Chronology. Critics often dispute the use of Jehoiakim's reign to date events. Jehoiakim served as king over Judah for only three months before being deported to Babylon and replaced by his nephew Zedekiah. Instead of dating by Zedekiah's reign, Ezekiel dates by Jehoiakim's. Supposedly, this reveals Ezekiel did not live contemporaneously with the captivity, else he would have known to use the reignal years of Zedekiah.

At the outset, the argument fails to impress. Had it clearly spoken for a late origin of the book, critics would have seized it during the naturalist revolution in the eighteenth century. That they did not do so reveals the weakness of the argument.

Twentieth century archaeological discoveries also doom the argument. These discoveries proved so significant that Albright claimed they offered an "inexpugnable argument in favor of its (the book of Ezekiel) genuineness."[5] In 1928-30, archaeologists unearthed jar handles stamped "Eliakim, steward of (Jehoiakim)" at both Tell-Beit-Mirsim and Bethshemesh. As Unger notes, these show that the people of Judah still viewed the deposed monarch as their rightful king, though he languished in Babylon detention.

Ezekiel's prophecy (30:7) that Egypt would "be desolate among desolate lands and their cities will lie among ruined cities," is evidence in the presence of poor farmers among the ruins of the fabled Memnon Colossi. (Photo courtesy, Dr. Marlin Connelly.)

Then, in 1925, publication of tablets found in Babylon outlining ration allotments for the Hebrew royal house confirmed that even his captors continued to regard Jehoiakim as Judah's rightful king.[7] The tablets, from the reign of Nebuchadnezzar, listed distribution of supplies to "(Jehoiakim), king of Judah."[8] Interestingly, Ezekiel (8:1) dates a vision from the "sixth year" of Jehoiakim's reign (592 B.C.), which is the exact date applied to the tablets uncovered at Babylon![9]

A Palestinian Background. Some argue that someone living in Palestine, rather than someone living in Babylon, wrote the book. As evidence, they point to detailed familiarity with both Palestinian events and settings. These arguments do little to establish a late date. Some who opt for this position claim the book was written before the exile, in the time of Manasseh, and not later.[10] Even if the book originated in Palestine, that alone does not demand it originated during the second or third century. As noted below, much in the book belies an in-depth understanding of events in the sixth century B.C. as opposed to events occurring in later centuries.

In addition, critics willfully ignore Ezekiel's 20-25 early years spent in Palestine before the Babylonian deportations. During that period he would have become familiar with many details of the culture and surroundings. Since his father, Buzi, was a Zadokite priest, Ezekiel's knowledge of the temple and religious structure in Judah should have been exemplary. Also, critics assume that no communication occurred between Ezekiel and the Jews in exile and those remaining in Jerusalem. Jeremiah (29:1f.) openly affirms such correspondence. Communication definitely existed when Jerusalem collapsed (Ezek. 33:21). In short, there are no valid reasons to assume that communication didn't exist earlier.[11]

Further, Thompson has noted several statements that presuppose a Babylonian as opposed to a Palestinian setting. The word for "brick" in the Hebrew (Ezek. 4:1) specifically refers to a mud-baked brick, common in Babylon, not in Jerusalem. Another vision orders Ezekiel (12:5-7) to "dig through" the wall of house. Since Babylonians constructed their houses of mud or adobe, that would not be insurmountable. Those who lived in Jerusalem, however, made their houses from stone. Ezekiel (13:10-15) refers to a house that would be destroyed by severe rainstorms. Again, Babylon's mud-based houses fit the text.[12]

Presence of Aramaisms. A third argument often half-heartedly advanced by critics claims that the presence of certain Aramaic elements in the book's language implies a late date. For a book containing well over a thousand verses, one would assume several such instances. That is not so.

As early as 1950, C. G. Howie lambasted critics for parroting assertions of Aramaic influence without taking time to confirm the validity of those assertions.[13] Howie's exhaustive study revealed only a few such instances. Other scenarios can easily explain each instance without resorting to a late origin for the material. Two decades later, Howie's argumentation still held as Harrison explained an inherent weakness in the critic's logic:

> ... only nine definite Aramaic roots occur, two of which were drawn from earlier Aramaic sources. ... Clearly, the amount of Aramaic influence on the book has been exaggerated, and on the basis of all available evidence there would seem to be nothing in the linguistic structure of the oracles and visions that is incompatible with a date in the early sixth century B.C.[14]

So weak is the linguistic argument that even Zimmerli concluded, "Nothing opposes the acceptance of the book's claim that its language comes from the sixth century B.C."[15]

Possible Use of Editors. Most critics assume that all prophetic books passed through a lengthy period of editing. During this period, critics further assume that editors freely embellished the prophet's original work. The evidence offered in support of this theory involves such items as the prophet's use of a variety of literary styles. Isaiah and Jeremiah are divided on that basis. That diversity is absent in Ezekiel. The effort by critics to manufacture diversity has not proven convincing.

First, the attempt to force the book of Ezekiel into the same literary mold as Isaiah and Jeremiah betrays the real motive. Everything must be forced to submit to a foundering philosophy of secular humanism. Consistency of argumentation means nothing.

Second, evidence for a single author is simply overwhelming. Zimmerli, who accepts editorial accretions, still finds himself admitting that

> ... it is not possible in the book of Ezekiel to remove the stylizing which has been outlined, as a dress that has been put on subsequently, and find beneath it a basic material which has been composed differently. This necessitates the view that, not only behind the book in its present form, but also behind the composition of its individual parts, there stands a definite plan which itself points back to a particular hand. Ezekiel's own hand has given his message this characteristic stamp.[16]

Harrison views the uniformity even stronger: "The work exhibits such homogeneity that serious questions must be raised about any theory of editorial activity by someone other than the prophet himself."[17] Also, Greenberg, in his latest commentary, admits the evidence comes down conclusively on the side of a sixth-century prophet who provided the picture if not the frame of the book.[18] Manweiler agrees: "Ezekiel is probably the most carefully dated of all the Old Testament books. ... the majority of biblical scholars, even those who reject the inspiration and unity of the Bible, believe most of the book was written in the sixth century B.C. by the prophet Ezekiel."[19] Smith's conclusion is apropos:

> The critical studies of the Book of Ezekiel over the past fifty years or so have largely canceled each other out. The situation now is much the same as it was prior to 1924 (the work of Holscher) when the unity and integrity of the book were generally accepted by the critics.[20]

Reasons for Accepting the Early Date

After reviewing theories for a late date offered by critics, Weevers concludes, "these contrary views have received little support. The evidence for the approximate correctness of the traditional date for Ezekiel's work seems overwhelming."[21]

Clear Relevance to the Period. As Weevers notes, "Clear references to the final rulers of Judah (Jehoahaz, Jehoiakim, Zedekiah) presuppose the traditional dates."[22] A second contemporary reference relates to the description of the temple gate (Ezek. 40:5ff.). Nebuchadnezzar's forces decimated Solomon's Temple. After all eyewitnesses to the building's design had died, only a general conception of the building would have remained. The Second Temple, though following the original pattern as closely as possible, never came close to being an exact duplicate. One change related to the design of the gates. Harrison explains the relationship between Ezekiel's description and the early dating of the book:

> That the vision of the Temple in Ezekiel 40:5ff. was a subconscious reflection of a real structure is indicated by the fact that the east gate, on reconstruction, proves to be of the same general type as that excavated from the Solomonic period of Megiddo by Nelson Glueck. Such a memory must have arisen, as Howie has observed, from one who was acquainted with the Solomonic Temple in some detail, since gates constructed after the general pattern described in Ezekiel were not found after the early ninth century B.C.[23]

Close Attention to Dates. Another factor pointing to an early origin for the book can be found throughout the book in the close attention given to the specific dates when various events occurred. Awareness of detail in this area can be consistently detected in non-biblical materials from the sixth century. On the other hand, close attention to dates had become far less important from the late fourth century through the Maccabean period.[24]

In conclusion, cogent arguments support placing the origin of the book of Ezekiel during the sixth century B.C. at the time claimed by the text.

Dating the Book of Daniel

Those interested in picturesque stories will find the book of Daniel to be a treasure-trove of excitement and mystery. From the vivid imagery of the blazing inferno to the surprising quiet of a lion's den, the book glistens with stories that, at first glance, seem incredible. Those stories are just one reason that many critics opt for a late writing of the book.

Reasons for Assigning a Late Date to Daniel

An Antisupernatural Bias. The usual reasons for assigning Daniel to some unknown second century author stem far more from antisupernatural presumptions than from the preponderance of evidence. Young writes that "the negative view of the book of Daniel took its rise in a non-Christian atmosphere, and has been ably advocated by men who were opposed to the supernaturalism of Christianity."[25] Allis supports Young's observation. He notes that "In textbooks which represent the critical or higher critical viewpoint it is regarded as a matter of prime importance to explain the supernatural, which often means to explain it away."[26] Goldingay writes in his recent commentary that "Critical scholarship has sometimes overtly, sometimes covertly approached the visions with the a priori conviction that they cannot be actual prophecies of events to take place long after the seer's day, because prophecy of that kind is impossible."[27]

The most scathing attack on the modern theological science that supports critical analysis of both Old and New Testaments comes from former adherent Eta Linnemann: "Scientific theology was born, not because people were committed to the Bible, but because they sought reasons to avoid obligation to its teachings."[28] She adds, "To a great extent the sacrificial, painstaking labor that scientific theology expends amounts to a working out in intricate detail the philosophical mold into which Scripture must be shaped."[29]

The Use of Aramaic Words. A second argument for a late origin involves the use of certain Aramaic words. Earlier scholars alleged these words could only come from Aramaic spoken in western Syria and Palestine after 300 B.C.[30] That argument no longer holds. Daniel's Aramaic style appears in wide use as early as the sixth century B.C. and in limited use centuries earlier.[31] Discoveries of the Elephantine Papyri in Egypt offer conclusive evidence that Daniel's Aramaic had spread throughout the Mediterranean world long before the second century. A. R. Millard concludes of these discoveries that they "invalidate such linguistic objections, especially in showing that the Aramaic is identified with the sixth and fourth centuries, not the second."[32]

Other linguistic evidence also denies the assertion.[33] Robert Dick Wilson, an accomplished linguist who could communicate in 45 languages, drove a stake through the heart of the critics' assertion:

> ... the composite Aramaic of Daniel agrees in most every particular of orthography, etymology and syntax, with the Aramaic of the North Semitic inscriptions of the 9th, 8th and 7th centuries B.C. and of the Egyptian papyri of the 5th century B.C., and the vocabulary of Daniel has an admixture of Hebrew, Babylonian and Persian words similar to that of the papyri of the 5th century B.C.; whereas, it differs in composition from the Aramaic of the Nabateans, which is devoid of Persian, Hebrew, and Babylonian words, and is full of Arabians, and also that of the Palmyrenes, which is full of Greek words, while having but one or two Persian words, and no Hebrew or Babylonian.[34]

In addition, the Aramaic used by Daniel shares marked similarities with documents unearthed at Ras Shamra that appear to go back as far as the 15th century B.C.[35] Besides, fully "nine-tenths of the vocabulary (in Daniel) is clearly old — established (fifth century B.C. and earlier)."[36]

The Use of Persian Words. Another tantalizing argument offered by early critics concerns the use of Persian words. Yet, why this should be problematic is difficult to understand. Daniel lived well into the days of the Persian Empire. Surely he would be acquainted with the Persian language. Clinton writes:

> Daniel lived part of his life under Persian rule. He may have reedited the early chapters himself including up-to-date terminology at these points. Most of these words concern government and administration and it would be fitting for Daniel to bring these more in line with the current situation.[37]

The Use of Greek Words. Critics claim the appearance of three Greek words (each naming a musical instrument) in Daniel "demands" a date after the conquest of Alexander.[38] The "demand" is comical. Three Greek words in an entire book hardly "demand" anything. Even if these words could not have originated until much later, their appearance may be explained easily. For example, the three words could have been "edited in" later by a scribe/translator who replaced an older name with one that was newer.

Even that simple alternative is unnecessary. Research shows extensive contacts between Persia/Babylon and the Greek world as early as the eighth century B.C.[39] The most significant contact — recorded by Neo-Babylonian ration tablets — included importing Greek musicians from the Philistine city of Ashkelon to Babylon before 600 B.C. A transfer of Greek names to Mesopotamian instruments could occur with ease under such conditions.[40]

Of the three Greek words used as evidence, one *(kitharos)* appears in the writings of Homer as early as the eighth century B.C. As such it can have no bearing on a possible second century origin of the book.[41] Besides, evidence now suggests that the Greek word itself may have originated in Mesopotamia.[42] One scholar marshals a wealth of evidence to support the thesis that both ancient Mesopotamian musical instruments and musical notation were among many elements of culture transmitted to the Greeks. He concludes, "The influence exerted by Mesopotamian culture on the western world was far reaching."[43]

Only two words, then, could have even remote relevance to supporting a second century origin for the book. As Kitchen explains, "this is only negative evidence, i.e., lack of evidence, and there is nothing to prevent earlier occurrences from turning up."[44]

Upon examination, evidence here appears just as ephemeral. The second instrument ("sackbut" in the KJV; "lyre" in the NIV) cannot be definitively traced to Greek origins.[45] The word could have originated either in Arabia or Akkad. Yet, even if the word is of Greek origin, current understandings show "it might be best to reverse the order of the borrowing, seeing the Greek ... as having been borrowed from the Near East."[46] Given the uncertainty, the word hardly "demands" anything.

Another reason for minimizing the "demand" centers on logical difficulties that arise should the critics' position be adopted. McGuiggan questions,

> ... what if the liberal (critic) was right? It would mean the book was written at a time when Palestine had been under Greek government and influence for about 160 years! And all we find are three Greek words designating instruments of music! Would this not rather speak for a pre-Alexander date? Why isn't the book riddled with Greek words? Why aren't there numerous words of Greek origin relating to government? The Aramaic of Daniel, we are told, was a linguistic medium which readily absorbed foreign terminology. Where are all the Greek words?[47]

Given the weaknesses, it is telling that modern critics admit that this argument provides "the strongest evidence in favour of the second century B.C." origin for the book of Daniel.[48] If this is the best evidence, surely those who accept the early date for the book's composition have little to fear.

The Style of Hebrew Words. Critics observe that the Hebrew language underwent key changes in vocabulary and syntax during the time of Nehemiah. They then assert that the Hebrew vocabulary and syntax in Daniel closely parallels the later style, not the earlier.[49]

Again, the flimsy nature of the supporting evidence collapses under investigation. First, Hebrew sections in the book contain Persian words but no Greek words. Archer adds, "If Daniel were written around 165 B.C., the absence of Greek terms, especially political and administrative terms, is inexplicable."[50]

Second, the Hebrew used in Daniel is remarkably similar to that found in Ezekiel, a book most critics assign to the period of the exile.[51] Coupled with that comparison, researchers note a significant difference in the Hebrew of Daniel and that of Ecclesiasticus, a book written simultaneously to the time critics assert Daniel came into existence.[52] Additional material originating at Qumran in the second century B.C. exposes glaring differences between Daniel's Hebrew usage and that of the Qumran authors.[53] If editors wrote the book of Daniel in the second century, the opposite should be true.

The Use of Apocalyptic. Another reason for adopting a late date involves the use of apocalyptic language. The argument draws parallels between the apocalyptic language/style in Daniel and the language/style found in other Near Eastern apocalyptics. Critics argue that Daniel's style could not possibly have existed in the sixth century B.C. Yet, as

Wilson ably pointed out years ago, the only examples of Hebrew apocalyptic writing (Jubilees, the 12 Patriarchs, Enoch, the Sibylline Oracles, and Baruch) thought to have been written in the second century B.C. differ radically from that of Daniel.[54] The attempt to tie Daniel with Akkadian apocalypses fares no better.

Jewish Placing of Daniel in the Hagiographa. The Hebrew Old Testament currently in use is partitioned into three sections the Law (Torah), the Prophets (Nebiim), and the Writings (Kethubim). Five books, those commonly credited to Moses (Genesis to Deuteronomy), comprise the Torah. The section of the Prophets houses eight books (Joshua, Judges, the books of Samuel, the books of the Kings, Isaiah, Jeremiah, Ezekiel, and the Book of the Twelve). All remaining books appear in the Writings. It is this last segment that contains the book of Daniel.

Because this segment appears in the Writings rather than in the Prophets, critics assert that the book must be a late addition to the Scriptures — probably originating in the second century B.C. Driver clearly outlines the argument:

> ... the division known as the 'Prophets' was doubtless formed prior to the Hagiographa [Writings]; and had the book of Daniel existed at that time, it is reasonable to suppose that it would have been ranked as the work of a prophet, and have been included among the former.[55]

Implicit in Driver's commentary are several assumptions. One, he assumes the three sections of the Hebrew Scriptures were completed in stages with the "Writings" being the final stage to be finished. Two, he assumes early Jewish scholars would have considered Daniel to be closely related to Isaiah or Jeremiah. Three, other critics also assume that, if the book did exist when the section known as the "Prophets" was completed, it found its way into the "Writings" because it was merely a historical book written in apocalyptic language.

All three assumptions are invalid.

As to the widely held three-stage development theory, no physical evidence has ever supported it. It is supported by assumptions and inferences. It also flies in the face of the oldest evidence that exists regarding the make-up of the Hebrew Bible. Josephus plainly states that the Old Testament Scriptures were completed in approximately 424 B.C. with Malachi's prophecy. No evidence older than Josephus contradicts that view. Also, no evidence for nearly 300 years after Josephus contradicts his statement.

Josephus divides the Scriptures into three sections. Section one includes the five books of the law. Section two includes all books currently listed in English Bible as 'historical' as well as all books in the modern category of major and minor prophets. Daniel sits snugly within this second section. The four remaining books are termed "psalms" and "hymns" and include Psalms, Proverbs, Ecclesiastes, and the Song of Solomon. This grouping compares favorably with Jesus' statement (Luke 24:44) that "All things must be fulfilled, which are written in the Law of Moses, and in the Prophets, and in the Psalms, concerning me."

Translators of the Septuagint evidently preceded Josephus. Completed well before either Jesus or Josephus, this Greek Old Testament used a grouping identical with that of Josephus. Daniel appeared among the prophets. Wilson then reasoned,

> All the direct evidence, then, that precedes the year 200 A.D., supports the view that Daniel was in the earliest times among the Prophets. Further, this conclusion is supported by all the direct evidence outside the Talmud, which is later than A.D. 200. Thus, Origen, at A.D. 250, and Jerome, at A.D. 400, both of whom were taught by Jewish Rabbis and claim to have gained their information from Jewish sources, put Daniel among the Prophets and separate the strictly prophetical books from those which are more properly called historical.[56]

In an attempt to explain the discrepancy between the current Hebrew grouping and the near unanimous testimony of antiquity, Boutflower suggests that Jewish scholars reworked the sectional divisions of the Hebrew Old Testament sometime between the middle of the third century A.D. and the beginning of the fourth.[57]

His scenario is certainly reasonable. We must remember that the anti-Christian apologist Porphyry released his attack on the book of Daniel during the third century. He maintained the book appeared during the time of the Maccabees. Since Jewish scholars were engaged in efforts to discredit Christianity at this time, his arguments may have offered them one way of defusing powerful time-frame arguments that link the time of the Messiah's coming with the Roman Empire.

The suggestion that Daniel best characterizes an apocalyptic history and pseudo-prophecy describing the times of the Syrian despot, Antiochus Epiphanes, fails to hold water. In addition to evidence just presented, material from both Qumran and New Testament writers call Daniel "the prophet." Besides, if critics are correct that the book is an ex post facto prophecy, they must explain an obvious blunder. McDowell explains:

> Critics claim the Egyptian campaign mentioned in Daniel 11:40-45 never happened. This means that the Jews who lived during this time, who must have known all about Epiphanes and his campaigns, accepted this book shortly after it was written as the genuine work of a great prophet of foregone

years, even though it speaks of a whirlwind conquest of Egypt which never occurred. Do the critics believe the people of that day to be so credulous?[58]

Such a position would be grossly unfair to the scholars of the time. Many religious writings appeared among the Jews during the intertestamental period. Some were the works of well-known, respected, national heroes. Many included strong religious and moral presentations. Yet, not a single one gained acceptance into the Hebrew Scriptures. As Anderson underscores,

> The Sanhedrin of the second century B.C. was composed of men of the type of John Hyrcanus; men famed for their piety and their learning; men who were heirs of all the proud traditions of the Jewish faith, and themselves the sons of successors of the heroes of the noble Maccabean revolt. And yet we are asked to believe that these men, with their extremely strict views of inspiration and their intense reverence for their sacred writings ... used their authority to smuggle into the sacred canon a book which, ex hypothesi, was a forgery, a literary fraud, a religious novel of recent date.[59]

Alleged Historical Errors. Critical scholars continue to allege that many historical errors surface in the twelve chapters of Daniel. Obviously, every alleged error cannot be answered in the current context. Three of the more well-known charges will be carefully examined. If the book withstands these attacks, students should feel confident of the book as a whole. The three areas involve Nebuchadnezzar's madness (Dan. 4), Belshazzar's kingship (Dan. 5), and his relationship to Nebuchadnezzar.

According to Daniel, the Babylonian king, "walking on the roof of the royal palace of Babylon," bragged, "Is not this the great Babylon that I have built as the royal residence, by my mighty power and for the glory of my majesty (4:29-30)?" His pride elicited a swift, decisive response from God. He was "driven away from people and ate grass like cattle. His body was drenched with the dew of heaven until his hair grew like the feathers of an eagle and his nails like the claws of a bird" (Dan. 4:33).

No valid reason denies Nebuchadnezzar's illness. First, his building endeavors were as considerable as Daniel suggests. Hardened clay bricks recovered at the site of ancient Babylon uniformly carry his name. Even at the turn of the century, scholars required more than 125 pages of text and translations just to catalog his building inscriptions.[60] Also, "the East India House inscription, now in London, has six columns of Babylonian writing telling of the stupendous building operations which the king carried on in enlarging and beautifying Babylon."[61] An extensive description of his building genius appears in chapter nine.

Second, Herodotus may include a veiled allusion to Nebuchadnezzar's pride.[62] He describes a Persian spokesman who warns Xerxes that "it is the great ones that God smites with his thunder" because of "their pride. ... It is always the great buildings and the tall trees which are struck by lightning. It is God's way to bring the lofty low." Persia supplanted Babylon as the world's leading power and the history of their predecessors was well known in Susa.

Third, Daniel paints an accurate picture of a rare mental disorder. His accuracy suggests an eyewitness observation. Harrison, who observed a similar occurrence in Great Britain just after World War II, explains:

> The illness described in Daniel ... constitutes a rare form of monomania, a condition of mental imbalance in which the sufferer is deranged in one significant area only. The particular variety of monomania described is known as boanthropy, another rare condition in which Nebuchadnezzar imagined himself to be a cow or a bull, and acted accordingly. ... the narrative present(s) the clinical facts with discrimination and good taste, and bears all the marks of a genuine contemporary or near-contemporary record.[63]

Fourth, other ancient sources confirm Daniel's record. Berosus, a Babylonian priest, alludes to some mysterious sickness that occurred in the later years of Nebuchadnezzar's reign.[64] Eusebius, quoting the second century B.C. historian Abydenus, relates that during his last years, Nebuchadnezzar, while being "possessed by some god," announced the coming of a "Persian mule" (Cyrus) who would enslave the nation. After making this prediction, the king "immediately disappeared."[65]

Also, the dearth of information available from Babylonian sources comes as no surprise. The presence of mental derangement "was held in universal awe and dread in antiquity."[66] Any evidence "of mental affliction was regarded as possession par excellence by demonic powers."[67] Because Nebuchadnezzar achieved legendary status, we would not expect his subjects to divulge any suspected mental illness.

Fifth, one of Nebuchadnezzar's inscriptions provides a fleeting glimpse at a possible confirmation of Daniel's record. The damaged tablet, recovered by Rawlinson, reads:

> For four years the seat of my kingdom in my city ... did not rejoice my heart. In all my dominions I did not build a high place of power, the precious treasures of my kingdom I did not lay out. In the worship of Merodach my lord, the joy of my heart in Babylon, the city of my sovereignty, I did not sing his praises and I did not furnish his altars, nor did I clear out the canals.[68]

Coupled with the inscription, excavators observed a significant decline in the king's building activities during the last portion of his reign.[69]

A second historical concern turns on Daniel's proclamation that Belshazzar was king in Babylon when the city fell to Medo-Persian armies. Critics first denied Belshazzar's existence. For years, all ancient sources available to scholars showed that Nabonidus, not Belshazzar, was the last king of Babylon. Later finds altered that denial. Several records spoke of a Belshazzar who was Nabonidus' son. Undaunted, critics took the discoveries in stride and switched their argument to claim that Daniel erred in calling Belshazzar a "king." He was, they insisted, never more than a prince.

That assertion falls as well. First, a cuneiform inscription reported by Finegan reads,

> He entrusted a camp to his eldest, first-born son; the troops of the land he sent with him. He freed his hand; he entrusted the kingship to him. Then he himself undertook a distant campaign.[70]

While we can argue incessantly over semantics, the inscription provides enough evidence to conclude that Belshazzar's father perceived him as "king" over Babylon. Two other tablets contain further proof. Found at Erech and reported by T. G. Pinches,[71] the tablets include contracts where two parties to a business deal took their oaths in the names of both Nabonidus and Belshazzar. Price, Sellers, and Carson conclude of the finds, "The inclusion of the son's name with his father's in the same oath puts him in the same class with the king himself."[72]

Also, records clearly show that Nabonidus was out of the city for an extended period before its fall. Since the father took up residence at Teima (in Arabia) during that time, Belshazzar served as de facto, if not de jure, king over the city.[73] Additional cuneiform documents record that Belshazzar "presented sheep and oxen at the temples in Sippar as an offering of the king."[74]

Finally, Babylonian sources use the term "king" to apply to those who serve under other, more powerful, kings. Gruenthauer reports,

> ... we know from the inscriptions of Nergal shar-usur that Bel-shum-ishkun was king of Babylon during the reign of Nebuchadnezzar. Still his name does not appear on any contract tablet. Nergal-shar-usur calls him "King of Babylon" without adding any qualification whatever to indicate that he was only a sub-king under Nebuchadnezzar.[75]

Boutflower reports a similar occurrence during the reign of Cyrus.[76] So, Daniel turns out to be far more accurate than most critics imagine. Even Belshazzar's promise (Dan. 5:30) to make Daniel "third ruler" in the kingdom makes sense.

The final investigation centers on Daniel's statements (5:2,11,13,18,22) that Belshazzar was the "son" of Nebuchadnezzar when records clearly state he was the "son" of Nabonidus. Also, Nabonidus was not related to Nebuchadnezzar in any way. Still, the answers are simple. First, the Aramaic word for "son" may be translated "grandson," "descendant," or "offspring."[77] If Belshazzar descended from Nebuchadnezzar, he could legitimately be called his "son." Second, Raven believes evidence shows that Nabonidus legitimatized his claim to the throne by marrying one of Nebuchadnezzar's daughters.[78] An earlier king, Neriglissar, did exactly that.[79]

Thus, the historical accuracy of the book rejects, rather than supports, an origin during the second century.[80]

Reasons for Rejecting the Late Date

Lack of Consistency by the Critics. Caves at Qumran yielded many materials relating to the book of Daniel. These materials show the book existed, in almost its present form, by the middle of the second century B.C. Waltke argues that discovery of the Qumran manuscripts "dating from the Maccabean period renders it unlikely that the book was composed during the time of the Maccabees."[81]

Here, a demonstrable lack of consistency plagues the critics. The same scholars who demand an origin of Daniel during the second century allow identical evidence from Qumran to push the dates of Ecclesiastes and the Chronicles back into at least the third, and often the fourth, century B.C.[82] Even a third century date invalidates the assumption of critics that the book describes events occurring during the Maccabean period. Payne suggests one possible reason for the inconsistency:

> Antisupernaturalism must bring the "prophecy" down to a time after the events described (especially after Antiochus's sacrilege of 168 B.C.); or, if the latest possible date has been reached, it must reinterpret the predictions to apply to other, already-accomplished events. Consequently, since Daniel was extensively quoted (and misunderstood) as early as 140 B.C. (Sibylline Oracles 3:381-400), rationalists have no alternative but to apply the supposed coming of the Messiah and the fulfillment of the seventy weeks to Maccabean times, rather than Christ's, even though this requires "surmising a chronological miscalculation on the part of the writer" (ICC, p. 393).[83]

Reference in I Maccabees. Mattathias Maccabaeus died in 166 B.C. Shortly after, I Maccabees was penned. Yet, I Maccabees quotes the patriarch as saying, "Ananias, Azarias, and Misael (Hebrew = Shadrach, Meshach, Abednego), by believing, were saved out of the flame. Daniel for his innocence was saved from the mouth of lions." If the general populace knew and accepted these stories from Daniel as fact during Mattathias' lifetime, surely the book itself had existed for some time. Of course, with no justification except a preconceived bias, the critics deny that Mattathias referred to the book.

References in Ezekiel. Another troublesome problem comes from references to Daniel in Ezekiel, a book that has long withstood the attacks of critics. Few deny that it existed well before the Maccabean period. Yet, twice (14:14,20) Ezekiel pairs Daniel with Noah and Job and once (28:3) asks, "Are you wiser than Daniel?"

Attempts by critics to avoid the obvious damage from these references to the late date for the book of Daniel show their open bias against supernaturalism. They claim that Ezekiel did not refer to the biblical Daniel but to another, obscure "Dn'il" spoken of in tablets found at Ras Shamra. Again, no physical evidence supports the critical view. No evidence shows that Ezekiel knew the Dn'il at Ras Shamra. Nothing in Hebrew literature speaks of him. No evidence explains why a Hebrew prophet, chiding his people on their unfaithfulness, would include an unknown pagan with two Hebrew heroes of faith. Noah and Job escaped severe physical dangers through their faith. The biblical Daniel did the same. Nothing suggests "Dn'il" escaped great physical danger. Only deep, preconceived biases can forge such a connection.

Reasons for Accepting an Early Date

Josephus and Alexander the Great. Josephus, the fabled but oft-maligned Jewish historian, recounts an interesting report regarding a threatened confrontation between Alexander the Great and the Jews.[84] Josephus explains that during Alexander's forays against the coastal cities of Tyre and Gaza, he often demanded supplies for his armies from smaller kingdoms in the interior. One of those kingdoms was Judah. Jaddua, the high priest, denied the request, saying Israel had vowed not to take up arms against Darius. Jaddua insisted the vow must be honored.

After a costly victory at Gaza, Josephus declared that Alexander turned his armies toward Jerusalem. On learning of his approach, Jaddua offered a sacrifice and asked for God's help in turning back their powerful enemy. In response to the prayer, the high priest was instructed to dress in his priestly garments, order other priests and the citizenry to dress in white, open the gates to the city, and walk, unarmed, to meet the Greek. Jaddua obeyed. Five miles from the city, the two groups met.

Two factors defused Alexander's anger. First, before the meeting, he had seen the high priest in a dream. That dream instructed Alexander to treat Jaddua and his people with kindness. Second, Jaddua informed

Alexander of Daniel's prophecy that a Greek would defeat the Persians. Pleased with the prophecy and the manner of his greeting, Alexander treated the Jews graciously.

The story carries what J. B. Phillips calls a "ring of truth." It fits. One, Alexander did demand supplies from small, nearby kingdoms. Two, he delayed his trek to Egypt for months to attend to Tyre and Gaza. It is reasonable that he would devote a few days to deal with Jerusalem. Jerusalem lay less than thirty miles east of Gaza. The short trip would require only a few hours. Three, Persia had freed the Jews from slavery in Babylon. Naturally, Judah would feel compelled to remain true to a vow made to their benefactors. Four, refusals of the type described by Josephus always incensed Alexander. His egotism could not allow such an affront. Both Tyre and Gaza lay deteriorating for that very reason.

Five, Alexander was deeply superstitious and often sought advice from mediums and sorcerers. He based many of his decisions on dreams and omens. Six, Alexander did grant special clemency to the Jews. But, why? Josephus' story gives the only explanation from antiquity why Alexander spared a city that swore allegiance to Persia. Seven, no evidence denies Josephus' story.

Neither Arrian nor Curtius recorded every detail of Alexander's campaigns. That neither mention such a short, militarily uneventful trip after the massive confrontations at Tyre and Gaza is hardly surprising. Besides, arguments from silence prove notoriously unreliable. Similar charges appear regarding the existence of the Hittites, Sargon, and Belshazzar. Each provides ample testimony to the ineffectiveness of such approaches. As Coffman and Coffman summarize, "There is no way to discredit the historical account of Alexander's sparing the city of Jerusalem from the ravages inflicted on cities like Tyre and Sidon, except by allowing Josephus' explanation of what happened."[85]

Eight, Alexander felt strongly about having a secure base from which to enter Egypt. A hostile Jerusalem threatened his security. Nine, Arrian admits Alexander planned to use Gaza as a base to conduct additional, though undisclosed, military operations.[86] Ten, Quintus Curtius Rufus noted that after Alexander "came in full force to the city of Gaza," he marched "against the cities still refusing the yoke of domination."[87]

Still, since Josephus alone specifically mentions the side-trip to Jerusalem, and since the trip runs afoul of accepted dogma, most modern writers, without the slightest evidence, consider it akin to a "pious legend."[88] A few admit the story must "contain a grain of truth."[89]

Coffman and Coffman note the inconsistency: "Critics of course disallow Josephus' testimony on any point where he contradicts their theories but enthusiastically accept him on practically anything else."[90] If Josephus does prove accurate, the book of Daniel clearly existed, as Scripture, in the late fourth century B.C.

Use of Words from Assyrio-Babylon. Finally, the book "contains several Assyrio-Babylonian words, such as might be expected in a book written at or near Babylon in the latter half of the sixth century B.C."[91] The presence of these words provides a logical base for traditional beliefs. Some words either disappeared completely or underwent major alterations in the following centuries. So, their appearance certainly links the book's material to a place and time of origin consistent with an early date of writing.

26

They Saw the Future
and It Really Happened

Dad passed from this earthly life on his birthday, February 28, 1994. During the last weeks, he seemed to sense his time here was rapidly drawing to a close. I understand his looks and actions during those days much better now. I think I know why there were tears in his eyes as he watched his granddaughters. He sensed the transition was near. He sensed the future.

So, too, though in different ways, biblical prophets sensed the future. They claimed to see future happenings — not intuitively, but because an Intelligence far greater than their own revealed them. We do not know how that Intelligence communicated the future. It is enough to know that it happened. More often than not, their simple explanation was, "The Word of the Lord came to me."

History reveals many such claims.

Even today, they permeate society. Announcements of impending doom and the end of the ages occur with increasing frequency as we near the millennium. Sounds of war rumble menacingly in the distance. Gaza, Grozny, Sarajevo, and Algiers shudder as the angel of death makes her rounds. Crime and violence rock society. Governments, designed to provide justice and equality, reek with corruption. Most of humanity chafes under the burden. There seems to be no escape. In worlds seething with fatalism, the oppressed seize even the slightest opportunity to better their lives. Many think that opportunity lies in the manipulation of the future. If they knew the future, they could sidestep its disasters. If they knew the future they could escape their onerous conditions. If they knew the future, they could forge a happier life. Since seers, psychics, and prophets claim to know the future, their services are in great demand. Unfortunately, as we have seen, their claims far outdistance reality.

Attracted by wealth and power, they prey on the weak and gullible. If there were no rewards, they would quickly surrender their profession.

But, there are rewards. Lots of them. Enough to attract waves of charlatans. Centuries ago, Ezekiel (21:21) described the hold of "seers" over
kings and nations: "For the king of Babylon will stop at the fork in the
road, at the junction of the two roads, to seek an omen: He will cast lots
with arrows, he will consult his idols, he will examine the liver." Modern
pretenders still gain huge followings by continually setting dates for the
end of the world. Jim Jones and David Koresh so controlled the minds of
their followers that even the marching orders of death were obeyed.

Failed predictions litter the landscape of history. The dogs of war have
been unleashed when no one predicted their devastation. Just as unex-
pectedly, they have been brought to bay. Good has appeared when evil
was predicted. Disaster has fallen when prosperity was expected. Sooner
or later, though, someone exposes the charades. With each exposure,
each failed prophecy, each revelation of fraud, more people join the
ranks of unbelievers and cynics. Who can blame them?

That's why demonstrations of the accuracy of biblical prophecy become
so vital. We need to know that some "prophets" delivered messages free
from motives of profit or self-aggrandizement. We need to know that some
seers paid for their predictions with their lives. We need to stand in the
gallery when Manasseh, as a result of Isaiah's prophecies, orders him sawn
in half. We need to choke back the revulsion as we visit Jeremiah in the
bloody mire of a Jerusalem prison. But we must remember much more.

We must sense the amazement of their peers as the biblical prophets
pronounce unthinkable predictions of future events. We must sense the
perplexity of their listeners as they outline the futures of cities, nations,
and peoples — futures that seemed far more unreasonable then than
space travel seemed to those living in the tenth century.

Listen as their explosive judgments fall.

Watch as history documents the fulfillment of their predictions.

Analyze the uncanny accuracy of their prophecies. As you do, you will
realize that they saw the future. They became God's amazing spokesmen.

They saw the future of age-old Egypt. They saw her power shattered, her
temples and monuments toppled and broken. They saw her culture disappear, her natural resources diminish, her dynasties end.

They saw the future of arrogant Assyria. They saw her ruthless, seemingly indestructible armies self-destruct in a drunken stupor. They saw
her defenses, supposedly unpenetrable by man-made implements of war,
savaged by nature's torrents. They saw her people disappear from the
table of nations.

They saw the future of magnificent Babylon burst onto the world's
stage, glow brightly for an instant, then fade rapidly from view. They

saw the crafty diversion of the Euphrates and the silent passing of centuries when only wild animals stood the night watches over the eroding, crumbling city.

They saw the pockmarked future of Phoenicia's twin cities of Tyre and Sidon. They saw Sidon survive the centuries. They saw Tyre vanish. They saw the cunning genius of a Greek conqueror forever alter the Tyrian landscape.

They saw Edom's ambitious businessmen dwindle away as the trade routes so critical to their survival inexplicably shifted northward. They saw merciless, blowing sands join with looters and a thousand years of obscurity to remove even the names of Petra's Edomite and Nabatean princes.

They saw the Philistines, the bane of Samson, Eli, Samuel, Saul, and David, grow quiet and still. They saw her cities conquered and overlaid with sand.

They saw the death throes of Samaria, Moab, and Ammon.

They saw the future of stiff-necked Jerusalem colored in the red of a first-century holocaust. They saw and identified signs warning of the approach of that dreadful, 70 A.D. nightmare. They saw the hurried escape of thousands of Christians from the capital and its environs. In the years following, as these Christians passed by the devastation left by Titus and the Roman legions, they surely offered prayers of thanks for the warnings that allowed their escape.

The biblical prophets also foretold the appearance of God's servant. They announced the time and place of his worldly arrival. They saw his miraculous works and the uniqueness of his resurrection.

In short, they saw the future.

Of course, others disagree with these conclusions.

Some reject prophecy because they reject God. Yet, the best evidence available infers the existence of God/a Divine Being. If God exists, why should anyone think it incredible that He would predict the future?

Some argue that the written records of the biblical prophets were composed *ex post facto*, after-the-event. The evidence for such is pitifully weak and based on the blindly-accepted, yet never-proven assumptions of nineteenth century German critics. Unless one begins by assuming the critics' world views are true, it is far more reasonable to believe the prophecies were given when they claimed to be than they are late additions.

Some complain that studies such as this one overlook many unfulfilled prophecies. Space does not allow an in-depth analysis of that complaint here. A few comments must suffice. First, the conditional nature of temporal predictions explains many of these so-called failures. Scripture plainly holds that the purpose of most prophecies related to nations, cities, and peoples is to produce a repentant spirit and a change of behavior. When changes were made, the predictions were lifted. Second, many predictions have been fulfilled symbolically. For example, predictions of peace for God's people may just as easily refer to inner peace rather than to physical peace. Many passages are fulfilled in exactly this manner. Third, some prophecies remain unfulfilled. This does not mean fulfillment will never come. Several predictions regarding ancient nations, cities, and cultures found fulfillment hundreds of years after the actual predictions were made. Fourth, even if there were prophecies that went totally unfulfilled, that does not deal with the amazing accuracy of many others. How these predictions could have been offered in such minute detail deserves an explanation.

Finally, some suggest that the biblical prophets were merely lucky in their predictions of future events. Such a solution is very unsatisfying. How is it that there are so many amazingly accurate predictions? Luck may explain a few; surely it cannot explain them all. A person may be lucky enough to win the lottery once. It would not be unthinkable for the same individual to win twice. Heads would be raised and questions asked, however, if the same individual, or group, won again, time after time. The same is true with biblical prophecies. You may pass off one or two as luck. You cannot do the same for hundreds of meticulously detailed, highly accurate predictions.

There is a reasonable explanation. The biblical prophets saw the future, and they saw it through visions, dreams, and actual communications with a supernatural being. Those communications provided the prophet motive. They provided these fascinating personalities a "fire in their bones" that left them no alternative but to warn, censure, plead, and encourage in the name of God. They believed they were God's spokesmen. The amazing accuracy of their predictions provides strong evidence that they were right.

Notes

Chapter 2

1. G. V. Smith, "Prophet," in *ISBER*, G. P. Bromiley, ed., (Grand Rapids: Eerdmans, 1986), 3: 986-992.

2. See, for instance, H. H. Rowley, *Prophecy and Religion in Ancient China and Israel* (New York: Harper & Brothers, 1956), and R. C. Zaehner, *The Comparison of Religions* (Boston: Beacon, 1962).

3. A. G. Auld, "Prophets through the Looking Glass: Between Writings and Moses," *JSOT* 27 (1983): 3-23.

4. A. G. Auld, "Prophets and Prophecy in Jeremiah and Kings," *ZAW* 96 (1984): 66-82.

5. A. G. Auld, "Word of God and Words of Man: Prophets and Canon," in *Ascribe to the Lord*, L. Eslinger and G. Taylor, eds., p. 247.

6. See, for instance, Hans M. Barstad, "No Prophets? Recent Developments in Biblical Prophetic Research and Ancient Near East Prophecy," *JSOT* 57 (1993): 39-60; S. A. Meier, *The Messenger in the Ancient Semitic World* (HSM, 45; Atlanta: Scholars Press, 1989); and J. T. Greene, *The Role of the Messenger and Message in the Ancient Near East: Oral and Written Communication in the Ancient Near East and in the Hebrew Scriptures: Communicators and Communiques in Context* (BJS, 169; Atlanta: Scholars Press, 1989), pp. 137-266. I do not claim that biblical prophecy is identical with neighboring Semitic prophecy. There are similarities, but also clear differences. See, for example, J.-G. Heintz, *Bibliographie de Mari — Archeologie et Textes* (1933-1988) (Wiesbaden: Otto Harrassowitz, 1990) for a listing of the many materials relating to the subject; also Heintz' "Bibliographie de Mari: Supplement I (1988-1990)," 77 *Akkadica* (1992): 1-37.

7. See I. Starr, ed., *Queries to the Sungod: Divination and Politics in Sargonid Assyria* (Helsinki: Helsinki University Press, 1990).

8. Hans M. Barstad, "Lachich Ostracon III and Ancient Israelite Prophecy," *Eretz-Israel* (1993).

9. For those in support of Auld's thesis see J. M. Ward, "The Eclipse of the Prophet in Contemporary Studies," *USQR* 42 (1988): 97-104, and F. E. Deist, "The Prophets: Are We Headed for a Paradigm Switch?" in *Prophet und*

Prophetenbuch, V. Fritz, K.-F. Pohlmann, and H.-C. Schmitt, eds. (BZAW, 185; Berlin: Walter de Gruyter, 1989), pp. 1-18.

10. Robert R. Wilson, "Prophecy," in *HBD*, Paul J. Achtemeier, ed. (San Francisco: Harper & Row, 1985), p. 826.

11. Abraham Kuenan, *Prophets and Prophecy in Israel* (1877; rprt. Amsterdam: Philo, 1969), p. 42.

12. Johannes Pedersen and Geoffrey Cumberlege, *Israel: Its Life and Culture. III-IV*, trans. by Annie J. Fausboll (London: Oxford University Press, 1940), p. 111.

13. T. H. Robinson, "Prophecy," *The London Quarterly and Holborn Review*, 184 (January, 1959), p. 37.

14. H. H. Rowley, *Prophecy and Religion in Ancient China and Israel* (New York: Harper & Brothers, Publishers, 1956), p. 4.

15. W. R. Arnold, *Ephod and Ark* (1917; rprt. Cambridge: Harvard University Press, 1969), p. 93.

16. See F. C. Eiselen, *Prophecy and the Prophets in their Historical Perspective* (Cincinnati: Jennings & Graham, 1909).

17. Ludwig Koehler and Walter Baumgartner, *LVTL*, 2d ed. (Leiden: E. J. Brill, 1953), p. 588.

18. J. A. Bewer, *AJSL* 18 (1901-02), p. 120.

19. See, for instance, J. Lindbloom, *Prophecy in Ancient Israel* (London: Basil Blackwell, 1962), p. 102.

20. Helmer Ringgren, "Prophecy in the Ancient Near East," in Richard Coggins, Anthony Phillips, and Michael Knibb, eds. *Israel's Prophetic Tradition* (Cambridge: Cambridge University Press, 1982), pp. 1-11.

21. Alfred Edersheim, *Prophecy and History in Relation to the Messiah* (Grand Rapids: Baker, 1955), p. 122.

22. Controversy continues to swirl over the presence of inspired prophecy during the inter-testamental period. David E. Aune, *Prophecy in Early Christianity* (Grand Rapids: Eerdmans, 1983), pp. 103-106, presents a comprehensive argument that all types of prophecy did not completely disappear during the interval in question.

23. Fruit from the sycamore fig required an unusual method of pruning. The sycamore fig had to be "pinched" or "pierced" a few days prior to harvesting, otherwise it would not ripen. See C. Hassell Bullock, *An Introduction to the Old Testament Prophetic Books* (Chicago: Moody, 1986), p. 56.

24. Emil G. Kraeling, *The Prophets* (Chicago: Rand McNally, 1969), p. 11.

25. T. J. Meek, *Hebrew Origins* (New York: Harper and Brothers, 1936), p. 148.

26. R. H. Charles, *Critical and Exegetical Commentary on the Book of Daniel* (Oxford: Oxford University Press, 1929), p. xxvi.

27. "Winston Leonard Spencer Churchill," *The Oxford Dictionary of Quotations*, 2d ed. (London: Oxford University Press, 1955), p. 143.

28. Abraham J. Heschel, *The Prophets* (New York: Harper & Row, 1962), pp. 3-5.

29. Bullock, *Prophetic Books*, p. 17.

30. Aune, *Prophecy in Early Christianity*, p. 339.

31. Samuel Sandmel, *The Hebrew Scriptures* (New York: Alfred A. Knopf, 1963), p. 48.

32. Frederick Meyrick, "Prophet," in *SDB*, rev. ed., H. B. Hackett, ed. (Boston: Houghton, Mifflin, 1881), Vol. III, p. 2594.

Chapter 3

1. Meek, *Hebrew Origins*, p. 148. Charles (*Daniel*, p. xxvi) captured the essence of this view when he wrote: "Prophecy is a declaration, a forthtelling, of the will of God—not a foretelling. Prediction is not in any sense an essential element of prophecy, though it may intervene as an accident—whether it be a justifiable accident is another question."

2. Bullock, *Prophetic Books*, p. 14.

3. Bernard Ramm, *Protestant Christian Evidences* (Chicago: Moody, 1953), p. 81.

4. Ramm, *Protestant Evidences*, p. 81.

5. J. Barton Payne, *EBP* (New York: Harper & Row, 1973), pp. 674-675, 681.

6. Payne, *EBP*, pp. 675, 681.

7. Gustav F. Oehler, *Theology of the Old Testament* (New York: Funk and Wagnalls, 1883), p. 487.

8. Jack Lewis, "The Word of Prophecy Made Sure," in *Pillars of Faith: Biblical Certainty in an Uncertain World*, Herman O. Wilson and Morris M. Womack, eds. (Grand Rapids: Baker, 1973), p. 156.

9. Raymond E. Brown, "Hermeneutics," in *JBC*, Raymond E. Brown, J. A. Fitzmeyer, and R. E. Murphy, eds. (Englewood Cliffs, N.J.: Prentice-Hall, 1968), Vol. II, p. 615.

10. Alfred Guillaume, *Prophecy and Divination* (London: Hodder and Stoughton, 1938), pp. 111-112.

11. John F. A. Sawyer, *Prophecy and the Prophets of the Old Testament* (Oxford: Oxford University Press, 1987), p. 2.

12. Sawyer, *Prophecy and the Prophets*, p. 15.

13. H. H. Rowley, *The Relevance of Apocalyptic* (London: Lutterworth, 1944), p. 34.

Chapter 4

1. Walter C. Kaiser, Jr. ("What about the Future?": in Walter C. Kaiser, Jr. and Moises Silva, eds., *An Introduction to Biblical Hermeneutics* [Grand Rapids: Zondervan, 1994], p. 149) has noted a close relationship between the obviously conditional prophecies in Leviticus and Deuteronomy and many later predictions that appear in later writings. He notes,: "The majority of prophecies in the Old Testament are conditional. Almost all of these predictions rest on Leviticus 26 or Deuteronomy 28-32. These two texts give a number of specific consequences that will result from either obedience of disobedience to God's word. The sixteen writing prophets of the Old Testament quote from or allude to these two texts hundreds of times." See, also, the specific application in the writings of Hosea-Jonah as described by Douglas Stuart (*Hosea-Jonah*, Word Biblical Commentary 31 [Waco: Word, 1987], pp. xxxii-xiii).

2. F. Furman Kearley, "The Conditional Nature of Prophecy: A Vital Hermeneutical Principle." (Montgomery, Ala.: Apologetics Press, n. d.).

3. Payne, *EBP*, p. 62.

4. Louis Berkhof, *Principles of Biblical Interpretation* (Grand Rapids: Baker, 1950), p. 150.

5. Kearley, "Conditional Nature of Prophecy."

6. Walter C. Kaiser, Jr., *Back Toward the Future: Hints for Interpreting Biblical Prophecy* (Grand Rapids: Baker Book House, 1989), pp. 36-37.

7. See chapters 13-15 relating to "Messianic Prophecies."

8. R. B. Girdlestone, *The Grammar of Prophecy* (London: Eyre and Spottiswoode, 1901), p. 29.

Chapter 5

1. Edith Hamilton, *Spokesmen for God*. (New York: W. W. Norton and Company, 1949), p. 71.

2. Gurdon C. Oxtoby, *Prophecy and Fulfillment in the Bible* (Philadelphia: The Westminster Press, 1966), pp. 12-13.

3. William Temple, *Nature, Man, and God* (New York: St. Martin's Press, 1934), p. 317.

4. C. H. Dodd, *The Authority of the Bible* (London: James Nisbet, 1952), p. 83.

5. For an in-depth study of this issue, see Ronald Nash, *The Word of God and the Mind of Man* (Grand Rapids: Zondervan, 1982).

6. J. I. Packer, *God Has Spoken* (Grand Rapids: Baker Book House, 1979), p. 21.

7. John Davidson, *Discourses on Prophecy: Its Structure, Use and Inspiration.* 2d ed. (London: John Henry & James Parker, 1856), viii, p. 378.

8. Robert D. Culver, "Were the Old Testament Prophets Really Prophetic?" In *Can I Really Trust the Bible?* Howard Vos, ed., (Chicago: Moody Press, 1963), p. 99.

9. Thomas H. Horne, *An Introduction to the Critical Study and Knowledge of the Holy Scriptures.* 8th ed. (1839; rprt, Grand Rapids: Baker, 1979), I, p. 272.

10. Kuenan, *The Prophets and Prophecy*, p. 277.

Chapter 6

1. Wilbur Smith, *Egypt in Biblical Prophecy* (Grand Rapids: Baker, 1957), p. 77.

2. Herodotus, *The Histories*, tr. by Aubrey de Selincourt (New York: Penguin, 1971), ii.147; Diodorus Siculus, *Bibliotheca Historica*, tr. by F. R. Walton, et al., ed. by T. E. Page (Cambridge: Harvard University Press, 1957), i. 66.

3. E. F. Wente, "From the Beginning of the 18th Dynasty to c. 330 B.C.," in "Egypt: History of," *EB-MAC*, 6, p. 479.

4. John Ruffle, *The Egyptians* (Ithaca, N.Y.: Cornell University Press, 1977), p. 92.

5. John Albert Wilson, *The Burden of Egypt* (Chicago: University of Chicago Press, 1951), p. 292.

6. Diodorus Siculus, *Bibliotheca Historica*, i. 66.

7. Francis Arundale, *Gallery of Antiquities Selected from the British Museum* (London: J. Weale, 1842), pp. 25-26. See, also, Gaston Maspero, *The Dawn of Civilization*, tr. by M. L. McClure (New York: Frederick Ungar, 1894), Vol. I, p. 37.

8. Maspero, *Dawn of Civilization*, I, p. 16.

9. Maspero, *Dawn of Civilization*, I, pp. 19-20.

10. Maspero, *Dawn of Civilization*, I, p. 24.

11. Maspero, *Dawn of Civilization*, I, p. 81.

12. Alexander Keith, *Evidence of the Truth of the Christian Religion Derived from the Literal Fulfillment of Prophecy*, 37th ed. (London: T. Nelson and Sons, 1859), p. 497.

13. John Urquhart, *The Wonders of Prophecy*, 9th ed. (Harrisburg, Pa.: Christian Publications, 1925), p. 49.

14. Villiers Stuart, *Egypt after the War* (London: John Murray, 1882), pp. 51, 241.

15. John Gardner Wilkinson, cited in Urquhart, *Wonders of Prophecy*, p. 49.

16. G. Plinius Secundus (Pliny the Elder), *Natural History*, tr. by H. Rackham and W. H. S. Jones (Cambridge: Harvard University Press, 1951), xiii, 11-12.

17. John Gardner Wilkinson, *Manners and Customs of the Ancient Egyptians* (London: John Murray, 1837), Vol. I, p. 168.

18. Maspero, *Dawn of Civilization*, I, p. 27. Also, see Wilkinson, *Manners and Customs*, Vol. II, p. 97.

19. Charles Leonard Irby and James Mangles, *Travels in Egypt and Nubia, Syria and the Holy Land* (London: John Murray, 1868), cited in Urquhart, *Wonders of Prophecy*, p. 53.

20. Margaret Alice Murray, *The Splendour that Was Egypt* (New York: The Philosophical Library, 1949), p. 282.

21. Wilkinson, *Manners and Customs*, Vol. II, pp. 75-80.

22. Wilkinson, *Manners and Customs*, Vol. III, pp. 113f.

23. Urquhart, *Wonders of Prophecy*, p. 57.

24. John Baines and Jaromir Malek, *Atlas of Ancient Egypt* (New York: Facts on File, 1980), pp. 90-91.

25. Reginald Stuart Poole and Stanley Lane Poole, "Egypt," *EB*, 9th ed. (Chicago: R. S. Peale, 1892), Vol. VII, p. 777.

26. Amelia B. Edwards, *A Thousand Miles Up the Nile* (London: G. Routledge and Sons, 1890), pp. 219-220.

27. The "Great Mother Goddess" Hathor was one of Thebes' dominant deities. Depicted either as a beautiful woman or a brown or golden cow, her preeminence was so pervasive that Israelite slaves, thinking Moses had perished on Sinai, forced Aaron to build "a golden calf." The calf represented Hathor. See John Romer, *People of the Nile* (New York: Crown, 1982), pp. 167-168.

28. Serapis was evidently a cross-cultural god with a mixture of Osiris and Apis (the sacred bull).

29. Baines and Malik, *Atlas of Ancient Egypt*, p. 96.

30. Wilkinson, *Manners and Customs,* Vol. II, pp. 144-145.

31. Diodorus Siculus, *Diodorus on Egypt*, tr. by Edwin Murray (London:

McFarland & Co., Inc., 1985), p. 61

32. Charles Perry, *A View of the Levant* (London: T. Woodward, 1743), preface.

33. Claude Etienne Savary, *Letters on Egypt* (London: G. G. J. and J. Robinson, 1787), 2d ed., cited in Urquhart, *Wonders of Prophecy*, p. 24.

34. Baines and Malik, *Atlas of Ancient Egypt*, p. 84.

35. Strabo, *The Geography of Strabo*, tr. by Horace Leonard Jones (Cambridge: Harvard University Press, 1932), 17.1.46. See also Elizabeth Riefstahl, *Thebes in the Time of Amunhotep III* (Norman, Okla.: University of Oklahoma Press, 1964), pp. 169-183.

36. William Turner, "Cambyses," in *EB*, IV, pp. 733-734.

37. Baines and Malik, *Atlas of Ancient Egypt*, p. 134.

38. Urquhart, *Wonders of Prophecy*, p. 45.

39. Urquhart, *Wonders of Prophecy*, p. 45.

40. L. Sprague de Camp, *Great Cities of the Ancient World* (New York: Dorsett Press, 1972), p. 168.

41. Strabo, *The Geography*, 8.88-89, 115.

42. Reginald Stuart Poole, *The Cities of Egypt* (London: Smith, Elder, and Co., 1882), p. 79.

43. de Camp, *Great Cities*, p. 168.

44. James Henry Breasted, *A History of the Ancient Egyptians* (New York: Charles Scribners Sons, 1908), pp. 404f; H. R. Hall, "The Restoration of Egypt," in *CAH* (Cambridge: Cambridge University Press, 1929), Vol. III, p. 299; Thomas. K. Cheyne, *Jeremiah*, The Pulpit Commentary (1881, Rprt. Grand Rapids: Eerdmans, 1950), Vol. II, p. 208.

45. Cheyne, *Jeremiah*, Vol. II, p. 208.

46. Smith, *Egypt in Biblical Prophecy*, pp. 105-124.

47. See Robert William Rogers, *A History of Babylonia and Assyria*, 6th ed., (New York: Abingdon, 1915), Vol. II, p. 530.

48. James Pritchard, ed. *ANET* (Princeton: Princeton University Press, 1950), p. 308.

49. S. R. Driver, *Archaeology and Authority, Sacred and Profane; Essays on the Relation of the Monuments to Biblical and Classical Literature*, ed. David Hogarth (London: John Murray, 1899), pp. 116-117.

50. M. C. F. Volney, *Travels through Syria and Egypt* (London: G. G. J. and J. Robinson), Vol. I, pp. 74, 103, 110, 198.

51. Rogers, *History of Babylonia and Assyria*, p. 408.

Chapter 7

1. Charles F. Pfeiffer, *The Biblical World* (Grand Rapids: Baker, 1966), p. 418.

2. Diodorus Siculus, *Bibliotheca Historica*, ii.9.12-13.

3. Strabo, *The Geography*, 16.

4. E. M. Blaiklock, "Nineveh," in *NIDBA*, E. M. Blaiklock and R. K. Harrison, eds., p. 337.

5. Merrill F. Unger, *Archaeology and the Old Testament* (Grand Rapids: Zondervan, 1954), pp. 89-90.

6. Walter Maier, *The Book of Nahum* (Grand Rapids: Baker, 1980), p. 94.

7. Austen Henry Layard, *Nineveh and Its Remains* (London: J. Murray, 1849), Vol. I, p. 248.

8. Layard, *Nineveh and Its Remains*, Vol. I, p. 247.

9. Layard, *Nineveh and Its Remains*, Vol. II, p. 356.

10. Andre Parrot, *Nineveh and the Old Testament*, tr. by B. E. Hooke (London: SCM Press Ltd., 1955), p. 49.

11. T. G. Pinches, "Nineveh," in *ISBE*, James Orr, ed., Vol. IV, p. 2150.

12. Layard, *Nineveh and Its Remains*, Vol. I, p. 277.

13. Albert Champdor, *Babylon* (London: Elek Books, Ltd., 1958), p. 90; See, also, Jack Finegan, *Light from the Ancient Past: The Archaeological Background of Judaism and Christianity* (Princeton: Princeton University Press, 1946-59), Vol. I, p. 203; also James B. Pritchard, ANET (Princeton: Princeton University Press, 1950-55), pp. 275-295.

14. Michael Roaf, *Cultural Atlas of Mesopotamia and the Ancient Near East* (New York: Facts on File, 1990), p. 191.

15. Pfeiffer, *The Biblical World*, p. 421. Also, see the description in G. Frederick Owen, *Archaeology and the Bible* (Westwood, N.J.: Fleming H. Revell Co., 1959), p. 96f.

16. Layard, *Nineveh and Its Remains*, Vol. I, p. 262.

17. Layard, *Nineveh and Its Remains*, Vol. I, p. 263.

18. Maier, *Nahum*, p. 106.

19. Maier, *Nahum*, pp. 106-107.

20. Diodorus Siculus, *Bibliotheca Historica*, ii.27.

21. R. Campbell Thompson and R. W. Hutchinson, *A Century of Exploration at Nineveh* (New York: Luzac and Co., 1929), pp. 122f.

22. Maier, *Nahum*, p. 97. Maier writes, "A system of dams to the west of the city regulated the waters of the Tigris, and another series of dams in a flood-control system on the east restrained the Khosr River. An irrigation canal brought water to the city's orchards from Kisir, 40 miles away."

23. Austen Henry Layard, *Popular Account of Discoveries at Nineveh* (New York: Harper and Brothers, 1857), p. 321.

24. Sir Henry Rawlinson, *The History of Herodotus* (London: John Murray, 1862), p. 448.

25. Maier, *Nahum*, p. 126.

26. Diodorus Siculus, *Bibliotheca Historica*, xxvi.4.

27. Diodorus Siculus, *Bibliotheca Historica*, xxvi.6-7.

28. Maier, *Nahum*, p. 127.

29. Xenophon, *The Anabasis of Cyrus*, tr. by Carleton L. Brownson (Cambridge: Harvard University Press, 1950), III.4.10-12.

30. Lucian, "Charon," in *Lucian*, Vol. 2, tr. by A. M. Harmon, London: William Heinemann, 1913.

31. Strabo, *The Geography*, 16.1.3.

32. Herodotus, *The Histories*, I.193.

33. Maier, *Nahum*, p. 135.

34. Archibald Henry Sayce, *Assyria: Its Princes, Priests, and People* (London:

Religious Tract Society, 1894), p. 171.

35. Sidney Smith, "Ashurbanipal and the Fall of Assyria," in *CAH*, J. B. Bury, S. A. Cook, and F. E. Adcock, eds. (Cambridge: Cambridge University Press, 1929), Vol. III, pp. 130-131.

36. Maier, *Nahum*, p. 134.

37. Smith, "Ashurbanipal," in *CAH*, Vol. III, p. 130.

Chapter 8

1. Herodotus, *The Histories*, i. 192; Strabo, *Geography*, 16.1.14.

2. Herodotus, *The Histories*, vii, 152.

3. Edwin Yamauchi, *Persia and the Bible* (Grand Rapids: Baker, 1990), p. 77.

4. Herodotus, *The Histories*, i. 178.

5. Strabo, *Geography,* 16.1.5.

6. Seton Lloyd, *The Archaeology of Mesopotamia*, rev. ed. (London: Thames and Hudson, 1984), p. 226.

7. Irving L. Finkel, "The Hanging Gardens of Babylon" in *The Seven Wonders of the Ancient World*, Peter Clayton and Martin Price eds. (London: Routledge, 1988), p. 48.

8. William White, "Babylon" in *NIDBA*, Blaiklock and Harrison, eds., p. 86.

9. R. G. Killick, "Northern Akkad Project: Excavations at Habl-as-Sahr," *Iraq* 46 (1984), pp. 125-139.

10. Robert Koldewey, *The Excavations at Babylon*, tr. by Agnes St. Johns (London: Macmillan, 1914).

11. O. E. Ravn, *Herodotus' Description of Babylon* (Copenhagen: Arnold Busck, 1942).

12. Seton Lloyd, *Archaeology of Mesopotamia*, p. 224.

13. Mark Healy, *Nebuchadnezzar* (Poole, Dorsett, United Kingdom: Firebird Books, 1989), p. 32.

14. D. J. Wiseman, "Babylon," *ISBER*, Vol. I, p. 386.

15. Wiseman, "Babylon," *ISBER*, p. 389.

16. Gerald A. Larue, *Babylon and the Bible* (Grand Rapids: Baker Book House, 1969), pp. 59-60.

17. Josephus, *Antiquities*, in *Josephus: Complete Works*, tr. by William Whiston (1867; rprt. Grand Rapids: Kregel, 1960), x.11.1.

18. Josephus, *Against Apion*, in *Josephus: Complete Works*, tr. by William Whiston (1867; rprt. Grand Rapids: Kregel, 1960), i.19.

19. Diodorus Siculus, *Bibliotheca Historica*, ii.10.

20. Keith, *Evidence of the Truth of the Christian Religion*, pp. 400-401.

21. Yamauchi, *Persia*, pp. 85-86. See, further, Edwin Yamauchi, "Nabonidus," *ISBER*, G. W. Bromiley, ed. (Grand Rapids: Eerdmans, 1986), Vol. 3: 468-470.

22. Keith, *Evidence of the Truth of the Christian Religion*, p. 412.

23. Xenophon, *The Anabasis of Cyrus*, tr. by Carleton L. Brownson (Cambridge: Harvard University Press, 1950), vii.4.

24. Sidney Smith, *Isaiah 40-55* (London: Published for the British Academy by

H. Miford, Oxford University Press, 1944), p. 46; A. R. Burn, *Persia and the Greeks* (New York: St. Martin's Press, 1962), pp. 54-56; A. K. Grayson, *Assyrian and Babylonian Chronicles* (Locust Valley: J. J. Augustin, 1975), pp. 109-110.

25. Herodotus, *The Histories*, i.191; Edwin Yamauchi, Persia, p. 96; John Oates, *Babylon* (London: Thames and Hudson, 1986), p. 135; D. J. Wiseman, "Babylon," *ISBER*, p. 389.

26. W. Hinz, *Darius und die Perser* (Baden-Baden: Holle, 1976), p. 105.

27. R. K. Harrison, "Nabonidus," in *NIDBA*, Blaiklock and Harrison, eds., p. 325; Oates, *Babylon*, pp. 133-134.

28. H. W. F. Saggs, *The Greatness that Was Babylon* (New York: New American Library, 1962), pp. 147-148.

29. Oates. *Babylon*, p. 133.

30. Wiseman, "Babylon," *ISBER*, p. 389.

31. Amelie Kuhrt, "The Cyrus Cylinder and Achaemenid Imperial Policy," *JSOT* 25 (1983), pp. 83-94.

32. Wiseman, "Babylon," *ISBER*, p. 390.

Chapter 9

1. Seymour Gitin, "Last Days of the Philistines," *Arch* (May/June, 1992), p. 26; Trude Dothan, "What We Know about the Philistines," *BAR* 8 (1982): 20-44.

2. See Trude Dothan and Moshe Dothan, *People of the Sea* (New York: Macmillan, 1992), pp. 13-96 and Neal Bierling, *Giving Goliath His Due* (Grand Rapids: Baker, 1992), pp.51-88. Similar positions can be found in Edward E. Hindson, *The Philistines and the Old Testament* (Grand Rapids: Baker, 1971), and R. A. Stewart Macalister, *The Philistines: Their History and Civilization* (London: The British Academy, 1914).

3. H. Guthe, "Philistines," in *SHERK*, Samuel M. Jackson and George W. Gilmore (eds.), Vol. IX (Grand Rapids: Baker, 1950), pp. 34f; J. C. Greenfield, "Philistines," in *IDB*, George Arthur Buttrick, ed. (Nashville: Abingdon, 1962), Vol. III, p. 792.

4. Greenfield, "Philistines," *IDB*, p. 793.

5. Gerald L. Mattingly, "Philistines," in *MDB*, Watson E. Mills, ed., p. 685.

6. An invasion of Judah during the reign of Ahaz (II Chron. 28:18) is the sole possible exception. The incompleteness of the records leave the seriousness of this conflict in question.

7. Timothy G. Crawford, "Gaza," in *MDB*, Watson E. Mills, ed., p. 318.

8. Yohanan Aharoni, *The Land of the Bible* (Philadelphia: Westminister Press, 1967), p. 23. Years earlier, the indomitable Sir Flinders Petrie reported evidence of an extensive population in the region surrounding the city. See his *Ancient Gaza* (London: British School of Archaeology in Egypt, 1931), Vol. I, p. 2.

9. Macalister, *The Philistines*, p. 114.

10. Macalister, *The Philistines*, p. 71.

11. Arrian, *The Campaigns of Alexander*, trans. by Aubrey de Selincourt, rev. by J. R. Hamilton (New York: Penguin Books, 1971), ii.27.

12. Albert Barnes, *The Minor Prophets: A Commentary* (Grand Rapids:

Baker, 1950), vol. I, pp. 245-246.

13. Josephus, *Antiquities of the Jews*, xi.8.4.

14. Arrian, *Campaigns*, ii.27.

15. Barnes, *The Minor Prophets*, vol. II, p. 254.

16. Josephus, *Wars of the Jews*, in *Josephus: Complete Works*, tr. by William Whiston (1867; rprt. Grand Rapids: Kregel, 1960), ii.18.1.

17. Barnes, *The Minor Prophets*, vol. I, p. 254.

18. Keith, *Evidence of the Truth of the Christian Religion*, p. 378. Keith's discoveries were corroborated by Sir Flinders Petrie and members of the British School of Archaeology who carried out extensive digs there in the 1930s. See Sir Flinders Petrie, *Ancient Gaza I-IV* (London: British School of Archaeology in Egypt, 1931-1934).

19. Urquhart, *The Wonders of Prophecy*, p. 105.

20. Strabo, *Geography*, ii, p. 1080.

21. Keith, *Evidences of the Truth of the Christian Religion*, p. 380.

22. Peter W. Stoner, *Science Speaks*, rev. ed. (Chicago: Moody, 1976), p. 82.

23. Timothy G. Crawford, "Ashkelon," in *MDB*, Watson E. Mills, ed., p. 69.

24. Crawford, "Ashkelon," *MDB*, p. 69.

25. R. K. Harrison and E. M. Blaiklock, "Ashkelon," in *NIDBA*, E. M. Blaiklock and R. K. Harrison, eds., (Grand Rapids: Zondervan, 1983), p. 76.

26. Crawford, "Ashkelon," *MDB*, p. 69.

27. "Ashkelon," in Avraham Negev, ed., *AEHL*, 3d ed. (New York: Prentice-Hall, 1990), p. 44.

28. Barnes, *The Minor Prophets*, vol. II, p. 258.

29. "Ashkelon," in *Archaeological Encyclopedia*, Avraham Negev, ed., p. 44. See also Lawrence E. Stager, "When Canaanites and Philistines Ruled Ashkelon," *BAR* 17 (1991), pp. 24-43, and Dothan and Dothan, *People of the Sea*, p. 254.

30. Barnes, *The Minor Prophets*, vol. II, p. 258.

31. Timothy G. Crawford, "Ekron," in *MDB*, Watson E. Mills, ed., p. 240.

32. Gitin, "Last Days of the Philistines," *Arch*, p. 27.

33. Gitin, "Last Days of the Philistines," *Arch*, pp. 27-28.

34. Gitin, "Last Days of the Philistines," *Arch*, pp. 28-29.

35. Gitin, "Last Days of the Philistines," *Arch*, pp. 30-31. See, also, Bierling, *Giving Goliath His Due*, p. 241.

36. Herodotus, *The Histories*, ii.157.

37. Avraham Negev, "Ashdod," *AEHL*, p. 42.

38. Timothy G. Crawford, "Ashdod," in *MDB*, Watson E. Mills, ed., p. 68.

39. George Davis, *Bible Prophecies Fulfilled Today* (Philadelphia: The Million Testaments Campaign, 1955), p. 46.

40. Bierling, *Giving Goliath His Due*, p. 246.

41. Gitin, "Last Days of the Philistines," *Arch*, p. 26.

Chapter 10

1. Strabo, *Geography*, 16.2.22.

2. Herodotus, *The Histories*, ii.44.

3. For a brief history, see Wallace Bruce Fleming, *The History of Tyre* (New York: AMS Press, 1966), pp. 1-15.

4. H. Jacob Katzenstein, "Tyre in the Early Persian Period (539-486 B.C.E.)," *BA*, (Winter, 1979), p. 30.

5. A. von Gutshmid, "Phoenicia," EB, vol. 18, p. 804. H. Jacob Katzenstein, *The History of Tyre from the Beginning of the Second Millenium B.C.E. until the Fall of the Neo-Babylonian Empire in 538 B.C.E* (Jerusalem: The Schocken Institute, 1973), p. 68f., still credits to Phoenicians with the origin of alphabetic writing.

6. M. C. F. Volney, *Travels through Syria and Egypt* (London: G. G. J. & J. Robinson, 1787), Vol. II, p. 210.

7. Strabo, *Geography*, 17.3.3.

8. There should be little doubt that Tyre was divided into two parts: the mainland city and the island fortress. A Canaanite poem dating from around 1500 B.C., refers to "two Tyres" (Cyrus Gordon, *Ugaritic Manual* [Roma: Pontificum Institutum Biblicum, 1955], p. 317). Herodotus, (*The Histories*, ii.44) and Quintius Curtius Rufus (*The History of Alexander*, trans. by John Yardley, ed. by Waldemar Heckel [New York: Penguin Books, 1984], iv.2.4) both describe two temples to the local god, Heracles, one on the mainland and one on the city. The one on the mainland is said to be the older of the two (Marcus Junianus Justinus, *Abrege des Histoires Philippiques de Trogue Pompee*, tr. and ed. by E. and L. T. Chambry, 2 vols. [Paris, Garnier, 1936], xi.10-11; Quintius Curtius Rufus, *Alexander*, iv.2.4).

9. Josephus, *Against Apion*, i.17. See also H. Jacob Katzenstein, *The History of Tyre*, p. 9.

10. Quintius Curtius Rufus, *History of Alexander*, iv.2.

11. Strabo, *Geography*, 16.2.23.

12. Quintius Curtius Rufus, *Alexander*, iv.2.2.

13. Katzenstein, *History of Tyre*, p. 16.

14. Josephus, *Antiquities of the Jews*, 8.3.2.

15. Katzenstein, *History of Tyre*, p. 16. See also the records of Diodorus Siculus, *Bibliotheca Historica*, xvii.46.1.

16. Strabo, *Geography*, 16.2.23.

17. Katzenstein, *History of Tyre*, p. 185.

18. Fleming, *History of Tyre*, p. 29.

19. Josephus, *Antiquities of the Jews*, 9.14.2.

20. Fleming, *History of Tyre*, pp. 35-36.

21. Fleming, *History of Tyre*, p. 35.

22. Fleming, *History of Tyre*, p. 39.

23. Josephus, *Antiquities of the Jews*, 10.6.1.

24. Fleming, *History of Tyre*, p. 46.

25. Quintius Curtius Rufus, *Alexander*, iv.2.

26. Fleming, *History of Tyre*, pp. 55-56. Fleming's theorizing is backed by Arrian, *Campaigns*, 2.15.6; Quintius Curtius Rufus, *Alexander* iv.1.15-26; Diodorus Siculus, *Bibliotheca Historica*, xvii.46.4-6, as well as other sources.

27. Arrian, *Campaigns*, 2.15.7; Quintius Curtius Rufus, *Alexander*, iv.2.2-5; Diodorus Siculus, *Bibliotheca Historica*, xvii.40.2.

28. Quintius Curtius Rufus, *Alexander*, iv.2.18. See, as well, the well-written narrative by Peter Green, *Alexander of Macedon, 356-323 B.C.: A Historical Biography* (Berkeley: University of California Press, 1991), pp. 247-263.

29. Quintius Curtius Rufus, *Alexander*, iv.2.

30. Arrian, *Campaigns*, 2.18.5.

31. Quintius Curtius Rufus, *Alexander*, iv.3. See, also, Arrian, *Campaigns*, 2.19, and Diodorus Siculus, *Bibliotheca Historica*, xvii.41.

32. Arrian, *Campaigns*, 2.19.1-5; Quintius Curtius Rufus, *Alexander*, iv.2.24.

33. Green, *Alexander*, p. 251, notes that the mole was as much as 200 feet wide.

34. Arrian, *Campaigns*, 2.19.6-2.20.3. See, also, Green, *Alexander*, p. 254.

35. Quitius Curtius Rufus, *Alexander*, iv.4.

36. Diodorus Siculus, *Bibliotheca Historica*, xvii.46.

37. Green, *Alexander*, p. 263.

38. Quintium Curtius Rufus, *Alexander*, x.10; Diodorus Siculus, *Bibliotheca Historica*, xviii.3.

39. Diodorus Siculus, *Bibliotheca Historica*, xix.61.

40. Fleming, *History of Tyre*, pp. 65f. Also, Richard S. Hanson, *Tyrian Influence in the Upper Galilee* (Cambridge: American Schools of Oriental Research, 1980), pp. 6-7.

41. Hanson, *Tyrian Influence*, p. 7.

42. Fleming, *History of Tyre*, pp. 65f.

43. Peter Stoner. *Science Speaks* (Chicago: Moody Press, 1963), pp. 76-77.

44. Floyd Hamilton, *The Basis of Christian Faith*, rev. ed. (New York: Harper & Row, 1964), p. 309.

45. Bert Hall, "The Book of Ezekiel," *The Wesleyan Bible Commentary*, vol. III, Charles W. Carter, ed. (Grand Rapids: Eerdmans, 1967), p. 437.

46. Nina Nelson, *Your Guide to Lebanon* (London: Alvin Redman, Ltd., 1965), p. 220.

47. Hans-Wolf Rackl, *Archaeology Underwater* (New York: Charles Srcibner's Sons, 1968), p. 179.

48. Philip Ward, *Touring Lebanon* (London: Faber and Faber, Ltd., 1971), p. 68.

49. Volney, *Travels*, vol. II, p. 212.

50. Floyd E. Hamilton, *The Basis of Christian Faith* (New York: George H. Doran Company, 1927), p. 300.

51. George T. B. Davis, *Fulfilled Prophecies that Prove the Bible* (Philadelphia: The Million Testaments Campaign, 1955), pp. 18-19.

52. George Davis, *Fulfilled Prophecies that Prove the Bible* (Philadelphia: The Million Testaments Campaign, 1931), p. 19.

53. Henry Morris, *The Bible and Modern Science* (Chicago: Moody, 1956), p. 113.

54. For evidence of a sixth century composition, see Joseph Free, *Archaeology and Bible History* (Wheaton: Scripture Press, 1950), pp. 226-227, and W. F. Albright, "The Old Testament and Archaeology," in *Old Testament Commentary*, H. C. Alleman and E. F. Flack, eds. (Philadelphia: Muhlenberg Press, 1948), pp. 164-165. Even a critic like Georg Fohrer (*Introduction to the Old Testament*, tr. by David Green [Nashville: Abingdon, 1968], p. 406) admits

that "whoever wrote or compiled the work" did so very close to the time period given in the text. He concluded, "There is no evidence in favor of a date different from that suggested in the book."

55. References in Ezek. 1:2; 8:1; 20:1; 24:1; 29:1; 30:20; 31:1; 32:1,17; 33:21; and 40:1 all date themselves from 593-573 B.C. See James E. Smith, *Ezekiel* (Joplin, MO: College Press, 1979, p. 38).

56. Josephus, *Antiquities of the Jews*, 10.5.1.

57. Smith, *Ezekiel*, pp. 25-39; Bullock, *Prophetic Books*, pp. 228-229; Peter C. Craigie, *The Old Testament: Its Background, Growth & Content* (Nashville: Abingdon, 1986), pp. 168-169; Werner E. Lemke, "Ezekiel, The Book of," in *HBD*, Paul J. Achtemeier, ed. (San Francisco: Harper & Row, 1985), pp. 293-294; Moshe Greenberg, *Ezekiel 1-20, A New Translation with Introduction and Commentary* (Garden City, N.Y.: Doubleday, 1983), p. 27; John B. Taylor, *Ezekiel: An Introduction & Commentary* (Downers Grove: InterVarsity Press, 1969), pp. 13-20; R. K. Harrison, *Introduction to the Old Testament* (Grand Rapids: Eerdmans, 1969), p. 832.

58. Stoner, *Science Speaks*, p. 80.

Chapter 11

1. Edom and Nabataea occupied the same geographical region south of Judea. A distinct Edomite culture came first, dating well back into the middle of the second millenium B.C. See James A Sauer, "Transjordan in the Bronze and Iron Ages: A Critique of Glueck's Synthesis," *BASOR* 263 (1986), pp. 1-26; John J. Bimson and David Livingston, "Redating the Exodus," *BAR* 13 (September/October, 1987), pp. 40-53 and 66-68; and Baruch Halpern, "Radical Exodus Redating Fatally Flawed," *BAR* 13 (November/December, 1987), pp. 56-61.) Sometime between the fourth to sixth centuries, B.C., Arabic tribes known as the Nabataeans, infiltrated the region, intermingling and eventually subsuming the Edomite culture into their own. The blending was both gradual and peaceful. (See, Avraham Negev, "Understanding the Nabataeans," *BAR* 14 (November/December, 1988), pp. 26-45 and John Irving Lawlor, *The Nabataeans in Historical Perspective* (Grand Rapids: Baker, 1974).

2. Ian Browning, *Petra* (Parkridge, N.J.: Noyes Press, 1973), p. 48f.

3. George L. Kelm, "Edom/Edomites/Idumaea," in *MDB*, Watson E. Mills, ed., p. 232.

4. Yohanan Aharoni, *The Land of the Bible: A Historical Geography*, 2d ed., trans. A. F. Rainey (Philadelphia: Westminster, 1979), p. 40.

5. W. Ewing, "Sela," in *ISBE*, vol. IV, p. 2714.

6. William Vincent, *The Commerce and Navigation of the Ancients in the Indian Ocean* (London: T. Cadell and W. Davies, 1807), vol. II, pp. 260ff.

7. Vincent, *Commerce and Navigation*, vol. II, p. 263.

8. Browning, *Petra*, pp. 19-20.

9. Virgil Fry, "Petra," in *MDB*, Watson E. Mills, ed., p. 679.

10. Browning, *Petra*, p. 48.

11. Browning, *Petra*, p. 48.

12. George Livingston Robinson, *The Sarcophagus of an Ancient Civilization*

(New York: Macmillan, 1930), p. 31. Robinson describes two other entrances into the city through small wadis. But these are extremely hazardous and would have proven terribly impractical for someone trying to move heavily laden animals out of the city or someone attempting to sneak a large army inside.

13. Robinson, *Sarcophagus*, pp. 43-45.

14. Robinson, *Sarcophagus*, p. 61.

15. Johann Ludwig Burckhardt, *Travels in Syria and the Holy Land* (London: John Murray, 1822), p. 425.

16. Robinson, *Sarcophagus*, p. 78.

17. Josephus, *Antiquities of the Jews*, xiv.8.5.

18. "Edomite," In John McClintock and James Strong, *CBTL*, (1879, rprt. Grand Rapids: Baker, 1970), Vol. III, p. 60.

19. Leslie C. Allen, *The Books of Joel, Obadiah, Jonah, and Micah* (Grand Rapids: Eerdmans, 1976), p.130. See also Thomas J. Finley, *Joel, Amos, Obadiah: The Wycliffe Exegetical Commentary* (Chicago: Moody, 1990), pp. 340-342.

20. Allen, Joel, *Obadiah, Jonah, and Micah*, p. 159.

21. J. M. Myers, "Edom and Judah in the Sixth-Fifth Centuries B.C.," in Hans Goedicke, ed., *Near Eastern Studies in Honor of W. F. Albright* (Baltimore: Johns Hopkins University Press, 1971), p. 386.

22. John Bright, *A History of Israel*, 2d ed. (London: SCM, 1972), p. 329.

23. Mitchell Dahood, *Psalms 101-50* (Garden City: Doubleday, 1970), p. 272.

24. J. R. Bartlett, "Edom and the Fall of Jerusalem," *PEQ* (1982), pp. 13-24.

25. Overall, Bartlett must be considered one of the leading experts on the Edomite nation. His 1989 book, *Edom and the Edomites* (Sheffield: Academic Press), is the most thorough discussion to date. Yet, on this issue, Bartlett assumes a supernatural bias throughout his presentation. His conclusion (*PEQ*, 1982, p. 23) that the "prophets... owe Edom an apology" is unjustified. First, he admits a long-standing rancor between the two nations dating from the time of the monarchy. Moreover, he can present no hard evidence that there was ever harmony between the two from the days of David forward. Second, his interpretation of an ostraca discovered in 1969 is not sufficient to overturn the thesis that Edom and Judah were bitter enemies and that Edom launched an attack on Ramath-negeb at almost the same time that Babylon was attacking Jerusalem. (See Yohanan Aharoni, "Three Hebrew Ostraca from Arad," *BASOR*, 197 (1970), pp. 16-42.)

26. Richard J. Coggins, "Judgment between Brothers: A Commentary on the Book of Obadiah," in *Israel among the Nations: Nahum, Obadiah, Esther*, Richard J. Coggins and S. Paul Re'emi, eds. (Grand Rapids: Eerdmans, 1985), pp. 41, 71).

27. Itzhaq Beit-Arieh, "New Light on the Edomites," *BAR*, 14 (March/April, 1988) 41.

28. Josephus, *Wars of the Jews*, iv.5.1.

29. Josephus, *Wars of the Jews*, iv.5.2.

30. Josephus, *Wars of the Jews*, iv.5.3.

31. In addition to Isaiah, Jeremiah, and Ezekiel, Obadiah, Amos (1:11), and Joel (3:19) raised their voices against Edom and her descendants.

32. Josephus, *Antiquities of the Jews*, xiv.2.1.

33. Nelson Glueck, *Rivers in the Desert* (New York: Grove Press, 1959), p. 193.
34. Glueck, *Rivers in the Desert*, p. 276.
35. Burckhardt, *Travels*, p. 436.
36. Count de Bertou, "Notes on a Journey from Jerusalem by Hebron, the Dead Sea, al-Ghor, and Wadi 'Arabah, to 'Akabah and back by Petra in April, 1838," *JRGSL* (1839), p. 280.
37. Robinson, *Sarcophagus*, p. 235.
38. Robinson, *Sarcophagus*, pp. 235, 238.
39. Burckhardt, *Travels*, p. 436.
40. John Wilson, *The Lands of the Bible Visited and Described* (Edinburgh: W. Whyte, 1847), Vol. I, p. 329.
41. Wilson, *Lands of the Bible*, Vol. II, p. 337.
42. Irby and Mangles, *Travels in Egypt*, p. 402.
43. Wilson, *Lands of the Bible*, Vol. II, p. 379.
44. "Edomite," in *CBTK*, vol. III, McClintock and Strong, eds., p. 60.

Chapter 12

1. "Ammonites," *EB*, 9th ed., Vol. I, p. 742.
2. J. Arthur Thompson, "Ammon, Ammonites," in *IBD*, vol. I, J. D. Douglas, ed. (Wheaton, Ill.: Tyndale House, 1980), p. 42.
3. Josh McDowell, *Evidence that Demands a Verdict*, rev. ed. (San Bernardino: Here's Life, 1979), p. 286.
4. Carl Edwin Armerding, "Rabbah," in *NIDBA*, E. M. Blaiklock and R. K. Harrison, eds. (Grand Rapids: Zondervan, 1983), p. 383.
5. Ulrich Jasper Seetzen, *A Brief Account of the Countries Adjoining the Lake of Tiberias, the Jordan, and the Dead Sea* (Bath: Published for the Palestine Association of London by Meyler and Son, 1810), pp. 35-37.
6. Burckhardt, *Travels*, p. 364.
7. Lord Claud Hamilton, cited in Keith, *Evidence of the Truth of the Christian Religion*, p. 269.
8. Lord Lindsay, cited in Keith, *Evidence of the Truth of the Christian Religion*, pp. 269-270.
9. Keith N. Schoville, *Biblical Archaeology in Focus* (Grand Rapids: Baker, 1978), p. 489.
10. Gerald L. Mattingly, "Moab/Moabites," in *MDB*, Watson E. Mills, ed., p. 579.
11. Burckhardt, *Travels*, pp. 363-367.
12. Seetzen, *A Brief Account*, p. 39.
13. See, for example, various references in *NIDBA*, Blaiklock and Harrison, eds., and Schoville, *Biblical Archaeology*. Among the older, but still valuable, works are A. H. Van Zyl, *The Moabites* (Leiden: Brill, 1960); Nelson Glueck, *The Other Side of the Jordan* (New Haven: The American Schools of Oriental Research, 1940); and G. Lankester Harding, *The Antiquities of Jordan* (New York: Crowell, 1959).
14. Cyril Graham, *The Ancient Bashan and the Cities of Og* (Cambridge:

Cambridge essays, 1868), cited in Keith, *Evidence of the Truth of the Christian Religion*, pp. 285-287.

15. Robert Ker Porter, *Travels in Georgia, Persia, Armenia, Ancient Babylonia, Etc. during the Years 1817, 1818, 1819, and 1820* (London: Longman, Hurst, Rees, Orme. and Brown, 1822), Vol. II, p. 187.
16. Burckhardt, *Travels*, p. 369.
17. Porter, *Travels*, Vol. II, p. 187.
18. Volney, *Travels*, Vol. II, p. 344.
19. Seetzen, *A Brief Account*, p. 26.
20. Irby and Mangles, *Travels*, p. 473.
21. Josephus, *Antiquities of the Jews*, x.9.7.
22. Van Zyl, *The Moabites*, p. 157.
23. H. Porter, "Moab, Moabites," *ISBE*, Vol. III, p. 2071.

Chapter 13

1. Zendavesta, *Vendidad*, 19.2.
2. Hesiod, *Works and Days*, T. A. Sinclair, ed. (London: Macmillan, 1932), 171.
3. Suetonius, "Vespasian," *Lives of the Twelve Caesars*, trans. by H. M. Bird (Chicago: Argus, 1930), c.4.
4. Tacitus, *The Histories*, trans. by Kenneth Wellesley (New York: Penguin Books, 1990), 5.13.
5. Raymond E. Brown, *The Birth of the Messiah* (Garden City: Doubleday, 1977), p. 506.
6. See F. F, Bruce, *Second Thoughts on the Dead Sea Scrolls* 2nd ed. (Grand Rapids: Eerdmans, 1961), pp. 80-91.
7. Paula Fredriksen, *From Jesus to Christ* (New Haven: Yale University Press, 1988), p. 20.
8. Alfred Edersheim, *The Life and Times of Jesus the Messiah* (1883, rprt. Grand Rapids: Eerdmans, 1969), vol. II, pp. 710-741.
9. A. T. Pierson, *God's Living Oracles* (London: James Nisbet, 1908).
10. James E. Smith, *The Promised Messiah* (Joplin, Mo.: College Press, 1984). See, especially, pp. 475-478.
11. J. Barton Payne, *EBP* (New York: Harper & Row, 1973), pp. 645-650.
12. Edersheim, *Life and Times*, II, p. 712.
13. J. W. Ethridge, *The Targum of Onkelos and Jonathan Ben Ussiel on the Pentateuch*, vol. I (New York: KTAV Publishing House, 1968), p. 331.
14. John Bowker, *The Targums and Rabbinic Literature* (London: Cambridge University Press, 1969), p. 278.
15. Josh McDowell, *Evidence that Demands a Verdict*, p. 168.
16. H. C. Leupold, *An Exposition of Genesis*, Vol. II (Grand Rapids: Baker, 1942), p. 1180.
17. Bruce, *Second Thoughts*, p. 80.
18. Bruce, *Second Thoughts*, p. 81.
19. Gerard Van Groningen, *Messianic Revelation in the Old Testament* (Grand Rapids, Baker, 1990), p. 182.

20. Van Groningen, *Messianic Revelation*, p. 173.

21. Van Groningen, *Messianic Revelation*, p. 184.

22. See Geerhardus Vos, *Pauline Eschataology* (Grand Rapids: Eerdmans, 1953), especially pp. 1-7.

23. Adam Clarke, *Clarke's Commentary*, Vol. 1, (1811, rprt. Nashville: Abindon, n.d.), p. 269.

24. McDowell, *Evidence that Demands a Verdict*, pp. 168-169.

25. Cited in M. M. LeMann, *Jesus before the Sanhedrin*, trans. by Julius Magath (Nashville: Southern Methodist Publishing House, 1886), pp. 28-30.

26. Josephus, *Antiquities of the Jews*, 20.9.1.

27. Van Groningen, *Messianic Revelation*, p. 800.

28. Edward J. Young, *The Prophecy of Daniel* (Grand Rapids: Eerdmans, 1949), p. 75.

29. Young, *Prophecy of Daniel*, p. 280.

30. Young, *Prophecy of Daniel*, pp. 285-286.

31. Young, *Prophecy of Daniel*, p. 286.

32. Josh McDowell, *Prophecy: Fact or Fiction?* (San Bernardino, Calif.: Here's Life Publishers, 1981), p. 23.

33. Gleason L. Archer, *A Survey of Old Testament Introduction* (Chicago: Moody Press, 1973), pp. 397-398.

34. See P. W. Coxon, "The Syntax of the Aramaic of Daniel. A Dialectical Study," *HUCA* (48) 1977, pp. 107-122; R. I. Vasholz, "Qumran and the Dating of Daniel," *JETS*. (21) 1978, pp. 315-321; Edwin M. Yamauchi, "Archaeological Backgrounds of the Exilic and Postexilic Era. Part I: The Archaeological Backgrounds of Daniel," BS (137) 1980, pp. 3-16; and Gerhard F. Hasel, "The Book of Daniel and Matters of Language: Evidence Relating to Names, Words, and the Aramaic Language," *AUSS* (19) 1981, pp. 211-225.

35. John C. Whitcomb, Jr., "Daniel, Book of," *IBD*, Vol. 1, (Wheaton: Tyndale, 1980), p. 361.

36. See Bruce K. Waltke, "The Date of the Book of Daniel," *BS* (133) 1976, pp. 319-329 and Edwin M. Yamauchi, "Daniel and Contacts between the Aegean and the Near East before Alexander," *EQ* 53. 1981, pp. 37-47.

37. Joyce G. Baldwin, "Some Literary Affinities of the Book of Daniel," *TB* (30) 1979, pp. 77-99.

38. See Klaus Koch, "Is Daniel among the Prophets?" *Int* (39) 1985, pp. 117-130 and Joyce G. Baldwin, "Is there Pseudonymity in the Old Testament?" *Themelios* (4) 1978, pp. 6-12.

39. J. A. Motyer, "Messiah. I. In the Old Testament," in *IBD*, Vol. 2, J. D. Douglas, ed., p. 993.

40. Harold W. Hoehner, *Chronological Aspects of the Life of Christ* (Grand Rapids: Zondervan, 1977), pp. 121-123.

41. See the account regarding Persian decrees offered in Esther 8:8-11 and compare with Ezra 4:21.

42. Michael J. Gruenthaner, "The Seventy Weeks," *CBQ* 1 (1939), p. 32.

43. C. F. Keil, *Biblical Commentary on the Book of Daniel*. trans. by M. G. Easton (Edinburgh: T. and T. Clark, 1876), pp. 379-380.

44. Albert Barnes, *Notes, Critical, Illustrative, and Practical, on the Book of Daniel* (New York: R. Worthington, 1881), p. 390.

45. Hoehner, *Chronological Aspects.*

46. Robert Anderson, *The Coming Prince,* 16th ed. (1895; rprnt. Grand Rapids: Kregel, 1967), pp. 67-75.

47. Hoehner, *Chronological Aspects,* p. 136.

48. Hoehner, *Chronological Aspects,* pp. 136-137.

49. Robert Newman, "The Time of the Messiah," in *The Evidence of Prophecy* (Hatfield, Penn: Interdisciplinary Biblical Research Institute, 1988), pp. 113-120.

Chapter 14

1. A fine overview is found in Colin Brown, *Miracles and the Critical Mind* (Grand Rapids: Eerdmans, 1984) and in his popularized version of the same material, *That You May Believe* (Grand Rapids: Eerdmans, 1985). Other treatises include David and Randall Basinger, *Philosophy and Miracle: The Contemporary Debate* (Lewiston, N.Y.: Edwin Mellen, 1986) and the older, but thoughtful, C. S. Lewis, *Miracles: A Preliminary Discussion* (London: Bles, 1947) and Alan Richardson, *The Miracle Stories of the Gospels* (London: SCM Press, 1941). For those interested in detailed philosophical studies, see Richard Swinburne, *The Concept of Miracle* (London: St. Martin's Press, 1970), and H. van der Loos, The Miracles of Jesus, *Supplements to Novum Testamentum IX* (Leiden: E. J. Brill, 1968).

2. For an excellent extended summary of the arguments in favor of the possibility of the miraculous, see Ronald H. Nash, *Faith and Reason* (Grand Rapids: Zondervan, 1988), pp. 225-272. A shorter, but well done discussion, is found in Millard J. Erickson, *The Word became Flesh* (Grand Rapids: Baker, 1991), pp. 481-487. See also, Arlie Hoover, *Dear Agnos* (Grand Rapids: Baker, 1976), pp. 137-167; Josh McDowell, *He Walked among Us* (San Bernardino: Here's Life, 1988), pp. 262-277; Norman Geisler and Ron Brooks, *When Skeptics Ask* (Wheaton, Ill.: Victor Books, 1990), pp. 75-99; and Robert C. Newman, "Miracles and the Historicity of the Easter Week Narratives," in John Warwick Montgomery, ed., *Evidence for Faith* (Dallas: Probe Books, 1991), pp. 275-302.

3. C. S. Lewis, *Miracles* rev. ed. (London: Collins, Fontana Books, 1960), p. 9.

4. Brown, *Miracles,* pp. 291-292.

5. Brown, *That You May Believe,* p. 73.

6. Nash, *Faith and Reason,* p. 243.

7. Josh McDowell, *Evidence that Demands a Verdict,* p. 125.

8. An in-depth discussion of the evidences for the existence of God are beyond the parameters of this particular study. Those interested in such studies might consult Charles B. Thaxton, Walter L. Bradley, and Roger L. Olsen, *The Mystery of Life's Origin* (New York: Philosophical Library, 1984); J. P. Moreland, *Scaling the Secular City* (Grand Rapids: Baker, 1987); Lawrence Richards, *It Couldn't Just Happen* (Ft. Worth: Sweet, 1987); John Warwick Montgomery, ed. *Evidence for Faith*; Terry Miethe and Anthony Flew, *Does God Exist? A Believer and an Atheist Debate* (San Francisco: Harper, 1991); J. P. Moreland and Kai Nielsen,

Does God Exist: The Great Debate (Nashville: Nelson, 1990); and William Lane Craig, *The Existence of God and the Beginning of the Universe* (San Bernardino: Here's Life Publishers, 1979). Many other materials could be added.

9. John P. Meier, *A Marginal Jew: Rethinking the Historical Jesus.* Volume 2. *Mentor, Message, and Miracles* (New York: Doubleday, 1994), p. 520.

10. Meier, *A Marginal Jew*, Vol. 2, p. 521.

11. See materials in notes 1 and 2 above. See, also, Francis J. Beckwith, *David Hume's Argument against Miracles. A Critical Analysis.* (Landover, MD: University Press of America, 1989; William Lane Craig, "The Problem of Miracles: A Historical and Philosophical Perspective," in David Wenham and Craig Blomberg, eds., *Gospel Perspectives. The Miracles of Jesus*, vol. 6, (Sheffield: JSOT, 1986), pp. 9-48; J.C.A. Gaskin, *Hume's Philosophy of Religion*, 2d ed. "Atlantic Highlands, NJ: Humanities, 1988), pp. 135-165; Michael P. Levine, *Hume and the Problem of Miracles: A Solution* (Dordrecht: Philosophical Studies Series, 41, London: Kluwer, 1989; and Keith E. Yandell, *Hume's Inexplicable Mystery: His Views of Religion* (Philadelphia: Temple University, 1990), pp. 315-338.

12. Brown, *That You May Believe*, pp. 73-74.

13. Brown, *Miracles*, p. 287.

14. Because of its obvious substantiation of early Christian biograhical descriptions of Jesus, this section of Josephus' work undergoes extensive criticism. Several excellent defenses of the section effectively rebut such criticisms. See, for example, McDowell, *He Walked among Us*, pp. 37-45; F. F. Bruce, *Jesus and Christian Origins Outside the New Testament* (Grand Rapids: Eerdmans, 1974), pp. 36-41; Everett Ferguson, *Backgrounds of Early Christianity* (Grand Rapids: Eerdmans, 1987), pp. 385-389; John P. Meier, *A Marginal Jew: Rethinking the Historical Jesus* (New York: Doubleday, 1991), pp. 56-69; Louis H. Feldman, *Josephus and Modern Scholarship 1937-1980* (New York: de Gruyter, 1984), pp. 679-703; and Louis H. Feldman and Gohei Hata, eds. *Josephus, Judaism, and Christianity* (Detroit: Wayne State University Press, 1987).

15. Josephus, *Antiquities*, 18.3.3.

16. Otto Betz, "Miracles in the Writings of Flavius Josephus," in *Josephus*, Louis H. Feldman and Gohei Hata, eds., p. 215.

17. Josephus, *Wars of the Jews* ii.13.45; vi.5.2; *Antiquities of the Jews* xx.5.1; xx.8.5-6; Betz, "Miracles," pp. 222-231.

18. Meier, *A Marginal Jew*, Vol. 2, p. 592.

19. Josephus, *Antiquities*, 9.7.6.

20. Joseph Klausner, *Jesus of Nazareth, His Life, Times and Teaching* (New York: Macmillan, 1925), pp. 18-19.

21. An English translation of the section under discussion can be found in I. Epstein, ed., *The Babylonian Talmud. Seder Nezikim in Four Volumes. III Sanhedrin*, trans. by Jacob Shachter (London: Soncino, 1935), pp. 281-282.

22. See Meier, *A Marginal Jew*, pp. 96-97; Morris Goldstein, *Jesus in the Jewish Tradition* (New York: Macmillan, 1950), p.25; and Joseph Klausner, *Jesus of Nazareth*, pp. 25-27.

23. Meier, *A Marginal Jew*, p. 97.

24. Justin Martyr, *Dialogue with Trypho*, in Alexander Roberts and James Donaldson, eds., *The Ante-Nicene Fathers* (1885; rprnt. Grand Rapids: Eerdmans, 1969), chapter 69.

25. R. T. France, *The Evidence for Jesus* (Downers Grove: InterVarsity Press, 1986), p. 70

26. E. Glenn Hinson, "Egerton 2, Papyrus," in *MDB*, Watson E. Mills, ed., p. 235.

27. For a more complete description of the materials, see Harold I. Bell and T. C. Skeat, *Fragments of an Unknown Gospel and Other Early Christian Papyri* (London: Trustees of the British Museum, 1935), and C. H. Dodd, "A New Gospel." *BJRL* 20 (1936), pp. 56f.

28. France, *Evidence for Jesus*, p. 71.

29. France, *Evidence for Jesus*, p. 70.

30. E. L. Sukenik, "The Earliest Records of Christianity," *AJA* LI (1947), pp. 351-365.

31. B. Gustafson, "The Oldest Grafitti in the History of the Church," *NTS* III (1956-57), pp. 64-69.

32. John A. T. Robinson, *Redating the New Testament* (Philadelphia: Westminster Press, 1976); Josh McDowell, *He Walked among Us*, pp. 109-174; Bo Reicke, *The Roots of the Synoptic Gospels* (Philadelphia: Fortress Press, 1986); Robert L. Thomas and Stanley N. Gundry, *A Harmony of the Gospels* (San Francisco: Harper & Row, 1978); France, *Evidence for Jesus*, pp. 86-139.

33. Meier, *A Marginal Jew.* Vol. 2, p. 4.

34. Alan Richardson, *The Miracle Stories of the Gospels* (London: SCM, 1941), p. 36.

35. Simon Greenleaf, *An Examination of the Testimony of the Four Evangelists by the Rules of Evidence Administered in the Courts of Justice* (1874; rprt. Grand Rapids: Baker Book House, 1965), p. 29.

36. J. P. Moreland, *Scaling the Secular City*, p. 128.

37. Murray J. Harris, *From Grave to Glory* (Grand Rapids: Zondervan, 1990), p. 149.

38. A. E. Harvey, *Jesus and the Constraints of History* (Philadelphia: Westminister, 1982), p. 110.

39. Craig Blomberg, *The Historical Reliability of the Gospels* (Downers Grove: InterVarsity Press, 1987), p. 81.

40. Will Durant, *The Story of Civilization*, vol. III *Caesar and Christ* (New York: Simon and Schuster, 1944), p. 557.

41. Jon A. Buell and O. Quentin Hyder, *Jesus: God, Ghost, or Guru?* (Grand Rapids: Zondervan, 1978), p. 64.

42. John A. T. Robinson, *The Priority of John* (London: SCM, 1985), p. 53.

43. Stephen Smalley, *John: Evangelist and Interpreter* (Exeter: Paternoster, 1978).

44. Erickson, *The Word became Flesh*, p. 426.

45. Erickson, *The Word Became Flesh*, pp. 427-428.

46. Douglas Groothuis, *Revealing the New Age Jesus* (Downers Grove: InterVarsity Press, 1990), p. 131.

47. John McRay, *Archaeology and the New Testament* (Grand Rapids: Baker, 1991); Alan Millard, *Discoveries from the Time of Jesus* (Oxford: Lion Publishing, 1990); Bill Humble, *Archaeology and the Bible* (Nashville: Christian Communications, 1990); Gonzalo BaezCamargo, *Archaeological Commentary on the Bible* (Garden City: Doubleday, 1984), pp. 195-235; E. M. Blaiklock, *The Archaeology of the New Testament* rev. ed. (Nashville: Nelson, 1984); Edward P. Myers, *Archaeology of the Bible* (West Monroe: School of Biblical Studies, 1980), pp. 96-99; Jack Lewis, *Archaeological Backgrounds to Bible People* (Grand Rapids: Baker, 1971), pp. 137-174.

48. Jack Finegan, *The Archaeology of the New Testament* (Princeton: Princeton University Press, 1969), p. 85.

49. Millard, *Discoveries*, pp. 36-37.

50. L. I. Levine, ed., *Ancient Synagogues Revealed* (Jerusalem: Israel Exploration Society, 1981); E. M. Meyers and J. F. Strange, *Archaeology, the Rabbis, and Early Christianity: The Social and Historical Setting of Palestinian Judaism and Christianity* (Nashville: Abingdon, 1981).

51. M. Stein, "How Herod Moved Gigantic Blocks to Construct Temple Mount," *BAR* 6 (1981), 42-46; James H. Charlesworth, *Jesus within Judaism: New Light from Exciting Archaeological Discoveries*, (New York: Doubleday, 1988), p. 117-119.

52. Charlesworth, *Jesus within Judaism*, pp. 103-130.

53. Zvi Greenhut, "Discovery of the Caiaphas Family Tomb," *Jerusalem Perspective* 4 (July-October, 1991), pp. 6-11 and Ronny Reich, "Ossuary Inscriptions from the Caiaphas Tomb," *Jerusalem Perspective* 4 (July-October, 1991), pp. 13-21.

54. Sir William Ramsay, *The Bearing of Recent Discovery on the Trustworthiness of the New Testament* (1911; rprt. Grand Rapids: Baker, 1953), p. 38.

55. Ramsay, *The Bearing of Recent Discovery*, p. 89.

56. Charlesworth, *Jesus within Judaism*, pp. 168-169.

Chapter 15

1. Richard A. Horsley with John S. Hanson, *Bandits, Prophets, and Messiahs: Popular Movements at the Time of Jesus* (New York: Harper & Row, 1985), p. 32.

2. Richard A. Batey, *Jesus & the Forgotten City* (Grand Rapids: Baker, 1991), p. 50.

3. Horsley and Hanson, *Bandits, Prophets, and Messiahs*, p. 56.

4. Josephus, *Wars of the Jews* 1.11.2; *Antiquities of the Jews* 14.11.2.

5. Kaari Ward, ed., *Jesus and His Times* (Pleasantville, N.Y.: The Reader's Digest, 1987), p. 75.

6. Henri Daniel-Rops, *Daily Life in the Time of Jesus* trans. by Patrick O'Brien (Ann Arbor: Servant Books, 1980), p. 151.

7. Paul L. Maier, *In the Fullness of Time: A Historian Looks at Christmas, Easter, and the Early Church*, rev. ed. (San Fransisco: Harper, 1991), p. 12.

8. Daniel-Rops, *Daily Life*, p. 62.

9. Josephus, *Wars of the Jews* 1.22.4-5; John C. H. Laughlin, "Herod," in

MDB, Watson E. Mills, ed., p. 376; F. F. Bruce, *New Testament History* (Garden City: Anchor Books, 1972), pp. 20-25.

10. Macrobius, *Les Saturnales*, trans. by Henri Bornecque (Paris: Garnier freres, 1937), ii.4.11.

11. Josephus, *Antiquities of the Jews*, 15.1.2; 14.9.4; H. W. Hoehner, "Herod," *ISBER*, vol. II, p. 690; Charles Ludwig, *Rulers of New Testament Times* (Denver: Accent Books, 1976), p. 23.

12. Josephus, *Wars of the Jews* 2.33.6.

13. The territory awarded Herod's third son, Philip, was, for the most part, outside Palestine proper.

14. Josephus, *Wars of the Jews* 2.1.1-3.

15. Josephus, *Wars of the Jews*, 2.5.1-2; *Antiquities of the Jews*, 17.10.10. See also Batey, *Forgotten City*, p. 53; Sean Freyne, *Galilee from Alexander the Great to Hadrian 323 B.C.E. to 135 C.E.* (Wilmington: Michael Glazier, 1980), p. 123.

16. Horsley, *Bandits, Prophets, and Messiahs*, p. 35.

17. Fredriksen, *From Jesus to Christ*, p. 79.

18. Josephus, *Antiquities of the Jews* 18.3,1-2

19. Philo, *Ad Gaium* 38.302.

20. See, A. N. Sherwin White, "Pilate, Pontius," *ISBER*, Vol. 3, G. W. Bromiley, ed., pp. 867-869.

21. Horsley, *Bandits, Prophets, and Messiahs*, p. 42.

22. Philo, *De. Spec. Leg.* I.64; See also the discussion in Richard N. Longnecker, *The Christology of Early Jewish Christianity* (London: SCM, 1970), pp. 32-41; Oscar Cullmann, *Christology of the New Testament*, trans. by S. C. Guthrie and C. A. M. Hall (London: SCM, 1963), pp. 13-15; H. M. Teeple, *Mosaic Eschatological Prophet* (Philadelphia: Society of Biblical Literature, 1917), pp. 74-85.

23. Smith, *The Promised Messiah*, pp. 122-128.

24. Smith, *The Promised Messiah*, pp. 145-154.

25. See F. F. Bruce, *Jesus and Christian Origins Outside the New Testament* (Grand Rapids: Eerdmans, 1974), pp. 66-81.

26. Among numerous materials, see Robert D. Culver, *The Sufferings and the Glory of the Lord's Righteous Servant* (Moline, Ill.: Christian Service Foundation, 1958); Allen R. MacRae, *The Gospel of Isaiah* (Chicago: Moody, 1977), pp. 129-150; Edward J. Young, *Isaiah Fifty-Three* (Grand Rapids: Eerdmans, 1953).

27. Even Rowley, *Servant of the Lord*, pp. 85-88, admitted the text provides an obvious connection between the promised Davidic king and the suffering servant.

28. Van Groningen, *Messianic Revelation*, p. 620.

29. S. R. Driver and Adolf Neubauer, *The Fifty-Third Chapter of Isaiah According to the Jewish Interpreters* (1876; rprt. New York: KTAV Publishing House, 1969).

30. Ernst Hengstenberg, *Christology of the Old Testament and a Commentary on the Messianic Predictions*, Vol. II (1847, rprt. Grand Rapids: Kregel, 1956), pp. 311-342.

31. Van Groningen, *Messianic Revelation*, p. 643.

32. Van Groningen, *Messianic Revelation*, p. 647.

33. See Michael Bauman, "Why Noninerrantists Are Not Listening: Six Tactical Errors Evangelicals Commit," *JETS* 29 (1986), 317-324.

34. Robert E. Picirilli, *Paul the Apostle* (Chicago: Moody Press, 1986), pp. 26-37.

35. Harris, *Grave to Glory*, p. 59. See also, C. R. North, *The Second Isaiah* (Oxford: Clarendon, 1964), p. 244.

36. See chapter 14 for the defense of the testimony of early eyewitnesses.

37. Joseph Klausner, *Jesus of Nazareth*, p. 51. See also, Goldstein, *Jesus in the Jewish Tradition*, p. 147.

38. Murray J. Harris, *Raised Immortal.* (Grand Rapids: Eerdmans, 1985), p. 40.

39. J. P. Moreland, *Scaling the Secular City*, pp. 162-163.

40. Edwin Yamauchi, "Easter—Myth, Hallucination, or History?" *ChT* 4 (March 15, 1974), pp. 4-16. See also Ulrich Wilkens, *Resurrection*, trans. by A. M. Stewart (Atlanta: John Knox, 1978), pp. 8-9; and William Lane Craig, *The Son Rises* (Chicago: Moody, 1981), p. 63.

41. Moreland, *Scaling the Secular City*, p. 161.

42. Rudolf Bultmann, *The History of the Synoptic Tradition*, trans. John Marsh, 2d ed. (Oxford: Basil Blackwell, 1963), p. 274.

43. Craig, *The Son Rises*, pp. 47-67.

44. Craig, *The Son Rises*, pp. 59-61.

45. Edward Lynn Bode, *The First Easter Morning: The Gospel Accounts of the Women's Visit to the Tomb of Jesus* (Rome: Biblical Institute Press, 1970), pp.160-161; Wilchens, *Resurrection*, pp. 37-39.

46. Moreland, *Scaling the Secular City,* p. 168.

47. *J. Sot* 19a.

48. *B. Kidd* 82b.

49. Moreland, *Scaling the Secular City*, p. 165.

50. Hoover, *Dear Agnos*, p. 233.

51. Harris, *Grave to Glory*, p. 108.

52. Pinchas Lapide, *The Resurrection of Jesus: A Jewish Perspective* (Minneapolis: Augsburg, 1983), p. 100.

53. Norman Anderson, *Jesus Christ: The Witness of History* (Downers Grove: Inter-Varsity, 1985), p. 123.

54. Charles Alford Guignebert, *Jesus* (New York: University Books, 1956), pp. 500f.

55. David Friedrich Strauss, *The New Life of Jesus Critically Examined*, 2d ed., trans. by G. Eliot (London: S. Sonnenschien, 1892); see also Ernst Renan, *The Life of Jesus*, trans. by Charles Edwin Wilbour (New York: Carleton, 1864).

56. Otto Pfleiderer, *Early Christian Conception of Christ* (London: Williams and Norgate, 1905), pp. 134-151; Wilhelm Bousset, *Kyrios Christos* 2d ed., trans. J. E. Steeley (Nashville, 1970, orig. 1921), pp. 56-60; Alred Loisy, *The Birth of the Christian Religion*, trans. L. P. Jacke (London: G. Allen and Unwin, 1948), pp. 93-95.

57. Bultmann, *Synoptic Tradition.*

58. Kirsopp Lake, *The Historical Evidence for the Resurrection of Jesus Christ* (New York: G. P. Putnam's Sons, 1907), pp. 250-253.

59. Hermann Samuel Reimarus, *Reimarus—Fragments*, trans. by R. S. Fraser (1879; rprt. London: Williams and Norgate, 1971).

60. Excellent treatments of the resurrection are found in Bode, *First Easter Morning*; Craig, *The Son Rises*; Gary Habermas, *The Resurrection of Jesus: An Apologetic* (Grand Rapids: Baker, 1980); Harris, *Grave to Glory*, pp. 101-128; McDowell, *The Resurrection Factor*; Moreland, *Scaling the Secular City*, pp. 159-183; W. J. Sparrow-Simpson, *The Resurrection and the Christian Faith* (Grand Rapids: Zondervan, 1968).

61. Gary Habermas, in Terry L. Miethe, ed. *Did Jesus Rise from the Dead? The Resurrection Debate* (New York: Harper & Row, 1987), pp. 20-21.

62. Among those modern scholars who Habermas identifies as demonstrating that these theories are inadequate: Karl Barth, *The Doctrine of Reconciliation*, vol. 4, part I of *Church Dogmatics*, ed. G. W. Bromiley and T. F. Torrence (Edinburgh: T. and T. Clark, 1956), p. 340; Raymond Brown, "The Resurrection and Biblical Criticism," *Commonweal* 87 (November 24, 1967), p. 233; Paul Tillich, *Systematic Theology*, vol. 2 (Chicago: University of Chicago Press, 1971), p. 156; Wolfhart Pannenberg, *Jesus—God and Man*, trans. Lewis L. Wilkens and Duane Priebe (Philadelphia: Westminster, 1968), pp. 88-97; Gunther Bornkamm, *Jesus of Nazareth*, trans. Irene and Fraser McLuskey with James M. Robinson (New York: Harper & Row, 1960), pp. 181-185; Ulrich Wilckens, *Resurrection*, trans. A. M. Stewart (Edinburgh: Saint Andrews Press, 1977), pp. 117-119; John A. T. Robinson, *Can We Trust the New Testament?* (Grand Rapids: Eerdmans, 1977), pp. 123-125; and A. M. Hunter, *Bible and Gospel* (Philadelphia: Westminster, 1969), p. 111.

63. "Acts and Martyrdom of the Holy Apostle Andrew," in Alexander Roberts and James Donaldson, eds., *The Ante-Nicene Fathers* (Grand Rapids: Eerdmans, 1951), pp. 511-516.

64. "Martyrdom of the Holy and Glorious Apostle Bartholomew," in Roberts and Donaldson, eds., *Ante-Nicene Fathers*, Vol. VIII, pp. 553-557.

65. "Consummation of Thomas the Apostle," in Roberts and Donaldson, eds., *Ante-Nicene Fathers*, Vol. VIII, pp. 550-552.

66. See Carsten P. Thiede, *Simon Peter: From Galilee to Rome* (Grand Rapids: Zondervan, 1988), pp. 185-194 for a summary of the evidence.

67. Although many scholars place John's humiliation at the whim of Domitian, sizable evidence suggests that this was more likely to have occurred under Nero. (See David Chilton, *The Days of Vengeance* [Forth Worth: Dominion Press, 1987] and Kenneth L. Gentry, Jr., *Before Jerusalem Fell* [Tyler, Tex: Institute for Christian Economics, 1989]). However, the identity of the Caesar in question is irrelevant to current concerns. Scholars may quibble over who inflicted the torture; that it happened is widely accepted.

68. J. T. Marlin, *The Seven Churches of Asia Minor* (Duncan, Okla.: J. T. Marlin, 1980), p. 2.

69. Pascal, in Robert W. Gleason, ed., *The Essential Pascal*, trans. G. F. Pullen (New York: Mentor-Omega Books, 1966), p. 187.

70. J. N. D. Anderson, *Christianity: The Witness of History*, (Downers Grove: InterVarsity, 1970), p. 92.

71. Edward Gibbon, *The History of the Decline and Fall of the Roman Empire* (1776; rprt. Chicago: William Benton, 1952), p. 179.

72. Craig effectively defends the historicity of the burial. See his *The Son Rises*, pp. 46-63.

73. Maier, *First Easter*, pp. 118-119.

74. Bruce, *New Testament History*, p. 391.

75. Harris, *From Grave to Glory*, p. 124.

76. George Curries, *The Military Discipline of the Romans from the Founding of the City to the Close of the Republic*. Abstract of thesis published under the auspices of the Graduate Council of Indiana University (Bloomington: Indiana University, 1928), pp. 41-43.

77. See, for instance, Flavius Vegetius-Renatus, *The Military Institutions of the Romans*, trans. by John Clark, ed. by Thomas R. Phillips (Harrisburg, Penn.: The Military Service Publishing Company, 1944).

78. McDowell, *Resurrection Factor*, p. 55.

79. Martin Hengel, *Crucifixion in the Ancient World and the Folly of the Message of the Cross*, trans. by John Bowden (Philadelphia: Fortress, 1977), p. 25.

80. Abundant references document the customary torture prior to crucifixion: Philo, *In Flaccum* 72; Seneca, *Dialogues* (Paris: L'Association Guillaume Books, 1927), 5; Plato, *Gorgias*, trans. by W. C. Helmhold (Indianapolis: Bobbs-Merrill, 1952), 473bc; Dionysius of Halicarnassus, *The Roman Antiquities*, trans. by Earnest Cary (Cambridge: Harvard University Press, 1948), 5.51.3; Livy 22.13.9; 28.37.3.

81. C. Truman Davis, "The Crucifixion of Jesus," *Arizona Medicine*, March, 1965, p. 185.

82. Eusebius, *Ecclesiastical History*, trans. by Christian Frederick Cruse (Grand Rapids: Baker, 1955), p. 371.

83. Maier, *First Easter*, p. 112.

84. Strauss, *Life of Jesus*, Vol. I, p. 412.

85. E. LeCamus, *The Life of Christ* Vol. III (New York: The Cathedral Library Association, 1908) pp. 485-486.

86. Michael Green, *The Day Death Died* (Downers Grove: InterVarsity, 1982), p. 47.

87. Paul F. Maier, *In the Fullness of Time: A Historian Looks at Christmas, Easter, and the Early Church*, rev. ed. (San Francisco: Harper, 1991), p. 181.

88. Maier, *Fullness of Time*, p. 180.

89. John Wenham, *Easter Enigma: Are the Resurrection Accounts in Conflict?* (Grand Rapids: Zondervan, 1984). p. 11.

90. Maier, *Fullness of Time*, p. 180.

Chapter 16

1. Kenny Barfield, *Why the Bible Is Number One* (Grand Rapids: Baker, 1988).

2. Voltaire, (*Oeuvres de Voltaire*, ed. A. Gotha, Tom. XVII, p. 107) cited in Keith, *Evidence of the Truth of the Christian Religion*, p. 106.

3. Tacitus, *The Histories*, 5.8.

4. Dion Cassius, *Dio's Roman History*, trans. by Earnest Cary (Cambridge: Harvard University Press, 1954), lxix, p. 798.

5. Josephus, *Wars of the Jews*, 3.3.2.

6. Robinson and Smith, *Palestine*, cited in Keith, p. 117.

7. Robinson and Smith, *Palestine*, cited in Keith, p. 117.

8. Keith, *Evidence of the Truth of the Christian Religion*, p. 117.

9. Josephus, *Antiquities of the Jews*, x.9.7.

10. Perhaps the term "capital" is too generous. At least in the early days of the northern kingdom, it might be better to simply refer to the cities as royal residences. See J. P. J. Olivier, "In Search of a Capital for the Northern Kingdom," *JNSL*, 11 (1983) 117-132.

11. John W. Crowfoot, Kathleen Kenyon, and E. L. Sukenik, *The Buildings at Samaria* (London: Palestine Exploration Fund, 1942), p. 1.

12. J. W. Jack, *Samaria in Ahab's Time* (Edinburgh: T. & T. Clark, 1929), pp. 2-3.

13. A. Van Selms, "Samaria," in *ISBER*, Vol. IV, G. W. Bromiley, ed., p. 296.

14. Crowfoot, Kenyon, and Sukenik, *Buildings at Samaria*, p. 1.

15. Crowfoot, Kenyon, and Sukenik, *Buildings at Samaria*, p. 1.

16. Edd Rowell, "Samaria," in *MDB*, Watson E. Mills, ed., p. 788.

17. Schoville, *Biblical Archaeology*, p. 466.

18. Carl Armerding, "Samaria," in *NIDBA*, E. M. Blaiklock and R. K. Harrison, eds., pp. 394-396; "Samaria," in *AEHL*, 3d ed., Avraham Negev, ed. (New York: Prentice-Hall, 1990), pp. 334-337; J. W. and G. M. Crowfoot, *Early Ivories from Samaria* (London: Palestine Exploration Fund, 1938); J. B. Hennessey, "Excavations at Samaria-Sebaste, 1968," *Levant* 2 (1970), pp. iv-v, 1-21.

19. Barnes, *Minor Prophets*, Vol. II, pp. 274-275.

20. Burton Coffman, *Commentary on the Minor Prophets* (Austin, TX: Firm Foundation, 1981), Vol. II, p. 223.

21. Rowell, "Samaria," in *MDB*, Watson E. Mills, ed., p. 788.

22. Rowell, "Samaria," in *MDB*, Watson E. Mills, ed., p. 789.

23. Josephus, *Antiquities of the Jews*, xiii.10.3.

24. Josias Leslie Porter, *A Handbook for Travelers in Syria and Palestine* (London: John Murray, 1858), p. 345.

25. Porter, *Handbook for Travelers*, p. 344.

26. Carl Willem Meredith Van de Velde, *Narrative of a Journey through Syria and Palestine in 1851 and 1852*, vol. I (Edinburgh: W. Blackwood and Sons, 1854), p. 384.

27. See G. A. Reisner, C. S. Fisher, and D. G. Lyon, *Harvard Excavations at Samaria* (Cambridge: Harvard University Press, 1924), 2 volumes, and Andre Parrot, *Samaria: The Capital of the Kingdom of Israel* (New York: Philosophical Library, 1958).

28. Jack, *Samaria in Ahab's Time*, p. 5.

29. Van de Velde, *Syria and Palestine*, Vol. I, p. 384.

Chapter 17

1. *Tacitus, The Histories*, v.13.4, says the normal population of Jerusalem (including its suburbs) approximated 600,000. See also, Josephus, *Wars of the Jews*, 5.9.3.
2. Batey, *Forgotten City*, p. 191.
3. For opposing views see Joachim Jeremias, *Jerusalem in the Time of Jesus*, tr. by F. H. Cave and C. H. Cave (Philadelphia: Fortress Press, 1975), pp. 77-84. His calculations do not seem to take into account numerous factors. For instance, he avoids noting that the suburbs were considered part of the city; he does not take into account the fact that, in time of war, people from the surrounding region crowd into the largest, best-fortified city; he refuses to consider the testimony of several independent witnesses as to the large population of first-century Palestine; he assumes that Tacitus borrowed his information from Josephus; and he assumes that Josephus uses erroneous numbers. Other sources include, Anthony Byatt, "Josephus and Population Numbers in First-Century Palestine," *PEQ* 105 (1973), 51-60, and John Wilkinson, "Ancient Jerusalem: Its Water Supply and Population," *PEQ* 106 (1974), 33-51.
4. Mishnah, *Sukkah*, iii.8.
5. Midrash Rabbah, *Lamentations*, 4.2 on 4.2.
6. Midrash Rabbah, *Lamentations*, 1.50 on 1.16.
7. Jeremias, *Jerusalem*, pp. 21-25.
8. Josephus, *Wars of the Jews*, 5.5.6.
9. Josephus, *Antiquities of the Jews*, 15.11.3.
10. Jeremias, *Jerusalem*, p. 22.
11. Mishnah, *Middoth*, ii.3; Josephus, *Wars*, v.5.2.
12. Josephus, *Wars of the Jews*, 5.5.6.
13. Tosephta, *Menahoth*, iii.19.
14. Mishnah, *Middoth*, iv.6.
15. William L. Lane, *The Gospel of Mark* (Grand Rapids: Eerdmans, 1974), p. 451.
16. Talmud, *Sukkah*, 51b; *Baba Bathra*, 4a.
17. Josephus, *Wars of the Jews*, 5.5. See also Jeremias, *Jerusalem*, p. 25 and information in Richard M. Mackowski, *Jerusalem: City of Jesus* (Grand Rapids: Eerdmans, 1980), pp. 113-137.
18. G. Plinius Secundus (Pliny the Elder), *Natural History*, 5.15.70.
19. Batey, *Forgotten City*, p. 36.
20. Michael Grant, *Herod the Great* (New York: American Heritage, 1971), p. 75.
21. Batey, *Forgotten City*, p. 44. See also, Josephus, *Antiquities of the Jews*, 15.8.1.
22. Josephus, *Antiquities of the Jews*, 15.8.1.
23. Batey, *Forgotten City*, p. 46. See also, Grant, *Herod the Great*, p. 127.
24. Josephus, *Wars of the Jews*, 5.4.2.
25. F. LaGard Smith, *The Narrated Bible* (Eugene, Ore.: Harvest House, 1984), p. 1449.
26. William R. Kimball, *What the Bible Says about the Great Tribulation* (Joplin, Mo: College Press, 1983), p. 3.

27. Josephus, *Wars of the Jews*, 7.1.1.
28. Jan Jozef Simons, *Jerusalem in the Old Testament* (Leiden: Brill, 1952), p. 435.
29. Josephus, *Wars of the Jews*, 2.19.5.
30. Josephus, *Wars of the Jews*, 2.19.4.
31. Josephus, *Wars of the Jews*, 2.19.6.
32. Josephus, *Wars of the Jews*, 2.19.7.
33. Will and Ariel Durant, *The Lessons of History* (New York: Simon and Schuster, 1968), p. 81.
34. Kimball, *The Great Tribulation*, p. 24; Josephus, *Antiquities of the Jews*, 18.9; *Wars of the Jews*, 2.10.
35. Josephus, *Antiquities of the Jews*, 18.8.2-9. See also, Tacitus, *The Histories*, v.9.
36. Josephus, *Wars of the Jews*, 2.10.1.
37. Tacitus, *The Histories*, v. 9.
38. Josephus, *Antiquities*, 18.8.7-9.
39. Josephus, *Wars of the Jews*, 2.13.
40. Josephus, *Wars of the Jews*, 2.13.2.
41. Origen and Jerome, cited in Kimball, *The Great Tribulation*, pp. 20-21.
42. Josephus, *Antiquities of the Jews*, 20.2.5.
43. Tacitus, *Annals*, xii.43; Suetonius, "Claudius," in *Twelve Caesars*, xviii.2; Jeremias, *Jerusalem*, p. 143; Mike Fuhrman, "First-Century Hunger," *BI*, ? (1992), 52-56; K. S. Gapp, "The Universal Famine under Claudius," *HTR*, 28 (1935), 258-261; Kimball, *The Great Tribulation*, p. 30.
44. Josephus, *Antiquities of the Jews*, 20.51.
45. Suetonius, "Nero," *Twelve Caesars*; Kimball, *The Great Tribulation*, p. 30.
46. Josephus, *Wars of the Jews*, 4.4.5.
47. Tacitus (*Annals* xiv.27; xv.22) describes the earthquakes near Laodicea and Pompeii in some detail.
48. Lane, *Gospel of Mark*, p. 466.
49. Edward J. Young, *The Prophecy of Daniel* (Grand Rapids: Eerdmans, 1949); Jim McGuiggan, *The Book of Daniel* (Lubbock: Montex, 1978).
50. Lane, *Gospel of Mark*, p. 467.
51. Josephus, *Wars of the Jews*, 4.3.7.
52. Josephus, *Wars of the Jews*, 4.4.4.
53. Josephus, *Wars of the Jews*, 4.3.10.
54. Lane, *Gospel of Mark*, p. 469.
55. Josephus, *Wars of the Jews*, 4.3.10.
56. Kimball, *The Great Tribulation*, p. 59.
57. Eusebius, *Ecclesiastical History*, iii.5.3.
58. Josephus, *Wars of the Jews*, 2.20.1.
59. Lane, *Gospel of Mark*, p. 469.
60. Lane, *Gospel of Mark*, p. 470.
61. Josephus, *Wars of the Jews*, 5.1.5.
62. Josephus. *Wars of the Jews*, 5.1.5.
63. Josephus, *Wars of the Jews*, 5.12.3.

64. Josephus, *Wars of the Jews*, 5.13.4.
65. Josephus, *Wars of the Jews*, 6.3.4.
66. Josephus, *Wars of the Jews*, 6.8.5.
67. Josephus, *Wars of the Jews*, 6.9.2-3.
68. Josephus, *Wars of the Jews*, 6.5.3.

Chapter 18

1. Robert F. Paget, *In the Footsteps of Orpheus: The Discovery of the Ancient Greek Underworld* (London: Robert Hale, 1967); Robert K. G. Temple, *Conversations with Eternity: Ancient Man's Attempts to Know the Future* (London: Rider & Company, 1984).
2. Strabo, *Geography*, v.4.5.
3. Temple, *Conversations with Eternity*, p. 11.
4. Peter Watson, *War on the Mind: The Military Uses and Abuses of Psychology* (New York: Basic Books, 1978), p. 253.
5. Paget, *Footsteps of Orpheus*, p. 163.
6. Vergil, *Aeneid*, Book VI, trans. by John W. Davidson, *The Works of Virgil* (London: Bell and Daldy, 1873), p. 253.
7. Temple, *Conversations with Eternity*, p. 19.
8. Philipp Vandenberg, *The Mystery of the Oracles*, trans. by George Unwin (New York: Macmillan, 1982), p. 8.
9. Temple, *Conversations with Eternity*, p. 50.
10. Eusebe Salverte, *The Occult Sciences: The Philosophy of Magic, Prodigies, and Apparent Miracles*, trans. by Anthony Todd Thompson (New York: Harper & Brothers, 1846), p. 40.
11. Jane Harrison, *Prolegomena to the Study of Greek Religion* (Cambridge: Cambridge University Press, 1903), p. 581.
12. Pausanias, *Guide to Greece*, Vol. 1, trans. by Peter Levi (New York: Penguin, 1971), ix.39.4.
13. G. Plinius Secundus (Pliny the Elder), *Natural History*, xxv.20.47.
14. Philostratus, *The Life of Apollonius of Tyana*, Vol. II, trans. by F. C. Conybeare (Cambridge: Harvard University Press, 1950), viii.19-20.
15. Temple, *Conversations with Eternity*, p. 46.
16. Temple. *Conversations with Eternity*, pp. 11-13.
17. Paget, *In the Footsteps of Orpheus*, p. 161.
18. Vandenberg, *Mystery of the Oracles*, p. 14f.
19. Herodotus, *The Histories*, i. 53.
20. Herodotus, *The Histories*, i.51-52.
21. Temple, *Conversations with Eternity*, p. 18
22. Vandenberg, *Mystery of the Oracles*, p. 132.
23. John Pollock, *The Apostle: A Life of Paul* (Wheaton: Victor Books, 1972), p. 95.
24. Herodotus, *The Histories*, i.46-48.
25. Those at Delphi, Trophonios, Abae, Dodona, Branchidae, Amphiaraus, and Siwa.

26. Vandenberg, *Mystery of the Oracles*, pp. 154-158.
27. Temple, *Conversations with Eternity*, pp. 32-39.

Chapter 19

1. Vandenberg, *Mysteries of the Oracles*, pp. 128-130.
2. Parke, *Greek Oracles*, pp. 80-81.
3. Marcus Tullius Cicero, *De divinatione*, trans. and ed. by E. E. Kellett (Cambridge: Cambridge University Press, 1936), i.34. See, also, David E. Aune, *Prophecy in Early Christianity and the Ancient Mediterranean World* (Grand Rapids: Eerdmans, 1983), p. 25. Aune also notes that the oracle of Herakles near Bura used divination exclusively.
4. Aune, *Prophecy in Early Christianity*, p. 23.
5. Aune, *Prophecy in Early Christianity*, p. 23. Following Cicero (*De divinatione*, i.6.12), Aune divides divination into two groups which he terms "technical divination" (based on the skill of interpreters) and "natural divination" which he considers trance, ecstasy, and visions (p. 24). "Somewhat uneasily" he places the oracles in the second category. Cicero's division (*ars* and *natura*) was much the same.
6. Cicero, *De Divinatione*, i.18.35.
7. Temple, *Conversations with Eternity*, p. 72.
8. Morris Jastrow, Jr., "The Liver as the Seat of the Soul," in *Studies in the History of Religions Presented to Crawford Howell Toy*, David Gordon Lynn and George Foot Moore, eds. (New York: Macmillan, 1912), p. 158.
9. E. A. Wallis Budge, *Egyptian Magic*, (1901; rprnt., New York: Dover, 1971), p. 224.
10. Arrian, *Campaigns*, vii.18.2-5.
11. Plutarch, "Alexander," in *The Age of Alexander*, trans. by Ian Scott-Kilvert, (New York: Penguin, 1973), 73, pp. 330-331.
12. Arrian, *Campaigns*, vii.18.2f.
13. Temple, *Conversations*, p. 75.
14. Green, *Alexander of Macedon*, pp. 473-477.
15. Xenophon, *Anabasis, or Expedition of Cyrus*, trans. J. S. Watson (London: Bohn's Library, 1891).
16. Xenophon, *Anabasis*, vi.4.9-25.
17. O. R. Gurney, "The Babylonians and Hittites," in *Oracles and Divination* Michael Loewe and Carmen Blacker, eds. (Boulder: Shambhala, 1981), p. 147.
18. See J. P. Vernant et al., *Divination et Rationalite* (Paris: Editions du Seuil, 1974), Auguste Bouche-Le Clerq, *Histoire de la Divinatione dans l'Antiquite*, 4 vols. (Paris: E. Leroux, 1879-1882); and Rencontre Assyriologique Internationale, *La Divination en Mesopotamie Ancienne et dans les Regions Voisines* (Paris: Presses Universitaires de France, 1966).
19. Gurney, "Babylonians and Hittites," p. 148.
20. A. L. Oppenheim, *Ancient Mesopotamia*, Rev. ed. (Chicago: University of Chicago Press, 1977), pp. 210, 216, 301, and 340.
21. Gurney, "Babylonians and Hittites," in *Oracles and Divination*, Loewe

and Blacker, eds., p. 151.

22. David Pingree, "Astrology," in *EB-MAC*, Vol. 2 (Chicago: University of Chicago Press, 1978), p. 219.

23. John Ankerberg and John Weldon, *Astrology: Do the Heavens Rule Our Destiny?* (Eugene, Ore.: Harvest House, 1989), p. 11.

24. Donald Ragan, *For the Record: From Wall Street to Washington* (New York: Harcourt Brace Jovanovich, 1988), pp. 3, 295-298.

25. John Ankerberg and John Weldon (*Astrology*, pp. 47-110) summarize the results of many scientific studies. The reader is refered to their in-depth treatment.

26. Roger B. Culver and Philip A. Ianna, *The Gemini Syndrome: A Scientific Evaluation of Astrology* (Buffalo: Prometheus, Books, 1984), pp. 169-170.

27. Geoffrey Dean, "Does Astrology Need to be True? Part 1: A Look at the Real Thing," *The Skeptical Inquirer* 9, no. 2, p. 169.

28. Dean, "Does Astrology Need to be True?", p. 170.

29. Robert Eisler, *The Royal Art of Astrology* (London: Herbert Joseph, Ltd., 1946), p. 21.

30. Roger B. Culver and Philip A. Ianna, *Astrology: True or False—A Scientific Evaluation* (Buffalo: Prometheus Books, 1988), p. 213.

31. James T. Braha, *Ancient Hindu Astrology for the Modern Western Astrologer* (North Miami: Hermetician Press, 1986), p. 306.

32. Culver and Ianna, *Gemini Syndrome*, p. 174.

33. Ankerberg and Weldon, *Astrology*, p. 107.

34. Ruth Montgomery, *A Gift of Prophecy* (New York: Bantam Books, 1966), p. 179.

35. See James Bjornstad, Jeanne Dixon, *Edgar Cayce: 20th Century Prophecy* (Minneapolis: Dimension Books, 1969), pp. 38-45.

36. Ankerberg and Weldon, *Astrology*, p. 109.

Chapter 20

1. Because I believe evidence indicates inspiration of the Scriptures, I accept an inevitable second advent of Jesus and the ultimate dissolution of the material universe. I strongly reject doomsday prophets who claim to discern the date of this event.

2. Edgar Leoni, *Nostradamus: Life and Literature* (New York: Exposition Press, 1961), p. 9.

3. Leoni, *Nostradamus*, p. 106.

4. Leoni, *Nostradamus*, pp. 42ff.

5. David Wallechinsky, Amy Wallace, and Irving Wallace, *The Book of Predictions* (New York: Bantam Books, 1981), pp. 354f.

6. Gabriel Naude, *Apologie pour tous les grand personages ... soupconnes de magie* (Paris: F. Targa, 1625), p. 472.

7. Anatole Le Pelletier, *Le Oracles de Michel de Nostredame ...* (Paris: Le Pelletier, 1867), pp. 8-13. See also Eugene F. Parker, *Michel Nostradamus — Prophet*, Unpublished doctoral dissertation, Cambridge: Harvard University, 1920.

8. Leoni, *Nostradamus*, p. 102f.

9. Leoni, *Nostradamus*, p. 112.

10. Leoni, *Nostradamus*, p. 109.

11. Leoni, *Nostradamus*, p. 107.

12. Leoni, *Nostradamus*, p. 37.

13. Leoni, *Nostradamus*, p. 29.

14. Leoni, *Nostradamus*, p. 110.

15. *Doctrine and Covenants* (Salt Lake City: Church of Jesus Christ of Latter Day Saints, 1974), 107:92.

16. B. H. Roberts, ed., *The History of the Church of Jesus Christ of Latter Day Saints* (Salt Lake City: Deseret Publishing Co., 1951), Vol. 2, p. 182.

17. Roberts, *History*, Vol. 5, p. 336.

18. *Millennial Star*, 15:206-207.

19. Cited from a photocopy of the original diary in Gerald and Sandra Tanner, *The Changing World of Mormonism* (Chicago: Moody, 1980), p. 419.

20. Max H. Parkin, *Conflict at Kirtland* (Salt Lake City: Deseret Publishing Co., 1966), pp. 53-55.

21. Roberts, *History*, Vol. 1, p. 323.

22. Oliver Cowdery, *Defense in a Rehearsal of My Grounds for Separating Myself from the Latter Day Saints* (Norton, Ohio: Pressley's Job Office, 1839), p. 1.

23. Klaus J. Hansen, "The Metamorphosis of the Kingdom of God: Toward a Reinterpretation of Mormon History," *D* 1 (Autumn, 1966), p. 76.

24. Parley P. Pratt, *Mormonism Unveiled — Truth Vindicated*, 4th ed. (New York: J. W. Harrison, 1842), p. 15.

25. *Doctrine and Covenants*, 57:1-13; 84:1-5.

26. A more complete discussion may be found in James D. Bales, *The Testing of Joseph Smith, Jr.* (Concord, Calif.: Pacific Publishing Co., 1967), p. 7f; William Brodie Crouch, *The Myth of Mormon Inspiration* (Shreveport: Lambert Book House, 1968), pp. 169-172; Gerald and Sandra Tanner, *Changing World*, pp. 420-424.

27. *Doctrine and Covenants*, 84:2-4; 115:7-17; 29:8.

28. See the *Millennial Star*, 7:47-48, and Orson Pratt, *Orson Pratt's Works* (1851; rprt. Salt Lake City: Modern Microfilm, n.d.), p. 5.

29. See Richard L. Bushman, "Taking Mormonism Seriously," *D* 1 (Spring, 1966), p. 81.

30. Although Mormons outside the Reorganized Church vehemently deny the prophecy occured, the evidence that it did is substantial. See Heman C. Smith, *Journal of History*, Lamoni, Iowa 2:5-9 and Wingfield Watson and W. W. Blair, *Watson-Blair Debate* (Clifford, Ontario: W. J. Smith, 1892), pp. 184-185.

31. Crouch, *Mormon Inspiration*, p. 168.

32. Gerald and Sandra Tanner, *Joseph Smith's Successor: An Important New Document Comes to Light* (Salt Lake City: Modern Microfilm, 1981), pp. 4-26.

33. Nephi Lowell Morris, *The Prophecies of Joseph Smith and their Fulfillment* (Salt Lake City: Deseret News, 1920), pp. 113, 115.

34. *Millennial Star*, 22:455.

35. *Times and Seasons*, 5:395.

36. Orson Pratt, *Journal of Discourses*, 12:344.

37. *Journal of Oliver B. Huntington*, 2:166. Copies of the Journal may be located at the Utah State Historical Society and the Henry E. Huntington Library in Pasadena, California.

38. David Whitmer, *An Address to all Believers in Christ* (Richmond, Missouri: David Whitmer, 1887), p. 31. See also Oliver Cowdery, *Defense*, pp. 1-2.

39. *Doctrine and Covenants*, 111:1-10. See also, Crouch, *Mormon Inspiration*, pp. 163-166.

40. Crouch, *Mormon Inspiration*, pp. 180-182.

41. *Doctrine and Covenants*, 114:1.

42. Floyd C. McElveen, *The Mormon Illusion* (Glendale, Calif.: Regal Books, 1979), p. 36.

43. *Doctrine & Covenants*, 87:1-8. The text first appeared in the 1851 Liverpool edition of *The Pearl of Great Price*, p. 35. One evidence of the importance attached to this prophecy can be seen in the book by Morris (*Prophecies of Joseph Smith*) where some 50 pages are devoted to proving the Civil War prophecy offers proof that Smith was a true prophet.

44. John D. Hicks, *The Federal Union* (New York: Houghton Mifflin Co., 1937), pp. 412-418.

45. "The Crisis," *Painesville Telegraph and Geauga Free Press*, December 21, 1832, p. 1.

46. Larry Jonas, *Mormon Claims Examined* (Grand Rapids: Baker, 1961), p. 52.

47. Melvin J. White, *The Secession Movement in the United States, 1847-1852* (Madison: University of Wisconsin Press, 1910), p. 111.

48. Tanner and Tanner, *Changing World*, p. 429.

49. Tanner and Tanner, *Changing World*, p. 429.

50. Joseph Smith, Jr., *History of the Church*, (Salt Lake City: Deseret News, 1902), vol. I, pp. 315-316.

51. For an evaluation of other, supposedly fulfilled prophecies, see Crouch, *Mormon Inspiration*, pp. 143-160. Also, Tanner and Tanner, *Changing World*, pp. 404-408, 417-430.

52. Norman Cohn, *The Pursuit of the Millennium* 2d ed. (New York: Harper Torchbooks, 1961), p. 21.

53. James J. Brookes, *Maranatha or the Lord Cometh* (St. Louis: Edward Bredell, 1878), p. 364.

54. See William M. Alnor, *Soothsayers of the Second Advent* (Old Tappan, N.J.: Revell, 1989), pp. 52-61.

55. Alnor, *Soothsayers*, pp. 56-57.

56. C. E. Sears, *Days of Delusion — a Strange Bit of History* (New York: Houghton-Mifflin, 1924), p. 144.

57. C. J. Woodworth and George H. Fisher, (comp. and eds.), *The Finished Mystery* (Vol. VII, *Studies in the Scriptures*, 7 vols., 1918 edition; Brooklyn: International Bible Students Association, 1917), p. 387.

58. Woodworth and Fisher, *Finished Mystery*, p. 53.

59. Woodworth and Fisher, *Finished Mystery*, p. 483. See, also, James D. Bales, *Jehovah's Witnesses?* (Dallas: Gospel Teachers, 1978), pp. 72-73.

60. *WT*, September 15, 1910.

61. "They Shall Know that a Prophet Is among Them," *WT*, April 1, 1972, p. 197.

62. *WT*, July 1, 1943, p. 203.

63. *WT*, January 15, 1959, pp. 40-41.

64. George Orwell, *Nineteen Eighty-Four* (New American Library, 1981), p. 32.

65. *Reasoning from the Scriptures*, (Brooklyn: Watchtower, 1985), pp. 136-137.

66. *WT*, January 1, 1980, p. 2.

67. Charles Taze Russell, *The Time Is at Hand*, Vol. II (*Studies in the Scriptures*, 7 vols., Brooklyn: Watchtower Bible & Tract Society, 1889), pp. 98-99.

68. Charles Taze Russell, *Thy Kingdom Come*, Vol. III (*Studies in the Scriptures*, 7 vols., Brooklyn: Watchtower Bible & Tract Society, 1891), p. 126.

69. *WT*, July 15, 1984, p. 1677.

70. Alnor, *Soothsayers*, p. 59.

71. See the following references in *WT*: October 1, 1917, p. 6149; January 1, 1918, p. 6191; and May 1, 1918, p. 6243.

72. Woodworth and Fisher, *Finished Mystery*, p. 128.

73. J. F. Rutherford, *Millions Now Living Will Never Die* (Brooklyn: Watchtower Bible & Tract Society, 1920), pp. 89-90.

74. *1980 Yearbook of Jehovah's Witnesses* (Brooklyn: Watchtower Bible & Tract Society, 1979), p. 62.

75. *Judge Rutherford Uncovers Fifth Column* (Brooklyn: Watchtower Bible & Tract Society, 1940), p. 15.

76. *WT*, December 15, 1941, p. 372.

77. *WT*, August 15, 1968, p. 494.

78. Edmond C. Gruss. *Jehovah's Witnesses and Prophetic Speculation* (Nutley, N.J.: Presbyterian & Reformed, 1974), p. 102. Other material relating to failed prophecy among the Witnesses may be found in David A. Reed, *How to Rescue Your Loved One from the Watchtower* (Grand Rapids: Baker, 1989), pp. 55-74; Duane Magnani, *The Watchtower Files* (Minneapolis: Bethany House, 1985), pp. 63-99; and Anthony A. Hoekema, *Jehovah's Witnesses* (Grand Rapids: Eerdmans, 1963), pp. 25-44.

79. See the account in Alnor, *Soothsayers*, pp. 65-142.

80. Richard Lacayo, "Cult of Death," *Time*, March 15, 1993, p. 36.

81. Lacayo, "Cult of Death," p. 36.

82. Edgar C. Whisenant, *88 Reasons Why the Rapture Will Happen in 1988!*. (Nashville: World Bible Society, 1988).

83. "Rapture Seer Hedges on Latest Guess," *ChT*, October 12, 1988, p. 43.

84. "Rapture Seer," p. 43.

85. Edgar C. Whisenant, *The Final Shout, Rapture Report 1989* (Nashville: World Bible Society, 1989), p. 24.

86. "Rapture Seer," p. 43.

Chapter 21

1. Louis de Broglie, "Reflexions sur la causalite," *Annales de la Foundation Louis de Broglie*, 2 (1977), p. 69. A recent, though technical, discussion of causality is Mario Bunge's *Causality and Modern Science*, 3rd rev. ed. (New York: Dover, 1979).

2. For an up-to-date discussion of the necessity for "causation," see R.C. Sproul, *Not a Chance* (Grand Rapids: Baker, 1994).

3. David Hume, *The Letters of David Hume*, ed. J. Y. T. Grieg (Oxford: Clarendon Press, 1932), vol. 1, p. 187.

4. On the impossibility of self-creation, see Sproul, *Not a Chance*, pp. 11-14, 168-180.

5. See the arguments advanced by William Lane Craig, *Apologetics: An Introduction* (Chicago: Moody Press, 1984), pp. 74-95, and his *The Kalam Cosmological Argument* (New York: Barnes & Noble, 1979).

6. Robert Jastrow, *God and the Astronomers* (New York: W. W. Norton & Company, Inc., 1978), p. 111.

7. Jastrow, *God and the Astronomers*, pp. 114-115.

8. Paul Davies, *The Runaway Universe*, (New York: Harper & Row, 1978), p. 27, in arguing for the Big Bang, writes, "The Universe cannot have existed forever — there must have been a creation." Even George Gamow (The Creation of the Universe, [New York: Viking, 1955]), the one generally credited for developing the modern Big Bang, uses terms such as "the creation of the universe" in his description of the theory.

9. Edward Milne, *Modern Cosmology and the Christian Idea of God* (Oxford: Clarendon Press, 1952).

10. Jastrow, God and the Astronomers, pp. 14, 16.

11. This is the definition used by Isaac Asimov, "In the Game of Energy and Thermodynamics, You Can't Even Break Even," *Journal of the Smithsonian Institute*, June, 1970, p. 8.

12. Paul Davies, "Chance or Choice: Is the Universe an Accident?" *NS* 80 (1978), p. 506.

13. Paul Davies, *God and the New Physics* (New York: Simon & Schuster, 1983), p. 11. See, also, Davies' most recent discussion in *The Last Three Minutes* (New York: Basic Books, 1994).

14. P. W. Bridgman, "Reflections on Thermodynamics," *AS*, 41 (October, 1953), p. 549.

15. Quoted in Stanley W. Angrist, "Perpetual Motion Machines," *SA* 218 (January, 1968), p. 120.

16. W. Stansfield, *The Science of Evolution* (1977), p. 57.

Chapter 22

1. A brief explanation may be found in Moreland, *Scaling the Secular City*, pp. 43-75.

2. William Paley, *Natural Theology or Evidence and Attributes of Deity*, 18th ed. (Edinburgh: Lackington, Allen and Co., and James Sawers, 1816).

3. See William Lane Craig, *Apologetics: An Introduction* (Chicago: Moody,

1984), pp. 68-69, for answers to attacks on this analogy.

4. One popularized effort at debunking Paley's analogy can be found in Richard Dawkins, *The Blind Watchmaker* (New York: Norton, 1986).

5. An excellent discussion and visualization of this concept may be found in Philip Morrison and Phylis Morrison, *Powers of Ten* (New York: Scientific American, 1982).

6. Neil McAleer, *The Mind-Boggling Universe* (Garden City: Doubleday, 1987), p. 165.

7. McAleer, *Mind-Boggling Universe*, pp. 18-19.

8. McAleer, *Mind-Boggling Universe*, p. 169.

9. A relatively easy-to-understand explanation may be found in Richard von Mises, *Probability, Statistics, and Truth* (New York: Dover, 1981).

10. Emile Borel, *Elements of the Theory of Probability* (Englewood Cliffs, NJ: Prentice-Hall, 1965), p. 57.

11. Emile Borel, *Probabilities and Life* (New York: Dover, 1962), p. 28.

12. P. Lafont, "Book Review," *Permanences*, (November, 1972), pp. 7-8.

13. Carl Sagan, *The Cosmic Connection* (New York: Dell, 1973), pp. 236-237.

14. R. L. Wysong, *The Creation - Evolution Controversy* (East Lansing: Inquiry Press, 1976), p. 104.

15. Paul S. Moorhead and Martin M. Kaplan, eds., *Mathematical Challenges to the Neo-Darwinian Interpretation of Evolution* (Philadelphia: The Wistar Institute Press, 1967).

16. Murray Eden, "Inadequacies of Neo-Darwinian Evolution as a Scientific Theory," in *Mathematical Challenges*, Moorhead and Kaplan, eds., p. 11.

17. M. P. Schutzenberger, "Algorithms and the Neo-Darwinian Theory of Evolution," in *Mathematical Challenges*, Moorhead and Kaplan, eds., pp. 74-75.

18. Harold Blum, *Time's Arrow and Evolution*, 3d ed. (Princeton: Princeton University Press, 1968), p. 158.

19. Cited in Edmund Ambrose, *The Nature and Origin of the Biological World* (New York: John Wiley, 1982), p. 135.

20. Charles-Eugene Guye, *L'Evolution Physico-Chimique*, 2d ed. (Paris: Hermann & Co., 1942).

21. F. Salisbury, "Doubts about the Modern Synthetic Theory of Evolution," *ABT* 33 (1971), pp. 335-336.

22. Hubert P. Yockey, "A Calculation of the Probability of Spontaneous Biogenesis by Information Theory," *JTB* 67 (1977), pp. 377, 387.

23. Fred Hoyle and Chandra Wickramasinghe, *Cosmic Life-Force: The Power of Life across the Universe* (New York: Paragon House, 1990), p. 134.

24. Ambrose, *Nature and Origin*, p. 135.

25. Harold J. Morowitz, cited by Duane Gish in "The Genesis War," *SD* (October, 1981), p. 83.

26. Henry Quastlar, *The Emergence of Biological Organization* (New Haven: Yale University Press, 1964).

27. L. E. Orgel, "Darwinism at the Very Beginning of Life," *NS* 94 (1982), pp. 149, 151.

28. Ambrose, *Nature and Origin*, p. 135.

29. Jacques Monod, *Chance and Necessity: An Essay on the Natural Philosophy of Modern Biology*, trans. by Autryn Wainhouse (New York: Knopf, 1971), p. 136.

30. Cited in Ambrose, *Nature and Origin*, p. 135.

31. Blum, *Time's Arrow*, p. 158.

32. Fred Hoyle, "The Big Bang in Astronomy," *NS*, 91 (1981), pp. 521, 527.

33. William H. Thorpe, "Reductionism in Biology," in F. Ayala and Theodosius Dobzhansky, eds., *Studies in the Philosophy of Biology* (Berkeley: University of California Press, 1974), p. 117.

34. John Keosian, "Life's Beginnings — Origin or Evolution?" in J. Oro, et al, eds., *Cosmochemical Evolution and the Origins of Life, International Conference on the Origin of Life* (Dordrecht: Reidel, 1974), vol. 1, p. 291.

35. Coppedge, *Evolution*, p. 120.

36. Lecomte du Nouy, *Human Destiny* (New York: Longmans, 1947), p. 34.

37. Fred Hoyle, *The Intelligent Universe* (New York: Holt, Rinehart and Winston, 1983), p. 12.

38. Freeman Dyson, *Disturbing the Universe* (New York: Harper & Row, 1979), p. 250.

39. Hugh Ross, *The Fingerprint of God*, 2d ed. (Orange, Calif.: Promise Publishing, 1991), p. 132.

40. Michael H. Hart, "Habitable Zones About Main Sequence Stars," *Icarus* 37 (1979), 351-357.

41. Corey S. Powell, "Livable Planets," *SA* 286 (February, 1993), 18, 20; "Our Friend Jove," *Discover* 14 (July, 1993), 15.

42. See Harold Morowitz, "Ice on the Rocks," *Science 82* (September, 1982), p. 26-27; "Water's Wondrous Talents," *SD* (May, 1982), p. 103; "Trademark of the Creator: The Incredible Wonder of Water," *Moody Monthly* (April, 1975), pp. 61-62.

43. John Barrow and Frank Tipler, *The Cosmological Anthropic Principle* (Oxford: Oxford University Press, 1986).

44. Robert T. Rood and James S. Trefil, *Are We Alone? The Search for Extraterrestrial Civilizations*, (New York: Scribner's Sons, 1983.

45. Barrow and Tipler, *Anthropic Cosmological Principle*, p. 133.

46. Julie Ann Miller, "A Skunk of a Beetle," *SN* 115 (May 19, 1979), p. 330.

47. Robert E. Kofahl and Kelly L. Seagraves, *The Creation Explanation* (Wheaton, IL: Shaw, 1975), p. 2.

48. Robert A. Ginskey, "Bombardier Beetle Blasts Evolution," *The Plain Truth*, (January, 1980), p. 17.

49. Nicolette Perry, *Symbiosis: Close Encounters of a Natural Kind* (Poole, Dorsett: Blandford Books, 1983), p. 8. Excellent treatises may be found in S. M. Henry, *Symbiosis*, 2 vols., (New York: Academic Press, 1966) and G. D. Scott, *Plant Symbiosis* (New York: St. Martin's Press, 1969).

50. Mary Batten, "Earth's Odd Couples," *SD* (Nov/Dec, 1980), p. 70.

51. Some sources argue for the seventh segment. See Perry, *Symbiosis*, p. 33.

52. Douglas Dewar, *The Transformist Illusion* (Murfreesboro, TN: Dehoff Publications, 1957), p. 259.

53. Geoffrey Taylor, cited in Dewar, *Transformist Illusion*, p. 260.

54. Perry, *Symbiosis*, p. 34.

55. See the list described in Perry, *Symbiosis*, pp. 35-62. An extremely interesting article is found in Conrad Limbaugh, "Cleaning Symbiosis," SA 205 (1961), pp. 42-49.

56. Perry, *Symbiosis*, p. 35.

57. Perry, *Symbiosis*, p. 36.

58. Perry, *Symbiosis*, p. 40.

59. Batten, "Odd Couples," p. 71.

60. Batten, "Odd Couples," p. 114.

61. Batten, "Odd Couples," p. 118.

62. Evan V. Shute, "Remarkable Adaptations," in Walter E. Lammerts, ed., *Scientific Studies in Special Creation* (Grand Rapids: Baker, 1971), pp. 262-263.

63. Shute, "Remarkable Adaptations," pp. 263-264.

64. See Francis Hitching, *The Neck of the Giraffe* (New York: New American Library, 1982), pp. 152-153.

65. Kofahl and Seagraves, *Creation Explanation*, p. 5.

66. A group of short examples of design may be found in John N. Clayton, *Dandy Designs* (South Bend, IN: Does God Exist, 1984).

67. Bert Thompson, "The Design Argument — "Eye" of the Storm," *RR* (October, 1988), pp. 41-44.

68. Andrew Snelling, "Australia's Amazing Kangaroos and the Birth of Their Young," *CEN* (Sept.-Nov., 1988), pp. 8-13; Dewar, *Transformist Illusion*, pp. 250-251; H. J. Frith and J. H. Coleby, *Kangaroos* (Australia: F. W. Cheshire, 1969); and G. D. Sharman, "They're a Marvellous Mob Those Kangaroos!" *National Geographic*, 155 (1979), pp. 192-209.

69. Werner Gitt, "The Biblical Teaching Concerning Creation," in E. H. Andrews, Werner Gitt, and W. J. Ouweneel, eds., *Concepts in Creationism* (Welwyn, Herts, England: Evangelical Press, 1986), pp. 36-41; Evan Shute, "Instinct," in Donald W. Patten, ed. *A Symposium on Creation: IV* (Grand Rapids: Baker, 1972), pp. 86-88; Robin Baker, et al, eds., *The Mystery of Migration* (Toronto: John Wiley & Sons, 1980).

70. Lawrence Richards, *It Couldn't Just Happen* (Fort Worth: Sweet, 1987), pp. 108-109.

71. Richards, *It Couldn't Just Happen*, pp. 105-106.

72. Richards, *It Couldn't Just Happen*, pp.103-104.

73. Robert E. D. Clark, *The Universe: Plan or Accident*, 3d ed. (Grand Rapids: Zondervan, 1961), p. 185.

Chapter 23

1. Suetonius, "Vespasian" in *The Twelve Caesars*, trans. by Robert Graves and Michael Grant (New York: Penguin, 1979), 4.5, p. 281.

2. Tacitus, *The Histories*, 5.13.

3. W. H. Brownlee, *The Meaning of the Dead Sea Scrolls* (New York: Oxford University Press, 1964), p. 36.

4. Attempts at denying fulfillments come by declaring materials in Daniel 2 refer to events contemporary with Antiochus Epiphanes rather than to the Roman Empire. These efforts are dealt with, in rigorous detail, in numerous sources and will not be addressed here. See, for instance, Arthur J. Ferch, "The Book of Daniel and the Maccabean Thesis," *AUSS*, (1983), pp. 129-141.

5. Gleason L. Archer, *A Survey of Old Testament Introduction* (Chicago: Moody, 1973), p. 399. See, also, Gleason C. Archer, Jr., "Modern Rationalism and the Book of Daniel," *BS* (1979), pp. 129-147.

6. Josh McDowell, *Prophecy: Fact or Fiction?* (San Barnardino: Here's Life, 1981), p. 25.

7. John Wenham, *Redating Matthew, Mark, and Luke* (Downers Grove: InterVarsity Press, 1992).

8. John A. T. Robinson, *Redating the New Testament* (Philadelphia: Westminster Press, 1976).

9. Joseph Blenkinsopp, *Prophecy and Canon: A Contribution to the Study of Jewish Origins* (South Bend: Notre Dame University Press, 1977), p. 3.

10. Roger Beckwith, *The Old Testament Canon of the New Testament Church* (Grand Rapids: Eerdmans, 1985), pp. 141-142.

11. David Ewert, *From Ancient Tablets to Modern Translations* (Grand Rapids: Zondervan, 1983), pp. 70-71.

12. R. K. Harrison, *Introduction to the Old Testament* (Grand Rapids: Eerdmans, 1969), p. 286.

13. Ewart, *Ancient Tablets*, pp. 69-70.

14. Aune, *Prophecy in Early Christianity*, pp. 103-106.

15. Aune, *Prophecy in Early Christianity*, p. 104.

16. Jack Lewis, "What Do We Mean by Jabneh?" JBR 32 (1964), pp. 125-132; Roger Beckwith, *The Old Testament Canon of the New Testament Church* (Grand Rapids: Eerdmans, 1985), pp. 138-166; Sid Z. Leiman, *The Canonization of Hebrew Scripture: The Talmudic and Midrashic Evidence* (Hamden, Conn.: Transactions of the Connecticutt Academy of Arts and Sciences. Archon Books, 1976), pp. 131-132.

Chapter 24

1. See, for instance, Michael Pfau, David A. Thomas, and Walter Ulrich, *Debate and Argument: A Systems Approach to Advocacy* (Glenview, IL: Scott, Foresman and Co., 1987), pp. 10, 48-49.

2. Norman Geisler and Ron Brooks, *When Skeptics Ask* (Wheaton, IL: Victor Books, 1990), p. 115.

3. See Archer, *Old Testament Introduction*, pp. 318-321.

4. Y. T. Radday, *The Unity of Isaiah in the Light of Statistical Linguistics* (Hildesheim: H. A. Gerstenberg, 1973).

5. A. Kasker, "The Book of Isaiah: Characterization of Authors by Morphological Data Processing," *Revue de l'Organizations Internationales pour l'Etude des Langues*, 3 (1972), pp. 1-62.

6. See such defenses as those raised by Joseph Addison Alexander, *The

Earlier Prophecies of Isaiah (1846; rprt. Grand Rapids, 1953); idem., *The Later Prophecies of Isaiah* (1847); Franz Delitzsch, *Biblische Kommentar uber den Propheten Jesaja* (1866; rprnt. Grand Rapids, 1949); L. D. Jeffreys, *The Unity of the Book of Isaiah: Linguistic and Other Evidence of the Undivided Authorship* (1899); D. S. Margoliouth, *Lines of Defense of the Biblical Revelation* (1903); G. L. Robinson, *The Book of Isaiah: In Fifteen Studies* (1910). Later defenses include W. A. Wordsworth, *En Roeh* (1939); E. J. Kissane, *The Book of Isaiah: Translated from a Critically Revised Hebrew Text with Commentary*, Vol. I (Dublin: 1941), Vol. II (Dublin: 1943); and Oswald T. Allis, *The Unity of Isaiah* (1950; rprt. Nutley, NJ: Presbyterian and Reformed, 1977).

7. Andrew E. Hill and John H. Walton, *A Survey of the Old Testament* (Grand Rapids: Zondervan, 1991), p. 320.

8. Barfield, *Why the Bible Is Number One.*

9. John N. Oswalt, *The Book of Isaiah, Chapters 1-39* (Grand Rapids: Eerdmans, 1986), p. 26

10. See R. Posner, "The Use and Abuse of Stylistic Statistics," *Archivum Linguisticum* 15 (1963), pp. 111-139.

11. L. L. Adams and A. C. Rincher, "The Popular Critical View of the Isaiah Problem in the Light of Statistical Style Analysis," *Computer Studies* 4 (1973), pp. 149-157.

12. A classic modern example can be found in Peter C. Craigie, *The Old Testament: Its Background, Growth, and Content* (Nashville: Abingdon, 1986), pp. 153-155. Craigie reviews a few arguments then succumbs to the current establishment. His reason for accepting the late date is not based on reasoning but on the fact that most modern scholars accept the late date.

13. Harrison, *Introduction to the Old Testament*, p. 769.

14. See, for example, Eta Linnemann, *Historical Criticism of the Bible: Methodology or Ideology?*, trans. by Robert W. Yarbrough (Grand Rapids: Baker, 1990); Gerhard Maier, *The End of the Historical-Critical Method*, trans. by Edwin W. Leverenz and Rudolph F. Norden (St. Louis: Concordia, 1977); and Gary North, *The Hoax of Higher Criticism* (Tyler, Texas: Institute for Christian Economics, 1989).

15. Calum M. Carmichael, *Law and Narrative in the Bible: The Evidence of the Deuteronomic Laws and the Decalogue* (Ithaca, N.Y.: Cornell University Press, 1985), p. 14.

16. Millar Burrows, *The Dead Sea Scrolls* (New York: Viking, 1955), p. 118.

17. Harrison, *Introduction to the Old Testament*, p. 786.

18. Josephus, *Antiquities of the Jews*, 11.1.1.

19. Edward J. Young, *The Book of Isaiah*, Vol. 1 (Grand Rapids: Eerdmans, 1965), p. 3.

20. Compare Isaiah 52:12 with Micah 2:13; 58:1 with Micah 3:8; 49:23 with Micah 7:17; and 41:15-16 with Micah 4:13).

21. Harrison, *Introduction to the Old Testament*, pp. 795-797. See also, W. O. E. Oesterley and T. H. Robinson, *Hebrew Religion: Its Origin and Development* (London: Macmillan, 1930), pp. 225f.

22. Additional evidence also points to a possible use of Isaiah's material by

the compiler of the Kings. See Harrison, *Introduction to the Old Testament*, p. 781.

23. See, for example, Isaiah 47:8 and Zephaniah 2:15; Isaiah 52:7 and Nahum 1:15.

24. Hill and Walton, *Survey of the Old Testament*, p. 320. See also John H. Walton, "New Observations on the Date of Isaiah," *JETS* 28 (1985): 129-132.

25. Harrison, *Introduction to the Old Testament*, pp. 790-791.

26. Harrison, *Introduction to the Old Testament*, p. 791.

27. Gleason L. Archer, Jr. *A Survey of Old Testament Introduction* (Chicago: Moody, 1994), pp. 375-379.

28. Oswalt, *Isaiah*, p. 18. See also Peter Ackroyd, "Isaiah I-XII: Presentation of a Prophet," *VTS* 29 (1978), p. 29.

29. Oswalt, *Isaiah*, p. 20.

30. Hill and Walton, *Survey of the Old Testament* (1991).

31. James Burton Coffman and Thelma B. Coffman, *Commentary on Isaiah* (Abilene, TX: ACU Press, 1990).

32. John H. Hayes and Stuart A. Irvine, *Isaiah, the Eighth-century Prophet: His Times and His Preaching* (Nashville: Abingdon, 1987). .

33. C. Hassell Bullock, *Prophetic Books*.

34. Oswalt, *Isaiah*.

35. Homer Hailey, *A Commentary on Isaiah* (Grand Rapids: Baker, 1985).

36. Jim McGuiggan, *The Book of Isaiah* (Lubbock: Montex Publishing Company, 1985).

37. William Sanford LaSor, David Allan Hubbard, and Frederic William Bush, *Old Testament Survey* (Grand Rapids: Eerdmans, 1982).

38. John T. Willis, *Isaiah* (Austin: Sweet, 1980).

39. Paul T. Butler, *Isaiah*, Vol. 1 (Joplin, Mo.: College Press, 1975).

40. Archer, *Old Testament Introduction*.

41. Approximately 621 B.C.

42. H. H. Rowley, *Men of God*, p. 161.

43. C. H. Gordon, *Before the Bible* (New York: Harper & Row, 1962), p. 293.

44. Bernard Duhm, *Das Buch Jeremia* (Tubingen: J. C. B. Mohr, 1901).

45. Sigmund Mowinckel, *Zer Komposition des Buches Jeremia* (Kristiania: J. Dybwad, 1914).

46. A candid assessment of the theory's development may be found in J. A. Thompson, *The Book of Jeremiah* (Grand Rapids: Eerdmans, 1980), pp. 33-50.

47. See the discussion in Harrison, *Introduction to the Old Testament*, pp. 815-817.

48. Harrison, *Introduction to the Old Testament*, pp. 817-818.

49. Bullock, *Prophetic Books*, pp. 198-207; Thompson, *Jeremiah*, p. 43; LaSor, Bubbard, and Bush, *Old Testament Survey*, p. 409; Donald Wiseman, "Jeremiah," in *The International Bible Commentary*, rev. ed., F. F. Bruce, ed. (Grand Rapids: Zondervan, 1986), p. 766, John B. Graybill, "Jeremiah, Book of," in *NIDB*, rev. ed., J. D. Douglas and Merrill C. Tenney, eds., (Grand Rapids: Zondervan, 1987), p. 508; J. G. S. S. Thompson, "Jeremiah," in *IBD*, J. D. Douglas, et al, eds. (Wheaton: Tyndale, 1980), Part 2, p. 747.

50. Willem A. VanGemeren, *Interpreting the Prophetic Word* (Grand Rapids: Zondervan, 1990), p. 294; also, Anthony Ash, *Jeremiah* (Abilene, Texas: ACU Press, 1987).

51. John Bright, "The Date of the Prose Sermons of Jeremiah," *JBL*, 70 (1951), pp. 15-35.

52. Walter Brueggemann, *Jeremiah 1-25: To Pluck Up, To Tear Down* (Grand Rapids: Eerdmans, 1988), p. 7.

53. Bullock, *Prophetic Books*, p. 203.

54. Graybill, "Jeremiah, Book of," p. 509. For a translation of the letters see James B. Pritchard, ed., *Ancient Near Eastern Texts Relating to the OT* (1955).

55. Josephus, *Antiquities of the Jews*, 10.5.1.

Chapter 25

1. Stuart Briscoe, *All Things Weird and Wonderful* (Wheaton, Ill.: Victor, 1978).

2. This is not to say opposing viewpoints were non-existent. As early as Spinoza (1632-1677), occasional rumblings could be heard. Still, these were always sporadic. Even the few attacks on the book during the eighteenth century gained few followers.

3. Such was the conclusion of even noted critics like S. R. Driver, *Introduction to the Literature of the Old Testament* (Edinburgh: T. & T. Clark, 1898), p. 261.

4. Gustav Holscher, *Hesekiel, der Dichter und das Buch* (Gissen: Topelmann, 1924).

5. W. F. Albright, "The Old Testament and Archaeology," in *Old Testament Commentary*, H. C. Alleman and E. E. Flack, eds. (Philadelphia: Muhlenberg, 1948), p. 164.

6. Merrill F. Unger, *Archaeology and the Old Testament* (Grand Rapids: Zondervan, 1954), p. 293.

7. Robert Koldewey, *Das Wieder Erstehende Babylon* (1925), p. 90ff.

8. W. F. Albright, "King Jehoiakim in Exile," *BA* 5 (1942), pp. 49-55.

9. Joseph P. Free, *Archaeology and Bible History*, rev. ed. by Howard F. Vos (Grand Rapids: Zondervan, 1992), p. 195.

10. See James S. Smith, *The Book of the Prophet Ezekiel: A New Introduction* (London: SPCK, 1931).

11. See Bullock, *Prophetic Books*, pp. 230-231. Another insightful refutation of the Palestinian argument may be found in H. H. Rowley, "The Book of Ezekiel in Modern Study," *BJRL* 36 (1953-54), pp. 146-190.

12. J. A. Thompson, *The Bible and Archaeology*, 3d ed. (Grand Rapids: Eerdmans, 1982), p. 194.

13. C. G. Howie, *The Date and Composition of Ezekiel* (Philadelphia: JBL Monograph Series 4, 1950).

14. Harrison, *Introduction to the Old Testament*, p. 847.

15. Walther Zimmerli, *Ezekiel 1*, trans. by Ronald E. Clements, ed. by Frank M. Cross and Klaus Baltzer (Philadelphia: Fortress, 1979), p. 21.

16. Zimmerli, *Ezekiel 1*, p. 25.

17. Harrison, *Introduction to the Old Testament*, p. 849.

18. Moshe Greenberg, *Ezekiel 1-20: A New Translation with Introduction and Commentary* (Garden City: Doubleday, 1983).

19. Robert W. Manweiler, "The Destruction of Tyre," in *The Evidence of Prophecy*, Robert C. Newman, ed. (Hatfield, Pa.: Institute for Biblical Research, 1988), p. 21.

20. James E. Smith, *Ezekiel* (Joplin, Mo.: College Press, 1979), p. 33.

21. John W. Weevers, *The New Century Bible Commentary: Ezekiel* (Nashville: Thomas Nelson, 1969), p. 21.

22. Weevers, *Ezekiel*, p. 21.

23. Harrison, *Introduction to the Old Testament*, p. 847. See, also, C. G. Howie, IDB, pp. 206ff.

24. Zimmerli, *Ezekiel 1*, p. 9.

25. Edward J. Young, *The Prophecy of Daniel* (Grand Rapids: Eerdmans, 1949), p. 24.

26. Allis, *Unity of Isaiah*, p. 1.

27. John E. Goldingay, *Daniel* (Dallas: Word, 1989), p. xxxix. See, also, Bruce K. Waltke, "The Date of the Book of Daniel," BS 133 (1976), pp. 319-329.

28. Eta Linnemann, *Is there a Synoptic Problem?*", trans. by Robert W. Yarbrough (Grand Rapids: Baker, 1992), p. 19.

29. Linnemann, *Synoptic Problem*, p. 20.

30. See S. R. Driver, *Literature of the Old Testament*, rev. ed. (Edinburgh: T & T Clark, 1909), pp. 471-473.

31. Charles Boutflower, *In and Around the Book of Daniel* (London: Society for Promoting Christian Knowledge, 1923), pp. 256-257.

32. A. R. Millard, *Daniel* (Grand Rapids: Zondervan, 1979), p. 902. See, also, Peter W. Coxon, "The Syntax of the Aramaic of Daniel," *HUCA* 48 (1977), pp. 107-122.

33. See McDowell, *Daniel*, pp. 82-89. also, Robert J. Vasholz, "Qumran and the Dating of Daniel," *JETS* 21 (1978), pp. 315-321.

34. Robert Dick Wilson, quoted in McGuiggan, *The Book of Daniel* (Lubbock: Montex, 1978), pp.17-18.

35. Edward J. Young, *Introduction to the Old Testament* (Grand Rapids: Eerdmans, 1956), p. 362.

36. Donald J. Wiseman, et al., *Notes on Some Problems in the Book of Daniel* (London: Tyndale, 1970), p. 34. See, also, Gerhard F. Hasel, "The Book of Daniel and Matters of Language: Evidence Relating to Names. Words, and the Aramaic Language," *AUSS* 19 (1981), pp. 211-225.

37. Stephen M. Clinton, "S. R. Driver and the Date of Daniel," *JCS*, 5 (Fall, 1969), p. 38.

38. Driver, *Literature of the the Old Testament*, p. 508.

39. Paul Butler, *Daniel*, rev. ed. (Joplin, Mo.: College Press, 1976), p. 6.

40. See William Stevenson Smith, *Interconnections in the Ancient Near East: A Study of the Relationships between the Arts of Egypt, the Aegean, and Western Asia* (New Haven, CT: Yale University Press, 1965); Edwin M. Yamauchi, *Greece and Babylon: Early Contacts between the Aegean and the Near East* (Grand Rapids: Baker, 1967); Kenneth Kitchen, "The Aramaic of Daniel," in

Notes on Some Problems in the Book of Daniel, Donald J. Wiseman, et al, eds. (London: Tyndale, 1965); E. Y. Kutscher, "Aramaic," in *Current Trends in Linguistics*, T. A. Sebeok, ed. (The Hague: Mouton, 1970), pp. 401-402; Edwin M. Yamauchi, *Persia and the Bible* (Grand Rapids: Baker, 1990), pp. 379-382; and T. F. R. G. Braun, "The Greeks in the Near East," in *CAH: The Expansion of the Greek World, Eighth to Sixth Centuries B.C.*, 2d ed., J. Boardman and N. G. L. Hammond, eds. (Cambridge: Cambridge University Press, 1982), vol. 3, part 3, pp. 25-26.

41. Kitchen, "The Aramaic of Daniel," pp. 48-49.

42. Maximilian Ellenbogen, *Foreign Loan Words in the Old Testament* (Mystic, CT: Verry, 1962), p. 148.

43. Egon Wellesz, ed., *Ancient and Oriental Music* (London: Oxford University Press, 1957), p. 250.

44. Kitchen, "The Aramaic of Daniel," pp. 48-49.

45. See Charles H. Dyer, "The Musical Instruments in Daniel 3," *BS* (October-December, 1990), pp. 431-432.

46. Dyer, "Musical Instruments," p. 432.

47. Jim McGuiggan, *The Book of Daniel* (Lubbock: Montex, 1978), p. 17. Also, Edwin M. Yamauchi, "Archaeological Backgrounds of the Exilic and Postexhilic Era. Part I: The Archaeological Backgrounds of Daniel," *BS* 137 (1980), pp. 3-16 and "Daniel and Contacts between the Aegean and the Near East before Alexander," *EQ* 53 (1981), pp. 37-47.

48. Peter W. Coxon, "Greek Loan-Words and Alleged Greek-Loan Translations in the Book of Daniel," *Glasgow University Oriental Society Transactions* 25 (1973-74), p. 24.

49. Driver, *Literature of the Old Testament*, p. 473.

50. Archer, *Survey of the Old Testament*, p. 376.

51. Edwin Jankins, *The Authorship of Daniel*. A thesis presented to the faculty of the Department of Old Testament at Talbot Theological Seminary, June, 1955, p. 81.

52. Archer, *Survey of Old Testament*, p. 391.

53. Archer, *Survey of Old Testament*, p. 378.

54. Robert Dick Wilson, *Studies in the Book of Daniel* Vol. 2, (1917; rprt. Grand Rapids: Baker, 1979), pp. 107-113.

55. Driver, *Literature of the Old Testament*, p. 467.

56. Robert Dick Wilson, *Studies in the Book of Daniel*, Second Series (New York: Revell, 1938), p. 49.

57. Boutflower, *Daniel*, p. 277.

58. McDowell, *Prophecy: Fact or Fiction?*, p. 39.

59. Sir Robert Anderson, *Daniel in the Critics' Den* (London: James Nisbet & Co. Ltd., 1902), pp. 104-105.

60. S. Langdon, *Building Inscriptions of the Neo-Babylonian Empire* (Paris: Leroux, 1905).

61. Joseph Free, *Archaeology and Bible History* (Wheaton, Ill.: Scripture Press, 1969), p. 228.

62. Herodotus, *The Histories*, 7.10.

63. Harrison, *Introduction to the Old Testament*, pp. 1115-1117.

64. Josephus, *Against Apion*, I.20. See, also, Young, *Introduction to the Old Testament*, p. 358.

65. Eusebius, *Preparation for the Gospel*, trans. by Edwin H. Gifford (Oxford: Clarendon, 1903), 9.41.

66. R. K. Harrison, *Old Testament Times* (Grand Rapids: Eerdmans, 1970), p. 272.

67. Harrison, *Introduction to the Old Testament*, p. 1115.

68. George Rawlinson, *Historical Evidences of the Truth of the Scriptural Records*, trans. by A. N. Arnold (London: J. Murray, 1859), pp. 185, 440 n. 29.

69. Harrison, *Introduction to the Old Testament*, p. 1115.

70. Jack Finegan, *Light from the Ancient Past*, 2d ed. (Princeton: Princeton University Press, 1959), vol. 1, pp. 220-221.

71. T. G. Pinches, "Fresh Light on the Book of Daniel," *The Expository Times*, April, 1915, pp. 297-299.

72. Ira Maurice Price, Ovid R. Sellers, and E. Leslie Carlson, *The Monuments and the Old Testament* (Philadelphia: The Judson Press, 1958), p. 307.

73. See the older, but excellent, study of Raymond P. Dougherty, *Nabonidus and Belshazzar* (New Haven: Yale University Press, 1929), pp. 59ff.

74. Archer, *Survey of the Old Testament*, p. 383.

75. Michael J. Gruenthauer, "The Last King of Babylon," *CBQ*, 11 (1949), p. 416.

76. Boutflower, *Daniel*, p. 118.

77. Harrison, *Introduction to the Old Testament*, p. 1120.

78. John H. Raven, *Old Testament Introduction* (London: Fleming H. Revell Co., 1910), pp. 321-322.

79. Joseph D. Wilson, *Did Daniel Write Daniel?* (New York: Charles C. Cook, n.d.), p. 29.

80. For a brief, but effective, review of the failure of the Maccabean position, see Arthur J. Ferch, "The Book of Daniel and the Maccabean Thesis," *AUSS* 21 (1983), pp. 129-141.

81. Bruce Waltke, "The Date of the Book of Daniel," *BS* (1976), p. 321.

82. Waltke, "Date of Daniel," p. 322; Millar Burrows, *More Light on the Dead Sea Scrolls* (New York: Viking, 1958), p. 171; Jacob M. Myers, "I Chronicles," *Anchor Bible* (New York: Doubleday, 1965), p. 165.

83. J. Barton Payne, "Daniel, Book of," in *NIDB*, J. D. Douglas and Merrill C. Tenney, eds., p. 253.

84. Josephus, *Antiquities of the Jews*, 11.8.3.

85. Coffman and Coffman, *Daniel*, p. 9.

86. Arrian, *Campaigns*, 2.27.

87. Quintius Curtius Rufus, *The History of Alexander*, trans. by John Yardley and Waldemar Heckel (New York: Penguin, 1984), iv.5.12-13.

88. Green, *Alexander of Macedon*, p. 266.

89. Werner Keller, *The Bible as History*, trans. by William Neil (New York: William Morrow and Company, 1956), p. 322.

90. Burton Coffman and Thelma Coffman, *Daniel* (Abilene: ACU Press, 1989), p. 9.

91. Boutflower, *Daniel*, p. 256.

Select Bibliography

Aharoni, Yohanan. *The Land of the Bible: A Historical Geography.* 2d ed. Translated by A. F. Rainey. Philadelphia: Westminster, 1979.

Allis, Oswald T. *The Unity of Isaiah.* Philadelphia: Presbyterian and Reformed, 1950.

Alnor, William M. *Soothsayers of the Second Advent.* Old Tappan, NJ: Revell, 1989.

Ankerberg, John, and Weldon, John. *Astrology: Do the Heavens Rule Our Destiny?* Eugene, OR: Harvest House, 1989.

Archer, Gleason L. *A Survey of Old Testament Introduction.* Chicago: Moody, 1973.

Archer, Gleason L., Jr. *A Survey of Old Testament Introduction.* Rev. and Updated ed. Chicago: Moody, 1994.

Arrian (Flavius Arrianus). *History of Alexander and Indica.* Translated by E. I. Robson. 2 vols. London: W. Heinemann, Ltd., 1929-1933.

_____. *The Campaigns of Alexander.* Translated by Aubrey de Selincourt, rev. by J. R. Hamilton. New York: Penguin, 1971.

Auld, A.G. "Prophets and Prophecy in Jeremiah and Kings." *ZAW* 96 (1984): 66-82.

_____. "Prophets through the Looking Glass: Between Writings and Moses." *JSOT* 27 (1983): 3-23.

Aune, David E. *Prophecy in Early Christianity.* Grand Rapids: Eerdmans, 1983.

_____. "The Use of PROPHETES in Josephus." *JBL* 101 (1982): 419-421.

Avi-Yonah, Michael, ed. *EAEHL.* 4 Vols. Englewood Cliffs: Prentice-Hall, 1975.

Baines, John, and Malek, Jeromir. *Atlas of Ancient Egypt.* New York: Facts-on-File, 1980.

Barfield, Kenny. *Why the Bible Is Number One.* Grand Rapids: Baker, 1988.

Barnett, R. D. "Xenophon and the Wall of Media." *JHS* 83 (1963): 13-15.

Barrow, John, and Tipler, Frank. *The Anthropic Cosmological Principle.* Oxford: Oxford University Press, 1986.

Barstad, Hans M. "No Prophets? Recent Developments in Biblical Prophetic Research and Ancient Near Eastern Prophecy." *JSOT* 57 (1993): 39-60.

Bartlett, J. R. *Edom and the Edomites*. Sheffield: Academic Press, 1989.

Batey, Richard A. *Jesus and the Forgotten City*. Grand Rapids: Baker, 1991.

Batten, Mary. "Earth's Odd Couples." *SD* (Nov.-Dec., 1980): 66-71, 114, 118.

Beckwith, Roger T. "Daniel 9 and the Date of Messiah's Coming in Essene, Hellenistic, Pharisaic, Zealot, and Early Christian Computations." *RdQ* 10 (1981): 521-542.

Bierling, Neal. *Giving Goliath His Due*. Grand Rapids: Baker, 1992.

Blaiklock, E. M. *The Archaeology of the New Testament*. Rev. ed. Nashville: Nelson, 1984.

_____., and R. K. Harrison, eds. *NIDBA*. Grand Rapids: Zondervan, 1983.

Blenkinsopp, Joseph. *A History of Prophecy in Israel*. Philadelphia: Westminster, 1983.

Blomberg, Craig. *The Historical Reliability of the Gospels*. Downers Grove: InterVarsity, 1987.

Bode, Edward Lynn. *The First Easter Morning: The Gospel Accounts of the Women's Visit to the Tomb of Jesus*. Rome: Biblical Institute Press, 1970.

Borel, Emile. *Elements of the Theory of Probability*. Englewood Cliffs, NJ: Prentice-Hall, 1965.

_____. *Probabilities and Life*. Translated by Maurice Baudin. 1943; rprt. New York: Dover,. 1962.

Boutflower, Charles. *In and Around the Book of Daniel*. London: Society for Promoting Christian Knowledge, 1923.

Brodie, Fawn M. *No Man Knows My History: The Life of Joseph Smith*. 2d ed. New York: Knopf, 1971.

Brown, Colin. *That You May Believe*. Grand Rapids: Eerdmans, 1985.

_____. *Miracles and the Critical Mind*. Grand Rapids: Eerdmans, 1984.

Brown, Raymond E. *The Death of the Messiah*. 2 Vols. New York: Doubleday, 1994.

_____. *The Birth of the Messiah*. Garden City: Double day, 1977.

Browning, Ian. *Petra*. Parkridge, NJ: Noyes, 1973.

Buckingham, James Silk. *Travels in Mesopotamia*. 2 Vols. London: H. Colburn, 1827.

Bullock, C. Hassell. *An Introduction to the Old Testament Prophetical Books*. Chicago: Moody, 1986.

Bunge, Mario. *Causality and Modern Science*. 3d rev. ed. New York: Dover, 1979.

Burckhardt, Johann Ludwig. *Travels in Arabia*. London: H. Colburn, 1829.

_____. *Travels in Syria and the Holy Land*. London: John Murray, 1822.

Buss, M. J. "Prophecy in Ancient Israel." *IDBS*, 1976, pp. 694-697.

Carr, David. "Reaching for Unity in Isaiah." *JSOT* 57 (1993): 61-80.

Cassius Dio. *The Roman History*. Translated by Ian Scott-Kilvert. New York: Penguin, 1987.

Charlesworth, James H., ed. *Jesus and the Dead Sea Scrolls*. New York: Anchor Bible Reference Library, Doubleday, 1993.

_____. *The Messiah: Developments in Earliest Judaism and Christianity*. The First Princeton Symposium on Judaism and Christian Origins. Philadelphia: Fortress Press, 1992.

_____. *Jesus within Judaism: New Light from Exciting Archaeological Discoveries*. New York: Doubleday, 1988.

Childs, Brevard S. *Isaiah and the Assyrian Crisis*. Naperville, Ill.: Alec R. Allenson, 1967.

Chilton, David. *The Days of Vengence*. Forth Worth: Dominion Press, 1987.

Cicero, Marcus Tullius. *De divinatione*. Translated and ed. by E. E. Kellett. Cambridge: Cambridge University Press, 1936.

Clarke, Adam. *Clarke's Commentary*. Vol. I. 1811; rprt. Nashville: Abingdon, n. d.

Clayton, John N. *Dandy Designs*. South Bend, IN: Does God Exist?, 1984.

Coppedge, James. *Evolution: Possible or Impossible?* Grand Rapids: Zondervan, 1973.

Coxon, Peter W. "The Syntax of the Aramaic of Daniel." *HUCA* 48 (1977): 107-122.

_____. "Greek Loan-words and Alleged Greek-Loan Translations in the Book of Daniel." *Glasgow University Oriental Society Transactions* 25 (1974): 24-40.

Craig, William Lane. *Assessing the New Testament Evidence for the Historicity of the Resurrection of Jesus*. Lewiston: Edward Mellen, 1989.

_____. "The Historicity of the Empty Tomb of Jesus." *NTS* 31 (1985): 39-67.

_____. The *Kalam Cosmological Argument*. New York: Barnes & Noble, 1979.

_____. "Philosophical and Scientific Pointers to Creation ex Nihilo." *JASA* 32 (1980): 5-13.

_____. *The Son Rises*. Chicago: Moody, 1981.

Crouch, William Brodie. *The Myth of Mormon Inspiration*. Shreveport: Lambert, 1968.

Culver, Robert D. "Were the Old Testament Prophets Really Prophetic?" In *Can I Really Trust the Bible?* Howard Vos, ed. Chicago: Moody, 1963, pp. 91-116.

Culver, Roger B., and Ianna, Philip A. *Astrology: True or False— A Scientific Evaluation*. Buffalo: Prometheus Books, 1988.

Davison, John. *Discourses on Prophecy: Its Structure. Use, and Inspiration*. 2d ed. London: John Henry & James Parker, 1856.

Dawkins, Richard. *The Blind Watchmaker*. New York: Norton, 1986.

Denton, Michael. *Evolution: A Theory in Crisis*. Bethesda, MD: Adler & Adler, 1986.

Diodorus Siculus. *Bibliotheca Historica*. Translated by F. R. Walton, et al. T. E. Page, ed. Cambridge: Harvard University Press, 1957.

Dothan, Trude. "Ekron of the Philistines, Part I: Where They Came From, How They Settled Down, and the Place They Worshiped In." *BAR* 16 (1990): 20-26.

_____. "The Philistines Reconsidered." *Biblical Archaeology Today*. Jerusalem: Israel Exploration Society, 1985, pp. 165-176.

Dothan, Trude, and Dothan, Moshe. *People of the Sea*. New York: Macmillan,

1992.

Dothan, Trude, and Gitin, Seymour. "Ekron of the Philistines." *BAR* 16 (1990): 26-36.

Dressler, Harold P. "The Identification of the Ugaritic DNIL with the Daniel of Ezekiel." *VT* 29 (1979): 152-161.

Dyer, Charles H. "The Musical Instruments in Daniel 3." *BS* 147 (1990): 426-436.

Erickson, Millard J. *The Word became Flesh*. Grand Rapids: Baker, 1991.

Eslinger, L., and Taylor, G., eds. *Ascribe to the Lord: Biblical and Other Studies in Memory of Peter C. Craigie* (JSOT Sup. 67; Sheffield: Sheffield Academic Press, 1988).

Fagan, Brian M. *The Rape of the Nile: Tomb Robbers, Tourists, and Archaeologists in Egypt*. New York: Scribner, 1975.

Feldman, Louis H. *Josephus and Modern Scholarship* (1937-1980). New York: de Gruyter, 1984.

_____, and Hata, Gohei, eds. *Josephus, Judaism, and Christianity*. Detroit: Wayne State University Press, 1987.

Ferch, Arthur J. "The Book of Daniel and the Maccabean Thesis." *AUSS* 21 (1983): 129-141.

Ferguson, Everett. *Backgrounds of Early Christianity*. Grand Rapids: Eerdmans, 1987.

Fisher, W. B., ed. *The Cambridge History of Iran I: The Land of Iran*. Cambridge: Cambridge University Press, 1968.

Fitzmeyer, J. A. "Crucifixion in Ancient Palestine, Qumran Literature, and the New Testament." *CBQ* 40 (1978): 493-513.

Fleming, Wallace Bruce. *The History of Tyre*. New York: AMS, 1966.

Fredriksen, Paula. *From Jesus to Christ: The Origins of the New Testament Images of Jesus*. New Haven: Yale University Press, 1988.

Free, Joseph P. *Archaeology and Bible History*. Rev. by Howard F. Vos. Grand Rapids: Zondervan, 1992.

Gentry, Kenneth L. *Before Jerusalem Fell: Dating the Book of Revelation*. Tyler, Tex: Institute for Christian Economics, 1987.

Gersevitch, I., ed. *The Cambridge History of Iran II: The Median and Achaemenian Periods*. Cambridge: Cambridge University Press, 1985.

Girdlestone, R. B. *The Grammar of Prophecy*. London: Eyre and Spottiswoode, 1901.

Gitin, Seymour. "Last Days of the Philistines." *Arch* 45 (May/ June, 1992): 26-31.

_____, and Dothan, Trude. "The Rise and Fall of Ekron of the Philistines." *BA* 50 (1987): 197-221.

Graham, Cyril. *The Ancient Bashan and the Cities of Og*. Cambridge: Cambridge Essays, 1868.

Grant, Michael. *Herod the Great*. New York: American Heritage, 1971.

Green, Joel B., McKnight, Scot, and Marshall, I. Howard, eds. *DJG*. Downers Grove: InterVarsity, 1992.

Gruenthaler, Michael J. "The Last King of Babylon." *CBQ* 11 (1949): 406-427.

Gruss, Edmond C. *Jehovah's Witnesses and Prophetic Speculation.* Nutley, NJ: Presbyterian & Reformed, 1974.

Guillaume, Alfred. *Prophecy and Divination among the Hebrews and Other Semites.* London: Hodder and Stoughton, 1938.

Habermas, Gary. "The Early Christian Belief in the Resurrection of Jesus: A Response to Thomas Sheehan." *MTJ* 3 (1992): 105-127.

_____. *The Resurrection of Jesus: An Apologetic.* Grand Rapids: Baker, 1980.

Hall, H. R. "The Eclipse of Egypt" In *CAH.* J. B. Bury, S. A. Cooke, and F. E. Adcock, eds. Cambridge: Cambridge University Press, 1929. 3:251-269.

Halpern, Baruch. "Radical Exodus Redating Fatally Flawed." *BAR* 13 (1987): 56-61.

Harris, Murray J. *From Grave to Glory.* Grand Rapids: Zondervan, 1990.

Harrison, R. K. *An Introduction to the Old Testament.* Grand Rapids: Eerdmans, 1969.

Hart, Michael H. "Habitable Zones About Main Sequence Stars," *Icarus* 37 (1979), 351-357.

Hasel, Gerhard F. "The Book of Daniel and Matters of Language: Evidence Relating to Names, Words, and the Aramaic Language." *AUSS* 19 (1981): 211-225.

Hayes, John H., and Irvine, Stuart A. *Isaiah, the Eighth-century Prophet: His Times and His Preaching.* Nashville: Abingdon, 1987.

Herodotus. *The Histories.* Translated by Aubrey de Selincourt. New York: Penguin, 1972.

Heschel, Abraham. *The Prophets.* New York: Harper & Row, 1962.

Hitching, Francis. *The Neck of the Giraffe.* New York: New American Library, 1982.

Hoehner, Harold W. "Herod." In *ISBER.* G. P. Bromiley, ed., 2: 688-698.

Hoover, Arlie J. *Dear Agnos: A Defense of Christianity.* Grand Rapids: Baker, 1976.

Horseley, Richard, with Hanson, John S. *Bandits, Prophets, and Messiahs: Popular Movements at the Time of Jesus.* New York: Harper & Row, 1985.

Huffman, Herman B. "Prophecy in the Ancient Near East." *IDBS,* 1976, pp. 697-700.

Humble, Bill. *Archaeology and the Bible.* Nashville: Christian Communications, 1990.

Irby, Charles Leonard, and Mangles, James. *Travels in Egypt and Nubia, Syria and the Holy Land.* London: John Murray, 1868.

Jastrow, Robert. *God and the Astronomers.* New York: W. W. Norton, 1978.

Jeremias, Joachim. *Jerusalem in the Time of Jesus.* Translated by F. H. Cave and C. H. Cave. Philadelphia: Fortress, 1975.

Josephus, Flavius. *Antiquities of the Jews.* In Josephus: Complete Works. Translated by William Whiston. 1867; rprt. Grand Rapids: Kregel, 1960.

Josephus. *Wars of the Jews*. In Josephus: Complete Works. Translated by William Whiston. 1867; rprt. Grand Rapids: Kregel, 1960.

Kaiser, Walter C., Jr. *Back toward the Future: Hints for Interpreting Biblical Prophecy*. Grand Rapids: Baker, 1989.

Katzenstein, H. Jacob. *The History of Tyre*. Jerusalem: The Schocken Institute, 1973.

Kearley, F. Furman. "The Conditional Nature of Prophecy: A Vital Hermeneutical Principle." Montgomery: Apologetics Press, n.d.

Keith, Alexander. *Evidence of the Truth of the Christian Religion Derived from the Literal Fulfillment of Prophecy*. 37th ed. London: T. Nelson & Sons, 1859.

Kimball, William R. *What the Bible Says about the Great Tribulation*. Joplin: College Press, 1983.

Kofahl, Robert E., and Seagraves, Kelly L. *The Creation Explanation*. Wheaton: Shaw, 1975.

Koldewey, Robert. *The Excavations at Babylon*. Translated by Agnes St. Johns. London: Macmillan, 1914.

Layard, Austen Henry. *Popular Account of the Discoveries at Nineveh*. New York: Harper & Brothers, 1857.

_____. *Discoveries in the Ruins of Nineveh and Babylon*. London: John Murray, 1853.

_____. *Nineveh and Its Remains*. London: John Murray, 1849.

LaSor, William Sanford, Hubbard, David Allan, and Frederic William Bush. *Old Testament Survey*. Grand Rapids: Eerdmans, 1982.

Leoni, Edgar. *Nostradamus: Life and Literature*. New York: Exposition Press, 1961.

Lewis, C. S. *Miracles*. Rev. ed. London: Collins, Fontana, 1960.

Lindbloom, J. *Prophecy in Ancient Israel*. London: Basil Blackwell, 1962.

Loewe, Michael, and Blacker, Carmen, eds. *Oracles and Divination*. Boulder: Shambhala, 1981.

MacQueen, J. G. *Babylon*. London: Robert Hale, 1964.

Maier, Walter. *The Book of Nahum*. Grand Rapids: Baker, 1980.

Margalioth, R. *The Indivisible Isaiah: Evidence for the Single Authorship*. New York: Yeshiva University Press. 1964.

Margenau, Henry, and Varghese, Abraham, eds. *Cosmos, Bios, Theos*. LaSalle, Ill: Open Court, 1992.

McDowell, Josh. *He Walked among Us*. San Bernardino: Here's Life, 1988.

_____. *Prophecy: Fact or Fiction?* San Bernardino: Here's Life, 1981.

_____. *The Resurrection Factor*. San Bernardino: Here's Life, 1981.

McRay, John. *Archaeology and the New Testament*. Grand Rapids: Baker, 1991.

Meier, John P. *A Marginal Jew: Rethinking the Historical Jesus*. Volume 1: *The Roots of the Problem and the Person*. New York: Doubleday, 1991.

_____. *A Marginal Jew: Rethinking the Historical Jesus*. Volume 2: *Mentor,*

Message,and Miracles. New York: Doubleday, 1994.

Mers, M. J. "Herodotus, the Bible, and Babylon." *NEASB* 17 (1981): 34.

Miethe, Terry L. "The Cosmological Argument: A Research Bibliography." *TNS* 52 (1979): 285-305.

_____, ed. *Did Jesus Rise from the Dead? The Resurrection Debate.* New York: Harper & Row, 1987.

_____, and Flew, Anthony, eds. *Does God Exist? A Believer and Atheist Debate.* San Francisco: Harper, 1991.

_____, and Habermas, Gary R. *Why Believe? God Exists!.* Joplin: College Press, 1991.

Mills, Walter, E., ed. *MDB.* Macon: Mercer University Press, 1990.

Montgomery, John Warwick, ed. *Evidence for Faith.* Dallas: Probe, 1991.

Moreland, J.P., ed. *The Creation Hypothesis.* Downers Grove: InterVarsity, 1994.

_____. *Scaling the Secular City.* Grand Rapids: Baker, 1987.

Morrison, Philip, and Morrison, Phyllis. *Powers of Ten.* New York: Scientific American, 1982.

Nash, Ronald. *The Word of God and the Mind of Man.* Grand Rapids: Zondervan, 1982.

Negev, Avraham, ed. *AEHL.* Rev. ed. New York: Prentice-Hall, 1990.

Newman, Robert C. *The Evidence of Prophecy.* Hatfield, Penn: Interdisciplinary Biblical Research Institute, 1988.

Olivier, J. P. J. "In Search of a Capital for the Northern Kingdom." *JNSL* 11 (1983): 117-132.

"Our Friend Jove." *Discover* 14 (July, 1993), 15.

Overholt, Thomas W. "Prophecy in History: The Social Reality of Intermediation." *JSOT* 48 (1990): 3-29.

Owen, G. Frederick. *Archaeology and the Bible.* Westwood, NJ: Revell, 1959.

Oxtoby, Gurdon C. *Prophecy and Fulfillment in the Bible.* Philadelphia: Westminster, 1966.

Paget, Robert F. *In the Footsteps of Orpheus: The Discovery of the Ancient Greek Underworld.* London: Robert Hale, 1967.

Parke, H. W. *A History of the Delphic Oracle.* Oxford: B. Blackwell, 1939.

Parker, S. B. "Possession Trance and Prophecy in Pre-exilic Israel." *VT* 28 (1978): 271-285.

Parrot, Andre. *Nineveh and the Old Testament.* Translated by B. E. Hooke. London: SCM, 1955.

Parrott, Andre. *Samaria: The Capital of the Kingdom of Israel.* New York: Philosophical Library, 1958.

Pausanias. *Guide to Greece.* Translated by Peter Levi. New York: Penguin, 1971.

Payne, J. Barton. *EBP.* New York: Harper & Row, 1973.

Petrie, Sir Flinders. *Ancient Gaza.* 4 Vols. London: British School of Archaeology in Egypt, 1931-1934.

Plutarch. *The Age of Alexander: Nine Greek Lives.* Translated by Ian Scott-

Kilvert. New York: Penguin, 1973.

Porter, Robert Ker. *Travels in Georgia, Persia, Armenia, Ancient Babylon, etc. during the Years 1817, 1818, 1819, and 1820*. 2 vols. London: Longman, Hurst, Rees, Orme, and Brown, 1822.

Powell, Corey S. "Livable Planets." *SA* 268 (February, 1993), 18, 20.

Pritchard, James, ed. *ANET*. Princeton: Princeton University Press, 1950.

Quastlar, Henry. *The Emergence of Biological Organization*. New Haven: Yale University Press, 1964.

Radday, Y. T. *The Unity of Isaiah in the Light of Statistical Linguistics*. Hildesheim: H. A. Gerstenberg, 1973.

Ramsay, Sir William. *The Bearing of Recent Discovery on the Trustworthiness of the New Testament*. 1911; rprt. Grand Rapids: Baker, 1953.

Ravn, O. E. *Herodotus' Description of Babylon*. Copenhagen: Arnold Busck, 1942.

Reisner, A. C., Fisher, C. S., and D. G. Lyon. *Harvard Excavations at Samaria*. Cambridge: Harvard University Press, 1924.

Rich, Claudius James. *Narrative of a Journey to the Site of Babylon in 1811*. Mary Rich, ed. London: Duncan & Malcolm, 1839.

Richards, Lawrence. *It Couldn't Just Happen*. Ft. Worth: Sweet, 1987.

Ringgren, Helmer. "Israelite Prophecy: Fact or Fiction?" Congress Volume, Jerusalem 1986 *VT* Sup., 40; Leiden: Brill, 1988, pp. 204-210.

_____. "Prophecy in the Ancient Near East." In *Israel's Prophetic Tradition*, Richard Coggins, Anthony Phillips, and Michael Knibb, eds. Cambridge: Cambridge U. Press, 1982, pp. 1-11.

Roaf, Michael. *Cultural Atlas of Mesopotamia and the Ancient Near East*. New York: Facts-on-File, 1990.

Robinson, John A. T. *Redating the New Testament*. Philadelphia: Westminster, 1976.

Ross, Hugh. *The Fingerprint of God*. Orange, CA: Promise Publishing, 1991.

Rowley, H. H. *Prophecy and Religion in Ancient China and Israel*. New York: Harper & Brothers, 1956.

Russell, J. M. *Sennacherib's Palace without Rival at Nineveh*. Chicago: University of Chicago Press, 1991.

Sawyer, John F. A. *Prophecy and the Prophets of the Old Testament*. Oxford: Oxford U. Press, 1987.

Shute, Evan. "Remarkable Adaptations." *In Scientific Studies in Special Creation*, Walter Lammerts, ed. Grand Rapids: Baker, 1971, pp. 258-268.

Secundus, G. Plinius (Pliny the Elder). *Natural History*. Translated by H. Rackham and W. H. S. Jones. Cambridge: Harvard University Press, 1951.

Seetzen, Ulrich Jasper. *A Brief Account of the Countries Adjoining the Lake of Tiberias, the Jordan, and the Dead Sea*. Published for the Palestine Association of London. Bath: Meyler and Sons, 1810.

Smith, G. V. "Prophecy." In *ISBER*, Vol. 3. G. P. Bromiley, ed. Grand Rapids: Eerdmans, 1986, pp. 986-992.

Smith, James E. *The Promised Messiah*. Joplin, MO: College Press, 1984.

Sproul, R.C. *Not a Chance*. Grand Rapids: Baker, 1994.

Stefanovic, Zdravko. *The Aramaic of Daniel in the Light of Old Aramaic*. Sheffield: Sheffield Academic Press, 1992.

Story, Dan. *Defending Your Faith: How to Answer the Tough Questions*. Nashville: Nelson, 1992.

Strabo. *The Geography*. 8 Vols. Translated by Horace Leonard Jones. Cambridge: Harvard University Press, 1917-1932.

Stronach, David. "When Assyria Fell: New Light on the Last Days of Nineveh." *MS* 2 (1989): 1-2.

Suetonius. *The Twelve Caesars*. Translated by Robert Graves. Rev. and ed. by Michael Grant. New York: Penguin, 1979.

Sukenik, E. L. "The Earliest Records of Christianity." *AJA* 51 (1947): 351-365.

Tacitus. *The Histories*. Translated by Kenneth Wellesley. Rev. ed. New York: Penguin, 1990.

_____. *The Annals of Imperial Rome*. Translated by Michael Grant. Rev. ed. New York: Penguin, 1989.

Tanner, Gerald, and Tanner, Sandra. *Joseph Smith's Successor: An Important New Document Comes to Light*. Salt Lake City: Modern Microfilm, 1981.

_____. *The Changing World of Mormonism*. Chicago: Moody, 1980.

Temple, Robert K. G. *Conversations with Eternity: Ancient Man's Attempt to Know the Future*. London: Rider & Company, 1984.

Thaxton, Charles B., Bradley, Walter L., and Olsen, Roger, L., *The Mystery of Life's Origin*. New York: Philosophical Library, 1984.

Thompson, Bert. "The Design Argument — "Eye" of the Storm." *RR* 8 (October, 1988): 39-44.

Tomasino, Anthony J. "Isaiah 1.1-2.4 and 63-66, and the Composition of the Isaianic Corpus." *JSOT* 57 (1993): 81-98.

Vandenberg, Philipp. *The Mystery of the Oracles*. Translated by George Unwin. New York: Macmillan, 1982.

VanGemeren, Willem A. *Interpreting the Prophetic Word*. Grand Rapids: Zondervan, 1990.

Van Groningen, Gerard. *Messianic Revelation in the Old Testament*. Grand Rapids: Baker, 1990.

Vasholz, Robert J. "Qumran and the Dating of Daniel." *JETS* 21 (1978): 315-321.

Vincent, William. *The Commerce and Navigation of the Ancients in the Indian Ocean*. London: T. Cadell and W. Davies, 1807.

Volney, M. Constantin Francois. *Travels through Syria and Egypt*. 2 vols. London: G. G. J. and J. Robinson, 1785-1788.

Waltke, Bruce. "The Date of the Book of Daniel." *BS* 133 (1976): 319-329.

Walton, John H. "New Observations on the Date of Isaiah." *JETS* 28 (1985): 129-132.

Wenham, John. *Redating Matthew, Mark, & Luke*. Downers Grove: InterVarsity, 1992.

_____. *Easter Enigma: Are the Resurrection Accounts in Conflict?* Grand Rapids: Zondervan, 1984.

Whisenant, Edgar C. *88 Reasons Why the Rapture Will Happen in 1988.* Nashville: World Bible Society, 1988.

Williamson, H. G. M. "A Response to A. G. Auld." *JSOT* 27 (1983): 33-39.

Wilkins, Michael J., and Moreland, J.P., eds. *Jesus Under Fire.* Grand Rapids: Zondervan, 1995.

Wilkinson, John. "Ancient Jerusalem: Its Water Supply and Population." *PEQ* 106 (1974): 33-51.

Wilkinson, John Gardner. *Manners and Customs of the Ancient Egyptians.* 3 Vols. London: John Murray, 1837.

Wilson, Robert R. "Prophecy and Ecstasy: A Reexamination." *JBL* 98 (1979): 321-337.

Wiseman, D. J. *Nebuchadnezzar and Babylon.* London: Oxford University Press, 1985.

Xenophon. *The Anabasis of Cyrus.* Translated by Carleton L. Brownson. Cambridge: Harvard University Press, 1950.

Xenophon. *Anabasis, or Expedition of Cyrus.* Translated by J. S. Watson. London: Bohn's Library, 1891.

Yamauchi, Edwin. "Daniel and Contacts between the Aegean and the Near East before Alexander." *EQ* 53 (1981): 37-47.

_____. *Persia and the Bible.* Grand Rapids: Baker, 1990.

Yockey, Hubert P. "A Calculation of the Probability of Spontaneous Biogenesis by Information Theory." *JTB* 67 (1977): 377-398.

Young, Edward J. *Isaiah Fifty-Three.* Grand Rapids: Eerdmans, 1953.

A more complete bibliography may be obtained from the publisher at: P. O. Box 150, Nashville, Tennessee 37202. Please write for additional information.

Printed in the United States
1425700002B/127-135

9 780892 254583